Terra/Wattel – European Tax Law

Student Edition

Terra/Wattel – European Tax Law

Seventh Edition

Abridged Student Edition

Volume II

Indirect Taxation

Marie Lamensch
Madeleine Merkx
Martijn Schippers
Ilona van den Eijnde

Wolters Kluwer

Published by:
Kluwer Law International B.V.
PO Box 316
2400 AH Alphen aan den Rijn
The Netherlands
E-mail: international-sales@wolterskluwer.com
Website: www.wolterskluwer.com/en/solutions/kluwerlawinternational

Sold and distributed by:
Wolters Kluwer Legal & Regulatory U.S.
7201 McKinney Circle
Frederick, MD 21704
United States of America
E-mail: customer.service@wolterskluwer.com

ISBN 978-94-035-4201-0

e-Book: ISBN 978-94-035-4202-7
web-PDF: ISBN 978-94-035-4203-4

PREFACE

This book is intended as a reference book for EU law and tax practitioners, administrators, academics, the judiciary, and tax law or Union law policy makers.

The present Volume 2 offers a systematic analysis of EU secondary legislation in the field of indirect taxation.

It is divided in four Chapters, as follows:
1. The Union Customs Code
2. The Recast VAT Directive
3. Excises and Energy taxation Directives
4. Administrative cooperation in the field of indirect taxes

This Seventh Edition has been edited by Marie Lamensch and Madeleine Merkx. They have also edited and elaborated the Chapters on the Recast VAT Directive and on administrative cooperation in the field of indirect taxes. The Chapters on the Union Customs Code and the Excises and Energy taxation Directives have been updated and elaborated by, respectively, Martijn Schippers and Ilona van den Eijnde.

Marie Lamensch is Professor of taxation at the UCLouvain and the Free University of Brussels and a lawyer at the Brussels' Bar. She is also a member of the VAT Expert Group of the European Commission.

Madeleine Merkx is Professor of indirect taxes at Erasmus University Rotterdam and a partner at the Tax Research Center of BDO the Netherlands.

Martijn Schippers is Assistant Professor in customs law and indirect taxation at the Erasmus School of Law, programme coordinator of EFS' Post-Master in EU Customs Law and member of EY's Global Trade & Customs team in the Netherlands.

Ilona van den Eijnde is Academic Teacher in customs law and indirect taxation at the Erasmus School of Law and a regular author for several publications including a PhD in progress. She is tax lawyer at EY in Rotterdam, specialized in customs, environmental & lifestyle taxation.

Manuscript dated 1 July 2021

CONTENTS

Preface / V

Introduction / XIII

CHAPTER 1
The Union Customs Code / 1
Update and elaboration by Martijn Schippers

1.1 Introduction / 1
1.2 Legal sources / 2
1.2.1 The international legal (customs) framework / 2
1.2.2 The EU Customs Union / 3
1.3 General Provisions (Titles I and IX) / 4
1.3.1 The General Provisions of Title I / 4
1.3.2 Final Provisions / 9
1.4 Methods of Levying Duties (Titles II and III) / 10
1.4.1 Customs Debt and Guarantees / 11
1.4.2 Factors on the basis of which import duties are applied / 18
1.5 The System of Formalities and Supervision (Titles IV, V, VI, VII and VIII) / 36
1.5.1 Entry of Goods (Title IV) / 36
1.5.2 Customs Status, Customs Procedure, Verification, Release and Disposal of Goods (Title V) / 39
1.5.3 Release for Free Circulation (Title VI) / 43
1.5.4 Special Procedure (Title VII) / 45
1.5.5 Export and re-export (Title VIII) / 55

CHAPTER 2
Value Added Tax – the Recast VAT Directive / 57
Update and elaboration by Marie Lamensch and Madeleine Merkx

2.1 Introduction / 57
2.2 Subject Matter / 58
2.3 Scope / 61
2.4 Territorial Application / 61
2.5 Taxable Persons / 62
2.5.1 Introduction / 62
2.5.2 Any person / 62

2.5.3 Economic activity / 63
2.5.4 Continuing basis / 65
2.5.5 Independence / 65
2.5.6 Holding companies and share dealings / 66
2.5.7 Public bodies / 67
2.6 Taxable Transactions / 68
2.6.1 Supply of goods / 68
2.6.2 Intra-Community supplies / 73
2.6.3 Supply of services / 74
2.6.4 Importation of goods / 77
2.6.5 Vouchers – provisions common to supply of good and service / 77
2.6.6 New Means of Transport / 77
2.7 Place of Taxable Transactions / 78
2.7.1 Place of Supply of Goods / 79
2.7.2 Place of Intra-Community Acquisition of Goods / 81
2.7.3 Place of Supply of Services / 83
2.7.4 Place of Importation / 92
2.8 Chargeable Event and Chargeability of Tax / 93
2.8.1 Goods and services / 93
2.8.2 Intra-community acquisitions / 96
2.8.3 Imports / 96
2.9 Taxable Amount / 97
2.10 Rates / 101
2.11 Exemptions / 103
2.11.1 Exemptions without the Right to Deduction / 103
2.11.2 Exemptions Relating to Intra-Community Transactions / 116
2.11.3 Exemptions on Importation / 118
2.11.4 Exemptions on Exportation / 119
2.11.5 Exemptions Related to International Transport / 119
2.11.6 Exemptions Relating to Certain Transactions Treated as Exports / 120
2.11.7 Exemptions for the Supply of Services by Intermediaries / 120
2.11.8 Exemptions for Transactions Relating to International Trade / 121
2.12 Deductions / 123
2.12.1 Preliminary remarks / 123
2.12.2 Origin and Scope of Right of Deduction / 126
2.12.3 Refunds / 130
2.12.4 Proportional Deduction / 132
2.12.5 Rules Governing the Exercise of the Right of Deduction / 134
2.12.6 Adjustment of Deductions / 137
2.12.7 Private Use / 139
2.12.8 Deductions and Shares and Dividends / 140
2.12.9 Fraud and abusive practices / 148
2.13 Obligations of Taxable Persons and Certain Non-Taxable Persons / 152
2.13.1 Obligation to Pay / 152
2.13.2 Identification / 157
2.13.3 Invoicing / 158

2.13.4 Accounting / 167
2.13.5 Returns / 167
2.13.6 Recapitulative Statements / 168
2.13.7 Other Provisions / 169
2.13.8 Obligations in Respect of Imports / 169
2.14 Special Schemes / 170
2.14.1 Small and Medium-Sized Enterprises / 170
2.14.2 Farmers / 171
2.14.3 Travel Agents / 172
2.14.4 Second-Hand Goods, Works of Art, Collectors' Items and Antiques / 173
2.14.5 Investment Gold / 174
2.14.6 Special schemes for reporting and remitting VAT by non-established businesses / 174
2.15 Derogations / 178
2.15.1 Derogations Applying until the Adoption of Definitive Arrangements / 178
2.15.2 Derogations Subject to Authorisation / 179
2.16 Miscellaneous / 180
2.16.1 Implementing Measures / 180
2.16.2 VAT Committee / 181
2.16.3 Conversion Rates / 184
2.16.4 Taxes Not to Be Characterised as Turnover Taxes / 184
2.17 Final Provisions / 185
2.17.1 Transitional Arrangements and Transitional Measures / 185
2.17.2 Transposition and Entry into Force / 186
2.18 Final words on the ECJ case law / 187

CHAPTER 3
Excises and Energy Taxation / 189
Update and elaboration by Ilona van den Eijnde

3.1 Introduction / 189
3.2 The Recast General Arrangements Directive / 193
3.2.1 General Provisions / 193
3.2.2 Taxable event, Time and place of chargeability, Irregularities during movement under duty suspension, Reimbursement, Remission, Exemption / 206
3.2.3 Production, Processing, Holding and Storage / 221
3.2.4 Movement of Excise Goods under a Suspension Arrangement / 222
3.2.5 Movement and Taxation of Excise Goods after Release for Consumption / 228
3.2.6 Miscellaneous / 234
3.2.7 Exercise of the Delegation and Committee on Excise Duty / 237
3.2.8 Reporting and Transitional and Final Provisions / 237
3.3 The ECMS Regulation / 238
3.3.1 General Provisions / 238
3.3.2 Implementing Provisions / 239

3.4 Mineral Oils / 250
3.4.1 The Original Rules with Regard to Mineral Oils / 250
3.4.2 The Rates on Mineral Oils / 252
3.5 Alcohol and Alcoholic Beverages / 253
3.5.1 Beer / 254
3.5.2 Wine / 255
3.5.3 Fermented Beverages other than Wine and Beer / 257
3.5.4 Intermediate Products / 258
3.5.5 Ethyl Alcohol / 258
3.6 Tobacco / 259
3.6.1 Definitions / 260
3.6.2 Provisions Applicable to Cigarettes / 261
3.6.3 Provisions Applicable to Manufactured Tobacco other than Cigarettes / 263
3.6.4 Determination of the Maximum Retail Selling Price of Manufactured Tobacco, Collection of Excise Duty, Exemptions and Refunds / 265
3.6.5 Final Provisions / 266
3.7 Environmental Taxation / 267
3.7.1 Introduction: VAT adjustments to reach environmental objectives / 267
3.7.2 Car Registration and Circulation Tax / 273
3.7.3 Plastic Tax / 278
3.8 The 2003 Directive on Energy Taxation / 279
3.8.1 The Scope / 280
3.8.2 Levels of Taxation / 282
3.8.3 Exemptions, Reductions and Tax Refunds / 286
3.8.4 Holding and Movement of Products / 291
3.8.5 Chargeable Event and Chargeability / 291
3.8.6 Final Provisions / 293

CHAPTER 4
Administrative Cooperation in the field of indirect taxes / 295
Update by Marie Lamensch and Madeleine Merkx

4.1 Legal Basis: 'Internal Market' or 'Fiscal' provisions? / 295
4.2 The Recovery Assistance Directive (applicable for direct and indirect taxes) / 296
4.2.1 History, Main Features, Scope / 296
4.2.2 Types of Recovery Assistance / 299
4.2.3 Limitations on the Obligations to Assist; National Treatment; (No) Preference / 300
4.2.4 Miscellaneous / 301
4.2.5 Evaluation of the RAD / 302
4.3 Trade Monitoring Provisions / 303
4.4 Administrative Cooperation and Combating Fraud in the Field of VAT / 304
4.4.1 Within the EU / 304
4.4.2 With third countries / 317

4.5 Administrative Cooperation in the Field of Excise Duties / 318
4.6 Administrative Cooperation in the Field of Customs Duties / 319

ANNEX I - Customs, VAT and excise legislation: territorial application / 323

Index / 327

INTRODUCTION

The EU Member States have been engaged into a process of harmonization of their national indirect tax systems since the early days of the European Community (now European Union). The 1957 Treaty of Rome indeed already provided for the suppression of customs duties and measures with equivalent effect on intra Community trade[1] and for the adoption of a common customs tariff and a common commercial policy towards third countries,[2] which materialized trough the adoption of a consistent body of rules and procedures applicable to goods brought into or taken out of the EU customs territory. The founding Member States[3] also committed to abide by a prohibition of indirect tax discrimination against imports from other Member States.[4]

The 1957 Treaty of Rome further called for the harmonization of Member States' "turnover taxes, excise duties and other forms of indirect taxation".[5] Notwithstanding the application of the unanimity rule in this field, the Member States have agreed to comply with a harmonized VAT framework in the form of a succession of directives and with a partially harmonized framework in the field of excise duties and environmental taxation. Customs duties and VAT revenue both constitute EU own resources.[6] The full revenue arising from customs duties (less a collection fee) accrues to the EU budget and represents 13% of the total EU revenue,[7] while a percentage of national VAT revenue accrues to the EU budget and represents 11% of the total EU revenue.[8] Since 1 January 2021, a new revenue source to the EU budget has been added: a contribution based on the non-recycled plastic packaging waste.[9] In contrast, revenue from excise duties and other environmental taxes fully accrue to the Member States (like all direct tax revenue).

---

1 Customs duties were a primary target of the 1957 Rome Treaty (see Article 12). Articles 13 to 17 provided for the gradual removal of customs duties (roll back or phase out) by providing an automatic annual reduction in the duty ceilings (applied duties) during a transitional period of ten years.

2 Article 3 of the 1957 Treaty of Rome, now Article 28 of the TFEU.

3 Belgium, France, West Germany, Italy, Luxembourg and the Netherlands.

4 Article 95 of the 1957 Treaty of Rome and current Article 110 Treaty on the Functioning of the European Union, "TFEU", analysed in Volume I, Section 3.1.0.

5 Then Article 99 of the 1957 Treaty of Rome, subsequently Article 93 of the 1922 Treaty of Maastricht and now 113 of the TFEU.

6 70/243/ECSC, EEC, Euratom: Council Decision of 21 April 1970 on the replacement of financial contributions from Member States by the Communities' own resources, OJ L 94, 28.4.1970, p. 19–22.

7 DG Budget, Revenue Statistics (year 2019).

8 DG Budget, Revenue Statistics (year 2019).

9 Council Decision (EU, Euratom) 2020/2053 of 14 December 2020 on the system of own resources of the European Union and repealing Decision 2014/335/EU, Euratom, OJ L 424, 15.12.2020, p. 1–10.

This book provides a systematic analysis of the current EU secondary legislation concerning customs duties (Chapter 1), value-added-taxes (Chapter 2) excise duties and environmental taxes including car registration and plastic tax (Chapter 3). Chapter 4 analyses current (secondary legislation) instruments regulating administrative cooperation in the field of indirect taxes (including exchange of information and recovery of taxes).

CHAPTER 1

The Union Customs Code

Update and elaboration by Martijn Schippers

1.1 Introduction

Article 28 TFEU provides that the Union shall comprise a customs union covering all trade in goods including the prohibition of customs duties between Member States on imports and exports and all charges having equivalent effect and the adoption of a common customs tariff in their relations with third countries. The provisions of the customs union apply to the products originating in Member States and to products coming from third countries which are in free circulation in the Member States.[1]

The general rules and procedures applicable to goods brought into or taken out of the customs territory of the Union[2] are laid down in the Union Customs Code (UCC), Regulation (EU) No. 952/2013.[3] The UCC is supplemented by the UCC Delegated Act (UCC DA), Regulation (EU) No. 2015/2446[4] with regards to non- essential elements. To ensure the existence of uniform conditions for the implementation of the UCC and a harmonized application of procedures by all Member States, the EC adopted the UCC Implementing Act (UCC IA), Regulation (EU) No. 2015/1447.[5] The UCC Transitional Delegated Act (UCC TA), Regulation (EU) 2016/341[6] establishes transitional rules for operators and customs authorities pending the upgrading or the development of the relevant IT systems to create a fully electronic

1 Article 28(2) TFEU.
2 See Annex I for a comparison table between the customs territory, the VAT territory and the excise territory.
3 Regulation (EU) No 952/2013 of the European Parliament and of the Council of 9 October 2013 laying down the Union Customs Code (O.J. L 269, 10.10.2013, p. 1– 101).
4 Commission Delegated Regulation (EU) 2015/2446 of 28 July 2015 supplementing Regulation (EU) No 952/2013 of the European Parliament and of the Council as regards detailed rules concerning certain provisions of the Union Customs Code (O. J. L 343, 29.12.2015, p. 1).
5 Commission Implementing Regulation (EU) 2015/2447 of 24 November 2015 laying down detailed rules for implementing certain provisions of Regulation (EU) No 952/2013 of the European Parliament and of the Council laying down the Union Customs Code (O.J. L 343, 29.12.2015, p. 558).
6 Commission Delegated Regulation (EU) 2016/341 of 17 December 2015 supplementing Regulation (EU) 952/2013 of the European Parliament and of the Council as regards transitional rules for certain provisions of the Union Customs Code where the relevant electronic systems are not yet operational and amending Delegated Regulation (EU) 2015/2446 (O.J. L 69, 15.3.2016, p.1).

customs environment. These regulations along with the UCC Work Programme[7] setting out the planning of the IT systems constitute the UCC legal package.[8]

The UCC contains 9 Titles and 288 Articles. The UCC DA and UCC IA follow the same structure as the UCC and contain 9 Titles each. Combined they consist out of the impressive amount of 606 Articles and 76 Annexes. Our commentary below is restricted to the basic ideas of the UCC, UCC DA and UCC IA. It does, however, in section 1.2 explain how EU customs legislation fits into a Union's and broader international legal (customs) framework as this helps to understand how the legal package of the UCC is being applied and why it consists out of a basic, delegated and implementing act.

Basically, the provisions of the UCC can be arranged according to three themes:
(1) General provisions (Titles I and IX) – section 1.3;
(2) Methods of levying duties (Titles II and III) – section 1.4;
(3) The system of formalities and supervision (Titles IV, V, VI, VII and VIII) – section 1.5.

1.2 Legal sources

1.2.1 The international legal (customs) framework

In the wake of World War II, initial steps have been taken to establish what are nowadays called the World Trade Organization (WTO) and the World Customs Organization (WCO). Under the auspices of these two organizations and their former appearances, international agreements have been concluded and soft law has been issued that regulate world trade. Examples of WTO agreements that found (partly) their way into the provisions of the UCC are the Agreement on Implementation of Article VII GATT 1994 (the Valuation Agreement) and the Agreement of Rules of Origin. Examples of WCO conventions that play an important role for the purpose of applying the UCC are the International Convention on the Harmonized Commodity Description and Coding System (HS Convention), the Customs Convention on the A.T.A. Carnet for the temporary admission of goods (A.T.A. Convention) (1961), the Istanbul Convention on Temporary Admission (1990) and the International Convention on the Simplification and Harmonization of Customs procedures (the Kyoto Convention) of which the revised version entered into force on 3 February 2006 (the revised Kyoto Convention).

As a member of the WTO, the EU is obliged to convert WTO law into its own legislation, and the EU should adhere to the WCO conventions to the extent they are a signatory party to those conventions. It is, however, established case-law of the ECJ that these agreements

7 Commission Implementing Decision (EU) 2019/2151 of 13 December 2019 establishing the work programme relating to the development and deployment of the electronic systems provided for in the Union Customs Code (O.J. L 325, 16.12.2019, p. 168–182), replacing the earlier version of the Programme set out in Commission Implementing Decision (EU) 2016/578 of 11 April 2016 (O.J. L 99 15.4.2016 p. 6).

8 COM(2018) 39 final.

and conventions do not confer rights on citizens of the EU which they can invoke before the EU and Member States courts.[9]

1.2.2 The EU Customs Union

The EU Customs Union has been existing since 1968 and is considered one of the greatest achievements of the EU and one of the fundamental pillars of the EU.[10] Its principles are that there is one external border, one common tariff and a common legislative framework. This common legislative customs framework consisted out of more than 100 regulations each regulating part of the Union's customs legislation until the Community Customs Code became applicable on 1 January 1994.

During the years 1992–1993 the European Commission completed what was hailed at that time as 'the most far-reaching project of legislative consolidation ever undertaken in a field subject to Community law', by introducing the Community Customs Code (CCC), Regulation (EEC) No. 2913/92[11] and the implementing code (CCIP), Regulation (EEC) No. 2454/93.[12] With one stroke of the pen (or actually two) over one hundred (106) regulations and directives were repealed and replaced by 1168 Articles and 113 Annexes.[13] In addition to the CCC and the CCIP, two other regulations remained in force, dealing with specific areas of customs law, Regulation (EEC) No. 2658/87 on the customs tariff[14] and Regulation (EEC) No. 918/83, replaced by Regulation (EC) No. 1186/2009 setting up a Community system of reliefs from customs duty (codified version) from 1 January 2010.[15]

In its Communication to the Council and the European Parliament on a simple and paperless environment for customs and trade the Commission announced that it would modernize

9 Case 21 to 24-72 (*International Fruit Company NV and others v Produktschap voor Groenten en Fruit*), [1972] ECR 01219. There seem to be only two exceptions to this rule which can be derived from the Case C-69/89 (*Nakajima All Precision Co. Ltd.*), [1991] ECR I-02069 and C-70/87 (*Fediol*), [1989] ECR 01781. The ECJ held in these cases that provisions of the WTO agreement cannot be directly invoked in the Union or Member State courts, unless the Union intended to implement a particular obligation assumed in the context of the WTO, or where the Community measure refers expressly to the precise provisions of the WTO agreements.

10 Celebrating the Customs Union: the world's largest trading bloc turns 50, press release of 30 June 2018 (https://ec.europa.eu/commission/presscorner/detail/en/ IP_18_4265) and M.L. Schippers & W. de Wit, Reflections on the 50th anniversary of the EU Customs Union, *Erasmus Law Review*, 13 (3), 217-218.

11 Council Regulation (EEC) No. 2913/92 of 12 October 1992 establishing the Community Customs Code (O.J. L 302, 19.10.1992, p.1).

12 Commission Regulation (EEC) No. 2454/93 of 2 July 1993 laying down provisions for the implementation of Council Regulation (EEC) No 2913/92 establishing the Community Customs Code (O.J. L 253, 11.10.1993, p. 1).

13 In Case C-161/06 (*Skoma-Lux*), [2007] ECR I-10841, the ECJ held that the obligations contained in the Customs Code which had not yet been published in the Official Journal of the European Union in the language of a new Member State (Czech), where that language is an official language of the European Union, from being imposed on individuals in that State, even though those persons could have learned of that legislation by other means.

14 Council Regulation (EEC) No 2658/87 of 23 July 1987 on the tariff and statistical nomenclature and on the Common Customs Tariff (O.J. L 256, 7.9.1987, p. 1.).

15 O.J. 2009 L 324 p. 23.

and simplify customs rules and processes.[16] On 23 April 2008, Regulation (EC) No. 450/2008 was adopted laying down the Modernised Customs Code (MCC).[17] As the Lisbon Treaty[18] introduced a new legal framework with new rules and procedures concerning the adoption of implementing provisions accompanying main regulations, the Commission was obliged to recast the MCC into the UCC.

On 20 February 2012 a proposal was published by the Commission to recast the MCC, including articles empowering the Commission to adopt detailed supplementing and implementing rules. This resulted in the UCC legal package consisting out of the UCC, UCC DA, UCC IA, UCC TA, and Work Programme (section 1.1).[19] The UCC, being the basic regulation of the UCC legal package, was published on 9 October 2013 and entered into force on 30 October 2013. Most substantive provisions of the UCC are, however, applicable since 1 May 2016 and on that date it repealed and replaced the previous framework for customs legislation, contained in the CCC and CCIP.

1.3 General Provisions (Titles I and IX)

The general provisions of the UCC can be found in Titles I (General provisions) and IX (Electronic systems, simplifications, delegation of power, committee procedure and final provisions).

1.3.1 The General Provisions of Title I

1.3.1.1 Scope of the customs legislation, mission of customs authorities and definitions

The 'general provisions' of Title I start in Article 1 and 5(2) UCC by stipulating that the Code, its supplementing and implementing provisions – at Union or national level –, the Common Customs Tariff, legislation setting-up a Union system for reliefs from customs duty and international agreements containing customs provisions, insofar as they are applicable in the Union, form the customs rules. They apply to trade between the EU and third countries, to goods covered by the Treaties.

16 COM(2003) 452.
17 O.J. 2008, L 145, p. 1.
18 O.J. C 306, 17.12.2007, p. 1–271.
19 In addition, explanatory notes and guidelines (commonly referred to as 'soft law') have been issued to provide guidance to Member States and/or stakeholders in applying and implementing EU customs law. The explanatory notes to the Combined Nomenclature and the TARIC (see section 1.4.2.1) are explicitly mentioned in Article 9(1)(a), second indent, of Regulation (EEC) No. 2658/87 and have been recognised by the ECJ as important aids to the interpretation of Union customs law. There is no fundamental structural difference between the explanatory notes and the guidelines. The "explanatory notes" explain, if anything, the content of a specific article whereas the "guidelines" describe the practices to be followed. Apart from the explanatory notes to the Combined Nomenclature and the TARIC, guidance documents also exist, for example, in the following fields: customs decisions, data integration and harmonization, AEO, decisions on binding information, origin, valuation, debts and guarantees, entry and import, simplifications, transit and customs status, special procedures, export, military mobility, customs representation and return-refill containers.

The second paragraph of Article 1(1) UCC provides:

> Without prejudice to international law and conventions and Union legislation in other fields, the Code shall apply uniformly throughout the customs territory of the Union.

The mission of the customs authorities is set-out in Article 3 UCC. It becomes clear from this article that the customs authorities are not only responsible for levying customs duties, but also has missions and competences in the field of safety, health, the economy and environmental protection.

Article 4 UCC defines the customs territory. Here we encounter the first problem with regard to the indirect taxes since the customs territory is not identical to the territory where the European VAT system applies. When goods are within the customs territory, but in an area where VAT does not apply the movement of these goods within the customs territory to and from the area where VAT does not apply must be treated as importation or exportation (see Chapter 2, section 2.4), which clearly complicates legislation and is difficult to supervise.

The rather extensive Article 5 UCC is extremely useful for those who are 'starters' in the field of customs law. It offers a range of definitions such as Union goods, import duties and the pivotal concepts of 'customs procedure' and 'special procedure'. The definition of what is referred to as 'Union goods'[20] is set forth below (Article 5(23) UCC):

> 'Union goods' means goods:
> - goods wholly obtained in the customs territory of the Union and not incorporating goods imported from countries or territories outside the customs territory of the Union, or
> - goods brought into the customs territory of the Union from countries or territories outside that territory and released for free circulation, or
> - goods obtained or produced in the customs territory of the Union, either solely from goods referred to in the second indent or from goods referred to in the first and second indent.

'Non-Union goods' are goods other than those referred above. In principle, Union goods lose their status as such when they are actually removed from the customs territory of the Union.

The heart of the UCC is Title V dealing with, among others, placing goods under a customs procedure which means that goods are either released for free circulation, placed under a special procedure (e.g. transit, storage, specific use or processing) or exported from the customs territory of the Union. See further, section 1.5 below.

1.3.1.2 Rights and obligations of persons with regard to the customs legislation

Articles 6 through 55 UCC deal with rights and obligations in customs law regarding:
- exchange and storage of information and common data requirements;
- the right of representation (the representation acting in the name and for the account of another person or – the indirect representation – acting in one's own name but for the account of another) (section 1.3.1.3);

20 See also Art. 153 UCC on which goods are deemed to be Union goods.

- the possibility to obtain decisions from the customs authorities, including decisions on binding information with regard to tariff classification (BTI) and origin (BOI), valid throughout the customs union (section 1.3.1.4);[21]
- obtaining the status for authorised economic operator (AEO) (section 1.3.1.5);
- the obligation of Member States to provide for penalties for failure to comply with the customs legislation in their own national legislation;
- the right to an administrative decision with the right to appeal (section 1.3.1.6);
- the right for customs authorities to carry out any customs controls they deem necessary;
- keeping of documents and other information, and charges and costs.

1.3.1.3 Representation

Performing acts and formalities under the customs legislation most often requires special IT systems/applications and 'in-house' customs expertise. In particular where customs operations are not a person's 'daily business', that person may want to appoint another person in the capacity of customs representative that carries out the acts and formalities required under the customs legislation in his or her dealings with customs authorities on his or her behalf (Art. 5(6) UCC). If a person wants to import goods into the customs territory of the Union and is not established in that customs territory, that person needs to appoint an indirect customs representative. The reason is that the declarant needs to be established in the customs territory of the Union (Art. 170(2) read in conjunction with Art. 5(15) UCC).

A distinction can be made between a direct and indirect customs representative. A direct customs representative is acting in name and on behalf of the other person, where an indirect customs representative shall act in its own name, but still on behalf of that other person (i.e. the represented party). Irrespective of whether a person appoints another person in the capacity as customs representative, the represented party remains (one of) the person(s) liable for any customs debt that may occur. In the event of indirect representation, the person on whose behalf the customs declaration is made shall also be a debtor (see section 1.4.1.1).

A person that acts as customs presentative needs to be empowered in accordance with the requirements laid down in Article 19 UCC, because without being empowered the representative shall be deemed to be acting in their own name and on their own behalf. Additionally, a customs representative needs, in principle, to be established in the customs territory of the Union. Member States may set further requirements. Without prejudice to the application of less stringent criteria by the Member State concerned, a customs representative who complies with the criteria for an AEOC license (see section 1.3.1.5) shall be entitled to provide such services in a Member State other than the one where he or she is established.

21 Article 35 UCC opens the possibility to obtain binding information regard to other factors referred to in Title II. As binding information with regard to tariff classification and origin can already be requested for based on Article 33 UCC, the only factor left from Title II is valuation. The lack of delegated and implementing acts seem at this point in time unable market operators from requesting for a binding information with regard to the valuation of imported goods.

1.3.1.4 Binding Tariff Information

A BTI includes information in respect of the tariff classification of goods and is binding for a period of three years on the customs authorities, as against the holder of the decision, and on the holder of the decision, against the customs authorities. Safeguards are built in, such as an amendment to the Combined Nomenclature (CN) or a judgment of the ECJ, in which cases the holder of the binding information may still use that information for a period of six months if the conditions of Article 34(9) UCC are fulfilled.[22] It should be noted that the tariff information is binding on the customs authorities, *i.e.* it is not restricted to the Member State where the holder of the information is established.[23]

On 15 September 2005, the ECJ decided Case C-495/03 (*Intermodal Transports*)[24] concerning the classification in the CN of certain vehicles referred to as 'Magnum ET 120 Terminal Tractors'. The first question referred for a preliminary ruling relates to the relevance of binding tariff information issued by customs authorities of a Member State for the purposes of assessing whether the national courts of another Member State before which a question of tariff classification is raised are under an obligation to ask for a preliminary ruling. The ECJ (First Chamber) ruled that Article 234 EC (now Article 267 TFEU) must be interpreted as meaning that when, in proceedings relating to the tariff classification of specific goods before a national court or tribunal, a binding tariff information relating to similar goods

---

22 In Case C-315/96 (*Lopex Export GmbH*), [1999] ECR I-1287, the ECJ held that the aim of binding tariff information is to enable the trader to proceed with certainty where there are doubts as to the classification of goods in the existing customs nomenclature, thereby protecting him against any subsequent change in the position adopted by the customs authorities with regard to the classification of the goods. However, such information is not aimed at, nor can it have the effect of, guaranteeing that the tariff heading to which the trader refers will not subsequently be amended by a measure adopted by the Community legislature. See also Joined Cases C-133/02 and C-134/02 (*Timmermans Transport* and *Hoogenboom Production*), [2004] ECR I-1125, in which the ECJ held that where, on more detailed examination, it appears to the customs authorities that the interpretation based on which a BTI is issued is wrong, following an error of assessment or evolution in the thinking in relation to tariff classification, they are entitled to consider that one of the conditions laid down for the issue of a BTI is no longer fulfilled and to revoke that BTI with a view to amending the tariff classification of the goods concerned.

23 In Case C-199/09 (*Schenker SIA*), [2010] ECR I-12311, the ECJ held that an application for BTI may relate to different goods provided that these all belong to one and the same type of goods. Only goods which have similar characteristics and whose distinguishing features are completely irrelevant for the purposes of their tariff classification may be regarded as belonging to one type of goods for the purposes of that provision. In Case C-153/10 (*Sony Logistics*), [2011] ECR I-02775, the ECJ held that a person who makes customs declarations in his own name and on his own behalf cannot rely on a binding tariff information of which he is not the holder, but which is held by an associated company on whose instructions he made those declarations. However, a BTI may be relied on as evidence by a person other than its holder. The Dutch customs authorities, responsible for applying European Union law, attributed to a BTI the same legal value whether it was invoked by a third party or its holder. According to the ECJ, those authorities, by applying the customs manual, acted in a manner which was inconsistent with European Union law and that conduct could not give rise to a legitimate expectation on the part of traders. In Joined Cases C-288/09 and C-289/09 (*BskyB, Pace*), [2011] ECR I- 02851, the ECJ held *inter alia* that, where a regulation updating the Combined Nomenclature is adopted and that regulation does not set a time period during which the holder of a BTI which has ceased to be valid can nonetheless continue to rely on it, that holder is not entitled to continue relying on that BTI.

24 Case C-495/03 (*Intermodal Transports*), [2005] ECR I-8151.

issued to a person not party to the dispute by the customs authorities of another Member State is submitted, and that court or tribunal takes the view that the tariff classification made in that information is wrong, those two circumstances:

- cannot result, in respect of a court or tribunal against whose decisions there is a judicial remedy under national law, in the court or tribunal being under an obligation to refer to the ECJ questions on interpretation;
- cannot, in themselves, automatically result, in respect of a court or tribunal against whose decisions there is no judicial remedy under national law, in the court or tribunal being under an obligation to refer to the ECJ questions on interpretation.

A court or tribunal against whose decisions there is no judicial remedy under national law is, however, required, where a question of Union law is raised before it, to comply with its obligation to make a reference, unless it has established that the question raised is irrelevant or that the Union provision in question has already been interpreted by the ECJ or that the correct application of Union law is so obvious as to leave no scope for any reasonable doubt. The existence of such a possibility must be assessed in the light of the specific characteristics of Union law, the particular difficulties to which its interpretation gives rise and the risk of divergences in judicial decisions within the Union; the existence of the above-mentioned binding tariff information must cause that court or tribunal to take particular care in its assessment of whether there is no reasonable doubt as to the correct application of the combined nomenclature, taking account, in particular, of the three criteria mentioned above.

1.3.1.5 Authorized Economic Operator

Member States grant the status of ***authorised economic operator*** (AEO) to any economic operator that meets common criteria relating to the operator's control systems, financial solvency and compliance record since 2005. An economic operator with the AEO status is considered a trusted trader in the eyes of the customs authorities and confers certain benefits for the economic operator. The status of AEO, once granted by one Member State, must be recognised by the other Member States, but does not confer the right to benefit automatically in the other Member States from simplifications provided for in the customs rules. However, the other Member States must allow the use of simplifications by authorised economic operators provided they meet all the specific requirements for use of the particular simplifications. In considering a request to use simplifications, the other Member States need not repeat the evaluation of the operator's control systems, financial solvency or compliance record, which already have been completed by the Member State that granted the operator the status of authorised economic operator, but should ensure that any other specific requirements for use of the particular simplification are met.

1.3.1.6 The Right to Appeal

Section 6 of Title I provides that any person has the right to appeal against decisions taken by customs authorities which concern him directly and individually. This right may be exercised initially before the designated customs authorities and subsequently before an independent body. Thus, appeal in two stages is guaranteed.

In Case C-1/99 (*Kofisa*)[25] two questions were referred to the ECJ. The first question was whether an appeal against the decisions of the customs authorities may be brought directly before the judicial authority or whether it must be brought before the customs authority first; in other words, is an appeal in two stages compulsory? According to the ECJ, the Union legislature did not preclude that national law might authorize a trader, in appropriate circumstances, to lodge an appeal directly before an independent authority. Nor is there anything in the Union legislation to support the conclusion that it authorizes a trader to bypass an appeal before the customs authority and appeal directly to the independent body, where under the applicable national law an appeal to the customs authority is mandatory.

The second question was whether Article 244 CCC (now Article 45 UCC) confers the power to suspend implementation of a contested decision exclusively on the customs authorities or whether it also confers such powers on the judicial authorities. (Kofisa has asked the Italian court suspension of the collection of ITL 1,112,526,600 in VAT plus interest on the ground of misapplying the ceiling of imports.) According to the ECJ, Article 244 CCC confers power exclusively on the customs authorities. But the ECJ held:

> 46. However, that provision cannot restrict the right to effective judicial protection. The requirement of judicial control of any decision of a national authority reflects a general principle of Community law stemming from the constitutional traditions common to the Member States and enshrined in Articles 6 and 13 of the European Convention for the Protection of Human Rights and Fundamental Freedoms (Case 222/86 *Unectef v. Heylens*, paragraph 14, and Case C-97/91 *Oleificio Borelli v. Commission*, paragraph 14).
>
> 47. In the exercise of their control, it is for the national courts, pursuant to the principle of cooperation laid down in Article 5 of the EC Treaty (now Article 10 EC), to ensure the legal protection which persons derive from the direct effect of provisions of Community law (Case C-213/89 *Factortame and Others*, paragraph 19). 48. With more specific regard to the possibility of suspending implementation of a decision of a customs authority, it should be pointed out that a court seized of a dispute governed by Community law must be in a position to grant interim relief in order to ensure the full effectiveness of the judgment to be given on the existence of the rights claimed under Community law (*Factortame*, cited above, paragraph 21).

Thus, an unequivocal provision must yield for a general principle of Union law and of the European convention (the requirement of judicial control), as well as for the fundamental principle of cooperation.[26]

1.3.2 Final Provisions

In Title IX, Articles 278 to 281 UCC deal with the development of electronical systems and provide for transitional measures for some explicitly mentioned provision where their application depend on electronic data-processing techniques that are not yet operational. Under conditions, Member States are allowed to test simplifications for a limited period.

25 Case C-1/99 (*Kofisa*) [2001] ECR I-0207.
26 See also Case C-130/95 (*Bernd Giloy*), [1997] ECR I-1492.

In the UCC, 39 provisions empower the Commission to adopt delegated acts and 47 provisions empower the Commission to adopt implementing acts, which aligns EU customs legislation with the requirements of the Lisbon Treaty. With regard to the delegation of power to the Commission, the conditions and committee procedure are laid down in Articles 284 and 285 UCC. In executing its delegating power, the Commission may only adopt non-legislative acts of general application to supplement or amend certain non-essential elements of the UCC according to Article 290(1) TFEU. When executing its implementing powers the ECJ held that '[...] *the Commission may neither amend nor supplement the legislative act, even as to its non-essential elements'.*[27] If the Commission nevertheless exceeds its delegated or implementing powers, the ECJ may seek action for annulment of the particular provision in the delegated or implementing act.[28]

The last Article of the Code provide that the Code applies from 1 May 2016.[29] The provisions conferring delegating and implementing power to the Commission and Articles 52 ('Cost and charges'), 284 ('Exercise of the delegation'), 285 ('Committee procedures') and 286 ('Repeal and amendment of legislation in force') UCC already applied as from 30 October 2013.[30] Finally, the MCC, CCC, CCIP and Regulation (EC) No. 1207/2001[31] have been repealed as of 1 May 2016.

1.4 Methods of Levying Duties (Titles II and III)

Two Titles deal with this subject:

II. Factors on the basis of which import duties and export duties are applied (section 1.4.2);

III. Customs debt and guarantees (section 1.4.1).

27 See Case C-65/13 (*European Parliament v European Commission*), [2014] ECLI: EU:C:2014:2289.

28 In literature it is argued that certain provisions in the UCC DA and UCC IA alter the scope of UCC and should therefore be declared invalid by the ECJ in case an action for annulment is started. In that regard reference can be made to Article 33 UCC DA which contains an anti-avoidance rule for non-preferential origin which should, according to Melin and Arnold, be declared invalid, see Y. Melin and D. Arnold, Non-Preferential Customs Origin Under EU Law, *GTCJ* 14(10), p. 455. Schippers argues that Article 128(1) UCC IA, prescribing that the transaction value in a succession of sales should be determined based on the last sale of export, should be declared invalid, see M.L. Schippers, A Series of Sales: Determining the Customs Value Under the Union Customs Code, *GTCJ* 13(2), p. 44-45.

29 Originally Article 288(2) UCC stipulated that the provisions of the UCC, other than those mentioned in Article 288(1) UCC, would apply as from 1 June 2016. This was corrected soon after the publication of the UCC in the Corrigendum to Regulation (EU) No 952/2013 of the European Parliament and of the Council of 9 October 2013 laying down the Union Customs Code (O.J. L 269, 10.10.2013, p. 1) O.J. L 287, 29.10.2013, p. 90–90.

30 Article 288(1) UCC.

31 Council Regulation (EC) No 1207/2001 of 11 June 2001 on procedures to facilitate the issue of movement certificates EUR.1, the making-out of invoice declarations and forms EUR.2 and the issue of certain approved exporter authorisations under the provisions governing preferential trade between the European Community and certain countries and repealing Regulation (EEC) No 3351/83, O.J. L 165, 21.6.2001, p. 1–12.

1.4.1 *Customs Debt and Guarantees*

1.4.1.1 *The incurrence and debtors of a customs debt*

The term 'customs debt' is defined in Article 5(18) UCC. It means the obligation on a person to pay the amount of the import duties (customs debt on importation) or export duties (customs debt on exportation) which apply to specific goods under the Union provisions in force. Article 56(1) UCC clarifies that such duties are laid down in the Common Customs Tariff (CCT). A customs debt can therefore only be incurred in cases where the CCT lays down a duty for the goods concerned.[32] It should be noted that no customs debt can be incurred upon importation of narcotic drugs and counterfeit currency (Art. 83(2) UCC). This provision was already incorporated in the former Code (e.g. the CCC), *inter alia*, based on the *Einberger* cases.[33]

Where no duty exemption applies, the customs debt is incurred at the time when the customs declaration requesting release for free circulation is accepted (Art. 77(2) UCC). The determination of the amount of import duties shall be determined by the customs authorities responsible for the place where the customs debt is incurred, or is deemed to have been incurred in accordance with Article 87 UCC, as soon as they have the necessary information (Art. 101(1) UCC). Subsequently the customs debt is entered into the accounts of the customs authorities (Art. 104 UCC) and notified to the customs debtor (Art. 102 UCC). The statute of limitation for notifying the customs debt to the customs debtor is three years from the date on which the customs debt was incurred. This three-year period can be extended if the customs debt is incurred as the result of an act which, at the time it was committed, was liable to give rise to criminal court proceedings. The three-year period can in that case be extended to a period of a minimum of five and a maximum of ten years in accordance with national customs legislation. The statute of limitation is suspended in cases where (Art. 103(3) UCC):
- an appeal is lodged; or
- the customs authorities have communicated to the debtor their intention to recover customs duties post-clearance.[34, 35]

The person liable for payment of the customs debt in case of a lawful importation of goods is the declarant, and – in the event of indirect representation (*i.e.* someone acting on his

32 See also C-1/77 (*Bosch*), [1977] ECR 01473, para 4.

33 Case 240/81 (*Senta Einberger I*), [1982] ECR 3699 and Case 294/82 (*Senta Einberger II*), [1984] ECR 1177. See also Case C-343/89 (*Witzemann*) on counterfeit currency prohibited in all the Member States, [1990] ECR I-4477.

34 If the customs authorities intend to make a decision that would adversely affect the applicant, the customs authorities shall communicate the grounds on which they intend to base their decision in accordance with Article 22(6) UCC. This also includes the case whereby the customs authorities intend to recover customs duties post-clearance. Article 22(6) UCC codifies the Court's decision in the Case C-349/ 07 (Sopropé), [2008] ECLI:EU:C:2008:746. In that case the Court confirms that the principle to be heard also to customs law.

35 Under the CCC the statute of limitation was not suspended following the communication of the customs authorities about the grounds on which they intend to base their decision upon.

own name but on behalf of another person, Art. 18(1) UCC) – also the person represented (Art. 77(3) UCC).[36]

Besides the lawful importation of goods, a customs debt is incurred in case of unlawful importation of goods into the customs territory of the Union. Under the CCC, a customs debt following the unlawful importation of goods could occur based on Article 202 ('smuggling'), Article 203 ('unlawful removal from customs supervision') or Article 204 ('non-fulfilment of an obligation') CCC. The question whether a customs debt occurred based on Article 203 or Article 204 CCC resulted in many court cases.[37] The reason for that being that an exception to the rule that a customs debt is incurred through the unlawful importation was provided for in Article 859 CCIP, but only applied to customs debts within the meaning of Article 204(1)(a) CCC. Article 859 CCIP contained an exhaustive set of rules on failures, within the meaning of Article 204(1)(a) CCC, which 'have no significant effect on the correct operation of the temporary storage or customs procedure in question' and which, being an exception to the rule that a customs debt is incurred through the non-fulfilment of one of the obligations arising from the temporary storage of goods or customs procedures concerned, do not give rise to a customs debt. In order to avoid difficulties in determining the legal basis on which the customs debt incurs, Article 79 UCC groups together all cases of incurrence of a customs debt by the unlawful importation of goods. Article 79(1) UCC sets out that a customs debt on import shall be incurred through non-compliance with any of the following:

a) one of the obligations laid down in the customs legislation concerning the introduction of non-Union goods into the customs territory of the Union, their removal from customs supervision, or the movement, processing, storage, temporary storage, temporary admission or disposal of such goods within that territory;[38]
b) one of the obligations laid down in the customs legislation concerning the end- use of goods within the customs territory of the Union;[39]
c) a condition governing the placing of non-Union goods under a customs procedure or the granting, by virtue of the end-use of the goods, of duty exemption or a reduced rate of import duty.

The customs debt is incurred at the moment when the non-fulfilment of the obligation which gives rise to the customs debt is not met or ceases to be met or the moment when

36 For a more detailed discussion about the circle of customs debtors, we refer to: P. Chao, Circle of Debtors on Importation Defined: Without Responsibilities No Liability, *GTCJ* 15(6), p. 288-294.

37 Many of these cases before the ECJ also involved the question whether the occurrence of the customs debt based on Articles 203 and 204 CCC should also result in chargeable event for VAT purposes, namely the importation, under Article 2(1)(d) of the VAT Directive (Chapter 2, section 2.6.4). See for example Case C-66/ 99 (Wandel), [2001] ECR I-00873, Case C-371/99 (Liberexim), [2002] ECR I-06227, Case C-337/01 (Hamann International), [2004] ECR I-01791, Case C-234/ 09 (DSV Road), [2010] ECR I-07333, Case C-273/12 (Harry Winston), [2013] ECLI: EU:C:2013:466, Case C-480/12 (X BV), [2014] ECLI:EU:C:2014:329, Case C-75/13 (SEK Zollagentur), [2014] ECLI:EU:C:2014:1759.

38 *E.g.* fail to discharge a special procedure within a certain time-limit *(Art. 215 UCC) or breaching one of the conditions relating to the fulfilment of the economic conditions (e.g. exceeding the limits stated in the authorization)* may lead to the incurrence of the customs debt under Article 79(1)(a) UCC.

39 *E.g.* incorrect classification of goods under a special procedure may lead to the incurrence of the customs debt under Article 79(1)(b) UCC.

a customs declaration is accepted if a situation described under point c applies (Art. 79(2) UCC). Summarized, the customs debtors are in cases referred to under points a and b (Art. 79(3) UCC):

- any person who was required to fulfil the obligations concerned;[40]
- the persons who knowingly either participated in this or acquired or held the goods.[41]

In cases referred to under point c (Art. 79(3) UCC) the customs debtors are:

- the person who is required to comply with the conditions for placing the goods under the procedure;
- (where a customs declaration in respect of one of the customs procedures referred to in point (c) of paragraph 1 is drawn up), the persons who knowingly provided false information for completing the customs declaration.

Where several persons are liable for payment of one customs debt, they are jointly and severally liable for such debt (Art. 84 UCC).[42]

The place where the customs debt is incurred is to be determined based on Article 87 UCC and depends on the legal basis of the incurrence of the customs debt. In sequence order the place where is customs debt is incurred is:

- The place where the customs declaration or the re-export declaration referred to in Articles 77, 78 and 81 is lodged.
- In all other cases, the place where a customs debt is incurred shall be the place where the events from which it arises occur.

---

40 This is also the case if the goods are stolen while they are placed under a special procedure, even if it concerns violent theft, see Case C-273/12 (*Harry Winston SARL*), [2013] ECLI:EU:C:2013:466. In that case the Court held that a customs debt incurs if goods are stolen from a customs warehouse and that this theft also give rise to the chargeable event 'importation of goods' and causes value added tax to become chargeable.

41 In Case C-414/02 (*Spedition Ulustrans*), [2004] ECR I-8633, the ECJ ruled that Article 202(3) CCC (now Art. 79(3)) is to be interpreted as meaning that it does not preclude national legislation which, in the event of unlawful introduction into the customs territory of the Community of goods subject to import duties, makes the employer co-debtor of the customs debt of the employee who introduced those goods in the conduct of the employer's affairs, so long as such legislation requires that the employer took part in the introduction of the goods and knew or ought reasonably to have known that such introduction was unlawful. See also Case C-195/03 (*Merabi Papismedov and Others*), [2005] ECR I-1667. In Case C-679/15 (*Ultra-Brag AG v Hauptzollamt Lörrach*), [2017] ECLI:EU:C:2017:40, the question was whether a legal person participates in an unlawful introduction (even) if one of its employees, who is not its statutory representative, was involved in that introduction while acting within the scope of his responsibility. The ECJ answered this question in the affirmative.

42 In Case C-78/10 (*Berel*), [2011] ECR I-0000, the ECJ held that Articles 213, 233 and 239 CCC (now Articles 84, 124 and 116) must be interpreted as precluding the application, in the context of joint and several liability for a customs debt within the meaning of Article 213 CCC, of a principle of national law which has the effect that a partial remission of duty granted on the basis of Article 239 CCC to one of the debtors may be relied on by all the other debtors, so that the extinction of the debt provided for in point (b) of Article 233 CCC relates to the debt as such and thus releases all the jointly and severally liable debtors from payment of the debt to the extent of the amount remitted.

- If it is not possible to determine that place, the customs debt shall be incurred at the place where the customs authorities conclude that the goods are in a situation in which a customs debt is incurred.

1.4.1.2 Repayment/Remission

In case the customs debt has been communicated to the debtor, the amount of duties may be repaid or remitted (the latter if the debt has not yet been paid). There are several grounds for repayment or remission included in the UCC. Article 116(1) UCC provides for the following grounds (the grounds are discussed in further detail further down below):
i. overcharged amount of import or export duty (Art. 117 UCC),
ii. defective goods or goods not complying with the terms of the contract (Art. 118 UCC).
iii. error by the competent authorities (Art. 119 UCC),
iv. equity (Art. 120 UCC), or
v. invalidation of the customs declaration (second subparagraph of Art. 116(1) UCC).

For the grounds mentioned under the first and second indent it is mandatory to submit an application for repayment or remission, while for the other grounds the repayment or remission can be granted either on own initiative of the customs authorities or following an application by the person concerned. The procedure for repayment and remission is laid down in Article 121 UCC. The general time-limit of three years laid down in Article 121(1)(a) UCC to submit the application applies for the grounds mentioned under the first, third and fourth indent. For defective or non-complying goods the application for repayment or remission should be submitted within one year of the date of the notification of the customs debt, whereas in case of invalidation of a customs declaration, the period is specified in the rules applicable to invalidation. Based on the provisions included in Section 3, Chapter 2, Title III of the UCC it does not seems necessary to file a request to amend the customs declaration (Art. 173(3) UCC) for a successful request of repayment or remission.

According to Article 172 UCC IA, the application should be submitted by the person who has paid or is liable to pay the amount of customs duties, or by any person who has succeeded him in his rights and obligations.

If the application for repayment or submission is submitted, the customs authorities are entitled to take a decision, except for those situations where customs authorities consider that repayment or remission should be granted on the basis of Article 119 or 120 UCC and one of the cases described in Article 116(3) UCC applies. In that case the Member State concerned shall transmit the file to the Commission. The case most frequently occurring is when the amount for which the person concerned may be liable in respect of one or more import or export operations equals or exceeds EUR 500 000 as a result of an error or special circumstances (Art. 116(3)(d) UCC).

i) Overcharged amount of import or export duty
A repayment or remission of overcharged customs duties shall be granted on the basis of Article 116(1)(a) UCC insofar the amount corresponding to the customs debt initially notified exceeds the amount payable, or in case a customs debt was notified to the debtor

contrary to points (c) and (d) of Article 102(1) UCC (Art. 117 UCC). 'Justifications' used to invoke Article 116(1)(a) are among others amendment of the tariff classification or customs valuation, omissions or errors (e.g. material mistakes where calculating the amount of duty), or a posteriori request for relief from import duty (for returned goods, Art. 203 UCC).[43] In case the 'justification' relates to a posteriori request for the benefit of a reduced or zero rate of import duty on the goods under a tariff quota, a tariff ceiling or other favourable tariff measures, the repayment or remission shall, according to Article 117(2) UCC, be granted provided that, at the time of lodging the application accompanied by the necessary documents, either of the following conditions are fulfilled: i) in the case of a tariff quota, its volume has not been exhausted; ii) in other cases, the rate of duty normally due has not been re-established.

ii) Defective goods or goods not complying with the terms of the contract

Repayment or remission is, according to Article 118 UCC, granted on the basis of Article 119(1)(b) UCC if the goods are refused by the importer, either because of non-conformity at the time of release with the terms of the contract on the basis of which they were imported, or since the goods appear defective at the time of release. In these cases the application for repayment or remission should be submitted within one year of the date of the notification of the customs debt.[44]

iii) Error by the competent authorities

On the basis of Article 119 UCC repayment or remission of customs duties is granted in case of an error of the customs authorities in the follow up of a tariff quota (paragraph 2) or an error by the competent authorities (paragraph 1).[45] According to Article 119(1) UCC, customs duties shall only be repaid or remitted in case of an error by the competent customs authorities if: i) the debtor could not reasonably have detected that error; and ii) the debtor was acting in good faith. The ECJ held that 'competent authority' is referring not only to '*authorities competent for taking action for recovery but any authority which, acting within the scope of its powers, furnishes information relevant to the recovery of customs duties and which may thus cause the person liable to entertain legitimate expectations*'.[46] In that same court case, the ECJ held that '*legitimate expectations of the person liable attract the protection provided for in that article* [now Art. 119(1) UCC] *only if it was the competent authorities 'themselves' which created the basis for those expectations. Thus, only errors attributable to acts of those authorities confer entitlement to the waiver of post-clearance recovery of customs duties*'.[47]

43 Guidelines on Repayment and Remission of Customs Debt of the Commission, p. 8.

44 This situation should be distinguished from price adjustments for defective goods within the meaning of Article 132 UCC IA. For the latter the general time- limit of three years laid down in Article 121(1)(a) UCC for claiming repayment or remission of overcharged duties applies. See section 2 of the preamble of Commission Implementing Regulation (EU) 2020/893.

45 Special conditions apply if the error by the competent authorities take the form of a certificate issued by a customs authority outside the customs territory of the Union on which basis preferential treatment is granted (Article 119(3) UCC).

46 Case C-251/00 (*Ilumitrónica*), [2002] ECR I-10433, paragraph 40.

47 Case C-251/00 (*Ilumitrónica*), [2002] ECR I-10433, paragraph 42.

iv) Equity

In other cases than provided for in the second paragraph of Article 116(1), and in Articles 117, 118 and 119, Article 119(1)(d) UCC provides for the repayment or remission of customs duties in the interest of equity (i.e. in case of special circumstances), provided there is no deception or negligence on the part of the economic operator. The second paragraph of Article 120 UCC indicates that a 'special circumstances' shall be deemed to exist where it is clear from the circumstances of the case that the debtor is in an exceptional situation as compared with other operators engaged in the same business, and that, in the absence of such circumstances, he or she would not have suffered disadvantage by the collection of the amount of import or export duty.

In the *British American Tobacco Manufacturing BV* case the ECJ dealt with the question whether the fact that infringements of the Community transit system originate in the conduct of an undercover agent belonging to the customs services constitutes a special situation which may, in appropriate cases, justify the remission or repayment of the duties paid by the principal. The ECJ found that although it may be legitimate for the national authorities, in order better to dismantle a network, identify perpetrators of fraud and obtain or consolidate evidence, deliberately to allow offences or irregularities to be committed, to place on the person liable the burden of the customs debt arising from the choices made in connection with the prosecution of offences is inimical to the objective of fairness which underlies the relevant Community rules in that it puts that person in an exceptional situation in comparison with other operators engaged in the same business. According to the ECJ, such a conclusion applies even more strongly where the infringements of the Community transit system have been committed or provoked by the customs authorities themselves.[48]

v) Invalidation of the customs declaration

Repayment or remission of a customs debt occur if the customs declaration is invalidated. According to Article 148 UCC DA this is the case if:

- goods declared in error for a customs procedure under which a customs debt is incurred instead of being declared for another procedure;
- goods have been declared in error instead of other goods for a customs procedure under which a customs debt is incurred;
- goods sold under a distance contract as defined in Article 2(7) of Directive 2011/ 83/ EU of European Parliament and of the Council have been released for free circulation and are returned;
- Union goods have been declared in error for a customs procedure applicable to non-Union goods and their customs status as Union goods has been proved afterwards by means of a T2L, T2F or customs goods manifest;
- goods erroneously declared under more than one customs declarations;
- authorisation with retroactive effect is granted in accordance with Article 211(2) UCC.

48 Case C-222/01 (*British American Tobacco Manufacturing BV*), [2004] ECR I- 4683. See also Case T-282/01 (*Aslantrans* AG), [2004] ECR II-693, in which the CFI held that there was no special situation and Case C-494/09 (*Bolton Alimentari*), [2011] ECR I- 00647, on the 'special situation' within the meaning of Article 239(1) CCC (now Art. 116(1)(d) UCC) where a tariff quota was exhausted on the day on which it was opened, namely a Sunday, that being a day on which the customs offices in the Member State in which the operator in question is established are closed.

The time-limits for submitting the application for repayment or remission are stipulated in Article 148 UCC and cannot be prolonged.

1.4.1.3 The extinguishment of a customs debt

The grounds for extinguishing a customs debt are enumerated in Article 124(1) UCC. Where the customs debt is incurred through irregularities, the customs debt can still be extinguished according to Article 124(1)(h) and (g) UCC. From Article 124(1)(h) UCC it can be extracted that a customs debt that incurs based on Article 79 UCC shall be extinguished if the following conditions are met:

- the failure which led to the incurrence of a customs debt had no significant effect on the correct operation of the temporary storage or of the customs procedure concerned and did not constitute an attempt at deception;
- all of the formalities necessary to regularise the situation of the goods are subsequently carried out.

Context to the phrase 'failures ...[with].... no significant effect' has been given in Article 103 UCC DA. Under the CCC, the situations with no significant effect were included in Article 859 CCIP. Compared to Article 124(1)(h) UCC, there are two, significant differences. First, Article 859 CCIP only refers to non-compliance with the obligations (Art. 204 CCC) and not to removal of the goods from customs supervision (Art. 203 CCC). Article 124(1)(h) UCC does not make a(n) (explicit) difference between customs debts incurred through non-compliance with the obligations and the removal of goods from customs supervision, but 'simply' refers to the incurrence of a customs debt through irregularities in the sense of Articles 79 and 82 UCC. The second difference is that if a failure has no significant effect, the customs debt shall not incur under Article 204 CCC, while under the UCC the customs debt will be extinguished. In the case of the latter, that means that when the customs debt as already been communicated to the debtor, a request for repayment or remission should be submitted (section 1.4.1.2).

A ground for the extinguishment of a customs debt without an equivalent provision in the CCC, concerns Article 124(1)(k) UCC that provides for the extinguishment of an irregular incurred customs debt where evidence is provided to the satisfaction of the customs authorities that the goods have not been used or consumed and have been taken out of the customs territory of the Union. In the Case C-476/19 (*Combinova*) goods were processed under an inward processing procedure (section 1.5.4.5) and subsequently re-exported on 11 December 2017.[49] In the underlying case the bill of discharge (a formal notice to the customs authorities to end the procedure) should have been submitted on 22 February 2018 at the latest, but was received by the customs authorities on 5 March 2018. Although the goods were re-exported, the goods had been processed in the EU. The question referred to the ECJ was therefore whether that would prevent the customs debt from being extinguished pursuant to Article 124(1)(k) UCC. According to the ECJ 'used' shall be understood '*as meaning that the use of the goods referred to in that provision concerns only use which goes beyond the processing operations authorised by the customs authority under the inward*

49 Case C-476/19 (*Combinova*), [2020] ECLI:EU:C:2020:802.

processing procedure provided for in Article 256 of that code, and not use in accordance with those authorised processing operations.' Another outcome would have resulted in a very limited scope of application of Article 124(1)(k) UCC, especially for cases whereby goods undergo authorized processing operations under a special procedure.

For both Article 124(1)(h) and (k) UCC, the customs debt only extinguishes where the failure did not constitute an attempt at deception.[50] With this condition the legislator seems to have set the bar higher compared to Article 859 CCIP, where a customs debt does not occur provided that the failures does not imply obvious negligence on the part of the person concerned. It seems namely that 'obvious negligence' is easier to hold against a customs debtor compared to 'an attempt at deception'.

1.4.2 *Factors on the basis of which import duties are applied*

Title II (the factors on the basis of which duties are applied) does not cover the simplest subjects of customs law. Even if one would analyse that customs law basically boils down to 'percentage x value = the debt incurred', one still must know the applicable percentage (*i.e.* the duty) and the value. Title II distinguishes between:
(a) the customs tariff (section 1.4.2.1);
(b) origin (section 1.4.2.2); and
(c) customs value (section 1.4.2.3).

1.4.2.1 *The Customs Tariff*

By its very nature the UCC cannot cover all the customs rules and measures applicable to trade between the EU and third countries. Since it is the task of the UCC to group together the general rules, arrangements and procedures applicable to goods irrespective of their nature in a coherent system, the whole of the tariff policy, determined product by product, is excluded from it. With regard to the Common Customs Tariff (CCT) the UCC is rather brief (3 Articles). The main rule is that duties legally owed where a customs debt is incurred are based on the CCT of the EU.

On 22 September 1987, the Community ratified the International Convention on the Harmonized Commodity Description, the 'Harmonized System' (HS), which replaced the Brussels Convention of 1950 on Nomenclature for the Classification of Goods in Customs Tariffs. As a result of the Harmonized System a product appears under an identical description adopted by all the participating countries. At present there are more than a hundred Contracting Parties to this Convention, however, it is applied by more than 190 administrations worldwide, mostly to set up their national customs tariff and for the collection of economic statistical data. The European Union and its Member States together represent a block of 27 Contracting Parties to the aforementioned Convention.

50 For Article 124(1)(h) UCC this condition has been laid down under (i), where this condition is laid down in paragraph 6 for Article 124(1)(k) UCC.

The HS Nomenclature comprises about 5,000 commodity groups which are identified by a 6-digit code and arranged according to a legal and logical structure based on fixed rules. The Combined Nomenclature (CN) of the EU integrates the HS Nomenclature and comprises additional 8-digit subdivisions and legal notes specifically created to address the needs of the Union.[51]

The Harmonized System has been adopted by Regulation (EEC) No. 2658/87[52] on the Tariff and Statistical Nomenclature and on the CCT. This Regulation instituted a system called 'Combined Nomenclature' (CN). The CN also includes preliminary provisions, additional section or chapter notes and footnotes relating to CN subdivisions. Each CN subdivisions has an 8-digit code number, the CN code, followed by a description.

Duties based on the CCT of the EU comprise (Art. 56(2) UCC):
(a) the Combined Nomenclature (laid down in a separate Regulation, mentioned above);
(b) any other nomenclature based on the CN adding subdivisions in specific fields;
(c) the rates;
(d) conventional preferential tariff measures (*e.g.* originally based on the Lomé Convention, now on the Cotonou Agreement[53]);
(e) autonomous Union preferential tariff measures (*e.g.* the General Scheme of Preferences (GSP));
(f) autonomous suspensive measures; and
(g) other tariff measures prescribed for by other Union legislation;
(h) other tariff measures provided for by agricultural or commercial or other Union legislation.

Since certain specific Union measures could not be dealt with in the framework of the Combined Nomenclature it was necessary to create additional Union subdivisions and to include them in the integrated Tariff of the European Community (TARIC: Tarifs intégrés des communautés européennes).[54]

51 Every five year, the World Customs Organization (WCO) in Brussels adopt amendments to the structure and nomenclature of the HS, which is the basis for the tariff and statistical nomenclature of the European Union, the CN. HS Nomenclature 2022 have been accepted as a result of the Council Recommendation of 25 June 2020. The European Union, as a signatory and therefore a Contracting Party to the international HS Convention, is required to adopt these amendments and implement them effective January 1, 2022.

52 Last amended by Commission Regulation (EU) No. 1006/201. O.J. 2011, L 282, p. 1.

53 See Council Decision 2010/648/EU of 14 June 2010 on the signing, on behalf of the European Union, of the Agreement amending for the second time the Partnership Agreement between the members of the African, Caribbean and Pacific Group of States, of the one part, and the European Community and its Member States, of the other part, signed in Cotonou on 23 June 2000, as first amended in Luxembourg on 25 June 2005. O.J. 2010, L 287, p. 1.

54 For an introduction see O.J. 2003, C 103. The European Commission has decided to discontinue the annual publication of the integrated tariff of the European Communities in the EU's Official Journal. The online version of TARIC which is updated daily can be consulted on the Internet, https://ec.europa.eu/taxation_customs/dds2/taric/taric_consultation.jsp?Lang=en.

Generalised Scheme of Preferences

The EU Generalised Scheme of Preferences, referred to above, is the system of preferential trading arrangements through which the European Union extends preferential access to its markets to developing countries. In 1968 the United Nations Conference on Trade and Development (UNCTAD) recommended the creation of a 'Generalised System of Tariff Preferences' under which developed countries would grant trade preferences to all developing countries. The EU was the first to implement a GSP scheme in 1971. The current GSP scheme applies from 20 November 2012 until 31 December 2023.[55] The following three tariff preference arrangements fall under the scheme:

(1) General arrangement: under this arrangement the EU grants tariff reductions from products covered by around 66 % of tariff lines and originating from low- income or lower-middle income countries, which do not benefit from other preferential access to the EU market.[56]

(2) A special incentive arrangement sustainable development and good governance (GSP+). It eliminates tariffs for products covered by the essential by the same tariff lines as under general arrangement. The beneficiaries must meet a number of criteria (see below) including ratification and effective application of 27 key international conventions on sustainable development and good governance.

(3) 'Everything but Arms', a special arrangement for least-developed countries (LDCs): for the world's poorest countries this allows duty free access to the EU for all products except arms and ammunition.

To benefit from 'GSP+' countries need to demonstrate that their economies are poorly diversified, and therefore dependent and vulnerable. Poor diversification and dependence is defined as meaning that the seven largest sections of its GSP-covered imports to the Union must represent more than 75% of its total GSP-covered imports. GSP-covered imports from that country must also represent less than 2% of total EU imports under GSP.

They also have to have ratified and effectively implemented all fifteen core conventions on human and labour rights and twelve of the conventions related to good governance and the protection of the environment.

Certain products from GSP beneficiaries can be graduated from the scheme if they become competitive on the EU market. This is a sign that these products no longer need the GSP to boost their exportation. Thus, graduation is not a penalty, but indicates that the GSP has successfully performed its function, at least in relation to the country and product in question. This ensures that the GSP focuses on the country's most in need and helps them play a greater role in international trade.[57]

55 Regulation (EU) No. 978/2012, O.J. 2012, L 303, p. 1-82. According to Article 43 of the aforementioned regulation the expiry date shall neither apply to the special arrangement for the least-developed countries, nor, to the extent that they are applied in conjunction with that arrangement, to any other provisions of this Regulation.

56 Report on the Generalised Scheme of Preferences covering the period 2018- 2019, JOIN(2020) 3 final.

57 During the period 1 January 2020 and 31 December 2022, the graduated industries of some GSP beneficiaries are set-out in Commission Implementing Regulation (EU) No. 2019/249, O.J. 2019, L 42, p. 6-8.

We refer to 1.4.2.2 for the rules of origin that apply within the framework of the GSP of the Union.

Classification rules

In order to know which rates are applicable, goods must be classified according to certain rules. The following classification rules apply:

1. The titles of sections, chapters and sub-chapters are provided for ease of reference only; for legal purposes, classification shall be determined according to the terms of the headings and any relative section or chapter notes and, provided such headings or notes do not otherwise require, according to the following provisions.
2. (a) Any reference in a heading to an article shall be taken to include a reference to that article incomplete or unfinished, provided that, as presented, the incomplete or unfinished article has the essential character of the complete or finished article. It shall also be taken to include a reference to that article complete or finished (or falling to be classified as complete or finished by virtue of this rule), presented unassembled or disassembled.
   (b) Any reference in a heading to a material or substance shall be taken to include a reference to mixtures or combinations of that material or substance with other materials or substances. Any reference to goods of a given material or substance shall be taken to include a reference to goods consisting wholly or partly of such material or substance. The classification of goods consisting of more than one material or substance shall be according to the principles of rule 3.
3. When by application of rule 2(b) or for any other reason, goods *art prima facie* classifiable under two or more headings, classification shall be effected as follows:
   (a) The heading which provides the most specific description shall be preferred to headings providing a more general description. However, when two or more headings each refer to part only of the material or substances contained in mixed or composite goods or to only part of the items in a set put up for retail sale, those headings are to be regarded as equally specific in relation to those goods, even if one of them gives a more complete or precise description of the goods.
   (b) Mixtures, composite goods consisting of different materials or made up of different components, and goods put up in sets for retail sale, which cannot be classified by reference to 3(a), shall be classified as if they consisted of the material or component which gives them their essential character in so far as this criterion is applicable.[58]
   (c) When goods cannot be classified by reference to 3(a) or (b), they shall be classified under the heading which occurs last in numerical order among those which equally merit consideration.

58 See for example with regard to rule 3b, Case T-243/01 (*Sony Computer Entertainment Europe Ltd*), [2003] ECR II-4189, where a classification regulation regarding the PlayStation 2 was annulled based on the reply to a question from the CFI, in which the Commission stated that the component which gives the PlayStation 2 its essential characteristic is the component called Emotion Engine. That statement was at odds with the reasons given in the classification regulation, according to which it is the video game function which gives the apparatus its essential characteristic; accordingly, it could not justify its being classified in the regulation under the heading for video games.

4. Goods which cannot be classified in accordance with the above rules shall be classified under the heading appropriate to the goods to which they are most akin.
5. In addition to the foregoing provisions, the following rules shall apply in respect of the goods referred to therein:
   (a) Camera cases, musical instrument cases, gun cases, drawing-instrument cases, necklace cases and similar containers, specially shaped or fitted to contain a specific article or set of articles, suitable for long-term use and presented with the articles for which they are intended, shall be classified with such articles when of a kind normally sold therewith. This rule does not, however, apply to containers which give the whole its essential character.
   (b) Subject to the provisions of rule 5(a) above, packing materials and packing containers presented with the goods therein shall be classified with the goods if they are of a kind normally used for packing such goods. However, this provision is not binding when such packing materials or packing containers are clearly suitable for repetitive use. (The terms 'packing materials' and 'packing containers' mean any external or internal containers, holders, wrappings or supports other than transport devices (e.g. transport containers), tarpaulins, tackle or ancillary transport equipment. The term 'packing containers' does not cover the containers referred to in general rule 5(a).)
6. For legal purposes, the classification of goods in the subheadings of a heading shall be determined according to the terms of those subheadings and any related subheading notes and *mutatis mutandis* to the above rules, on the understanding that only subheadings at the same level are comparable. For the purposes of this rule the relative section and chapter notes also apply, unless the context otherwise requires.

Needless to say, these rules have been a source of controversy and have resulted in extensive case-law by the ECJ. To obtain legal certainty about the classification of goods, a binding tariff information (BTI decision) can be obtained from the customs authorities (section 1.3.1.4).

One of the issues of controversy relates to the notion of 'parts'. In principle every imported good is classified based on its own characteristics and properties, except for those cases where a good is treated as a 'part'. In that case a good, that is treated as a part, is classified under the same classification code as the good of which it is a part. It is established case-law that 'the notion of 'parts' implies a whole for the operation of which the part is essential.'[59] With regard to the Chapters 84, 85 and 90 the ECJ held that 'in order to classify an article as 'parts' [...] *it is not sufficient to show that, without that article, the machine or apparatus is not able to carry out its intended functions. It must also be established that the mechanical or electrical functioning of the machine or apparatus in question is dependent on that article'.*[60] Based on these criteria, the ECJ held that LED bulbs are not a part of lamps and lighting fittings,[61] ink- cartridges are not considered a part of a printer,[62] stove pipe set are

59 Case C-600/15 (*Lemnis Lighting BV*), [2016] ECLI:EU:C:2016:937, paragraph 48.
60 Case C-600/15 (*Lemnis Lighting BV*), [2016] ECLI:EU:C:2016:937, paragraph 48.
61 Case C-600/15 (*Lemnis Lighting BV*), [2016] ECLI:EU:C:2016:937.
62 Case C-276/00 (*Turbon International*), [2002] ECLI:EU:C:2002:88.

considered a part of a stove,[63] and polishing pads intended exclusively for semiconductor wafer- polishing machines are not considered parts of a polishing machine.[64]

Another issue relates to regulations of the Commission concerning the classification of certain goods in the CN. These regulations intend to ensure the uniform application of the CN, but gave rise to a good deal of litigation over the last couple of decades. These are either court cases that deal with a request for the annulment of a classification regulation, or, in other cases it concerns preliminary requests about the scope of the regulation,[65] or the application in time of the particular regulations.

Suspensions and Tariff Quota
The suspensions adopted on the basis of now Article 31 TFEU constitute an exception to the normal state of affairs (application of normal customs duty rate) since, during the period of validity of the measure and for an unlimited quantity they permit the total (total suspension) or partial waiver (partial suspension) of the normal duties applicable to imported goods (anti-dumping duties are not affected by these suspensions).

In this connection, it should be pointed out that goods imported under the suspension arrangements are in free circulation and enjoy freedom of movement throughout the Union. Furthermore, once a suspension is granted, normally any operator in any Member State is eligible to benefit from it. In the framework of several agreements that the European Union has concluded with third countries, as well as in the framework of autonomous preferential arrangements for some beneficiary countries, tariff concessions are provided for a pre-determined volume of goods. These tariff concessions are called 'preferential tariff quotas'. Within these preferential tariff quotas, a predetermined volume of goods originating in a specified country can benefit at import into the Union from a more favourable rate of duty than the normal third countries duty mentioned in the combined nomenclature. Entitlement to benefit from preferential tariff quotas is of course subject to presentation of the necessary evidence of origin.

1.4.2.2 Origin

The concept of origin can be divided between:
- Non-preferential origin
- Preferential origin

Non-preferential and preferential origin are not each other's opposites, but have their own purpose and set of rules. *Non-preferential origin* is used for the purposes of applying the CCT (with the exception of conventional and autonomous Union preferential tariff measures), non-tariff barriers, and other Union measures relating to the origin of the goods. *Preferential origin* relates to preferential measures that provide for the granting of preferential tariff

63 Case C-450/12 (*HARK*), [2013] ECLI:EU:C:2013:824.
64 Case C-336/11 (*Rohm & Haas Electronic Materials CMP Europe and others*), [2012] ECLI:EU:C:2012:500.
65 See e.g. Case C-106/94 and C-139/94 (*Colin and Dupré*), [1995] ECR I-04759, Case C-130/02 (*Krings*), [2004] ECR I-02121, Case C-376/07 (*Kamino*), [2009] ECR I-01167.

treatment to goods originating from certain countries, groups of countries or territories (a reduced duty or zero-rate).

Non-preferential origin

According to Article 60(1) UCC, goods wholly obtained in a single country or territory shall be regarded as having their origin in that country or territory. Article 31 UCC DA lists the goods that shall be considered wholly obtained in a single country or territory (e.g. mineral products extracted within that country or territory). Goods whose production involved more than one country (and that is normally the case) are deemed to originate in the country where they underwent their last, substantial economically justified processing or working.[66] In Article 34 UCC DA operations are listed that are not considered substantial, economically justified processing or working for the purposes of conferring origin ('minimal operations'). No origin is conferred when the facts justify the presumption that the sole object is circumvention of the applicable rates.

Preferential origin

To benefit from conventional preferential tariff measures, autonomous Union preferential tariff measures (GSP) and non-tariff preferential measures, the rules on origin are laid down in the UCC legal package. In case goods are benefiting from preferential measures contained in agreements which the Union has concluded with certain countries or groups of countries, the rules on origin are determined in those agreements.[67]

For the purpose of preferential tariff measures adopted within the framework of GSP, the rules are embedded in Articles 41 to 58 UCC DA. The rules are based on the criterion that goods are considered originating from a GSP beneficiary country if the goods are wholly obtained and, for goods whose production involved more than one country, on the criterion that goods result from sufficient processing or working. The rules for determining whether goods have been sufficiently worked or processed are adapted to each sector. The rules are based on the calculation of the content of non-originating materials, change of tariff heading, a specific processing requirement or the use of wholly obtained inputs, according to the case. Besides bilateral and cumulation with Norway, Switzerland and Turkey, the rules on origin provides for regional cumulation of origin which allows countries with identical rules of origin to work together for the purpose of manufacturing products eligible for preferential tariff. From 2017 on, a new procedure for demonstrating proof of origin whereby statements on origin are made out directly by exporters registered via an electronic system (Registered Exporter system, 'REX') has gradually replaced the former system of certification of origin carried out by the third country authorities. This will allow

66 The ECJ held that 'substantial' means that the product resulting from the processing should have 'its own properties and a composition of its own, which it did not possess before that process or operation', see Case 49/76 (*Gesellschaft für Überseehandel*), [1997] ECR I-41. In that regard, the ECJ held, for example, that the separation, crushing and purification of silicon metal blocks and the subsequent sieving, sorting and packaging of the silicon grains resulting from the crushing does not constitute origin-conferring processing or working for the purposes of Article 24 CCC (Art. 60(2) UCC), see Case C-373/08 (*Hoesch*), [2010] ECR I-951.

67 Examples of such agreements are the EU-UK Trade and Cooperation Agreement (EU-UK TCA), the EU-Canada Comprehensive Economic and Trade Agreement (CETA) and EU-Japan Economic Partnership Agreement (EU-Japan EPA).

the authorities of the exporting country to re-focus their resources on better controls against fraud and abuse, while reducing red tape for businesses. It does, however, place more responsibility on the operators.

As mentioned above, the rules on preferential origin with regard to bi- or multilateral agreements (often referred to as free trade agreements, FTAs) are laid down in those agreements. The rules in these agreements are also based on the criterion that goods are considered originating from a FTA country or territory if the goods are wholly obtained and, for goods whose production involved more than one country, on the criterion that goods result from sufficient processing or working. Depending on the applied FTA, demonstrating proof of origin takes the form of a movement certificate EUR.1, a movement certificate EUR-Med and/or invoice declaration. In more recent FTAs these means of evidence are replaced by statements on origin and importer's knowledge.[68],[69] An invoice declaration and statement on origin are both based on a principle of self-certification. For making out an invoice declaration or statement on origin for exports from the EU it is required that an economic operator obtained a license for approved exporter or is registered via an electronic system (REX) respectively.

1.4.2.3 The Customs Value

Even if one knows when a customs debt is incurred, which rate is applicable (taking into account the origin), the amount of duties cannot be calculated if one does not know the value for customs purposes, insofar as *ad valorem* duties are applied, *i.e.* a percentage of the value, which is normally the case. Customs duties may also be levied on a specific basis a fixed amount based on weight, quantity, volume, etc. Even a combination of *ad valorem* and specific duties is possible. The advantage of specific duties is that they are easy to apply. The advantage of *ad valorem* duties is that they tax expensive and low-cost products proportionally, they are easier to compare in international trade, they adapt to

68 The EU-Japan Economic Partnership Agreement and the EU-UK Trade Cooperation Agreement provide for the possibility to use importer's knowledge as means to claim preferential origin.

69 In Case C-66/99 (*Wandel*), [2001] ECR I-873, the ECJ decided that when goods are removed, before an examination of goods by the customs authorities could take place, a customs debt is incurred, based on the removal from customs supervision. A technically correct certificate of origin allowing a zero preferential tariff has then no bearing on the incurrence of the debt. In Case C-253/99 (*Bacardi*), [2001] ECR I- 6493, the ECJ held that Article 236(1) CCC (now Art. 116(1) UCC) does not permit the repayment of import duties where, after a complete customs declaration has been accepted by the customs authorities and the goods covered by it have been released into free circulation, the declarant presents a certificate of authenticity by virtue of which the goods would, supposing the certificate to have been produced with the goods, have been eligible for favourable tariff treatment. The fact that repayment or remission of duties pursuant to Article 236(1) is excluded because one of the legal conditions laid down for that repayment or remission has not been satisfied does not, of itself, exclude repayment or remission of those duties on the basis of Article 239 (1) CCC (now Art. 120 UCC) provided however that the legal conditions for the application of those provisions are satisfied. Factors 'which might constitute a special situation resulting from circumstances in which no deception or obvious negligence may be attributed to the person concerned', exist where, having regard to the objective of fairness underlying Article 239 CCC, factors liable to place the applicant in an exceptional situation as compared with other operators engaged in the same business are found to exist.

monetary fluctuations. Times of inflations have tilted the balance to *ad valorem* duties. In the CN only a few specific duties can be found.

The source of customs valuation legislation comes from the WTO Customs Valuation Agreement. These rules have been transposed into the UCC (Articles 69 to 76), the UCC DA (Article 71) and the UCC IA (Articles 127 to 146). The Commission provided for some further guidance on the application of the provisions in the UCC legal package in its Compendium of Customs Valuation Texts (edition 2021).

The customs valuation methods

The primary and preferred method to determine the customs value of goods is the transaction value method. Where the customs value cannot be determined because the goods are not subject to a sale for export or the conditions to apply the transaction value method are not fulfilled, it is to be determined by proceeding sequentially through the following four, alternative valuation methods:

(1) the transaction value of identical goods sold for export to the Union and exported at or about the same time as the goods being valued;
(2) the transaction value of similar goods sold for export to the Union and exported at or about the same time as the goods being valued;
(3) the value based on the unit price at which the imported goods for identical or similar imported goods are sold within the Union in the greatest aggregate quantity to persons not related to the sellers ('deducted value method');
(4) the computed value, consisting of the sum of:
    - the cost or value of materials and fabrication or other processing employed in producing the imported goods;
    - an amount for profit and general expenses equal to that usually reflected in sales of goods of the same class or kind as the goods being valued which are made by producers in the country of exportation for export to the Union;
    - the cost or value of the items referred to below with regard to items to be added to the value.

The order of application of methods 3 and 4 may be reversed if the declarant so requests. Where the customs value of imported goods cannot be determined under any of the methods mentioned above, the fall-back method applies, whereby the customs value of the imported goods must be determined, on the basis of data available in the Union, using reasonable means.

The transaction value method

The main rule (Art. 70 UCC) is that the customs value of imported goods is the transaction value, that is, the price actually paid or payable for the goods when sold for export to the customs territory of the Union, with some adjustments discussed below, provided that:

(a) there are no restrictions as to the disposal or use of the goods by the buyer, other than restrictions which:
    - are imposed or required by a law or by the public authorities in the Union;
    - limit the geographical area in which the goods may be resold;
    - do not substantially affect the value of the goods.

(b) the sale or price is not subject to some condition or consideration for which a value cannot be determined with respect to the goods being valued;
(c) no part of the proceeds of any subsequent resale, disposal or use of the goods by the buyer will accrue directly or indirectly to the seller, unless an appropriate adjustment can be made as discussed below; and
(d) the buyer and seller are not related, or, where the buyer and seller are related, that the relationship did not influence the price.

Price paid or payable
The price actually paid or payable is the total payment made or to be made by the buyer to or for the benefit of the seller for the imported goods and includes all payments made or to be made as a condition of sale of the imported goods by the buyer to the seller or by the buyer to a third party to satisfy an obligation of the seller. The payment need not necessarily take the form of a transfer of money. Payment may be made by way of a letter of credit or a negotiable instrument and may be made directly or indirectly.

Activities, including marketing activities, undertaken by the buyer on his own account, other than those for which an adjustment is provided, as discussed below, are not considered to be an indirect payment to the seller, even though they might be regarded as of benefit to the seller or have been undertaken by agreement with the seller, and their cost are not added to the price actually paid or payable in determining the customs value of imported goods.

Case C-491/04 (*Dollond & Aitchison Ltd*)[70] deals with the question whether the customs value of goods delivered from Jersey includes the value of services supplied in the United Kingdom. Dollond and Aitchison ('D&A') is a firm of opticians with branches throughout the United Kingdom. Dollond & Aitchison Lenses Direct Ltd ('DALD'), a company in the group, incorporated under Jersey law, dispensed disposable contact lenses by post from Jersey to the United Kingdom between 1 July 1999 and 30 June 2001. Subscribers paid a fixed monthly amount, for which they received a periodic supply of disposable contact lenses together with solutions and soaking cases. In addition, the price covered an initial contact lens examination or consultation, a contact lens check at least once a year and any other aftercare relating to the use of the lenses.

Until 1998, D&A operated a similar scheme under which customers collected disposable contact lenses from a branch every three months. They were entitled to receive certain professional services and were required to undergo an annual eye check. The tax authorities treated that scheme as involving two separate supplies: a supply of goods, taxable at the standard rate of VAT, and a supply of services, which was exempt from VAT. The proportion of the price attributed to the services was greater than that attributable to the goods.

In 1998, the system changed so that a company not connected with the appellant in the main proceedings dispatched the lenses, solutions and cases from Scotland. The appellant company did not change its method of accounting for VAT even though, following a judgment of the High Court in the case of *Leightons Ltd v. CEC*, the tax authorities had

70 Case C-491/04 (*Dollond & Aitchison Ltd*), [2006] ECR I-2129.

found it necessary to conclude that supplies of contact lenses are a mixed supply of goods and services in which the service element extends to all types of professional services, including measuring and fitting.

With effect from July 1999, the company moved its warehousing operation to Jersey to take advantage of cheaper postal services.

The Commissioners of Customs and Excises held, by decision of 18 October 1999, that when DALD dispensed contact lenses from Jersey to customers in the United Kingdom, the company in question made single supplies of goods, rather than supplies of goods and services. By a second decision of 6 September 2001, they held that the true value of a consignment included all amounts payable as a condition of the sale, that is to say, its full price.

D&A brought an appeal against both those decisions. By order of 24 November 2004 the VAT and Duties Tribunal, Manchester, decided to stay the proceedings and to refer the case to the ECJ for a preliminary ruling. In its judgment the ECJ started with pointing out that the Island of Jersey is an integral part of the customs territory but constitutes a third territory as regards the rules established by the VAT Directive. Consequently, the supply of goods by a company established in Jersey to a customer resident in the United Kingdom constitutes an importation within the meaning of Article 2(2) of the Directive. The taxable amount is thus defined by (then) Article 11B(1) of the Sixth Directive as 'the value for customs purposes', determined in accordance with Article 29 CCC (now Art. 70 UCC).

With regard to the question whether the payment made by a customer for the supply of specified services, such as examination, consultation or aftercare required for contact lenses, must be added to the total payment for the specified goods, which include contact lenses, cleaning solutions and soaking cases, in order to constitute together the transaction value within the meaning of Article 29 CCC the ECJ extensively referred to its case-law regarding customs valuation starting with *Van Houten* in which it already held that in order to determine what constitutes the 'transaction value' the calculation must be made on the basis of the conditions on which the individual sale was made.[71] It also held in *Brown Boveri* that, although software is not 'goods' but intangible property not subject to the Common Customs Tariff, the cost of acquiring it must be regarded as an integral part of the price paid or payable for the goods where it is embodied in them.[72] The ECJ also referred to its judgment in *Sommer* in which it held, after finding that the analyses carried out after importation were necessary in order for the goods to be delivered in accordance with the provisions of the contract, that the costs of those analyses, which the importer invoices to the buyer in addition to the price of the goods, must be regarded as an integral part of the 'transaction value' of the latter.[73] And, finally, the ECJ recalled that in *Overland Footwear* it held that Articles 29, 32 and 33 CCC (now Art. 70, 71 and 72 UCC) must be construed as meaning that a buying commission which is included in the customs value declared and is not shown separately from the selling price of the goods in the import declaration must

71 See Case 65/85 (Van Houten), [1986] ECR 447, paragraph 13.
72 See Case C-79/89 (Brown Boveri), [1991] ECR I-1853, paragraph 21.
73 See Case C-15/99 (Sommer), [2000] ECR I-8989, paragraphs 24 and 27.

be considered to be part of the transaction value within the meaning of Article 29 of that Code and is, therefore, dutiable.[74]

The ECJ then examined whether the services supplied in the United Kingdom are an integral part of the price of the goods dispatched from Jersey so that the two elements may be regarded as constituting together the transaction value within the meaning of Article 29 CCC.

Referring to yet another customs case,[75] the ECJ noted that in this respect, the fact that one of the two elements is effected in the customs territory and the other one outside that territory is of no relevance for determining the transaction value.

The ECJ then looked at the special offer called 'Contact Lenses by Post' which includes, in addition to delivery of disposable lenses and solutions from Jersey directly to the customer's home, specified services including an initial contact lens consultation, followed by dispensing and fitting services, and a professional aftercare service as and when requested by the customer. All the services are provided by D&A or its franchisees. Furthermore, the customer makes an advance monthly payment to DALD by direct debit, which does not distinguish consultations and other services from goods, the contract does not provide for any additional options and the supply of the services in question is an obligation under national law, thus amounting to a condition of sale.[76]

The ECJ concluded that the offer is a global one in respect of which a single payment is made. Accordingly, the supplies of services must be regarded as part of the 'payments made or to be made as a condition of sale of the imported goods by the buyer to the seller ... to satisfy an obligation of the seller' within the meaning of Article 29 CCC and, therefore, as an integral part of the customs value. From a customs case-law perspective the case it not surprising, we just wonder why the ECJ did not leave it to the referring court to decide whether the services in question amounted to a condition of sale.

Sale for export to the customs territory of the Union

The term sale should be interpreted in the widest sense.[77] In the case *Unifert* the ECJ held that 'the criterion which emerges from the term 'sold for export' relates to the goods and not to the situation of the seller. Placed in its proper context, the term suggests that it is agreed, at the time of sale, that the goods originating in a non- member country will be transported into the customs territory of the Community.'[78] If the buyer and seller agree, at the time of sale, that goods originating in a third country will be transported to another third country, the transaction value cannot be utilized, even if these goods are removed from customs supervision during their transit in the customs territory of the European Union.[79]

74 See Case C-379/00 (Overland Footwear I), [2002] ECR I-11133, paragraph 17.
75 See Case C-116/89 (BayWa), [1991] ECR I-1095, paragraph 15.
76 The ECJ also observed that, according to D&A, the supplies of services are invoiced separately if the customer does not adhere to the CLBP offer described earlier.
77 See also Case C-116/12 (*Christodoulou*), [2013] ECR 825. In this case the ECJ held that the transaction value can even be applied for 'the determination of the customs value of goods imported on the basis of a contract which, although described as a contract of sale, in fact proves to be a working or processing contract.'
78 See Case C-11/89 (*Unifert*), [1990] ECR I-2275, paragraph 11.
79 See Case C-46/16 (*LS Customs Services*), [2017] ECLI:EU:C:2017:839.

In the event of a series of sales, Article 128(1) UCC IA prescribes that transaction value should be established based on the sale occurring immediately before the goods were brought into that customs territory.[80] If the goods are not subject to a sale for export at the time of acceptance of the customs declaration, the transaction value cannot be applied and the customs value needs to be determined on an alternative valuation method, except for the situation described under Article 128 (2) UCC IA. Based on this provision the transaction value can still be used, namely on the first sale while the goods are in temporary storage or while placed under a special procedure other than internal transit, end-use or outward processing.[81]

Software imported on carrier media[82]

It should be noted that upon importation of software, the customs value is no longer restricted to the value of the carrier,[83] see Commission Regulation (EC) No. 444/ 2002 of 11 March 2002. According to the preamble of this Regulation:

> (7) The purpose of Article 167(1) of Regulation (EEC) No. 2454/93 was to avoid the levying of customs duties on software imported on carrier media. That objective has since been achieved by the Agreement on trade in information technology products (ITA), approved by Council Decision 97/359/EC. Without prejudice to the application of GATT Decision 4.1 of 12 May 1995, it is therefore no longer necessary to provide special implementing provisions for the determination of the customs value of carrier media.

This also applies to the UCC. In the *Compaq Computer International Corporation*- case[84] the ECJ held that in order to determine the customs value of imports of computers equipped by the seller with software for one or more operating systems made available by the buyer to the seller free of charge, in accordance with Article 32 (1)(b) or (c) CCC (now Art. 71(1)(b) or (c) UCC), the value of the software must be added to the transaction value of the computers if the value of the software has not been included in the price actually paid or payable for those computers. The same is true when the national authorities accept as the transaction value, in accordance with Union law, the price of a sale other than that made by the Union purchaser. In such cases, 'buyer' for the purposes of Article 32(1)(b) or (c) CCC must be understood to mean the buyer who concluded that other sale.

80 M.L. Schippers, A series of sales: determining the Customs Value Under the Union Customs Code, *Global Trade and Customs Journal*, 13 (2), p. 36-48.

81 Commentary No 13: Guidance on Articles 128 and 136 UCC IA of the Customs Expert Group, Valuation section.

82 For further reading, reference is made to M.L. Schippers, 'Some thoughts about imposing import duties on electronic transmissions in an era of digitalisation', in: P. Kavelaars (Ed.), *European Fiscal Essays*, Amsterdam: NLFiscaal 2021, p. 153-166 and M.L. Schippers, Software and customs valuation, *Global Trade and Customs Journal*, 16 (6), p. 222-228.

83 With regard to VAT and the importation of software see Case C-41/04 (*Levob*), [2006] ECR I-9433, on the absorption of standard software by customisation.

84 Case C-306/04 (*Compaq Computer International Corporation*), [2006] ECR I- 109991.

Defected goods
The price paid or payable can be adjusted in case of defected goods, provided that the adjustment is made by the seller for the benefit of the seller and if the following conditions are fulfilled (Art. 132 UCC IA):

- the goods were defective at the time of acceptance of the customs declaration for release for free circulation;
- the seller made the adjustment to compensate for the defect in order to fulfil either of the following:
  - a contractual obligation entered into before the acceptance of the customs declaration;
  - a statutory obligation applicable to the goods.

According to the ECJ, a good is also considered defective if at the time of acceptance of the declaration for entry to free circulation for specific goods, there was a manufacture-related risk that the goods might become defective in use.[85]

In the *Mitsui & Co*-case[86] the ECJ held that Article 29 CCC (now Art. 70 UCC) must be interpreted as meaning that, reimbursements which correspond to the costs of repairs invoiced by the buyer's own distributors, can result in a reduction of the transaction value of the goods and, as a result, of their customs value, which was declared on the basis of the price initially agreed between the seller/manufacturer and the buyer under the defected good scheme.

Related party transactions
Where the customs authorities have reasonable doubts that the declared transaction value represents the total amount paid or payable as referred to in Article 70(1) UCC, they may ask the declarant to provide additional information. The customs authorities may also ask for evidence that supports that a related sales transaction has not been influenced by the relationship of a related buyer and seller, but only insofar there are doubts about the acceptability of the price. If a declarant cannot meet this request or the doubts are not dispelled, the customs authorities may decide that the value of the goods cannot be determined in accordance with Article 70(1) UCC.

The declarant successfully shows that the price has not been influenced by the relationship of a related buyer and seller, if he is able to demonstrate that the declared transaction value closely approximates one of the test values (Art. 134(2) UCC IA). Since test values are not easy to identify given the tight conditions, and therefore, as part of the circumstances of sale test (Art. 134(1) UCC IA), any other detailed information surrounding the sale may be provided by the declarant to support that the relationship of a related buyer and seller did not influence the related sales transaction. In practice, transfer pricing studies are used to support the uninfluenced nature of the price paid or payable in case of related sales transactions. Although instruments of the Technical Committee on Customs Valuation of the WCO suggest that transfer pricing studies may be a good source of information for examining the circumstances of sale, no provision in the UCC or guidelines of the

85 Case C-661/15 (*X BV*), [2017] ECLI:EU:C:2017:753.
86 Case C-256/07 (*Mitsui & Co*), [2009] ECR I-1951.

Commission supports this view, although some Member States issued local guidance that approve the use of transfer pricing studies for examining the circumstances of the sale. If the view is taken that transfer pricing studies are indeed considered a valuable aid for this purpose, it raises the question whether transfer pricing adjustment should be taken into account for determining the price paid or payable between related parties. This is a very controversial issue given the existence of contradictory local court decisions and the infamous decision of the ECJ in the case *Hamamatsu*.[87, 88]

Hamamatsu Photonics, a Japanese established company, sold optoelectronic devices to Hamamatsu Germany, its subsidiary. The intra-groups prices of that group of companies have been established in accordance with an advance pricing agreement concluded between that group of companies and the German tax authorities on the basis of the 'Residual Profit Split Method'. Between 7 October 2009 and 30 September 2010, Hamamatsu Germany released for free circulation various goods from more than 1,000 consignments from their parent company, declaring a customs value corresponding to the price charged. A rate of between 1.4% and 6.7% was levied on the taxable goods. After those imports, it turned out that the operating margin of Hamamatsu Germany fell below the range for the operating margin, and consequently the transfer prices were being adjusted downwards. As the initially invoiced price was used to determine the customs values of the imported goods at stake, Hamamatsu Germany applied for a (partial) repayment of customs duties. There was no allocation of the adjustment amount to the individual imported goods. The local customs authorities refused this request. In the appeal procedure, the Finanzgericht München decided to stay the procedure and ask the ECJ if the customs valuation provisions in the CCC allow the transaction value to be based on an agreed transfer price, which is composed of an amount initially invoiced and declared and a flat-rate adjustment made after the end of the accounting period, to form the basis for the customs value, using an allocation key, regardless of whether a subsequent debit charge or credit is made to the declarant at the end of the accounting period.

The ECJ states that the transaction value must reflect the real economic value of the imported good and take into account all of the elements of that good that have economic value. Under reference to the case *Mitsui*[89] the ECJ recalls that a subsequent adjustment of the transaction value is limited to specific situations relating, *inter alia*, to quality defects or faulty workmanship in the goods discovered after their release for free circulation. The ECJ considers that the CCC does not impose any obligation on importer companies to apply for adjustment of the transaction value where it is adjusted subsequently upwards and it does not contain any provision enabling the customs authorities to safeguard against the risk that those undertakings only apply for downward adjustments. Therefore, according to the Court, the CCC does not allow account to be taken of a subsequent adjustment of the transaction value, such as that at issue in the case *Hamamatsu*.

87 See Case C-529/16 (*Hamamatsu*), [2017] ECLI:EU:C:2017:984.

88 M.L. Schippers & M. Friedhoff, EU ECJ's judgment in Hamamatsu: An Abrupt End to Interaction Between Transfer Pricing and Customs Valuation?, *EC Tax Review*, 28 (1), p. 32-42.

89 See Case C-256/07 (*Mitsui*), [2009] ECR 167.

Adjustments – Price additions

The price elements to be *added* to the price actually paid or payable for the imported goods are the following, to the extent that they are incurred by the buyer but are not included in the price actually paid or payable for the goods (Art. 71 UCC):

- commissions and brokerage fees, except buying commissions (the term 'buying commissions' means fees paid by an importer to his agent for the service of representing him in the purchase of the goods being valued);
- the cost of containers which are treated as being one, for customs purposes, with the goods in question, the cost of packing, whether for labour or materials; and
- the value, apportioned as appropriate, of the following goods and services where supplied directly or indirectly by the buyer free of charge or at reduced cost for use in connection with the production and sale for export of the imported goods, to the extent that such value has not been included in the price actually paid or payable (so-called 'assists'):
  - materials, components, parts and similar items incorporated in the imported goods;
  - tools, dies, moulds and similar items used in the production of the imported goods;
  - materials consumed in the production of the imported goods;
  - engineering, development, artwork, design work, and plans and sketches undertaken elsewhere than in the Union and necessary for the production of the imported goods.
- royalties and licence fees related to the goods being valued that the buyer must pay, either directly or indirectly, as a condition of sale of the goods being valued, to the extent that such royalties and fees are not included in the price actually paid or payable;
- the value of any part of the proceeds of any subsequent resale, disposal or use of the imported goods that accrues directly or indirectly to the seller; and
- the following costs up to the place where goods are brought into the customs territory of the Union:
  - the cost of transport and insurance of the imported goods; and
  - loading and handling charges associated with the transport of the imported goods.

The concepts of assists, royalty and license fees, and transport costs are discussed in greater detail below.

The ECJ held in the *BMW-case*[90] that the value of software could be added to the price paid or payable as assist under Article 71(1)(b)(i) or (iv) UCC. BMW provided software to manufacturers of control units free of charge. BMW imported the control units which included the software installed on them outside the EU. The referring court asked the ECJ whether the value of software could constitute an assist. The ECJ held that the argument that software is not listed in Article 71(1)(b) UCC cannot be accepted and that the ECJ already decided in the *Compaq Computer International Corporation*-case, discussed above, that the value of free of charge provided software for one or more operating systems made available by the buyer to the seller, should be added to the transaction value as either an assist (Art. 71(1)(b) UCC) or royalty and license fee (Art. 71(1(c) UCC). An assist can, in other words, also be an intangible asset such as software which follows also from the wording of the provision, that explicitly refers to 'goods' and 'services'. The ECJ is not asked

90 Case C-509/19 (*BMW Bayerische Motorenwerke AG v Hauptzollamt München*), [2020] ECLI:EU:C:2020:694.

to judge within which of the categories of assists the value of software supplied free of charge by BMW should fall. Nevertheless the ECJ held that software may be covered by both Article 71(1)(b)(i) and Article 71(1)(b)(iv) UCC. Under reference to the Compendium of Customs Valuation Texts, the ECJ gives guidance as to the scope of application of both categories by explaining that intellectual services necessary for the manufacture of the goods, fall within the scope of Article 71(1)(b)(iv) UCC, while intangible components incorporated into the imported goods to make them function and which are not necessary for their production, fall within the scope of Article 71(1)(b)(i) UCC.

The concept of royalties and licence relate solely to payments made by a buyer to a seller for the use of intellectual property rights,[91] that include, among other things, payments in respect to patent, trade marks and copyrights. Payments made for royalty and license fees shall be added where three cumulative conditions are satisfied, namely that, first, the royalties or licence fees have not been included in the price actually paid or payable, second, they are related to the goods being valued and, third, the buyer is required to pay those royalties or licence fees as a condition of sale of the goods being valued.[92] Unless proven otherwise, the royalty and license fees are related to the imported goods where the method of calculation of the amount of a royalty or licence fee derives from the price of the imported goods (Art. 136(2) UCC IA). The royalty or license fees can also be related to the imported goods if the amount of royalties or licence fees cannot be determined at the time when a licence agreement was concluded or when the customs debt was incurred.[93] Royalty and license fees can be related to the imported goods not only where the imported goods are themselves the subject of the licence agreement, but also where the imported goods are components of the product covered by the licence. This is, according to the Court, the case if there is '[...] *a sufficiently close link between those royalties or licence fees, on the one hand, and the [imported] goods concerned, on the other.*'[94] The royalty and license fees are considered to be paid as condition of sale if (Art. 136(4) UCC IA):

- the seller or a person related to the seller requires the buyer to make this payment;
- the payment by the buyer is made to satisfy an obligation of the seller, in accordance with contractual obligations;
- the goods cannot be sold to, or purchased by, the buyer without payment of the royalties or license fees to a licensor.

A payment is thus made as a condition of sale where that payment is so important to the seller that, without such a payment, the seller would not have concluded the sales contract.[95]

Finally, the costs of transport and insurance of the imported goods, and loading and handling charges associated with the transport of the imported goods to the place of introduction

91 Case C-775/19 (*5th Avenue Products Trading GmbH*), [2020] ECLI:EU: C:2020:948, paragraph 29.
92 For example, when a Chinese exporter sells T-shirts with the logo 'Paris 2024' and a licence fee is separately payable to the French Olympic committee, the fee should be added. If, however, the European importer has acquired the right to use the Olympic emblem separately from the committee, the fee is not to be added, since it is not a condition of sale.
93 Case C-173/15 (*GE Healthcare*), [2015] ECLI: EU:C:2017:195, paragraph 54.
94 Case C-76/19 (*'Curtis Balkan' EOOD*), [2020] ECLI:EU:C:2020:543, paragraph 49.
95 Case C-173/15 (*GE Healthcare*), [2015] ECLI: EU:C:2017:195, paragraph 60.

into the customs territory of the Union must be added to the price. According to the Court the term 'cost of transport' should be interpreted broadly as it includes '[...] *all the costs, whether they are main or incidental costs, incurred in connection with moving the goods to the customs territory of the Community.*'[96] It even includes '[...] *the supplement charged by the forwarding agent to the importer, corresponding to that agent's profit margin and costs, in respect of the service which it provided in organising the transport of the imported goods to the customs territory of the European Union.*'[97]

Adjustments – Price deductions
Provided that they are shown separately from the price actually paid or payable, the following price elements are *not included in* the customs value:
- charges for the transport of goods after their arrival at the place of introduction into the customs territory of the Union;
- charges for construction, erection, assembly, maintenance or technical assistance, undertaken after importation of imported goods such as industrial plant, machinery or equipment;
- charges for interest under a financing arrangement entered into by the buyer and relating to the purchase of imported goods, irrespective of whether the finance is provided by the seller or another person, provided that the financing arrangement has been made in writing and where required, the buyer can demonstrate that:
  - such goods are actually sold at the price declared as the price actually paid or payable, and the claimed rate of interest does not exceed the level for such transactions prevailing in the country where, and at the time when, the finance was provided.
- charges for the rights to reproduce the imported goods in the Union;
- buying commissions;
- import duties or other charges in the Union by reason of the import or sale of the goods;
- notwithstanding point (c) of Article 71(1) UCC, payments made by the buyer for the right to distribute or resell the imported goods, if such payments are not a condition of the sale for export to the Union of the goods.[98]

With regard to charges for interest not included in the customs value, the ECJ held that this also applies when a declaration does not mention the interest due or paid.[99]

Charges for the right to reproduce imported goods in the Union, as well as buying commissions and import duties or other charges payable in the Union by reason of the importation

96 See Case C-11/89 (*Unifert*), [1990] ECR I-2275, paragraph 30.
97 See Case C-59/16 (*Shirtmakers*), [2017] ECLI:EU:C:2017:362.
98 See also C-775/19 (*5th Avenue Products Trading GmbH*), [2020] ECLI:EU: C:2020:948. In that case the ECJ held that Article 29(1) and (3a) CCC (now Art. 70 (1) and (3a) UCC) must be interpreted as meaning that a payment made for a limited period of time by the buyer of imported goods to the seller of those goods, in return for the granting by the seller of an exclusive right to distribute those goods in a given territory, calculated on the basis of the turnover achieved in that territory, must be included in the customs value of those goods, see Case C-775/19 (*5th Avenue Products Trading GmbH*), [2020] ECLI:EU:C:2020:948, paragraph 47.
99 See Case C-152/01 (*Kyocera Electronics Europe GmbH*), [2003] ECR I-13821.

or sale of the goods are excluded from the customs value as mentioned above. See however Case C-379/00 (*Overland Footwear I*)[100] where the ECJ, *inter alia* held that:

> Articles 29, 32 and 33 of the Customs Code must be construed as meaning that a buying commission which is included in the customs value declared and is not shown separately from the selling price of the goods in the import declaration must be considered to be part of the transaction value within the meaning of Article 29 of that code and is, therefore, dutiable.

See also Case C-468/03 (*Overland Footwear II*)[101] where the ECJ added:

> On a proper interpretation of Articles 78 and 236 of Regulation No. 2913/ 92: after the release of the imported goods, the customs authorities, presented with an application from the declarant seeking revision of his customs declaration in relation to those goods, are required, subject to the possibility of a subsequent court action, either to reject the application by a reasoned decision or to carry out the revision applied for; where they find, at the conclusion of that revision, that the declared customs value erroneously included a buying commission, they are required to regularise the situation by reimbursing the import duties applied to that commission.

1.5 The System of Formalities and Supervision (Titles IV, V, VI, VII and VIII)

The heart of the matter, the core of the UCC is the system of formalities and supervision as laid down in Title IV dealing with goods brought into the customs territory, Title V dealing with general rule on customs status, placing goods under a customs procedure, verification, release and disposal of goods, Title VI dealing with the release of goods for free circulation and relief from import duty, Title VII with the so-called special procedures, and Title VIII with goods leaving the customs territory.

1.5.1 Entry of Goods (Title IV)

Bringing goods into the customs territory of the Union concerns a four-staged process. First an entry summery declaration needs to be submitted, secondly there is the arrival of the goods (*i.e.* the goods enter the customs territory of the Union), thirdly the goods shall be presented to the customs authorities and then, as a fourth step, the non-Union goods will be kept in temporary storage until the goods are placed under a customs procedure or re-exported from the customs territory of the Union.

1.5.1.1 The Entry Summary Declaration

Customs controls and risk analyses improve the security and safety of goods crossing the outer borders of the customs territory of the Union. The customs authorities of the EU Member States are tasked with performing a risk analysis and inspecting goods that represent a threat to security. Therefore, all goods that enter the customs territory of the Union shall be covered by an entry summary declaration (ENS) except for those enumerated in Article 104 UCC DA. The ENS contains (pre-arrival) information that enables the customs

100 Case C-379/00 (*Overland Footwear I*), [2003] ECR I-11133.
101 Case C-468/03 (*Overland Footwear II*), [2005] ECR I-8937.

authorities to perform a risk analysis for primarily security and safety purposes.[102] Where a consignment has been identified as posing a threat, the customs office of first entry shall take the necessary measures based on the results of the risk analysis. The customs office of first entry shall make the results of the completed risk analysis available to the customs authorities of the Member States that contributed to the risk analysis and to those that are potentially concerned by the movement of the goods (Art. 186(2)(d) UCC IA).

The ENS shall in principle be lodged electronically by the carrier of the goods[103] at the customs office of first entry within a specific time-limit before the goods are brought into the customs territory of the Union.[104]

1.5.1.2 Arrival of the Goods

According to Article 133(1) UCC the operator of a sea-going vessel or of an aircraft entering the customs territory of the Union shall notify the arrival to the customs office of first entry upon arrival of the means of transport. The arrival of the goods into the customs territory of the Union marks an important step with regard to the entry of the goods into the customs territory of the Union. From the time of their entry the goods will be subject to customs supervision and may be subject to customs controls (Art. 134(1) UCC). Non-Union goods shall remain under such supervision for as long as is necessary to determine their customs status and shall not be removed therefrom without the permission of the customs authorities. Union goods shall not be subject to customs supervision. Non-Union goods shall remain under customs supervision until their customs status is changed, or they are taken out of the customs territory of the Union or destroyed.

1.5.1.3 Presentation, Unloading and Examination of the Goods

Upon arrival of the goods into the customs territory of the Union, the goods shall be presented to customs to enable the competent customs authorities that the goods have been arrived and are available for inspection at the designated customs office or any other place designated or approved by the customs authorities. According to Article 140(2) UCC the customs authorities may at any time require goods to be unloaded and unpacked for the purpose of examining them, taking samples or examining the means of transport carrying them.

The presentation of the goods to customs is the responsibility of one of the following persons (Art. 139(1) UCC):
- the person who brought the goods into the customs territory of the Union;

---

102 The information that included in the ENS is enumerated in Appendix B UCC DA.
103 Besides the carrier, the UCC allows other persons to lodge the ENS instead (Art. 127(4) UCC).
104 The specific time-limit for lodging the ENS depends on the transport mode. In case of transport by sea the time-limits are stipulated in Article 105 UCC DA, in case of transport by air in Article 106 UCC DA, in case of transport by rail in Article 107 UCC DA, in case of transport by road in Article 108 UCC DA, in case of transport by inland waterways in Article 109 UCC DA, and in case of combined transportation the time- limits can be found in Article 110 UCC DA.

- the person in whose name or on whose behalf the person who brought the goods into that territory acts;
- the person who assumed responsibility for carriage of the goods after they were brought into the customs territory of the Union.

If the before-mentioned persons are not able to present the goods to customs, the following persons may present the goods instead notwithstanding the obligations of the previously mentioned persons (Art. 139(3) UCC):
- any person who immediately places the goods under a customs procedure;
- the holder of an authorisation for the operation of storage facilities or any person who carries out an activity in a free zone.

1.5.1.4 *Temporary Storage of Goods*

From the moment that the goods have been presented to the customs authorities, the non-Union goods must remain under customs supervision and are held in 'temporary storage' (Arts. 144-152 UCC), either at the customs office of presentation or at any other place designated, approved and controlled by that office until their placing under a customs procedure of re-export.

The goods are normally placed in an approved temporary storage facility (Art. 115 UCC DA) operated either by the importer or by a storage-keeper; the person holding the goods may be required to provide a guarantee to cover any customs debt that may arise (Art. 148(1) read in conjunction with Art. 89 UCC).[105]

During the temporary storage the goods may only be handled or treated in order to ensure their preservation, *e.g.* by cooling (Art. 147(2) UCC) but, with the permission of the customs authorities, the importer may examine the goods or take samples (Art. 134(2) UCC).

Non-Union goods in temporary storage shall be placed under a customs procedure or re-exported within 90 days (Art. 149 UCC). If the goods have not been placed under a customs procedure or re-exported within the prescribed period, the customs authorities shall, at the expense of the importer or the holder of the goods, take all necessary measures including (Art. 198(1)(a) UCC):
- removing the goods to a place under their supervision, and/or
- selling the goods, or
- destroying them.

105 A customs warehouse may also be used for temporary storage (Art. 147(1) UCC).

The effect of not placing the goods under a customs procedure or re-export on time were, *mutatis mutandis*, discussed in Case C-213/99 (*de Andrade*).[106] In Case C-371/99 (*Liberexim*)[107] the ECJ held that the time and place at which goods cease to be covered by external Community transit arrangements is necessarily the time and place at which the first irregularity is committed which can be regarded as a removal of the goods from customs supervision.[108]

1.5.2 Customs Status, Customs Procedure, Verification, Release and Disposal of Goods (Title V)

1.5.2.1 *Customs status of goods*

According to Article 153(1) UCC all goods in the customs territory of the Union shall be presumed to have the customs status of Union goods, unless it is established that they are not. Making a distinction between Union and non-Union goods is essential, because non-Union goods are subject to customs controls (section 1.5.1.2). Goods lose their status of Union goods in one of the following cases (Art. 154 UCC):

- where they are taken out of the customs territory of the Union, insofar as the rules on internal transit do not apply (Art. 155(1) and 227(2) UCC, section 1.5.4.2);
- where they have been placed under the external transit procedure, a storage procedure or the inward processing procedure, insofar as the customs legislation so allows;
- where they have been placed under the end-use procedure and are either subsequently abandoned to the State, or are destroyed and waste remains;
- where the declaration for release for free circulation is invalidated after release of the goods.

As discussed in the above, goods that are temporarily taken out of the customs territory of the Union keep their Union status if they are placed under the internal transit procedure. In some cases placing goods under an internal transit procedure is not necessary to preserve the Union status if the Union status of the goods can be proven by other means (Art. 155(2)

106 Case C-213/99 (*de Andrade*), [2000] ECR I-11083. The Tribunal Fiscal Advaneiro de Porto referred to the ECJ a series of questions. The first question was whether Article 53 CCC (Art. 147(4) UCC) precludes automatic application, without prior notification, of the sale of goods. According to the ECJ, Article 53 is clear. It expressly provides that the customs authorities are, without delay, to take all measures necessary, including the sale of the goods, to regularize the situation. Automatic application without prior notification is, thus permitted. The questions whether the 5% extra *ad valorem* duty violates the principle of proportionality was answered by the ECJ in a negative sense, albeit it is for the national court to determine whether such a penalty applies to infringements which are comparable under national law of the same nature and gravity. The questions with regard to the payment of VAT were answered by the ECJ as follows. The surcharge seeks to penalize the economic operators who have not complied with the prescribed formalities and time limits. It constitutes therefore a penalty and not consideration for a supply. By its nature it cannot be subject to VAT. If we see it correctly there was one bright spot in the decision for De Andrade, the penalty was inclusive stamp duty *and* VAT.

107 Case C-371/99 (*Liberexim*), [2002] ECR I-6227.

108 In Case C-66/99 (*Wandel*), [2001] ECR I-00873 the ECJ already held that the 'removal' must be understood as encompassing any act or omission the result of which is to prevent, if only for a short time, the competent authority from gaining access to goods under customs supervision and from monitoring them as provided for by the Union customs rules.

UCC and Art. 119(3) UCC DA) and in some specific cases no proof of the Union status is necessary at all (Art. 119(3) UCC DA).

1.5.2.2 Placing goods under a customs procedure

For placing goods under a customs procedure it is essential that goods shall be covered by a customs declaration appropriate for the particular procedure (i.e. release for free circulation, special procedures or (re-)export). The general rules with regard to for example the content of such declarations, the competent customs office where a customs declaration needs to be lodged and simplified declarations are embedded in Chapter 2 of Title V.

A customs declaration is thus the act whereby a person indicates the wish to place goods under a given customs procedure as provided for by the UCC (Arts. 5 (12) and 158 to 187 UCC). In general this task is performed by the owner of the goods, or by the person having control over the goods (*e.g.* a logistic company), or a person acting on behalf of these persons (a customs representative) could lodge the declaration. It may also be performed by the person having control over the goods. These persons may be individuals or companies, as well as in certain cases associations of persons (Art. 170(2) UCC). As a general rule these persons should be established in the Union. The declaration is in principle to be lodged with the customs office where the goods are presented (Art. 159(3) UCC). Upon application, the customs authorities may either authorize a person to lodge a customs declaration at a customs office responsible for the place where such person is established while goods are presented to customs at another customs office ('centralized clearance') or authorise a person to lodge a customs declaration, including a simplified declaration, in the form of an entry in the declarant's records ('entry in the declarant's records').

Centralised clearance can be used within one Member State or between several Member States (Art. 179(1) UCC and Art. 229 UCC IA). The person applying for the authorisation must be an authorised economic operator for customs simplifications (Art. 179(2) UCC). Centralised clearance is, however, not fully available until 2023 as the electronic systems to support the process will not be available until then. During the transitional period the Single Authorisation for Simplified Procedures (SASP) remains available. 'Single authorisation' means an authorisation involving different customs administrations (*i.e.* customs authorities in different Member States) covering entry for and/or discharge of the arrangements, storage, successive processing operations or uses. Single authorisations may be granted for a customs procedure with economic impact (customs warehousing, inward processing, temporary importation, outward processing) or end-use relief.[109] For example, when a company intends to carry out processing operations under the inward processing procedure in Spain, France and Italy, these operations may be covered by a single authorisation. Single authorisation for simplified procedures is the possibility of using the local clearance procedures (in few cases the simplified declaration procedure) to effect the customs formalities in the Member State where the economic operator is established, for their imports/exports wherever they occur in the Union. A transfer of the goods to the authorised location under a transfer procedure is possible; subsequently a

109 Under the UCC customs procedures with economic impact are referred to as 'special procedures'.

supplementary declaration is lodged. Under the CCC a number of customs authorities had, on the basis of agreement with each other, authorised centralised clearance involving entry of goods in another Member State, notably for inward processing, customs warehousing and, less frequently, for release for free circulation.[110] However, these arrangements between Member States are difficult and take a long time to be implemented, as they require long negotiations and considerable compromise between Member States, in order to find the best way of overcoming practical and legal difficulties, including the perception cost to be received by the importing Member State.

'Entry in the declarations records' means, as the name suggests, that the customs declaration is lodged in the form of an entry in the declarants records. All the particulars necessary for application of the provisions governing the customs procedure must be available in the declarant's electronic system at the moment of lodging (i.e. entry in the records) of the declaration. The moment the declaration is accepted is the moment the goods are entered in the declarant's records. The entry of goods for the customs procedure may thus be carried out at the premises of the person concerned, and the goods do not have to be presented to the customs before removal of the goods. A recapitulative/supplementary declaration must be submitted and the period of time covered by the supplementary declaration shall not exceed one calendar month.

A distinction can be made between standard and simplified customs declarations. Standard customs declarations shall contain all the particulars necessary for application of the provisions governing the customs procedure for which the goods are declared (Art. 162 UCC). The standard declaration can be distinguished between declarations:

- in writing;
- by a data processing technique;
- orally; or
- by any other act.

An example of the latter is passing through the 'green channel' at an airport.

The single administrative document or its electronic equivalent (SAD) is the standard form which is used for the various customs procedures.[111] A simplified customs declaration omits certain of the particulars necessary for application of the provisions governing the customs procedure for which the goods are declared *or* lacks supporting documents required for the application of the provisions governing the customs procedure for which the goods are declared. A supplementary declaration containing the missing particulars shall be lodged within a certain time-period (Art. 167(1) UCC in conjunction with Art. 146 UCC DA). In case supporting documentation is lacking at the time the goods are placed under a customs procedure, the necessary supporting documents shall be in the declarant's possession and

110 This is a major facilitation measure as the operator can:
- concentrate in-house customs expertise at a single location;
- deal with only one customs administration; and
- conduct the formalities, etc. in only one language.

111 Introduced in 1988, SAD legislation needed to take full account of today's environment and adapt with the evolution that occurred since its inception.

at the disposal of the customs authorities within a specific time-limit (Art. 167(1) UCC read in conjunction with Art. 147 UCC DA).

Clearly the simplified declaration procedure centralised clearance and the entry into the declarant's records are subject to (detailed) authorisations.

The declarant can by mistake include incorrect particulars in the customs declaration (*e.g.* wrong classification code, customs value, origin). If the declarant discovers the mistakes before the customs declaration is accepted, he or she can amend the customs declaration without permission of the customs authorities. If the customs declaration has been accepted, the declarant is permitted to amend one of more particulars of the customs declaration unless:

- by making the amendment the customs declaration becomes applicable to goods other than those which it originally covered (Art. 170(1) UCC);
- the customs authorities have informed the declarant that they intend to examine the goods (Art. 170(2) UCC);
- the customs authorities have established that the particulars of the customs declaration are incorrect (Art. 170(2) UCC);
- the customs authorities have released the goods (Art. 170(2) UCC).

An exception to this rule is provided for in Article 170(3) UCC. Based on this provision a declarant may be permitted to amend a customs declaration after release of the goods, provided that (i) the request is submitted within three years of the date of acceptance of the customs declaration, (ii) by amending the customs declaration the declarant complies with his or her obligations relating to the placing of the goods under the customs procedure concerned and (iii) an invalidation of the customs declaration has not been required.[112]

1.5.2.3 Verification and release of goods

The customs authorities are entitled to verify the accuracy of the particulars contained in the customs declaration which has been accepted. This entails the possibility to:

- examine the declaration and the supporting documents;
- require the declarant to provide other documents;
- examine the goods;
- take samples for analysis or for detailed examination of the goods.

The customs authorities may request the goods to be transported to a place suitable for the examination or where samples are to be taken. The transport shall be carried out by or under the responsibility of the declarant, and the related costs shall be borne by the declarant. The outcome of a partial examination and sampling of the goods apply to all goods covered by the same declaration, although the declarant may request further examination or sampling of the goods.

112 The last condition can be derived from the Guidance document on Customs Formalities on Entry and Import into the European Union, Ref. Ares (2018).

If the conditions for placing the goods under the procedure concerned are fulfilled and provided that any restriction has been applied and the goods are not subject to any prohibition, the goods will be released unconditionally provided that:
- the particulars in the customs declaration have been verified;
- the customs debt, if any, is settled;
- a guarantee is set (if required by the provisions governing the customs procedure for which the goods are declared).

1.5.2.4 Disposal of goods

One can also have non-Union goods be confiscated and sold, destructed, disposed or abandoned to the Exchequer. These and other measures are taken by the customs authorities if one of the cases described in Article 198(1) UCC occurs. Abandoned goods, or goods that are seized or confiscated shall be deemed to be placed under the customs warehousing procedure. The costs connected to the measures taken by the customs authorities are born by the person mentioned in Article 198(3) UCC and depend on why the actions are taken.

1.5.3 Release for Free Circulation (Title VI)

One of three customs procedures non-Union goods can be placed under is the procedure 'release for free circulation'. By releasing goods for free circulation, goods obtain the status of Union goods, which, in principle, can be freely moved within the Union. (See also Articles 28-29 TFEU.)

After releasing the goods for free circulation, the goods are no longer under customs supervision. However, a few situations require continued customs supervision, even after ending the customs procedure:
- when goods are released for free circulation at a reduced or zero rate of duty on account of their end-use (the end-use has to be checked by customs);
- when goods fall within the system of reliefs from customs duty and conditions have to be complied with after importation (some reliefs, like for household effects), see Regulation (EC) No. 1186/2009.

Goods usually enter the 'free circulation' by placing them under this procedure. Imported goods are entered for the procedure by means of a customs declaration. (With regard to the pre-arrival information, see sections 1.5.1.1 and 1.5.2.2 above.)

The second chapter of Title VI of the UCC is providing relief from import duties in specific cases. Firstly, an exemption of import duties for returning goods is provided for in Articles 203 to 207 UCC, granting an exemption on the return of originally Union goods which have been exported previously. In principle goods must be returned within three years in the state they left the Union, in order to enjoy the exemption. Certain provisions prevent abuse such as:
- the return of goods which previously were imported under a reduced or zero-rate duty by reason of their end-use;
- in situations of inward processing (section 1.5.4.5).

Secondly an exemption on products of sea-fishing taken from the territorial waters of third countries by a ship registered within the EU is provided for in Articles 208 and 209 UCC.

Besides relief from import duties for returned goods and products of sea-fishing, Regulation (EC) No. 1186/2009, that replaced Council Regulation (EC) No. 918/83, provides for the cases in which, on account of special circumstances, relief from import duties shall be granted where goods are released for free circulation. The relief from import duties applies to personal property when returning from a third country, or in case of marriage, personal luggage, etc., but also advertising materials, coffins, funerary urns, etc.

In Case C-170/03 (*Feron*)[113] the employer put a car at the exclusive disposal of Mr Feron both for private use and in connection with his work for that employer. During that period the employer was the owner of the car. According to the ECJ, a car such as that at issue is to be regarded as personal property within the meaning of Article 1(2)(c) of Council Regulation (EC) No. 918/83 and thus eligible for relief from import duty under Articles 2 and 3 of the Regulation. According to the relevant provisions of that Regulation, imports of a non-commercial nature are imports which consist exclusively of goods for the personal use of travellers or their families, or of goods intended as presents, where the nature or quantity of the goods is not such as to indicate that they are being imported for commercial reasons.

In Case C-99/00 (Criminal proceedings against *Kenny Roland Lyckeskog*)[114] the ECJ held that personal use, by definition, varies from one person to another, and from one culture to another, and the designation, for reference purposes, of a typical use would for that reason be unsatisfactory. It is therefore essential, for the proper application of Regulation (EC) No. 918/83, that a case-by-case assessment be made as to whether importation is commercial in character, account being taken, where appropriate, of the lifestyle and habits of each traveller. While the nature and quantity of the goods under consideration are among the indicators to be taken into account, customs authorities cannot confine themselves to those indicators in assessing whether or not the importation is commercial.

In Case C-7/08 (*Har Vaessen Douane Service*)[115] the ECJ held that grouped consignments of goods, with a combined intrinsic value which exceeds the value threshold of a small consignment, but which are individually of negligible value, can be admitted free of import duties, provided that each parcel of the grouped consignment is addressed individually to a consignee within the EU.[116] In that respect, the fact that the contractual partner of those consignees is itself established in the EU is not relevant where the goods are dispatched directly from a third country to those consignees.

113 Case C-170/03 (*Feron*), [2005], ECLI:EU:C:2005:176.
114 Case C-99/00 (*Lyckeskog*), [2002], ECLI:EU:C:2002:329.
115 Case C-7/08 (*Har Vaessen*), [2009], ECLI:EU:C:2009:417.
116 At the time of this judgment imports of goods below 22 EUR were also exempt from VAT and this decision was also relevant for the application of the VAT exemption. The VAT exemption on 'low value goods' is no longer applicable (since 1 July 2021).

1.5.4 Special Procedure (Title VII)

1.5.4.1 Import duties due by default, suspension by exception

Import duties are due by default and are non-recoverable, contrary to for example VAT where taxable persons have the right to reclaim import-VAT (see section 2.12.2). Customs duties can therefore be considered to be a true cost-price increasing 'levy'. To avoid customs duties become dutiable and goods losing subsequently their status of Union-good, customs duties are suspended while they are placed under a special procedure (except for end-use, which is not a suspension regime but a duty exemption, see section 1.5.4.4). As the special procedures form the exception to the rule that import duties become dutiable upon arrival of the goods in the customs territory of the Union, the procedural rules safeguarding that the goods remain under customs supervision are strict and comprehensive. A customs debt shall be incurred through the removal from customs supervision.

The ECJ held that the concept of removal from customs supervision encompass '[...] *any act or omission the result of which is to prevent the competent customs authority, if only for a short time, from gaining access to goods under customs supervision and from monitoring them* [...].'[117]

The UCC distinguish four categories of special procedures in Article 210 UCC:
- transit, which shall comprise external and internal transit (section 1.5.4.2);
- storage, which shall comprise customs warehousing and free zones (section 1.5.4.3);
- specific use, which shall comprise temporary admission and end-use (section 1.5.4.4);
- processing, which shall comprise inward and outward processing (section 1.5.4.5).

A standard set of rules regarding the application for an authorisation, record keeping, discharge goods from a special procedure, transfer of rights and obligations, usual forms of handling and equivalent goods are part of Chapter 1 of Title VII. Deviations to these rules are set-out in the subsequent chapters that provide for more detailed rules about each of the specific procedures.

An authorisation should be requested to use the special procedures, except for transit and where the storage facility operator is the customs authority itself (Art. 211(1) UCC). The authorisation is granted provided that the conditions in paragraphs 3 and 4 of Article 211 UCC are fulfilled.[118] One of these conditions is that the essential interest of Union producers should not be adversely affected by granting an authorisation.[119] This condition is intended to take account of various interest, including the interests of processors of raw materials and those of Union producers of similar goods. Where there is evidence that this is the case, examination of the economic conditions takes place at Union level. The procedure

117 C-337/01 (*Hamann*), [2004] ECR I-01791, paragraph 31.

118 Customs authorities may include conditions in the authorisation that are specifically designed for the situation the applicant of the authorisation finds itself in.

119 For inward processing there are exceptions to the rule that the economic conditions should be examined (Art. 166 UCC DA). If one of the exceptions apply, there are cases in which the economic conditions are deemed to be fulfilled (Art. 167 UCC DA).

of examining the economic conditions at Union level are laid down in Article 259 UCC IA. Provided that the conditions are fulfilled (Art. 211(2) UCC), the authorisation for inward and outward processing, end-use and temporary admission can be granted retroactively.

Appropriate records in a form approved by the customs authorities shall be kept by the holder of the special procedure as well as the persons carrying on an activity involving the storage, working or processing of goods, or the sale or purchase of goods in free zones (Art. 214 UCC). The records contain the information enumerated in Article 178 UCC DA.

A declaration shall be filled to place goods under a special procedure. If goods are placed under a subsequent customs procedure or – in case of a transit procedure – the procedure has ended correctly, the special procedure shall be ended by issuing a bill of discharge within a time-limit for discharge specified in the authorisation (Article 215 UCC in conjunction with Articles 174 and 175 UCC DA).

The rights and obligations the holder of a procedure has with regard to the goods placed under a special procedure other than transit can be transferred fully or partial (Art. 218 UCC). The customs authorities shall decide whether the rights and obligations can be transferred and under which conditions (Art. 266 UCC IA).

Goods placed under a customs warehouse procedure or in a free zone shall not be processed, while goods under the inward processing undergo one or more processing operations as provided for the authorisation. In both cases goods may undergo usual forms of handling intended to preserve them, improve their appearance or marketable quality or prepare them for distribution or resale (Art. 220 UCC). A list of permitted usual forms of handling has been included in Annex 71-3 UCC DA.

Under certain conditions, Union goods may take the place of non-Union goods under a special procedure (or non-Union goods take the place of Union goods under the outward processing procedure). The Union goods replacing the non-Union goods under the special procedure (or vice versa in case of outward processing) should take the form of equivalent goods. In principle, equivalent goods shall have the same eight-digit CN-code, the same commercial quality and the same technical characteristics as the goods which they are replacing (Art. 223(1) UCC). The use of equivalent goods can be best explained by giving an example.

> Company X has a customs warehouse authorisation for a location in MS 1 and MS 2 and is allowed to use equivalent compensation. On 1 January 2021 Company X receives 1,000 non-Union bottles in its storage location in MS 1. 700 equivalent bottles and 300 non-Union bottles arrive on 5 January 2021 at its storage location in MS 2. On 10 January 2021 an order is received for a delivery of 1,000 bottles to a third country. The bottles will be delivered from the storage location of Company X in MS 2. The 300 non-Union bottles are declared for re- export and the 700 equivalent bottles are declared for export. At the same time the equivalent bottles leave the customs territory, 700 bottles in Company X's storage location in MS 1 become Union goods.

1.5.4.2 Transit

The UCC mentions transit as first special procedure. A distinction is made between internal transit (in the past also referred to as T2 transport), and external transit (in the past also referred to as T1 transport). Additionally, other types of transit procedures exist.

Internal transit
Not in all cases when goods leave the customs territory do they lose their status of Union goods. When goods are transported from one part of the Union to another via the territory of a third country, the provisions regarding internal transit provide that the goods in question do not lose their status (Art. 227(1) UCC). Internal transit was in the past also referred to as T2 transport. The internal transit provisions allow special simplifications for so-called authorized consignors and consignees (Art. 233(4) read in conjunction with Arts. 313-320 UCC IA).

External transit
External transit is a suspension regime based on which non-Union goods can be transported between two parts of the Union (and/or EEA or EFTA countries) without payment of duties. This regime can also be applied to Union goods which have been declared for exportation, especially in the case of restitution of agricultural levies. In general a guarantee is required. In the early 1990's the Commission identified a number of ways in which the transit system was disfunctional: in particular there was a lack of coordination between the administrations and departments involved and a lack of consistency resulting from the multiplicity of systems, the existing systems were slow and a paper-based system was not adequate to combat fraud effectively (circulation of the transit documents lasts much longer than the movement of the goods they cover). Subsequently numerous studies stressed the need to reform the system to respond to the growth of trade flows. It was therefore decided in 1994 to computerise the administration of the international transit system and create the New Computerised Transit System (NCTS), replacing paper forms with electronic ones and exchanging them by e-mail.

Other transit procedures
Apart from the internal/external Union transit procedures use is also made of other transit procedures. The common transit procedure (CTP)[120] is the arrangement to transport goods from the Union to another country that also applies the same transport arrangement and forms, so that no customs formalities are necessary at the outer borders. For instance, if goods are moved from free circulation of the Union to Switzerland, they may be transported (after a declaration for export) with a T2 document.[121] Also, T1 status goods from a customs warehouse in the Union can be transported into Switzerland using the common transit procedure. The goods can cross the border and be transported to the place of destination in Switzerland, where they can be declared for (Swiss) free circulation.

120 CTP is currently used for all modes of transport in Iceland, Norway, Switzerland, EU countries, Turkey, North Macedonia, Serbia and in the United Kingdom of Great Britain and Northern Ireland.

121 See the Convention on a Common Transit Procedure dated 20 May 1987 (O.J. 1987, L 226, p.1). The CTP is administered by means of the NCTS (New Computerized Transit System), except for transports subject to the simplified procedure for rail, air, sea, or pipe.

In addition to the internal and external transit, there is the TIR procedure. The Customs Convention on the International Transport of Goods under cover of TIR Carnets (the TIR Convention) was signed in Geneva (Switzerland) on 14 November 1975. The EU is a party to the Convention.[122] The TIR Convention provides, in particular, that goods carried under the TIR procedure it establishes are not to be subject to the payment or deposit of import or export duties and taxes at customs offices *en route*. For those facilities to be applied, the TIR Convention requires that the goods be accompanied throughout the transport operation by a standard document, the TIR carnet, which serves to check the regularity of the operation. It also requires that the transport operations be guaranteed by associations[123] approved by the contracting parties, in accordance with the provisions of Article 6 of the Convention, which provides that subject to such conditions and guarantees as it shall determine, each Contracting Party may authorize associations to issue TIR carnets, either directly or through corresponding associations, and to act as guarantors.[124]

Other transit procedures are the following. The ATA carnet procedure is similar to TIR but it is limited to certain types of goods. The Rhine manifest procedure applies to water transport of non-Union goods on the Rhine and its associated tributaries. The NATO movement procedure applies to goods transported to NATO forces and the postal package procedure applies to goods sent by post.

The ATA Convention introduced the ATA Carnet, an international customs document that permits duty-free and tax-free temporary import of goods for up to one year. The initials

122 The EC approved it by Council Regulation (EEC) No. 2112/78 of 25 July 1978 (O.J. 1978, L 252, p. 1). See also Council Decision 2009/477/EC publishing in consolidated form the text of the TIR Convention as amended, O.J. 2009, L 165, p. 1.

123 In Case C-488/09 (*ASTIC*), [2010] ECR I- 14067, the ECJ held that Article 455(1) CCIP read in conjunction with Article 11(1) of the Customs Convention on the international transport of goods under cover of TIR carnets, is to be interpreted as meaning that a guaranteeing association cannot rely on the limitation period provided for in those provisions where the customs authorities of the Member State for whose territory it is responsible notify it, within a period of one year from the date on which those authorities were informed of an enforceable judgment identifying them as competent, of the facts which gave rise to the customs debt for which it is liable up to the amount that it guarantees.

124 A TIR carnet consists of a set of sheets each comprising vouchers No. 1 and No. 2 with the corresponding counterfoils, on which appears all the necessary information, one pair of vouchers being used for each territory crossed. At the start of the transport operation, counterfoil No. 1 is left with the customs office of departure; discharge takes place once counterfoil No. 2 is returned from the customs office of exit in the same customs territory. The procedure is repeated for each territory crossed, using the pairs of vouchers in the one carnet. TIR carnets are printed and distributed by the International Road Transport Union (IRU), established in Geneva, for issue to users by the national guaranteeing associations authorized to do so by the administrations of the contracting parties. The TIR carnet is issued by the guaranteeing association of the country of departure, the guarantee provided being covered by the IRU and a pool of insurers established in Switzerland. In Case C-161/08 (*Internationaal Verhuis- en Transportbedrijf Jan de Lely*), [2009] ECR I- 4075, the ECJ held that failure to comply with the period within which the holder of a TIR carnet is to be notified of its non-discharge does not have the consequence that the competent customs authorities forfeit the right to recover the duties and taxes due in respect of the international transport of goods made under cover of that carnet.

'ATA' are an acronym of the French and English words 'Admission Temporaire/Temporary Admission.' ATA Carnets cover:
- commercial samples;
- professional equipment;
- goods for presentation or use at trade fairs, shows, exhibitions and the like.[125]

That means almost anything: computers, repair tools, photographic and film equipment, musical instruments, industrial machinery, vehicles, jewellery, clothing, medical appliances and aircraft, race horses, old masters, prehistoric relics, ballet costumes and rock group sound systems are just some of the items that can cross borders duty-free and tax-free, thanks to ATA Carnets. The ATA Carnet is a simple international customs document with two sheets for presentation for each foreign country one wishes to visit, and two sheets for presentation to customs when leaving and returning the home country. One sheet is given to the foreign customs officials when entering their country and the other when leaving it. The same applies when exiting and entering the own country.

The Rhine manifest procedure was established to facilitate the movement of goods on the Rhine and its associated tributaries across national frontiers. The legal bases for this procedure are the Mannheim Convention of 17 October 1868 and the Protocol adopted by the Central Rhine Navigation Commission on 22 November 1963. The Union legislation which provides for the Rhine manifest to be used as a transit document is laid down in Articles 226(3)(d) and 227(2)(d) UCC. The Mannheim Convention concerns the following countries bordering the Rhine: the Netherlands, Belgium, Germany, France and Switzerland, which for the purposes of the Convention are considered as forming a single territory.

The rules concerning the import, export and transit of goods for NATO forces are contained in the Agreement between the Parties to the North Atlantic Treaty Organisation regarding status of their forces, signed in London on 19 June 1957. The document used for the movement of such goods is NATO Form 302. The Union legislation which provides for NATO Form 302 to be used as a transit document is Articles 226(3)(e) and 227(2)(e) UCC.

The Union legislation which provides for the transit procedure for post are Articles 226(3)(f) and 227(2)(f) UCC. Where non-Union goods are carried by post (including parcel post) from one point to another in the customs territory of the Union, the packaging and any accompanying documents shall bear a yellow label as foreseen in annex 72-01 UCC IA. Where Union goods are carried by post (including parcel post) to or from a part of the Union where the VAT Directive does not apply, the packaging and any accompanying documents shall bear a yellow label as foreseen in Annex 72-02 UCC IA.

In Case C-383/98 (*Polo/Lauren*)[126] the ECJ held that provisions that are part of Regulation (EU) No 608/2013 that contains measures concerning customs enforcement of intellectual property rights must be interpreted as being applicable to goods under external transit.

125 ATA carnets do not cover perishable or consumable items or goods for processing or repair.
126 Case C-383/98 (*Polo/Lauren*), [2000] ECR I-2519.

This case is different from Case C-115/02 (*Rioglass SA, Transremar SL*)[127] which involves goods lawfully produced which are in transit in a Member State where such goods infringe a trade mark. In this case a consignment of windows and windscreens, lawfully produced in Spain, was exported from Spain to Poland under cover of a Community transit certificate EX T2 and thus qualified for the duty- suspension arrangements which allow movement between two points in the customs territory of the Union and Poland free of import duty, tax or commercial policy measures. French customs officers carried out an inspection near Bordeaux and seized of the goods on suspicion of infringement of trade mark. According to the ECJ, the fact that the goods were intended for export to a non-member country does not necessarily lead to the conclusion that those goods do not fall within the scope of the Treaty provisions on the free movement of goods between Member States. Given that the present case involves goods lawfully manufactured in one Member State in transit within another Member State, the ECJ pointed out that the customs union established by the Treaty necessarily implies that the free movement of goods between Member States should be ensured. That freedom could not itself be complete if it were possible for Member States to impede or interfere in any way with the movement of goods in transit. It is therefore necessary, as a consequence of the customs union and in the mutual interest of the Member States, to acknowledge the existence of a general principle of freedom of transit of goods within the Union.

Given that the detention under customs control in issue was carried out on the basis of the *Code de la propriété intellectuelle*, the ECJ found it necessary to determine whether the obstacle to the free movement of goods created by that detention under customs control may be justified by the need to ensure the protection of industrial and commercial property referred to in Article 30 EC (now Art. 36 TFEU). Article 30 EC allows derogations from the fundamental principle of the free movement of goods within the common market only to the extent to which such derogations are justified for the purpose of safeguarding rights which constitute the specific subject-matter of such property. The goods in issue in the present case were detained on suspicion of infringement of trade mark. With respect to trade marks, it is settled case-law that the specific subject-matter of a trade mark is, in particular, to guarantee to the owner that he has the exclusive right to use that mark for the purpose of putting a product on the market for the first time and thus to protect him against competitors wishing to take unfair advantage of the status and reputation of the trade mark by selling products illegally bearing it. The implementation of such protection is therefore linked to the marketing of the goods. Transit, such as that in issue, which consists in transporting goods lawfully manufactured in a Member State to a non-member country by passing through one or more Member States, does not involve any marketing of the goods in question and is therefore not liable to infringe the specific subject-matter of the trade mark.

According to the ECJ, Article 28 EC (now Art. 34 TFEU) is to be interpreted as precluding the implementation, pursuant to a legislative measure of a Member State concerning intellectual property, of procedures for detention by the customs authorities of goods lawfully

127 Case C-115/02 (*Rioglass SA, Transremar SL*), [2003] ECR I-12705.

manufactured in another Member State and intended, following their transit through the territory of the first Member State, to be placed on the market in a non-member country.

In the context of piracy see also Council Regulation (EC) No. 1383/2003 of 22 July 2003 concerning customs action against goods suspected of infringing certain intellectual property rights and the measures to be taken against goods found to have infringed such rights.

1.5.4.3 Storage (Customs Warehousing and Free Zones)

Customs warehousing

Warehousing of goods is a special procedure (thus, authorization is required) and provides for a suspensive arrangement.

A warehouse is a place where non-Union goods can be stored without being subject to duties or Union goods can be stored, which are deemed to be exported in the framework of pre-financing agricultural levies. The amount of working or processing allowed on goods held in warehouses is limited essentially to keeping them preserved with a view to subsequent distribution. However, it is possible to process goods under inward processing or to an end-use procedure to take place on the premises of a customs warehouse, subject to the conditions provided for by those procedures.

A distinction is made between public and private warehouses. Public warehouses are available for use by any person, private warehouses are reserved for warehousing of the goods by the holder of an authorisation for customs warehousing.

Public warehouses are divided into (which type is available differs between EU Member States):

- Type I: under the responsibility of the holder of the authorisation and with the holder of the procedure (Art. 1(32) UCC DA);
- Type II: under responsibility of the holder of the procedure (Art. 1(33) UCC DA);
- Type III: operated by the customs authorities (Art. 1(2)(11) UCC IA).

In a customs warehouse goods have to be kept in the same condition. However, 'usual forms of handling' are allowed (in general, keeping the goods in good condition or preparing them for the next phase in distribution).

Public and private warehouses can be cross-border warehouses. Typically, the Member State where the main administration of the applicant is available, becomes the authority that issues the authorisation and is the place where the monthly summary declarations are lodged. This is also the authority where payment of import duties has to take place, even if the goods left the warehouse in another Member State. This may lead to some difficulties for the applicable VAT, for which the consequences are not clear. (Two solutions could be considered. A first solution may be to levy import VAT in the Member State where the goods have left the warehouse. Another solution is to levy import VAT in the Member State where the customs declaration has been filed. This (exempt) import is subsequently followed by a (deemed) intra-Community supply from the Member State of import to the Member State where the goods have left the warehouse.)

Free zones
A free zone is a part of the customs territory separated from the rest of it where non-Union goods are considered as not being on customs territory of the Union. Non-Union and Union goods can both enter the premises of a free zone. Non-Union goods stored in the zone are considered as not yet imported to the customs territory of the Union. They will not be considered under the free zone procedure if they remain in the free zone, but are released for free circulation or placed under the inward processing, temporary admission or end-use procedure. Union goods may be entered, stored, moved, used, processed or consumed in a free zone and will then also not be regarded as being under a free zone procedure.

On importation, free zones are mainly for storage of non-Union goods until they are released for free circulation. No import declaration has to be lodged as long as the goods are stored in the free zone. Import and export declarations have only to be lodged when the goods leave the free zone. In addition, there may be special reliefs available in free zones from other taxes, excises or local duties. These will differ from one zone to another. The free zones are mainly a service for traders to facilitate trading procedures by allowing fewer customs formalities.

1.5.4.4 Specific use

Temporary admission
This customs procedure (again with an economic impact and being a suspensive arrangement) allows the use in the customs territory with total or partial relief from import duties, of non-Union goods intended for re-export (without having undergone any change except due to the use of them).

In case of partial relief with a maximum of two years per month 3% is payable of the amount of duty which would have been payable if the goods were released for free circulation. There is a list of goods in respect of which partial relief may not be used. Examples of goods with total relief are professional and scientific equipment, goods for display at exhibitions and means of transport.

End-use
In certain cases the customs tariff allows goods to benefit from favourable treatment on account of their end use, such as:
- lobster meat, cooked, for the manufacture of lobster butter or of lobster pastes, pâtés, soups or sauces (*e.g.* CN code 1605 30 10); or
- fitting bumpers into motor vehicles during their manufacture (*e.g.* CN code 8708 10 10).

The end-use provision (Article 254 UCC), and guidelines thereto provide for a procedure allowing:
- the immediate release for free circulation of goods destined for a certain type of treatment or use; but

- customs supervision of their end use.

The use of the procedure requires a written authorisation.

1.5.4.5 Processing

Inward processing

Inward processing is a special procedure (authorization is thus required) and may be a suspensive arrangement. It is a trade facilitation measure, intended to encourage processing in the Union by allowing certain raw materials or components to be imported under duty suspension arrangements. After processing, the finished products are re-exported. Under the UCC the inward processing procedure has been merged with what was called the procedure for processing under customs control under the CCC. Finished goods may therefore also be declared for free circulation at the lower rate that applies to them rather than the rate which applies to the raw materials under the UCC (*e.g.* PVC materials subject to a duty rate of 8.3% may be processed into film screens with a duty rate of 2.7%).[128] The import duty advantage obtained in either case should contribute to creating or maintaining processing activities in the Union.

The products resulting from processing operations are known as compensating products. Prior exportation is possible, *i.e.* (so-called compensating) products processed from equivalent goods are exported before the import goods are entered for the procedure in the Union. Triangular traffic refers to the entry of the import goods at another customs office than that where the prior exportation of the compensating products took place.

A person intending to carry out processing operations must apply for an authorization. The customs authorities set him a time limit, on the expiry of which the inward processing procedure is to be discharged.

Union goods which have been exported and which it is subsequently intended to re-import into the Union are known as returned goods. Under Article 203 UCC, they may be reimported within a period of three years with relief from import duties. Under the first paragraph of Article 205 UCC, compensating products originally re- exported subsequent to an inward processing procedure may also qualify for application of the procedure for returned goods and be reimported with relief from import duties. However, relief applies only to the proportion of the value of the product which corresponds to inward processing carried out in the Union, whereas the proportion of the value of the product which corresponds to the import goods used in the manufacture of that product will give rise to the payment of import duties. Article 86(3) UCC applies when determining the amount of import duties.

128 The customs tariff is organised in such a way that, in most cases, imported goods carry higher rates of duty than the raw materials or components from which they are manufactured. In some cases however, processed products attract a lower rate of duty than the goods from which they are made. In some cases these tariff anomalies tend to make it more economical to import finished products directly from outside the Union, than to import the raw materials and manufacture the products in the Union.

Case C-166/94 (*Pezzullo Molini Pastifici Mangimifici*)[129] deals with default interests and inward processing. On 21 May 1982 Pezullo temporarily imported 1,000 tonnes of durum wheat from Canada in order to process it into wheat semolina and re-export it. Having done so, Pezullo released for consumption in Italy the by- products of the processing (middling, bran and meal), which were thus definitively imported on 15 January 1985.

In respect of the definitive import of those by-products, the Palermo customs authorities required the payment of a levy and of value added tax. It also required, under Article 191 of the Italian Customs Law the payment of default interest for the period between temporary importation and definitive importation. Pezullo paid the levy and the VAT, and also the default interest. However, considering that the Italian legal provisions pursuant to which the interest had been charged were incompatible with Union law, it instituted proceedings before the Tribunale di Salerno for recovery of the interest paid.

This resulted in the preliminary question whether the imposition of default interest provided for in Article 191 of the Italian Customs Law in respect of definitive importation at the time of the import operation at issue in the proceedings (1982) is prohibited by provisions of Union law which took precedence over national law.

The ECJ held that Directive 69/73, as in force at the material time, allowed a Member State to provide that, in the case of release for home use in the Union of goods previously subject to inward processing arrangements, the agricultural levy payable is to bear default interest for the period between temporary importation and definitive importation.

With regard to the charging of default interest on VAT it was different. The VAT Directive (see section 2.8 below) provides that the chargeable event and the date when the tax becomes chargeable shall occur only when the goods cease to be covered by the inward processing arrangements.

Outward Processing
Outward processing (OPR) is a special procedure (authorization is thus required) and the mirror of inward processing. Under this regime Union goods can be temporarily exported in order to undergo processing operations, while the products resulting from those operations are released for free circulation with total or partial relief from import duties.

OPR can take place with use of the standard exchange system, which offers the possibility that a replacement product replaces the product (the so-called compensating product) which results from the processing. Even prior importation is possible and also triangular traffic, *i.e.* importation into another Member State than the one from where the goods have been exported temporarily.

Goods that are exported only to be repaired (*i.e.* bringing back the product into its original condition) can be re-imported after repair with full relief from import duties in case of warranty. In case of repair against payment, the relief can be effectuated by applying

129 Case C-166/94 (*Pezzullo Molini Pastifici Mangimifici*) [1996] ECR I-331.

the applicable tariff to the repair costs as the final settlement, which is also the basis of assessment for VAT on importation, see section 2.9 below.

1.5.5 Export and re-export (Title VIII)

The procedure of exportation allows Union goods to leave the customs territory of the Union, while the procedure of re-exportation allows non-Union goods to leave the customs territory of the Union. Exported goods lose their status of Union goods when they are actually exported, with the exception of returned goods in Title V, see section 1.5.3. For goods under customs supervision (goods placed under a warehouse procedure, temporary imports, etc.) the goods to be exported have to be placed under a customs procedure or use re-exportation. The procedural rules with regard to (re)exporting goods are embedded in Title V (section 1.5.2).

Other arrangements dealing with goods leaving the territory: are outward processing (section 1.5.4.5) and internal transit (over the territory of a third country, for instance goods shipped from Germany to Italy, through Switzerland, see section 1.5.4.2).[130]

In case goods are exported from the customs territory of the Union, an exporter should be mentioned on the export declaration. At the time the substantive provisions of the UCC became applicable on 1 May 2016, the exporter definition embedded in Article 1(19) UCC DA was articulated, as follows:

> 'Exporter'
> (a) the person established in the customs territory of the Union who, at the time when the declaration is accepted, holds the contract with the consignee in the third country and has the power for determining that the goods are to be brought to a destination outside the customs territory of the Union;
> (b) the private individual carrying the goods to be exported where these goods are contained in the private individual's personal baggage,
> (c) in other cases, the person established in the customs territory of the Union who has the power for determining that the goods are to be brought to a destination outside the customs territory of the Union.

For the situations described under the first and third indent, the exporter needs to be established in the customs territory of the Union.[131] Guidance of the Commission allowed for these cases that a non-established person could still export goods if he/she appointed an indirect customs representative (*i.e.* person that acts in his own name, but for account of the represented party, see section 1.3.1.3).[132] This transitional period was supposed to apply until the deployment of the Automated Export System (expected launch date is 31 December 2025). On 1 August 2018 the exporter's definition, with regard to person other than private individuals, was amended *'[...] in order to allow greater flexibility to business*

---

130 See also Coucil Regulation (EC) No. 116/2009 on the export of cultural goods (codified version, O.J. 2009, L 39, 10.2.2009, p. 1) requiring the presentation of a licence issued by the competent Member State prior to the export of cultural goods.

131 According to Article 5(31) UCC a person is established in the customs territory:
- in the case of a natural person, any person who has his or her habitual residence in the customs territory of the Union;
- in the case of a legal person or an association of persons, any person having its registered office, central headquarters or a permanent business establishment in the customs territory of the Union.

132 Annex A, Definition of 'Exporter', Article 1(19) UCC DA, Ares(2016)2418814 (20 May 2016).

partners in the choice of the person which may act as exporter.'[133] The exporter's definition which is currently applicable reads as follows:

> 'Exporter'
> [...]
> (b) in other cases, where (a) does not apply:
> (i) a person established in the customs territory of the Union, who has the power to determine and has determined that the goods are to be taken out of that customs territory;
> (ii) where (i) does not apply, any person established in the customs territory of the Union who is a party to the contract under which goods are to be taken out of that customs territory.

Following the reform of Article 1(19) UCC DA, the Commission revised its Guidance on the exporter's definition twice.[134] In the '2018-edition', the Commission no longer explicitly allowed non-EU established entities to be named as exporter in the export declaration, while it did refer to a transitional period, suggesting it still implicitly allows non-established entities to act as exporter provided an indirect customs representative was being appointed. In the '2019- edition', the reference to the transitional period was removed from the Guidance document. One by one, EU Member States no longer applied the transactional period from the date the new exporter definition became applicable in 2018, while to this day a small minority of the EU Member States still allow non-EU established entities to act as exporter provided they appoint an indirect customs representative.

According to the Commission, the obligation to be established in the EU to act as exporter does not apply in case non-Union goods are re-exported from the customs territory of the Union.[135]

Completing the export procedures as set out in the UCC legal package is in some instances only one of the requirements attached to bringing the goods outside the customs territory of the EU. Export control laws and regulations may force exporters to fulfil additional requirements depending on the type of goods and the country the goods are exported to. Exports of, *inter alia*, strategic goods[136] and cultural goods[137] require for instance an export license for the purpose of preventing misuse and protection respectively. Exports may also require export licenses or can be restricted in case the EU, as part of its common foreign and security policy, had imposed sanctions against persons, organisations or countries.

133 Commission Delegated Regulation (EU) 2018/1063 of 16 May 2018 amending and correcting Delegated Regulation (EU) 2015/2446 supplementing Regulation (EU) No 952/2013 of the European Parliament and of the Council as regards detailed rules concerning certain provisions of the Union Customs Code (O.J. L 192, 30.7.2018, p. 1-28).

134 Annex A, Definition of 'Exporter', Article 1(19) UCC DA Revised, Ares(2018) 4012836 (30 July 2018) and Annex A, Definition of 'Exporter', Article 1(19) UCC DA Revised, Ares(2019)4346407 (8 July 2019).

135 Annex A, Definition of 'Exporter', Article 1(19) UCC DA Revised, Ares(2019) 4346407 (8 July 2019).

136 Strategic goods cover both military goods and dual-use items (i.e. goods, software and technology that can be used for both civilian and military applications). Regulation (EC) No. 2021/821 governs the EU's export control regime, see Regulation (EU) 2021/821 of the European Parliament and of the Council of 20 May 2021 setting up a Union regime for the control of exports, brokering, technical assistance, transit and transfer of dual-use items (recast) (O.J. L 206, 11.6.2021, p. 1–461).

137 Council Regulation (EC) No 116/2009 of 18 December 2008 on the export of cultural goods (O.J. L 39, 10.2.2009, p. 1–7).

CHAPTER 2

Value Added Tax – the Recast VAT Directive

Update and elaboration by Marie Lamensch and Madeleine Merkx

2.1 Introduction

On 28 November 2006, Council Directive 2006/112/EC on the common system of value added tax, recasting the Sixth VAT Directive, was adopted. The Recast VAT Directive (RVD) repeals and replaces the Sixth VAT Directive (and the First VAT Directive). It incorporates all the amendments made to the Sixth Directive by subsequent acts. It also contains any relevant provisions previously to be found in separate legal acts and excludes provisions which properly belong in other acts. In order to improve the drafting quality, the text of the Sixth Directive has undergone numerous changes. Although the changes do not affect its substantive content, they do alter the format, with the 53 Articles of the Sixth Directive divided into 414 new Articles and 12 Annexes. Annex XII contains a correlation table.

The RVD entered into force on 1 January 2007 and has been subject to numerous amendments ever since.[1] Significant amendments were introduced by (the list is not exhaustive):

- Directive 2008/8/EC changing the place of supply of services.[2]
- Directive 2010/45/EU introducing new rules on invoicing.[3]
- Directive 2016/1065 introducing new rules on vouchers.[4]
- Directives 2017/2455[5] and 2019/1995[6] introducing new rules for companies carrying out cross-border sales of goods or service (e-commerce VAT package).
- Directive 2018/2057 introducing thc possibility of a temporary application of a generalised reverse charge mechanism in relation to supplies of goods and services above a certain threshold.[7]
- Directive 2020/1756 following the United Kingdom (UK)'s withdrawal from the EU.[8]

---

1 The complete list of amendments is updated in the consolidated version of the RVD available on the European Commission website, at: https://eur-lex.europa.eu/ legal-content/EN/TXT/?uri=celex%3A02006L0112-20201212.
2 O.J. 2008, L 44, p. 11.
3 O.J. 2010, L 189, p. 1.
4 OJ L 177, 1.7.2016, p. 9–12.
5 OJ L 348, 29.12.2017, p. 7–22.
6 OJ L 310, 2.12.2019, p. 1–5.
7 OJ L 329, 27.12.2018, pp. 3-7.
8 OJ L 396, 25.11.2020, p. 1–2.

- Directive 2020/284 introducing certain requirements on payment service providers to keep records of e-commerce cross-border payments (applicable from 1 January 2024).[9]
- Directive 2020/285 introducing simplified rules to reduce the administrative burden and compliance costs for small businesses (applicable from 1 January 2025).[10]

On 15 March 2011, the Council adopted the implementing Regulation 282/2011 laying down implementing measures for the VAT Directive (see Section 2.16.1 below).[11] The Implementing Regulation (IR) has also been amended several times.[12]

2.2 Subject Matter

Article 1 RVD replaces the First VAT Directive and outlines the main characteristics of the EU VAT system. It provides the following:

1. This Directive establishes the common system of value added tax (VAT).
2. The principle of the common system of VAT entails the application to goods and services of a general tax on consumption exactly proportional to the price of the goods and services, however many transactions take place in the production and distribution process before the stage at which the tax is charged.
   On each transaction, VAT, calculated on the price of the goods or services at the rate applicable to such goods or services, shall be chargeable after deduction of the amount of VAT borne directly by the various cost components.
   The common system of VAT shall be applied up to and including the retail trade stage.

A general tax on consumption
The EU VAT is a general tax on consumption. It is in principle due on all supplies of goods and services made by taxable persons acting as such (see however exemptions in section 2.11). In general, a broad based tax is more equitable because it affects all consumers and products in the same way. It also allows for a lower tax rate in order to generate a satisfactory level of revenue. A broad-based tax therefore has the advantage of generating significant amounts of revenue while interfering as little as possible with economic behaviour and avoiding inequitable consequences on consumers depending on their consumption needs.

A tax proportional to the price of goods and services
Under the VAT system the tax is assessed strictly on the price of goods and services and does not vary depending on the quantity (contrary to excise taxes) nor on the ability to pay of the taxpayer (contrary to personal income taxes), not even when reduced rates are applicable (on reduced rates, see section 2.10).

applied up to and including the retail trade stage …
… chargeable after deduction of the amount of VAT borne directly by the various cost components

9 OJ L 62, 2.3.2020, p. 7–12.
10 OJ L 62, 2.3.2020, p. 13–23.
11 O.J. 2011, L 77, p. 1.
12 The complete list of amendments is updated in the consolidated version of the IR available on the European Commission website, at: https://eur-lex.europa.eu/ legalcontent/EN/TXT/?uri=CELEX%3A02011R0282-20200101.

One of the key features of the VAT system is that the tax is due on all taxable supplies, including transactions preceding the retail stage (contrary to "single stage" retail taxes).[13] The mechanism of deduction of input VAT (or refund, section 2.12) however ensures that taxable persons are relieved from the burden of the tax. Taxable persons indeed only remit a fraction of the VAT due, i.e. the difference between the output tax charged and the input VAT they have themselves incurred. This ensures the neutrality of the tax as described by the second sentence of Article 1 (2) RVD and the objective to tax consumption only. Accordingly, although a value added tax is levied on each transaction, only the final supply from the retailer to the end-consumer is subject to a net tax under the VAT system (because the final consumer may not deduct it). This applies regardless of how many stages a production or distribution chain has, different from the cumulative cascade systems that the EU Member States had before the introduction of the EU VAT system in 1968 (except for France). In early forms of multi- staged consumption taxes, the tax imposed in the subsequent stages was indeed imposed not only on the value of the product but also on the tax paid in the previous stages (a "tax on tax"). Such "cascading" tax could not be reclaimed by the intermediate supplier and therefore became part of the sales price, so that the tax component of the end-price became larger, the more stages there were between the producer and the end consumer. This resulted in potential distortions of competition and trade. Since the end price was dependent on the number of intermediate stages in the supply chain between the producer and the end consumer, potential distortions of competition indeed arose because vertically integrated cycles of production and distribution could offer lower end prices.[14] The neutrality of the VAT and the obstacle that cumulative cascade systems would present for the internal market was the reason why the EU VAT system has been harmonized in an early stage of the European Union (at that time "European Community").

Designing a consumption tax as a retail tax (i.e. a tax collected in full from retailers) or as a multiple stage tax (i.e. a tax collected fractionally throughout the production and distribution process) should, in principle, not affect the tax revenue yield. However, the fractioned collection of the tax in multi-staged systems is thought to yield more revenue

13 Single stage consumption taxes are levied by most US states and some provinces in Canada. In single stage systems the tax is levied once, traditionally at the retail stage. It is also possible to levy tax on more than a single stage, but still not on all stages like for example in Louisiana where a sales tax is imposed at the wholesale and retail levels. A single stage tax could also be imposed at the manufacturing level. Single-staged taxes are thus classified according to the stage of the production and distribution at which the tax is applied as "manufacturer tax", "wholesaler tax" or "retailer tax".

14 Vertical integration refers to integrating the different stages of production and distribution within a single legal person so that in the end only one taxable supply takes place between the integrated producer/distributor and the end-consumer. In the case of cascading taxes, a tax is due and cannot be recovered whenever a taxable supply takes place between the different persons involved in production and distribution. When a company vertically integrates all stages of production and distribution within its legal personality, there is no taxable supply between production and retail stage, and therefore no unrecoverable tax. Accordingly, cascading taxes distort business decisions by encouraging vertical integration even when there is no other economic reason to proceed that way. It also favours larger groups who can afford such vertical integration, as compared to smaller companies specialized in a specific domain and not willing or having the means to manage other production stages.

because it has an impact on the enforcement of the tax. As a matter of fact, in single- staged taxes, tax liability is concentrated at the retail stage, whereas in the VAT system, tax liability is spread over all economic transactions, so that the amount at risk of tax fraud is smaller in case of non-compliance. In addition, multi-staged taxes are thought to have a "self-enforcing effect" because a deduction (or refund) of input tax is only available if the taxable person provides evidence of VAT paid by means of an invoice. The self-enforcing effect should however not be overestimated, because it depends on administrative, including audit, efficiency. Revenue leaks may occur in multi staged systems in particular because of the possibility to deduct input VAT and obtain refunds. Finally, a major drawback of multi-staged systems as compared to single-staged systems, is that they impose non-negligible compliance burdens and costs on the supply side, related to filing and reporting requirements and refund procedures.

Under the VAT, the person liable for the payment of to the Treasury is indeed usually the supplier. The latter must assess, on a transaction basis, the amount of tax due in accordance with the applicable rules and remit that amount to the tax administration in the jurisdiction having taxing rights over the transaction. Suppliers bear the costs related to these collection obligations and are liable for the correct payment of the tax, although they do not receive any payment for that activity. This is why they often see themselves as "unpaid tax collectors". In some transactions between taxable persons the collection obligations may be shifted from the supplier to the (business) taxpayer, who will then be liable for correctly self-assessing the tax due and remitting it to the competent tax administration on a voluntary basis (also known as "reverse charging"). Even in this case, however, suppliers remain responsible for verifying that self-assessment/reverse charging rules apply, before making a (tax-free) supply (on which the tax will subsequently be paid by the business customer, on its initiative).

The fact that the tax increases the sales price raises the question of the incidence of the tax, or, in other words, the question whether the supplier will actually be able to fully shift the tax burden forwards to the consumer. In general, consumption taxes are designed on the assumption that the tax is fully shifted to the final consumer. However, it is generally accepted that the ability of the supplier to shift the tax burden forwards to consumers in the form of higher prices actually depends on his market position and on the price elasticity of demand.[15] Accordingly, to the extent the tax burden cannot be shifted by the supplier to the consumer, it should be acknowledged that the value added tax in effect becomes a tax on production rather than on consumption.

15 In practice, if demand is very price elastic, i.e. very responsive to price changes, then, even if the price will not increase very much when the tax is imposed, the quantity demanded will fall significantly. In that case, it is likely that suppliers will not be able to pass the (entire) tax burden to the consumer. In contrast, in case of price inelastic demand, all or the bulk of the tax can be passed on by the supplier because consumers are much less sensitive to price changes. In this case the quantity demanded will only fall very slightly or not at all even if the price will incorporate (almost) the full amount of the tax. Accordingly, when demand for a product is inelastic, the burden of the tax can be forwarded to the consumer.

2.3 Scope

The RVD distinguishes between the scope, *i.e.* the field of application, and, under a separate title, the territorial scope (for the latter see section 2.4 below). For the territorial allocation, generally referred to as the place of supply rules, see section 2.7 below.

Subject to value added tax are (further described under Section 2.6.):

1. the supply of *goods* and *services* effected for consideration within the territory of a Member State by a taxable person acting as such (Article 2(1)(a) and (c) RVD).
2. *intra-Community acquisitions* of goods for consideration by taxable persons and by non-taxable persons provided certain conditions are fulfilled (Article 2(1)(b) RVD) as well as the intra-Community acquisition of new means of transportation by anyone (see section 6.6.1 below).
3. the *importation* of goods by anyone (Article 2(1)(d) RVD).

2.4 Territorial Application

The VAT applies to the supply of goods and/or services and to intra-Community acquisitions of goods for consideration *within the territory* of a Member State[16] by a taxable person acting as such and to the importation of goods (Article 2(1) RVD). This territorial application is further defined in Articles 5 to 8 RVD, mainly by referring to the territorial application of the EC Treaty. As will be seen, in section 2.5 below, this application does not exclude the global concept regarding the taxability of persons.

See Annex I for a comparison table between the customs territory, the VAT territory and the excise territory.

Pursuant to the Withdrawal Agreement and the related Political Declaration setting out the framework for the future relationship dated 17 October 2019,[17] the UK left the EU from 1 February 2020. A transition period started during which the UK was still part of the EU's single market and customs union and applied the relevant EU Treaty and secondary legislation including the VAT legislation. The transition period ended on 30 December 2020. From 1 January 2021, the UK (including the Channel islands and the Isle of Man to the extent that Union law was applicable to them before the withdrawal) has left the EU VAT territory. Pursuant to the Protocols Annexed to the Withdrawal Agreement, first, the United Kingdom Sovereign Base Areas of Akrotiri and Dhekelia remains in the EU customs

---

16 See Case 283/84 (*Trans Tirreno*), [1986] ECR 0231, and Case C-30/89 (*Commission v. France*), [1990] ECR I-0691, on taxation of transport services outside the territorial waters and Case C-111/05 (*Aktiebolaget NN*), [2007] ECR I-2697, on the laying of a cable on the sea bottom between two Member States.

17 Agreement on the withdrawal of the United Kingdom of Great Britain and Northern Ireland from the European Union and the European Atomic Energy Community2019/C 384 I/01, O.J. *C 384I, 12.11.2019, p. 1–177* and Political declaration setting out the framework for the future relationship between the European Union and the United Kingdom2019/C 384 I/02 XT/21050/2019/ INIT *OJ C 384I, 12.11.2019, p. 178–193.*

Union and the VAT territory.[18] Second, special rules were introduced with respect to movements of goods to and from Northern Ireland[19] (see section 2.11.2 below). These rules are temporary (in principle they only apply until 1 August 2024 at the latest).

On 1 January 2020 the UK VAT system was identical to the EU VAT system and the ECJ case law was still applicable (concept of "retained EU law").[20] The ECJ case law decided after 31 December 2020 is no longer mandatory for UK courts.

2.5 Taxable Persons

2.5.1 Introduction

According to Article 9 RVD, "taxable person" means any person (or better "anyone") who independently carries out in any place any economic activity, whatever the purpose or result of that activity. Thus, a global concept is applied. Any person may be a taxable person and therefore be entitled to recovery of input VAT. Whether a person is subject to (European) VAT depends on the performance of (taxable) economic activities within the territory as defined in Articles 5 to 8 RVD. Activities that do not take place on a continuing basis or that are carried out by a dependent person are not activities of a taxable persons.

The elements that will be elaborated on in the following sections are:
- Any person (2.5.2)
- Economic activities (2.5.3)
- Continuing basis (2.5.4)
- Independency, including VAT grouping (2.5.5)

The VAT position of holding companies and public bodies is a special one and will be addressed in sections 2.5.6 and 2.5.7 respectively.

Due to recent developments the question arose whether participants in the sharing or gig economy should be treated as taxable persons for VAT purposes. For the time being, there is no specific harmonized VAT rules that applies to these sectors. Therefore, to determine the tax treatment of these persons, one should go through the same analysis than for any other business or entrepreneur.

2.5.2 Any person

"Any person" is not only an individual, but also a legal person, such as a private or public limited company. Also co-operations, joint ventures and partnerships, even when lacking legal personality, can be treated as taxable persons. Whether for income tax they are treated as separate taxpayers is not relevant. What counts for VAT purposes is that the

18 Articles 2 and 3 of the Protocol relating to the sovereign base areas of the United Kingdom of Great Britain and Nortern Ireland in Cyprus.
19 Article 8 of the Protocol on Ireland/Northern Ireland.
20 "As a general rule, the same rules and laws will apply on the day after exit as on the day before", The Explanatory Notes to the European Union (Withdrawal) Act 2018, para 10.

entity acts as a single unit. In the *Nigl* case,[21] the ECJ ruled that a number of cooperating winegrowers did not act as a single unit. The ECJ considered it important that each of the cooperatives in question exploits separate vineyards, that they each use almost exclusively their own business resources and employ their own staff, and that they act independently in relation to their suppliers, the authorities and, to a certain extent, their customers. Even in the situation where the partnership is a taxable person the partner can also be a taxable person when it carries out activities independent from the partnership. In the *Heerma*[22] case the ECJ ruled that leasing an immovable property to the partnership is such an independent activity.

2.5.3 *Economic activity*

An economic activity is specified as comprising all activities of producers, traders and persons supplying services, including mining and agricultural activities, and activities of the professions and the exploitation of tangible or intangible property for the purpose of obtaining income therefrom on a continuing basis. The ECJ has held that the "exploitation" of tangible property within now Article 9(1) refers to all transactions, whatever their legal form, by which it was sought to obtain income from goods on a continuing basis. The grant of building rights, whereby the grantee was authorized to use the immovable property for a specified period of time in return for a consideration, was to be considered to be the exploitation of tangible property for the purpose of obtaining income therefrom on a continuing basis. It was therefore an economic activity which generated a right to deduct input tax.[23] A private person operating a photovoltaic installation on the roof of a house which is used as a dwelling that had a contract for an indefinite period to supply electricity produced by this installation to a power company was also regarded as a taxable person by the ECJ.[24]

The RVD mentions any activity "whatever the purpose or result". However, the ECJ has decided that certain illegal transactions fall outside the scope of the VAT, such as the importation and supply of drugs, even when such sales are not systematically prosecuted in a Member State,[25] and the importation of counterfeit currency notes.[26] This only applies to activities that are *inherently* illegal, meaning that they could not be carried out legally.

---

21 Case C-340/15 (*Nigl*), ECLI:EU:C:2016:764. See also case C-312/19 (*XT*), ECLI:EU:C:2020:711 that deals with a silent partnership and answers the question who qualifies as the taxable person in that situation.

22 Case C-23/98 (*Heerma*), ECLI:EU:C:2000:46.

23 Case C-186/89 (*Van Tiem*), [1990] ECR I-4363. See also Case C-230/94 (*Renate Enkler*), [1996] ECR I-4517. The purely occasional commercial exploitation of property does not constitute an economic activity for the purposes of Article 4(1) and (2) of the Sixth Directive (now Article 9(1) RVD). It is of no relevance how often a taxable person concludes comparable transactions; what is relevant is whether the particular property provides long-term revenue.

24 Case C-219/12 (*Fuchs*), ECLI:EU:C:2013:413.

25 See for example Case 289/86 (*Happy Family*), [1988] ECR 3655.

26 Case C-343/89 (*Witzemann*), [1990] ECR I-4477.

In case these activities can also be carried out legally the neutrality principle requires that the illegal transactions are taxed as well.[27]

Furthermore, a person who supplies goods or services that are in all cases free of charge cannot be regarded as a taxable person.[28] This does not mean that taxable activities are performed whenever money is received. In addition to a direct link between the activity and the payment, there must be a legal relationship between the person receiving money and the person(s) paying it.[29] The ECJ held in a case regarding a Dutch organ grinder that the supply of services effected for consideration does not include an activity consisting of playing music on the public highway, for which no remuneration is stipulated, even if the musician solicits money and receives sums whose amount is, however, neither quantified nor quantifiable.[30] Even a charitable trust selling its shares in a foundation for an amount in excess of £ 1.8 billion must, according to the ECJ, be regarded as confining its activities to managing an investment portfolio in the same way as a private investor.[31] In fact, since the ECJ case *gemeente Borsele*[32] it became clear that a two-step-approach is necessary to determine whether an economic activity exists. First it must be established whether a transaction against consideration takes place. When applying this test, the fact that the price paid for an economic transaction is higher or lower than the cost price is irrelevant to the question whether a transaction is to be regarded as a "transaction effected for consideration". As a second step it must be established whether the activity is indeed an economic activity. In respect of the municipality of Borsele that carried out pupil transport for which approximately one third of the parents paid an own contribution which covered only 3% of the costs, the ECJ ruled that even though there was a supply of services against consideration the activity did not qualify as an economic activity. According to the ECJ there was a lack of symmetry between the costs and the contributions received with the result that there was no genuine link between the amount paid and the services supplied. The conditions under which the services are supplied too are different from those under which passenger transport services are usually provided, since the municipality of Borsele does not offer services on the general passenger transport market, but rather appears to be a beneficiary and final consumer of transport services which it acquires from transport undertakings with which it deals and which it makes available to parents of pupils as part of its public service activities. In the *EQ case*[33] the ECJ ruled that the VAT position of a lawyer was different from that of the municipality Borsele, because in his situation the income was not insufficient in respect of his operating costs. It therefore seems that an

27 Case C-283/95 *(Fischer)*, ECLI:EU:C:1998:276 regarding the organization of games of chance without having received the required authorisation. Other examples of illegal supplies that could be carried out legally include: the sale of goods without having obtained the required licences.

28 Case 89/81 (*Hong Kong Trade Development Council*), [1982] ECR 1277.

29 Such a legal relationship exists even when the obligations of one of the parties are "binding in honour only". Case C-498/99 (*Town & County Factors Ltd*), [2002] ECR I-7173.

30 Case C-16/93 (*Tolsma*), [1994] ECR I-0743. The theft of goods, by definition, does not give rise to any financial counterpart for the victim of the theft. It therefore cannot as such be regarded as a supply of goods "for consideration" within the meaning of Article 2 of the Directive on a *Tolsma* analysis. Case C-435/03 (*British American Tobacco International Limited &. N.V. Newman Shipping & Agency Company NV*), [2005] ECR I-7077.

31 Case C-155/94 (*Wellcome Trust*), [1996] ECR I-3013.

32 Case C-520/14 (*gemeente Borsele*), ECLI:EU:C:2016:334.

33 Case C-846-19, ECLI:EU:C:2021:277.

economic activity is absent only if a small part of the operating costs are covered by the income. This test will not be applied on a transaction-by-transaction basis, but the activity as a whole needs to be considered.

With regard to the question of *when* a person becomes a taxable person, the ECJ has ruled that initial investment expenditure incurred for the needs of, and with the view to carrying on, an enterprise should be considered an economic activity.[34] The same applies concerning the transactions entered into with the objective to wind up a business.[35] However, this does not prevent the fiscal authorities from requiring that the stated intention to carry out such activities be confirmed by objective circumstances.

2.5.4 *Continuing basis*

When activities are not carried out on a continuing basis, this does not confer the status of taxable person. If, however a person has obtained the status of taxable person, his tax liability extends to occasional activities.[36] The activity will however need to exceed the mere exercise of the right of ownership by its holder. If a person takes active steps, for the purpose of concluding sales, to market property by mobilising resources similar to those deployed by a producer, a trader or a person supplying services that person must be regarded as carrying out an "economic activity" and must, therefore, be regarded as a taxable person for that transaction.[37]

It is at the discretion of Member States to tax occasional transactions by non- taxable persons (Article 12(1) RVD) irrespective of whether the transaction is carried out on a continuing basis or whether the person who effected the supply carries out an activity of a producer, a trader or a person supplying services, *to the extent that that transaction does not constitute the mere exercise of the right of ownership by its holder.* In other words, the transaction must be an economic activity similar to those deployed by a producer, a trader or a person supplying services within the meaning of the second subparagraph of Article 9(1) of the VAT Directive.[38]

2.5.5 *Independence*

The requirement that a taxable person acts in an "independent" capacity excludes employees from an obligation to charge value added tax on services provided to their employers. In the *Van der Steen*[39] case the ECJ held that a natural person carrying out all work in the name and on behalf of a company that is a taxable person pursuant to a contract of employment binding him to that company of which he is also the sole shareholder, the sole manager and the sole member of staff, is not himself a taxable person. The *IO* case[40] shows that the

34 See *ex multis* Case 268/83 (*Rompelman*), [1985] ECR 0655, and Case 147/98 (*Gabalfrisa S.A. a.o.*), [2000] ECR I-1577.
35 Case C-32/03 (*Fini H*), [2005] ECR I-1599.
36 Case C-62/12 *(Kostov)*, ECLI:EU:C:2013:391.
37 Joined Cases C-180/10 and C-181/10 (*Sáaby and Kuc)*, ECLI:EU:C:2011:589.
38 Joined Cases C-180/10 and C-181/10 (*Sáaby and Kuc*), ECLI:EU:C:2011:589.
39 Case C-355/06 (*van der Steen*), [2007] ECR I-8863.
40 Case C-420/18 (*IO),* ECLI:EU:C:2019:490.

criterion of independency can be read both in Article 10 RVD that excludes employees from the concept of taxable person and in Article 9 RVD. Even though IO was not to be regarded as an employee, he was not an independent person under Article 9 RVD. As a member of a Supervisory Board IO was not acting in his own name, on his own behalf or under his own responsibility, but on behalf of and under the responsibility of the Supervisory Board. He also does not bear the economic risk arising from his activities, since he receives a fixed remuneration which is not dependent on his participation in meetings or hours actually worked. In the *FCE Bank* case[41] the ECJ ruled on the basis of Article 9 RVD that a fixed establishment which is not a legal entity distinct from the company of which it forms part is not to be regarded as an independent taxable person. Supplies between a head office and a branch are therefore generally not subject to VAT.

Member States may treat associated enterprises as a single, taxable entity, although they are legally independent, provided they are closely bound to one another by financial, economic and organizational links (so-called "VAT group", Article 11 RVD). Not all Member States apply this group registration, which is restricted to persons established within the territory of a Member State.[42] Where that provision is implemented by a Member State, the closely linked person or persons within the meaning of that provision cannot be treated as a separate taxable person or persons within the meaning of Article 9 RVD. Treatment as a single taxable person precludes persons who are thus closely linked from continuing to submit VAT declarations separately and from continuing to be identified, within and outside their group, as individual taxable persons, since the single taxable person alone is authorized to submit such declarations.[43]

As indicated above, supplies between a head office and a branch (fixed establishment) are not subject to VAT. If however the fixed establishment is part of a VAT group without its foreign head office or, *vice versa* (i.e. a head office is part of a VAT group without its fixed establishment) there are two separate taxable persons and supplies are subject to VAT.[44]

2.5.6 Holding companies and share dealings

With regard to economic activities, the ECJ has ruled that a "pure" holding company, *i.e.* a company whose activities concern solely the holding of shares in subsidiary companies, cannot be regarded as a taxable person.[45] A certain degree of interference in their management against consideration (dividends do not qualify as such[46]) is necessary for such companies to become taxable persons. Any services provided on a continuing basis can be regarded as interference in management.[47] In case a holding company qualifies as

41 Case C-210/04 (*FCE Bank*), ECLI:EU:C:2006:196.
42 Altough there are some EU Member States though that include foreign establishments in the VAT group in case the entitiy has a fixed establishment or head office in that Member State's territory. Whether this is allowed remains unclear.
43 Case C-162/07 (*Ampliscientifica*), [2008] ECR I-4019.
44 Case C-7/13 (*Skandia America Corporation*), ECLI:EU:C:2014:2225 and C-812/ 19 (*Danske Bank*), ECLI:EU:C:2021:196.
45 Case C-60/90 (*Polysar*), [1991] ECR I-3111.
46 Case C-142/99 (*Floridienne/Berginvest*), ECLI:EU:C:2000:623.
47 Case C-320/17 (*Marle Participations*), ECLI:EU:C:2018:537.

a taxable person because of the interference in the management of its subsidiaries VAT deduction on costs made will not be limited by the shareholding activity.[48] In other words, if a holding company provides services on a continuing basis to all its subsidiaries it has a full right to deduct VAT unless these services are exempt from VAT (see also section 2.11 and 2.12 below). The activities of open-ended investment companies, which go beyond the compass of the simple acquisition and the mere sale of securities, and which aim to produce income on a continuing basis, constitute economic activities within the meaning of Article 9(1) of the Directive as well.[49]

The question whether a holding company qualifies as a taxable person has direct consequences on the right to deduct. See section 2.12.8 for a more detailed analysis thereof.

2.5.7 Public bodies

Public bodies are normally considered to be non-taxable legal persons in respect of activities engaged in in that capacity, except if they compete with commercial enterprises (Article 13 RVD).

Annex I to the Directive mentions certain activities in relation to which public bodies must be treated as taxable persons, since they are typically also offered by the private sector, for example, telecommunication services,[50] transportation of goods and passengers, and the supply of water, gas and electricity.

There is no uniform interpretation of what is covered by public activities, since the ECJ has ruled that the distinction between public and private activities can only be derived pursuant to the legal system applicable to public authorities under national law.[51] The ECJ, however, has held that notaries and bailiffs in the Netherlands are considered to perform economic activities since they do not pursue their activities in the form of a body governed

48 Case C-108/14 and C-109/14 *(joined cases Larentia + Minerva and Marenave Schifffahrt)*, ECLI:EU:C:2015:496.

49 Case C-8/03 (*Banque Bruxelles Lambert SA* (*BBL*)), [2004] ECR I-10157.

50 In Case C-284/04 (*T-Mobile Austria*), [2007] ECR I-5189 and Case C-369/04 (*Hutchison 3G a.o.*), [2007] ECR I-5247, the ECJ held that the allocation, by auction by the national regulatory authority responsible for spectrum assignment, of rights such as rights to use frequencies in the electromagnetic spectrum with the aim of providing the public with mobile telecommunications services does not constitute an economic activity and, consequently, does not fall within the scope of the Directive.

51 Case 231/87 (*Carpaneto Piacento*), [1989] ECR 3233.

by public law.[52] A private body under civil law can be considered a public body for VAT purposes because public body is an autonomous concept of Union law.[53]

In a series of cases dealing with road tolls, the ECJ held that the activity of providing access to roads on payment of a toll carried out exclusively by traders governed by private law is subject to VAT, resulting in the fact that road tolls in Ireland are taxed, in France and the UK partially (insofar as carried out by private traders) and in Greece and the Netherlands not at all (carried out by public bodies).[54] In its case law the ECJ seems to narrow the "exemption" for public bodies and emphasises that it is clear from the scheme and purpose of the RVD, as well as from the place of Article 13 thereof in the structure of the Directive, that any activity of an economic nature is, in principle, to be taxable.[55]

2.6 Taxable Transactions

The RVD distinguishes between four types of taxable supplies:
1. Supply of goods
2. Intra-Community acquisition
3. Supply of services
4. Importation of goods

2.6.1 Supply of goods

Article 14 (1) RVD provides that a "supply of goods" means the transfer of the right to dispose of tangible property as owner. Tangible property for VAT purposes includes electric current, gas, heat, refrigeration and the like (Article 15(1) RVD) but also animals.[56]

According to the ECJ it is clear from the wording of Article 14(1) RVD that "supply of goods" does not refer to the transfer of ownership in accordance with the procedures prescribed

52 Case 235/85 (*Commission v. Netherlands*), [1987] ECR 1471. See also Case C- 202/90 (*Recaudadores de Tributos*), [1991] ECR I-4247 and Case C-456/07 (*Mihal*) [2008] ECR I-79*,. Case C-154/08 (*Commission v. Spain*), [2009] ECR I-187*, deals with the fact that the Tribunal Supremo (Supreme Court) of Spain held that land registrars, as regards the specific activities entrusted to them by the Autonomous Communities, consisting in the settlement and collection of certain taxes, are simply public officials and form part of the public administration. The ECJ declared the Kingdom of Spain liable for a failure to fulfil obligations through an interpretation of EU law and held that the Spanish administration may not seek protection from the judgment of the Tribunal Supremo to justify its failure to fulfil its obligations under EU law.

53 Case C-174/14 (*Saudaçor*), ECLI:EU:C:2015:733, where a private body was considered a public body for VAT purposes and C-182/17 (*Nagyszénás Településszolgáltatási Nonprofit*), ECLI:EU:C:2018:91, where a private body did not qualify as public body for VAT purposes.

54 Cases C-359/97 (*Commission v. UK*), [2000] ECR I-6355, C-276/97 (*Commission v. France*), [2000] ECR I-6251, C-358/97 (*Commission v. Ireland*), [2000] ECR I- 6301, C-408/97 (*Commission v. Netherlands*), [2000] ECR I-6417 and C-260/98 (*Commission v. Greece*), [2000] ECR I-6537.

55 Case C-288/07 (*Isle of Wight Council*), [2008] ECR I-7203 and Case C-554/07 (*Commission v. Ireland*), [2009] ECR I-128*.

56 Case 10/87 (*The Queen v. Commissioners and excise ex parte Tattersalls Ltd*), [1988] ECR 03281. See also Case C 209/14 (*NLB Leasing*), [2015], ECLI:EU: C:2015:440 in which the ECJ confirmed that a distinction must be made between an *operating lease* and *finance lease* (in which all risks are rewards of legal ownership are transferred to the lessee).

by the applicable national law but covers any transfer of tangible property by one party which empowers the other party actually to dispose of it *as if he were the owner* of the property.[57] The mere economic conveyance and not the transfer of legal ownership does therefore not prevent transactions to be treated as supplies of goods. If the legal transfer were decisive for the occurrence of a taxable supply, VAT would indeed be imposed at different intervals in the various Member States depending on whether property was transferred by contract (*e.g.* as in France, Italy and Belgium) or by the formal act of delivery (*e.g.* as in the Netherlands).[58]

Article 14(2) (b) RVD provides that transfers made in the context of a hire/ purchase or a conditional sale are also supplies of goods. As clarified by the ECJ, this applies to the case of a leasing contract with an option to purchase if it can be inferred from the financial terms of the contract that exercising the option appears to be the only economically rational choice that the lessee will be able to make at the appropriate time if the contract is performed for its full term[59] (see also section 2.8).

According to Article 14(2), (a) and (b) RVD, transfers made in connection with a compulsory transaction (*i.e.* by order made in the name of a public body against payment of compensation) are also to be treated as a supply of goods for VAT purposes.

The transfer of goods pursuant to a contract under which commission is payable on purchase or sale must likewise be considered a supply of goods (Article 14(2), (c) RVD). A similar provision exists with regard to supplies of services (Article 28 RVD): where a taxable person acting in his own name but on behalf of another (the so-called undisclosed agent) takes part in a supply of services, he must be considered to have received and supplied those services. Without these provisions an agent should always be required to reveal the name of his principal which would have been necessary for correct invoicing procedures. The RVD therefore introduces the fiction of a supply to and by the undisclosed agent, to whom and by whom proper invoices can be issued. In this case the commissionaire's fee is the difference between the purchase price and the sales price of the commissionaire. In several cases concerning supply of fuel,[60] the ECJ has however decided that an intermediary acting in his own name is not buying and selling the goods. According to the ECJ, in these cases the intermediary should be ignored because the right to dispose of the tangible property as owner was already with the customer at the time when the supplier could transfer his legal rights. In *Vega International*, a parent company organised and managed the supply of fuel cards, issued by different fuel suppliers, to all its subsidiaries. The parent company received invoices from the fuel suppliers (with VAT) and passed on the cost to the subsidiaries on a monthly basis with a surcharge of 2%. The ECJ decided that the supply of fuel was made directly to the subsidiaries (and so ignored the parent company

57 Case C-320/88 (*Staatsecretaris van Financïen v. Shipping and Forwarding Enterprise Safe BV*), [1990], ECR I-00285; Case C-185/01 (*Auto Lease Holland BV*), [2003] ECR I-1317.
58 Case C-320/88 (*SAFE*), [1990] ECR I-0285.
59 Case C-164/16 (*Commissioners for Her Majesty's Revenue & Customs v. Mercedes- Benz Financial Services UK Ltd*), [2017], ECLI:EU:C:2017:734.
60 Cases C-185/01 (*Auto Lease Holland*), [2003], ECLI:EU:C:2003:73; C-526/13 (*Fast Bunkering Klaipeda UAB*), [2015], ECLI:EU:C:2015:536; C-235/18, (*Vega International*), ECLI:EU:C:2019:412.

as an intermediary) and that the parent was providing (exempt, see Section 2.11.1) credit services to its subsidiaries.

According to Article 14(3) RVD Member States may regard the handing over of certain works of construction as a supply of goods and based on Article 15(2) RVD, Member States may consider the transfer of certain interests in immovable property and rights *in rem* as taxable supplies. If they do choose not to do so, these transfers are supplies of services.

Applicable from 1 July 2021, Article 14(1) RVD provides new definitions for the concepts of *intra-community distance sales of goods* and *distance sales of goods imported from third territories or third countries*. Both definitions concern supplies of goods (except new means of transport, goods supplied after assembly or installation by or on behalf of the supplier) to either non-taxable persons or persons whose intra- Community acquisitions are not taxable (see below, intra-Community acquisition) in which the goods are transported or dispatched by or on behalf of the supplier, including when the supplier intervenes indirectly in the transport or dispatch.

Article 5a of the IR clarifies that the goods shall be considered to have been transported or dispatched on behalf of the supplier in particular when the transport or dispatch of the goods is subcontracted by the supplier to a third party, if the supplier bears responsibility for the delivery of the goods to the customer, if the supplier invoices and collects transport fees and remits them to a third party arranging the dispatch or transport or if the supplier promotes the delivery services of a third party, puts the customer and a third party in contact or otherwise provides the information needed for the delivery (Article 5a, (a) to (d) of the IR). The goods will not be considered to have been dispatched or transported on behalf of the supplier if the customer transports the goods himself or arranges the delivery with a third party without the supplier intervening *either directly or indirectly* to provide or to help organizing the transport or dispatch (Article 5a, (d) IR *in fine*).

Also applicable from 1 July 2021, Article 14a RVD provides that a taxable person who *facilitates*, through the use of an electronic interface, either a distance sale of goods imported from third countries or territories with an intrinsic value of no more than 150 euros (Article 14a (1)) or an intra-community distance sale of goods or a local B2C-supply of a supplier not established in the EU (Article 14a (2)), shall be deemed to have received and supplied those goods. This *deeming provision* is a key provision of the e-commerce VAT package adopted by the Member States in 2017. In practice it means that platforms and other marketplaces that *facilitate* supplies are deemed to purchase and sell onward the goods sold online to final consumers. The concept *facilitate* is defined in a very broad manner under Article 5b IR as "the use of an electronic interface to allow a customer and a supplier offering goods for sale through the electronic interface to enter into contact which results in a supply of goods through that electronic interface". Article 5b IR further lists a set of actions that trigger the application of the deeming provision, e.g. setting the terms and conditions of the underlying supply or authorizing the charge to the client. It also clarifies that taxable person who only process payment, list or advertise goods or redirect customers to another platform do not qualify as deeming suppliers under Article 14a RVD. Platforms and other marketplaces that are deemed to receive and supply goods to final consumers may use the various schemes in place to simplify the declaration and payment of the VAT on the supplies to the final consumers (see Section 2.14.6.2-2.14.6.4). Article 5c IR contains a safeharbour clause that relieves the taxable persons acting as deemed suppliers from the liability to pay VAT in excess of the VAT that they have declared and paid when they received wrong information from the initial supplier regarding the supply and were dependent from that information and can demonstrate that they did not and could not reasonably know that this information was incorrect. Guidance regarding the correct application of the deeming provision (and other elements of the e-commerce VAT package) is offered by the European Commission in the "Explanatory notes on VAT e-commerce rules" published on 20 September 2020 (on explanatory notes, see Section 2.16.2).[61]

In accordance with Article 16 RVD the private use by a taxable person or other application free of charge for non-business purposes[62] must also be treated as a supply made for (a deemed) consideration (the so-called self-supply) when input VAT was (at least partially) deductible. By exception, the application for business use as samples or as gifts of small value are not treated as a self-supply.[63] The purpose of this provision is to ensure equal treatment between a taxable person who applies goods for private use (on which it could deduct the input VAT) and a final consumer who acquires goods of the same type (without the right to deduct input VAT).[64] In other words, this provision was inserted to prevent situations in which final consumption is untaxed.[65] In a case that concerned land owned by a building contractor in a private capacity on which, in the course of his professional activities, he had constructed a private dwelling for himself, the ECJ ruled that, since such land had never belonged to the assets of the undertaking, the land could never have been applied for a self-supply.[66] It should be noted that a person cannot keep a certain asset in his private assets simply because he desires so. A person should also use the asset in the course of the management and the administration of his private assets. If a person has taken active steps to market property by mobilising resources similar to those deployed by producers, traders or persons supplying services these activities do not normally fall within the scope of the management of private assets so those supplies regarding the asset

61 Available at: https://ec.europa.eu/taxation_customs/sites/taxation/files/vatecommerceexplanatory_notes_30092020.pdf.

62 In Kuwait Petroleum the ECJ decided that this provision could also apply if the disposal is made for business purposes. Case C-48/97, (*Kuwait Petroleum*), [1999], ECLI:EU:C:1999:203, para 22.

63 According to the ECJ a "sample is a specimen of a product which is intended to promote the sales of that product and which allows the characteristics and qualities of that product to be assessed without resulting in final consumption, other than where final consumption is inherent in such promotional transactions." That term cannot be limited, in a general way, by national legislation to specimens presented in a form which is not available for sale or to the first of a series of identical specimens given by a taxable person to the same recipient. The concept of "gifts of small value", must be interpreted as not precluding national legislation which fixes a monetary ceiling, for example GBP 50, for gifts made to the same person in the course of a 12-month period or forming part of a series or succession of gifts. Case C-581/08 (*EMI*), [2010] ECR I-08607.

64 Cases C-230/94, (*Enkler*), [1996], ECLI:EU:C:1996:352; C-258/95, (*Fillibeck*), ECLI:EU:C:1997:491.

65 Case C-581/08, (*EMI Group*), [2010], EU:C:2010:559.

66 Case C-20/91 (*De Jong*), [1992] ECR I-2847. More recently: C-36/16, (*Posnania Investment*), EU:C:2017:361.

(such as a sale) cannot be regarded as the mere exercise of the right of ownership by its holder, but instead must be regarded as economic activities.[67]

According to 17 RVD the transfer by a taxable person of goods forming part of his business assets to another Member State shall be treated as a supply of goods for consideration, except in a number of situations listed under 17 (2) RVD and under 17a RVD concerning call-off stock arrangements (on the latter, see under intra- Community acquisitions in this section further below).

In accordance with Article 18 RVD, Member States may treat the following transactions as a supply of goods for consideration: (a) the application of self-constructed goods, where the VAT on such goods, had they been acquired from another taxable person, would not be wholly deductible, the so-called internal supply;[68] (b) the application of goods by a taxable person for the purpose of a non-taxable area of activity (when VAT was deducted upon purchase) and (c) the retention of goods by the taxable person, or by his successors, when he ceases to carry out a taxable economic activity (again when VAT was deducted upon purchase).

Finally, Article 19 RVD provides that Member States may consider that no supply of goods (and services (Article 29 RVD)) has taken place in the event of a transfer of a totality of assets or part thereof, the so-called transfer of a going concern. In that event the recipient is treated as the successor to the transferor. This provision prevents large amounts of VAT from becoming due that would be deductible anyway. The ECJ clarified that this no-supply rule applies only when the transferee at least intends to operate the business or the part of the undertaking transferred and not simply to immediately liquidate the activity concerned and sell the stock, if any;[69] that it may apply when the stock and fittings of a retail outlet are transferred concomitantly with the conclusion of a contract of lease of the premises of that outlet, to the transferee, provided that the assets transferred are sufficient for the transferee to be able to carry on an independent economic activity on a lasting basis,[70] but that in contrast, the no supply rule does not cover a transaction by which an immovable property which was used for commercial purposes is let with all capital equipment and inventory items necessary for that use, even if the lessee pursues the activity of the lessor under the same name.[71] Since VAT is only deductible insofar as goods and services are used for taxable supplies, the question arises whether VAT can be deducted (and if so by whom) in cases of a transfer of a going concern. According to the ECJ the costs incurred by the transferor of a business for supplies made to him regarding that transfer form part of that taxable person's overhead.[72] This even applies when the transferor does not intend

67 Case C-331/14 (*Petar Kezi/ s.p. Trgovina Prizma*), ECLI:EU:C:2015:456.

68 Taxation of such internal supplies may be necessary to prevent regular supply patterns from becoming meaningless. When the tax is not fully deductible, the application of self-constructed goods results in a lower tax burden since the wage (and profit) components are not taxed. See Case 299/11, (*Gemeente Vlaardingen*), [2012], ECLI:EU:C:2012:698. See also Opinion of Advocate General Mengozzi in Case C-128/14, (*Het Oudeland Beheer*), [1992], ECLI:EU:C:2016:306.

69 Case C-497/01, (*Zita Modes*), [2003], ECLI:EU:C:2003:644.

70 Case C-444/10, (*Schriever*), [2011], ECLI:EU:C:2011:724.

71 Case C-17/18, (*Mailat, Apcom Select SA*), [2018], ECLI:EU:C:2018:1038.

72 Case C-408/98 (*Abbey National*), [2001] ECR I-1361.

to perform taxable activities himself, for example a German *Vorgründungsgesellschaft*, *i.e.* a company in formation.[73]

2.6.2 Intra-Community supplies

Intra-Community acquisition of goods is defined as "the acquisition of the right to dispose as owner of movable tangible property dispatched or transported to the person acquiring the goods by or on behalf of the vendor or the person acquiring the goods to a Member State other than that from which the goods are dispatched or transported" (Article 20 RVD).[74]

As a general rule, supplies of goods by taxable persons in one Member State to taxable persons in another Member State are exempt from VAT (Article 138 RVD), with the right to deduction. As the direct counterpart of supplies of goods being exempt in the country of departure, the corresponding intra-Community acquisitions are taxable in the country of destination (Article 2(1), point b RVD). In most cases the acquisition is made by a taxable person. However, non-taxable legal persons may also be subject to VAT when they make an intra-Community acquisition. In accordance with Article 3 RVD, there is no intra-Community acquisition when the customer is: (a) a farmer eligible for the flat-rate scheme (see section 2.14.2 below); (b) a taxable person not entitled to deduction of VAT (exempt, see 2.11.1) or (c) a non-taxable legal person, provided these customers purchase goods (excluding new means of transport and excise products) in another Member State for an amount not exceeding EUR 10 000 yearly (Member States may determine a higher threshold). Instead, their purchase is taxed (and not exempt) in the Member State from which the goods are dispatched or transported. Conversely, when the above-mentioned persons purchase goods in other Member States exceeding the threshold or when they exceeded the threshold in the previous calendar year, such purchases result in taxed intra-Community acquisitions (*i.e.* in the Member State of destination).

When a taxable person makes a cross-border transfer of own goods (eg. transfer of stocks), this qualifies as an exempt supply of goods followed by a taxed acquisition in the Member State of arrival of the goods (Article 17 RVD, see also Section 2.7.2). A series of transfers are excluded from this provision because the goods are eventually meant to return to the Member State of departure (see Article 17(2) RVD) or because the rules regarding the place of supply already provide for taxation (*e.g.* in cases when goods are assembled or installed or when electricity or gas is supplied, see sections 2.7 and 2.7.2 below or, in cases of distance sales, see section 2.7.1 below). Since 1 January 2020, new rules apply to call-off stock arrangements (whereby a taxable person dispatches or transports goods to a stock in another Member State for an intended acquirer whose identity and VAT identification number are known at the time of the transport or dispatch and who has the right to take goods out of this stock at his own discretion, at which time the property on the goods is transferred). Under the normal rules, an intra-Community supply of goods followed by an intra-Community acquisition takes place at the time when the goods are being transferred to the stock in the other Member State. Since at that time the customer has not yet been

73 Case C-137/02 (*Faxworld Vorgründungsgesellschaft*), [2004] ECR I-5547.
74 See Case C-409/04 (*Teleos*), [2007] ECR I-7797, on the meaning of the term "dispatched".

transferred the right to dispose of the goods, the acquisition is to be made in the country of arrival of the goods by the supplier, which implies the obligation to register in that Member State. New Article 17a RVD provides for a simplification: no intra-Community supply and no intra-Community acquisition take place at the time of dispatch or transport of the goods to the stock located in another Member State. An exempt intra-Community supply in the Member State of departure and a taxed intra-Community acquisition in the Member State where the stock is situated only take place at a later stage when the acquirer takes ownership of the goods. The intra-Community acquisition is thus reported by the acquirer and the simplification avoids VAT registration of the supplier in the Member State of the acquirer. The simplification only applies when several conditions are met (see Article 243(3) and 262(2) RVD and Article 54a IR).[75]

2.6.3 *Supply of services*

"Supply of services" is defined in Article 24 RVD on a residual basis. It covers any transaction "that does not constitute a supply of goods", which may include assignments of intangible property, the obligation to refrain from an act (e.g. a non-compete clause) and the performance of services in pursuance to the law (Article 25 RVD). Since a transaction may only qualify as a supply of goods if it involves tangible assets, the sale of intangible software or of any downloadable content is excluded from that category (even if the supply of the same software or content in a tangible form would qualify as a supply of good). Thanks to the residual wording of Article 24 RVD, these transactions fall into the category of services for VAT purposes.[76]

Not all transactions are subject to VAT though. A case for the ECJ dealt with the situation in which a German farmer received a subsidy for the definitive discontinuation of milk production. The ECJ held that by compensating farmers the Community does not acquire goods or services for its own use but acts in the common interest.[77] No benefits entail which would enable the Community or the competent national authorities to be considered consumers of a service within the meaning of Article 6(1) of the Sixth Directive (now Article 24 RVD). The German government disagreed and argued in a second case that the subsidy to farmers for the extensification of potato production was a payment for services.[78] The question of who benefits from a supply of a service or from its economic impact is entirely irrelevant. The ECJ held that a farmer, by not harvesting a percentage of his potato crop, does not provide services to an identifiable consumer or any benefit capable of being regarded as a cost component of the activity of another person in the commercial chain. In *Astra Zeneca* the ECJ held that the provision of a retail voucher by a company, which acquired

75 See also: European Commission, Explanatory Notes on the EU VAT changes in respect of call-off stock arrangements, chain transactions and the exemption for intra-Community supplies of goods ("2020 Quick Fixes"), December 2019, available at: https://ec.europa.eu/taxation_customs/sites/taxation/files/explanatory_notes_2020_quick_fixes_en.pdf.

76 Accordingly, while the sale of a hardcover book qualifies as a supply of goods for VAT purposes, the sale of the same book in an intangible format qualifies as a supply of services.

77 Case C-215/94 (*Mohr*), [1996] ECR I-0959.

78 Case C-384/95 (*Landboden-Agrardienste*), [1997] ECR I-7387.

that voucher at a price including VAT, to its employees in exchange for their giving up part of their cash remuneration constitutes a supply of services effected for consideration.[79]

The distinction between a supply of good and a supply of service is not always straightforward. The ECJ decided that reprographics activities have the characteristics of a supply of goods to the extent that they are limited to mere reproduction of documents on materials, where the right to dispose of them has been transferred from the reprographer to the customer who ordered the copies of the original. Such activities must however be classified as a "supply of services", where it is clear that they involve additional services liable, having regard to the importance of those services for the recipient, the time necessary to perform them, the processing required by the original documents and the proportion of the total cost that those services represent, to be predominant in relation to the supply of goods, such that they constitute an aim in themselves for the recipient thereof.[80] The ECJ also decided that restaurant transactions do not qualify as supplies of goods[81] but that the supply of prepared food for immediate consumption qualifies as a supply of goods if the elements of supply of services preceding and accompanying the supply of the food are not predominant.[82] The legislator eventually introduced specific definitions for restaurant and catering activities in the IR. As will be further developed in Section 2.16.1, the IR lays down specific definitions, notably for restaurant and catering services (Article 6 IR),[83] telecommunication services (Article 6a IR), broadcasting services (Article 6b IR), electronically supplied services (Article 7 IR), supply of services connected with immovable property (article 31a IR), supply of cultural, artistic, sporting, scientific, educational, entertainment, and similar services(Article 32 IR) and means of transport in context of a hire contract (Article 38 IR). These are harmonized VAT concepts, meaning that national definitions would not be relevant when applying VAT.

The use[84] of goods forming part of the assets of a business and the supply of services carried out free of charge[85] by a taxable person for his private use or of his staff (for example the use, free of charge, of a vehicle forming part of the assets of the business, by employees of the taxable persons)[86] or, more generally, for purposes other than those of his business,

79 In Case C-40/09 (*Astra Zeneca UK Limited*), [2010] ECR I- 07505.
80 Case C-88/09 (*Graphic Procédé*), [2010] ECR I-1049.
81 Case C-231/94 (*Faaborg-Gelting Linien*), [1996], ECLI:EU:C:1996:184.
82 Case C-497/09, (*Bog and others*), [2011], ECLI:EU:C:2011:135.
83 Consistent with previous ECJ case law. See C-231/94, (*Faaborg-Gelting Linien*), [1996], ECLI:EU:C:1996:184; C-497/09, (*Bog and others*), ECLI:EU:C:2011:135.
84 The difference with Article 16 RVD (applied goods) is that the use of the goods is only temporary.
85 Neither Article 16 RVD nor Article 26 RVD may be applied if there is a consideration. In Case C-412/03 (*Hotel Scandic*), [2005] ECR I-0743, the ECJ held that the fact that the price paid for an economic transaction is higher or lower than the cost price is irrelevant to the question whether a transaction is to be regarded as a "transaction effected for consideration". See, however, Article 80 in section 2.9.
86 See C-288/19, (*QM V Finanzamt Saarbrücken*), [1996], ECLI:EU:C:2021:32 in which the ECJ inter alia confirmed that the provision does not apply if there is a counterparty paid by the employee. If there is a counterparty the supply will qualify as a taxable hiring of a means of transport under Article 56(2) RVD if that employee has a permanent right to use that vehicle for private purposes and to exclude other persons from using it, in exchange for rent and for an agreed period of more than 30 days.

is treated as a taxable transaction. Member States may derogate from this rule, provided this does not lead to distortion of competition (Article 26 RVD).[87] The taxation of private use is not allowed where the input tax on the goods was not deductible or in so far as the use includes services on which the VAT was not deductible.[88] The question arose whether the provision of free transport or meals in canteens by an employer serves the employees' private purposes or those of a business. The ECJ has introduced a "business purpose test". According to the ECJ, Article 26 RVD must be interpreted in such a way that, on the one hand, it does not cover the provision, free of charge, of meals in company canteens to business contacts in the course of meetings held on the company premises where objective evidence indicates – this being a matter for the referring court to determine – that those meals are provided for strictly business-related purposes. On the other hand, Article 26 RVD applies in principle to the provision, free of charge, of meals by a company to its staff on its premises, unless – this likewise being a matter for the referring court to determine – the needs of the company, such as the need to ensure that work meetings are run smoothly and without interruptions, require the employer to ensure that meals are provided.[89] According to the ECJ, Article 26 RVD is not intended to establish a rule that transactions outside the scope of the system of VAT may be considered to be carried out for "purposes other than" those of the business within the meaning of that provision. Such an interpretation would have the effect of rendering Article 2(1) of the Directive meaningless. Articles 26(1)(a) RVD must therefore be interpreted as not being applicable to the use of goods and services allocated to the business for the purpose of transactions other than the taxable transactions of the taxable person, as the VAT due in respect of the acquisition of those goods and services, and relating to such transactions, is not deductible.[90]

Based on Article 27 RVD, Member States may subject the internal supply of services to taxation where the VAT on such services, had they been supplied by another taxable person, would not be fully deductible. This provision has the same *ratio legis* than Article 18 (a) RVD (see above).

87 This provision must generally be interpreted as meaning that the Member States may refrain from treating certain supplies or uses as supplies of services for consideration, in particular in order to simplify administrative procedures relating to collection of VAT. It cannot have the result that it is possible for the Member States to refuse to allow taxable persons who have chosen to treat capital goods used both for business and private purposes as business goods to deduct immediately and in full the input VAT due on the acquisition of those goods, which they are entitled to do. Such a restriction on the right to deduct would be contrary to that provision. Case C-434/03 (*P. Charles and T.S. Charles-Tijmens*), [2005] ECR I-7037.

88 See, *ex multis*, Case 50/88 (*Kühne*), [1989] ECR 1925 and Case C-193/91 (*Mohsche*), [1993] ECR I-2615.

89 Case C-371/07 (*Danfoss A/S AstraZeneca A/S*), [2008] ECR I-9549.

90 Case C-515/07 (*Vereniging Noordelijke Land- en Tuinbouw Organisatie* (*VNLTO*)), [2009] ECR I-839.

2.6.4 *Importation of goods*

"Importation of goods" means the entry into the Community of goods which are not in free circulation within the meaning of Article 24 of the Treaty, now Article 29 TFEU.[91] In addition, the entry into the Community of goods which are in free circulation, coming from a third territory forming part of the customs territory of the Community (see reference to Annex I, section 2.4 above), is regarded as importation of goods. A difference with other taxable supplies is that it is not necessary that the importation be made by a taxable person acting as such in order to be subject to VAT.

It should be noted that this concept of "importation" is proper to the VAT legislation and that it is not relevant for customs duties purposes. Also, the "VAT territory" and the customs territory do not coincide (see section 2.4. and also Chapter 1, section 1.3.1. and also Annex 1). As a consequence, goods imported from some territories may be qualified as import for VAT purposes and not for customs purposes (e.g. goods transported from the Canary Island to mainland Spain).

2.6.5 *Vouchers – provisions common to supply of good and service*

Article 30b (1) RVD provides that each transfer of a single purpose voucher by a taxable person acting in its own name is to be regarded as a supply of the goods or services to which the voucher relates. This means that the subsequent actual handing over of the goods or actual provision of the service in return for such a single purpose voucher is not to be regarded as an independent transaction. In contrast, Article 30 (2) RVD provides that only the actual handing over of the goods or actual provision of the services in return for a multiple-purpose voucher accepted as consideration will be subject to VAT. Preceding transfers of the voucher are not subject to VAT (Article 30 (2) in fine RVD clarifies that services such as distribution or promotion services in relation to multiple purpose vouchers are subject to VAT). A *single purpose voucher* is defined as a voucher where the place of supply of the goods or services to which the voucher relates, and the VAT due on those goods and services, are known at the time of the issue of the voucher. *Multi-purpose voucher* covers any other voucher (which is defined as an instrument where there is an obligation to accept it as (part) consideration for an identified supply of good or service (see Article 30a (1) RVD).

2.6.6 *New Means of Transport*

As mentioned in section 2.6.2 above, the general rule is that all supplies of goods to another Member State are exempt, provided that the acquirer has a certain status. In Article 2(2)

---

91 In Case C-181/97 (*Kooy*), [1999] ECR I-0483, the ECJ held that the entry into the Netherlands of goods coming from the Netherlands Antilles had to be regarded as entry into the EC for the purposes of applying Article 7(1) of the Sixth Directive (now Article 30 RVD). The fact that certain products which are in free circulation in the Overseas Countries and Territories can be imported into the Community free of customs duties and charges having equivalent effect, does not alter this. VAT on importations of products does not have the ingredients of a charge having the equivalent effect of customs duties.

RVD, this rule is extended in cases of intra-Community supplies of new private vehicles and other new means of transport; such supplies are exempt regardless of the status of the acquirer or the vendor. Thus, whether the purchaser or vendor is a private person, a non-taxable legal person or a totally exempt person, the supply from another Member State of a new means of transport is also exempt, followed by an intra-Community acquisition.

The following is considered to be a "means of transport"for VAT purposes: boats with a length exceeding 7.5 m, aircraft with a take-off weight exceeding 1 550 kg, and motorized land vehicles with a capacity exceeding 48 cc or with a power exceeding 7.2 kW, intended to transport persons or goods. In order not to be considered as "new" means of transport, both of the following conditions must be fulfilled: (1) they must be supplied more than six months after the date of first entry into service; and (2) they must have travelled more than 6 000 km (in the case of land vehicles), sailed more than 100 hours (in the case of boats),[92] or flown more than 40 hours (in the case of aircraft). The fact that any person who occasionally supplies a new means of transport to another Member State is regarded as a taxable person requires that the Member State in which the supply is made grants the taxable person the right of deduction of VAT. Article 172 RVD provides that the right to deduct arises and may be exercised only at the time of the supply and that the deduction is restricted to the amount of VAT not exceeding the tax which would have been payable if the supply had not been exempt. This provision prevents a lively intra-Community trade between individuals who would purchase new cars and deduct the VAT in order to sell the car for a nominal consideration in exchange for a purchase of another car in another Member State also against a nominal consideration.

2.7 Place of Taxable Transactions

Harmonised and consistently implemented place of supply rules are necessary to prevent double (and unintentional non-) taxation. This was confirmed by the ECJ who decided that the object of the specific place of supply provisions contained in the RVD is: "in accordance with, inter alia, recitals 17 and 62 of that directive, to avoid conflicts of jurisdiction which may result in double taxation or non-taxation".[93] It should however be noted that harmonisation does not mean that in practice double taxation cannot arise. Double taxation will indeed arise when the Member States have inconsistent interpretations of the rules. In this respect, the ECJ decided that the fact that one Member State made a wrong interpretation of a place of supply rule does not mean that the Member State where the VAT is due should misapply the RVD for the sake of avoiding double taxation.[94]

92 Whether or not a means of transport which is the subject-matter of an intra- Community acquisition is to be regarded as "new" is determined at the time when the right to dispose of those goods as owner is transferred from the vendor to the purchaser and not at the time the goods arrive in the Member State of acquisition for example after having sailed more than 100 hours. See Case C-84/09 (*X v Skatteverket*), [2010] ECR I-0000.

93 Cases C-276/18, (*KrakVet Marek Batko sp.k.*), [2020], ECLI:EU:C:2020:485; C- 111/05, (*Aktiebolaget NN*, [2007], EU:C:2007:195; C-327/94, (*Dudda*), [1996], EU: C:1996:355; of 9 March 2006, C-114/05, (*Gillan Beach*), [2006], EU:C:2006:169; C-291/07, (*Kollektivavtalsstiftelsen TRR* Trygghetsrådet), [2008], EU:C:2008:609, C-37/08, (*RCI Europe*), [2009], EU:C:2009:507.

94 Case C-278/18, (*KrakVet Marek Batko*), [2020], ECLI:EU:C:2020:485.

Depending on the nature of the supply,[95] the RVD provides for general and specific place of taxation rules.

2.7.1 *Place of Supply of Goods*

The general rule with regard to the place of supply of goods is clear. Goods that are not dispatched or transported are treated as being supplied at the place where the goods are when the supply takes place (Article 31 RVD).

The question of allocation will occur only when goods are transported or dispatched, by the seller or purchaser or by a third person. In this case the place of supply is deemed to be the place where the goods are located at the time when dispatch or transport of the goods to the customer begins (Article 32 RVD). When goods are exported or when an intra-Community supply is made the supply is exempt with the right to deduction (*i.e.* effectively zero-rated).

In cases of sales by connected contract, the so-called "ABC-contracts" (in which A sells to B and B to C, the goods are directly delivered to C, and A imports the goods directly into the Community), without a special provision, B and C could claim that the supply of the goods took place in the country of departure, *i.e.* outside the Community. Article 32(2) RVD) provides that in these circumstances the supplies by the importer (A) and any subsequent supply (the supply by B to C) are deemed to take place in the Member State of importation.

Without a close(r) alignment of VAT rates (see section 2.10 below for the agreement on the rate structure in the EU), unrestricted taxation of purchases by individuals in the Member State of purchase could result in a diversion of trade, through distance selling (*i.e.* by mail order, teleshopping and any other sale when the goods are shipped to the customer in another Member State) from the Member State with the lowest VAT rates. Therefore Article 33 RVD (a) and (b)[96] provides that by way of derogation from Article 32, intra-Community distance sales of goods and distance sales of goods imported from third countries or territories shall respectively be taxed in the Member State where the dispatch or transports ends, in other words in the country of destination (see Section 2.14.6.4 regarding the special scheme for distance sales of imported goods). This rule is applicable to purchasers who are non- taxable persons or persons whose intra-Community acquisitions are not taxed (because they remain below EUR 10 000 threshold, see section 2.2 above). Article 33 (a) RVD (concerning intra-Community distance sales) does however not apply when the following conditions are met: (a) the supplier is established in only one Member State, (b) goods are dispatched or transported to another Member State than the Member State of establishment of the supplier and (c) the total value (excl. VAT) of intra-Community distance sales and telecommunications, broadcasting and electronically

95 An inconsistent categorisation of the supplies based on the rules discussed in Section 2.6. would in turn result in an inconsistent location of a taxable supply, hence to double (or unintentional non) taxation.

96 This provision was amended by Directive 2017/2455 (as part of the e-commerce VAT package). It is applicable from 1 July 2021. Previous Article 34 RVD providing for national thresholds to determine the place of taxation was rescinded.

supplied services made by the supplier does not exceed EUR 10 000 (also in the previous calendar year).[97] Article 33 RVD does not apply at all to second-hand goods, works of art, collectors' items or antiques and second-hand means of transport covered by a special scheme (see Section 2.14.4).[98]

When goods are installed or assembled by or on behalf of the supplier, the place of supply is deemed to be the place where the installation or assembly takes place (Article 36 RVD). This rule prevents goods from being sold, for example in a third country, against the zero rate, for a price including the costs of installation, while upon importation VAT is only payable on the value of the goods, *i.e.* exclusive the costs of installation.

In accordance with Article 36a RVD, applicable from 1 January 2020, when the same goods are supplied successively (A-B-C sales, also referred to as chain transactions) and the goods are dispatched or transported from one Member State to another directly from the first supplier to the last customer in the chain, the dispatch or transport shall be ascribed[99] to the supply made to the intermediary operator, except when the intermediary operator communicates a VAT number issued to him by the Member State from which the goods are dispatched or transported. An *intermediary operator* is defined as a supplier within the chain, other than the first supplier in the chain who dispatches or transports the goods either himself or through a third party acting on his behalf (Article 36a (3) RVD). Extensive guidance is offered on chain transactions and the qualification of the subsequent supplied in the European Commission's explanatory notes on the so- called "quick fixes" (on explanatory notes, see section 2.16.2).[100]

In accordance with Article 37 RVD, when goods are supplied for consumption on board ships, aircraft or trains during the section of a passenger transport operation effected within the Community, the place of supply is the place where the goods are at the time of departure of the transport. "The section of a transport of passengers effected in the Community" is to be regarded as the part of the transport effected, without a stop in a third territory, between the point of departure and the point of arrival of the transport of passengers. By excluding the existence of "part of a transport of passengers effected within the Community", in the case of a stop in a third territory, Article 37 RVD aims to avoid the risks of conflicts of jurisdiction with the tax systems of third countries which would arise in the event of goods being supplied whilst an intra-Community journey was

---

97 Article 59c RVD. In accordance with Article 59c (4) RVD, the Member States must grant taxable persons the right to opt for the application of Article 33 RVD (taxation at destination irrespective of the value of intra-Community distance sales and supplies of electronically supplied services).

98 Article 35 RVD.

99 Before the entry into application of Article 36 RVD the ECJ had decided that in the case of chain transactions, only one supply can be qualified as the intra- Community supply to which the transport can be ascribed. See: Cases C-245/04, (*EMAG*), [2006], ECLI:EU:C:2006:232; C-430/09, (*Euro Tyre*), [2017], ECLI:EU: C:2017:106; C-386/16, (*Toridas*), [2017], ECLI:EU:C:2017:599; C-580/16, (*Firma Buhler*), [2018], ECLI:EU:C:2018:261 and (*Kreuzmayr*), [2018], ECLI:EU: C:2018:84.

100 European Commission, Explanatory Notes on the EU VAT changes in respect of call-off stock arrangements, chain transactions and the exemption for intra- Community supplies of goods ("2020 Quick Fixes"), December 2019, available at: https://ec.europa.eu/taxation_customs/sites/taxation/files/explanatory_notes_2020_quick_fixes_en.pdf.

interrupted by a stop in a third territory. Any supply of goods effected on a ship during a stop in a third territory is deemed to be made outside the scope of the EU VAT system, the tax treatment of the supply of goods falling, in that case, within the tax jurisdiction of the State in which the stop is made.[101]

In accordance with Article 38 RVD, the supply of gas and electricity, heat and cooling energy, before the final stage, is taxed at the place *where the customer has established his business* or has a fixed establishment to which the gas, electricity, heat and cooling energy are supplied. To simplify taxation, this taxation principle is combined with a reverse-charge mechanism (*i.e.* the recipient of a supply is held liable for payment of the VAT to the Revenue rather than the supplier, see section 2.13 below) if the supplier (called "taxable dealer", not to be confused with a person dealing in second-hand goods, works of art, collector's items and antiques also referred to as a "taxable dealer" in Article 311 RVD) and the buyer are not established in the same territory. On the other hand, the rules ensure that the supply of gas, electricity, heat and cooling energy at the final stage, mainly from distributor to final consumers, will be taxed at the place where the actual consumption takes place (Article 39 RVD). This is necessary, because the consumption of energy does not always take place where the final consumer is established or has his permanent address, whereas the objective of the VAT system is to try to ensure that tax accrues to the Member State of final consumption. In practice, the place of use and enjoyment will be the place where the gas and electricity are metered, which coincides often with the place where the final consumer is established, has his permanent address or where he usually resides.

2.7.2 *Place of Intra-Community Acquisition of Goods*

In accordance with Article 40 RVD the place of intra-Community acquisitions of goods is the place where the goods are at the time when dispatch or transport to the person by whom they are acquired ends.[102] Article 41 RVD however provides that the place of an intra-Community acquisition of goods shall be deemed to be within the territory of the Member State which issued the VAT identification number under which the person acquiring the goods made the acquisition, unless the person acquiring the goods establishes that VAT has been applied to that acquisition in accordance with Article 40 RVD. If VAT is applied

101 Case C-58/04 (*Antje Köhler*), [2005] ECR I-8219.

102 According to AG Kokott, in her Opinion in Case C-409/04 (*Teleos plc and Others*), the distinction between dispatch and transportation is as follows. Dispatch takes place when the seller or the acquirer uses an independent third party for transportation, such as the post office, which, during the transportation, does not follow instructions from either the seller or the acquirer. By handing the goods over to the third party, the dispatch, the seller loses control over the goods, without the acquirer yet obtaining the powers of an owner. That power is not transferred to the acquirer until the third party hands the goods over to him in the Member State of destination. At that moment, intra- Community acquisition takes place. Transportation within the meaning of the directive takes place, by contrast, if the seller or the acquirer carries out the transport of the goods himself, or through agents who follow his instructions. If the seller is responsible for transport, intra-Community acquisition takes place when the seller or his agent delivers the goods to the acquirer in the State of destination. If the acquirer assumes responsibility for transport, he obtains, directly or through his agent, the power to dispose of the goods as owner in the country of origin. But even in this case intra-Community acquisition does not take place until the transportation to another Member State has been completed.

to the acquisition in accordance with Article 41 RVD and subsequently applied, pursuant to Article 40 RVD, to the acquisition in the Member State in which dispatch or transport of the goods ends, the taxable amount must be reduced accordingly in the Member State which issued the VAT identification number under which the person acquiring the goods made the acquisition. VAT due on the basis of Article 41 RVD cannot simply be deducted in the VAT return, because its purpose is to create an incentive for the acquirer to establish that the intra-Community acquisition has been taxed in the Member State of arrival.[103]

When a sale of goods is negotiated and concluded, the final place of destination of the goods is not always already known. In particular in ABC contracts (or chain transactions), the same goods may be sold subsequently by various parties, and it is not until the end of the chain of transactions that it becomes known that the goods are to be delivered by the first party directly to the last party in the chain. The RVD states that the place of acquisition is deemed to be within the territory of the Member State which issued the VAT identification number under which the goods are acquired, without prejudice to the main rule which prescribes that the place of acquisition is the place where the dispatch or transport ends (Article 41 RVD). Thus, when goods are sold by A to B, both established in different Member States, the legal presumption is that the intra-Community acquisition takes place in the Member State of B. When B is selling the goods to C, who is established in a third Member State, the intra-Community acquisition of the goods by C is deemed to take place in the Member State of C. However, when A is delivering the goods directly to C, based on the main rule, B acquires the goods in the Member State of C and performs a domestic supply to C there. The Directive prescribes that in these circumstances the Member State of B must take measures to avoid double taxation, *i.e.* reduce the taxable amount accordingly. Article 42 RVD provides for a simplification. When A, registered in Member State A, sells goods to B, under B's VAT registration number issued by Member State B, and the goods are directly delivered to C in Member State C, the acquisition by B in Member State C (*i.e.* in accordance with the main rule) is deemed to have been subject to VAT in Member State C when two conditions have been met (in other words the acquisition will not be subject to VAT in Member State C because it is exempt (Article 141 RVD) and the taxable amount in Member State B will not have to be reduced accordingly because there is no intra-Community supply subject to VAT in Member State B):

(1) the acquirer (B) establishes that he has made this intra-Community acquisition for the needs of a subsequent supply made in Member State C for which the consignee (C) has been designated liable (*i.e.* the reverse charge is applicable); and
(2) the acquirer (B) satisfies certain administrative obligations, namely in his EC sales listing (see section 2.13.6) in Member State B he reports that C has been designated as the liable consignee.

Article 197 RVD states that the reverse charge on the B-C supply applies if the following conditions have been met:

(a) the taxable transaction is a supply of goods carried out in accordance with the conditions laid down in Article 141;

103 Cases C-536/08 and C-539/08 (*X and Facet BV/Facet Trading BV*), ECLI: EU:C:2009:65.

(b) the person to whom the goods are supplied (C) is another taxable person, or a non-taxable legal person, identified for VAT purposes in the Member State in which the supply is carried out;
(c) the invoice issued by the taxable person not established in the Member State of the person to whom the goods are supplied is drawn up in accordance with Articles 220 to 236 (see section 2.13.3).

Article 141 RVD states that an exemption applies for the intra-Community acquisition of B normally subject to VAT in the Member State of arrival if the following conditions have been met:
(a) the acquisition of goods is made by a taxable person (B) who is not established in the Member State C, but is identified for VAT purposes in another Member State;(b)
(b) the acquisition of goods is made for the purposes of the subsequent supply of those goods, in the Member State concerned, by the taxable person (B) referred to in point (a);
(c) the goods thus acquired by the taxable person (B) referred to in point (a) are directly dispatched or transported, from a Member State other than that in which he is identified for VAT purposes (Member State A), to the person (C) for whom he is to carry out the subsequent supply. It should be noted that in case B acquires the goods using a VAT identification number from an EU Member State different from the Member State of dispatch (Member State A), but is established in that latter Member State (Member State A) this condition is still met;[104]
(d) the person to whom the subsequent supply is to be made (C) is another taxable person, or a non-taxable legal person, who is identified for VAT purposes in Member State C;
(e) the person (C) referred to in point (d) has been designated in accordance with Article 197 as liable for payment of the VAT due on the supply carried out by the taxable person who is not established in the Member State in which the tax is due.

This seemingly complicated simplification (see also section 2.11.2) has effectively simplified chain contracts between three parties located in different countries. Under the original rules, direct deliveries by A to the final purchasers in the chain established in different Member States, while B would be established in a third country, would make it necessary for B to register in all Member States where the goods were to be delivered. Under this simplification it is sufficient that B is registered in one Member State (other than that of A and the final customers).[105] The use of the VAT registration number of B in that Member State triggers the reverse charge in the country of delivery, provided B fulfils the administrative obligations mentioned.

2.7.3 *Place of Supply of Services*

The rules for the place of supply consist of two main rules and particular rules. Different from exemptions (section 2.11.1) and rates (section 2.10) these particular rules are not to be

104 Case C-580/16 (*Firma Hans Bühler*), ECLI:EU:C:2018:261.
105 The Directive does not specifically mention that the simplification does not apply if B is registered in Member State C. However, a number of Member States will not allow the application of the rules if B is registered in Member State C.

interpreted strictly.[106] According to the *Dudda* case[107] the particular rules take precedence over the main rules, meaning that it first must be established whether one of the particular rule applies before the main rules are applied. The hierarchy between the different particular rules is yet unclear. A clarification could have been offered by the ECJ in the *Geelen* case,[108] but the ECJ ruled that in that particular case the question did not need to be answered, because only one of the particular rules was applicable at that time.

For taxable persons the main rule (*i.e.* the B2B general rule) is that the place of supply of services is the place where the customer/taxable person has established his business or has a fixed establishment to which the service is supplied (Article 44 RVD, further analysed below).

The place of supply of services to non-taxable persons is as a main rule (*i.e.* the B2C general rule) the place where the supplier has established his business or has a fixed establishment from which the service is supplied (Article 45 RVD, further analysed below).

Different rules for taxable and non-taxable persons could create problems when a person is acting both in the capacity of a taxable person and a non-taxable person, *e.g.* charities or government departments. Article 43 RVD therefore provides that for the purpose of applying the rules concerning the place of supply of services a taxable person who also carries out activities or transactions that are not considered to be taxable supplies of goods or services must be deemed to be a taxable person in respect of all services rendered to him and also that a non-taxable legal person who is identified for VAT purposes must be deemed to be a taxable person.[109] Article 18 IR provides for practical arrangements to establish the customers status for the purpose of applying the place of supply rules, while Article 19 IR states that in case of services purchased exclusively for private use, including use by staff, the customer must be regarded as a non-taxable person.

The VAT Directive is unclear on the issue of single or multiple supplies. Fortunately, guidance is to be derived on this subject from the case law of the ECJ. Every supply of a service must normally be regarded as distinct and independent and a supply which comprises a single service from an economic point of view should not be artificially split; the essential features of the transaction must be ascertained in order to determine whether the taxable person is supplying the customer, being a typical consumer, with several distinct principal services or with a single service. There is a single supply in particular in cases where one or more elements are to be regarded as constituting the principal service, whilst one or more elements are to be regarded, by contrast, as ancillary services which share the tax treatment of the principal service. A service must be regarded as ancillary to a principal service if it does not constitute for customers an aim in itself, but a means of better enjoying the principal service. In those circumstances, the fact that a single price is charged is not

106 Case C-568/17 (*Geelen*), ECLI:EU:C:2019:388.
107 Case C-327/94 (*Dudda*), [1996] ECR I-04595.
108 Case C-568/17 (*Geelen*), ECLI:EU:C:2019:388.
109 See C-459/19 (*Wellcome Trust*), 2021, ECLI:EU:2021:209, in which the Court further clarifies that this rule does not apply when the services are received for purely private purposes of the taxable person.

decisive.[110] This case law, which was developed in cases concerning supplies of services, is also applicable when the complex supply includes goods.

(1) Supplies to Taxable Persons (B2B)

Article 44 RVD sets as general B2B rule, which in practice is the fall-back or default rule, *i.e.* when no particular rules apply:

> The place of supply of services to a taxable person acting as such shall be the place where that person has established his business. However, if those services are provided to a fixed establishment of the taxable person in a place other than the place where he has established his business, the place of supply of those services shall be the place where the fixed establishment is located. In the absence of such a place of establishment or fixed establishment, the place of supply of services shall be the place where the taxable person has his permanent address or usually resides.

Thus, this general rule with respect to the place of supply of services to taxable persons is determined on the basis of where the taxable person receiving the service is established, rather than the jurisdiction in which the supplier of the services is established. The taxable person receiving the supply must therefore rely on the reverse charge mechanism for supplies made by persons established in different countries (see section 2.13.1).[111]

A first point of reference is the place of establishment of the business. Article 10 (1) IR defines the place where a business is established as the place where the functions of the business's central administration are carried out. According to the second paragraph of Article 10 IR when establishing where this place of business is located account shall be taken of the place where essential decisions concerning the general management of the business are taken, the place where the registered office of the business is located and the place where management meets. Where these criteria do not allow the place of establishment of a business to be determined with certainty, the place where essential decisions concerning the general management of the business are taken takes precedence. A postal address is not to be regarded as place of business according to the third paragraph of Article 10 IR.

The second point of reference is the fixed establishment. For purposes of Article 44 RVD only, Article 11 (1) IR defines the fixed establishment as:

> any establishment, other than the place of establishment of a business referred to in Article 10 of this Regulation, characterised by a sufficient degree of permanence and a suitable structure in terms of human and technical resources to enable it to receive and use the services supplied to it for its own needs.

---

110 Case C-349/96 (*Card Protection Plan* (*CPP*)), [1999] ECR I-0973.

111 Based on Article 196 VAT shall be payable by any taxable person, or non- taxable legal person identified for VAT purposes, to whom the services referred to in Article 44 are supplied, if the services are supplied by a taxable person not established within the territory of the Member State. It is noted here that it is added to Article 214 prescribing that Member States shall take the measures necessary to ensure that the following persons are identified by means of an individual number: "(d) every taxable person who within their respective territory receives services for which he is liable to pay VAT pursuant to Article 196; (e) every taxable person, established within their respective territory, who supplies services within the territory of another Member State for which VAT is payable solely by the recipient pursuant to Article 196".

Under this definition it is not required that the fixed establishment carries out taxable supplies of goods or services to third parties. Establishments that carry out preparatory or ancillary activities only can be regarded as a fixed establishment in that respect. As confirmed by the ECJ, a fixed establishment for VAT purposes is different than a permanent establishment for direct tax purposes.[112] In spite of the definition offered in the IR, based on previous ECJ case law, more recent case law has shown that the concept may still be difficult to apprehend.[113]

When a supplier provides a service to a taxable person with establishments in more than one country, he will need to establish to which of the establishments he has provided the service. Art, 22 (1) IR provides a step-by-step-approach:

Step 1: Firstly, the supplier must consider whether he can establish from the nature or the use of the service that it is intended for the fixed establishment. We can imagine that this would be possible, for example, if the supplier were to provide training for staff at the fixed establishment's location. But there are many cases where it is not possible to establish who uses the service. The supplier may then go to step 2.

Step 2: The supplier determines from the contract, the order, the VAT identification number of the customer and the payment whether the fixed establishment is the one that has purchased the service. If this is also not successful, the supplier must go to step 3.

Step 3: Step 3 is a catch-all clause. If, on the basis of step 1 and step 2, the supplier does not succeed in attributing the service to the fixed establishment, he may assume that the service has been provided to the head office. The same applies for services that are supplied to a taxable person under a contract covering one or more services used in an unidentifiable and non-quantifiable manner (i.e. global contracting).

The second paragraph of Article 22 IR states that the application of Article 22 (1) IR shall be without prejudice to the customer's obligations. In our view this means that the customer will need to establish to which of its fixed establishments the supplier has provided the service, regardless of the conclusions that the supplier draws from applying Article 22 (1) IR). He may be obliged to report the VAT in a different country under Article 196 RVD. In our view this means that he will need to establish the place of supply based on the use that is being made of the supply. To avoid situations of double taxation we assume that the customer in case it is liable to pay the VAT in the country of the fixed establishment informs the supplier of the fixed establishment being the customer.

As a fall-back scenario Article 44 RVD provides to additional points of reference: the permanent address and the place where a person usually resides. These are defined by Article 12 and 13 IR respectively.

112 CJEU, Case 210/04 (*FCE*), ECLI:EU:C:2006:196, para 34.

113 See for example Case C-615/12 (*Welmory*), ECLI:EU:C:2014:2298; C-547; C- 547/18 (*Dong Yang Electronics*), ECLI:EU:C:2020:350; C-213/11 (*Fortuna*), ECLI: EU:C:2012:495.

(2) Supplies to Non-Taxable Persons (B2C)
Article 45 RVD provides that the place of supply of services to non-taxable persons shall be the place where the supplier has established his business or has a fixed establishment from which the service is supplied. In the absence of such a place of establishment or fixed establishment, the place of supply of services shall be the place where the taxable person has his permanent address or usually resides. The place where the business is established, permanent address and where a person usually resides are defined the same for the purpose of applying Article 44 and 45 RVD. For the purpose of applying Article 45 RVD, Article 11 (2) defines the fixed establishment as: any establishment, other than the place of establishment of a business referred to in Article 10 IR, characterised by a sufficient degree of permanence and a suitable structure in terms of human and technical resources to enable it to provide the services which it supplies. An establishment carrying out preparatory or ancillary activities for the main place of business will therefore not qualify as a fixed establishment for the purpose of applying Article 45 RVD.

(3) Particular Provisions
Under the heading "particular provisions" Articles 46 to 59b provide for specific place of supply rules. The rules may apply to B2B and B2C supplies of services or to B2B or B2C-supplies of services only.

Particular rules applying to both B2B and B2C-services
According to Article 47 RVD the place of supply of services connected with immovable property, including the services of experts and estate agents, the provision of accommodation in the hotel sector or in sectors with a similar function, including the provision of accommodation in holiday camps or on sites developed for use as camping sites, the granting of rights to use immovable property and services for the preparation and coordination of construction work, such as the services of architects and of firms providing on-site supervision, shall be the place where the immovable property is located.[114] Article 13b IR defines immovable property, while Article 31a IR provides for a definition and examples of services connected with immovable property.[115]

Article 48 RVD provides that the place of supply of passenger transport services is the place where the transport takes place, proportionate to the distances covered.[116] Article 56 (1) RVD provides that the place of short-term hiring of a means of transport is the place where the means of transport is actually put at the disposal of the customer, *i.e.* taxable or

114 See Case C-111/05 (*Aktiebolaget NN*) on the laying of a cable on the sea bottom between two Member States; Case C-166/05 (*Heger Rudi*), [2006] ECR I-7749, on fishing right and Case C-37/08 (*RCI Europe*), [2009] ECR I-7533, on the exchange of timeshare interests.

115 See also the non-binding Explanatory notes on EU VAT place of supply rules on services connected with immovable property that enter into force in 2017, https://ec.europa.eu/taxation_customs/sites/taxation/files/resources/documents/taxation/vat/how_vat_works/explanatory_notes_new_en.pdf, that explain those rules even in more detail.

116 See, *inter alia*, Case C-116/96 (*Reisebüro Binder*), [1997] ECR I-6103. See also Case 283/84 (*Trans Tirreno Express*) [1986] ECR 00231; Case C-331/94 (*Commission v. Greece*), [1996] ECR I-2675, dealing with the Greek exemption of sea voyages in territorial waters from VAT. The Commission applied to the ECJ for a declaration that this was in breach of the Sixth Directive, contending that the place of supply was entirely within Greece. The ECJ upheld this contention.

non-taxable person. In Article 56 RVD, paragraph 3, "short-term" is defined as meaning the continuous possession or use of the means of transport throughout a period of not more than 30 days. For vessels this period must be increased to a period of not more than 90 days.

Particular rules applying to B2B-services only

Article 53 RVD provides that the place of supply of services *in respect of admission to* cultural, artistic, sporting, scientific, educational, entertainment, or similar events, such as fairs and exhibitions and of similar services related to the admission, supplied to *a taxable person* shall be the place where those events actually take place. In the *srf Konsulterna* case[117] the ECJ ruled that this provision covers a service in the form of a five-day course on accountancy and management which is supplied solely to taxable persons and requires advance registration and payment.

Exceptions applying to B2C-services only

According to Article 46 RVD the place of supply of services to non-taxable persons by an intermediary acting in the name and for the account of another person is the place where the underlying transaction is supplied in accordance with the VAT Directive. (The underlying transaction is either a supply of goods or a supply of a service.) There is no case law on the concept of intermediation in the context of this exception to the main rule for the place of supply of services to non-taxable persons. However, the ECJ has defined negotiation in the context of exemptions (see section 2.11). We assume that this case law is also relevant for determining whether there is intermediation with regard to the place of supply of services rules. The ECJ ruled that negotiation refers to the activity of an intermediary who does not occupy the position of any party to a contract relating to a financial product, and whose activity amounts to something other than the provision of contractual services typically undertaken by the parties to such contracts. Negotiation is a service rendered to, and remunerated by, a contractual party as a distinct act of mediation. It may consist, amongst other things, in pointing out suitable opportunities for the conclusion of such a contract, making contact with another party or negotiating, in the name of and on behalf of a client, the detail of the payments to be made by either side. The purpose of negotiation is therefore to do all that is necessary in order for two parties to enter into a contract, without the negotiator having any interest of his own in the terms of the contract.[118]

Article 54 (1) RVD provides that the place of supply of services and ancillary services relating to cultural, artistic,[119] sporting, scientific, educational, entertainment,[120] or similar activities, such as fairs and exhibitions including the supply of services of the organizers of such activities *to a non-taxable person* shall be the place where those services are carried out. It should be noted that in a digitalized economy these type of services can be provided at distance. In the *Geelen* case[121] the ECJ ruled that a supplier of erotic entertainment services

117 Case C-647/17 (*SRF Konsulterna*) ECLI:EU:C:2019:195.

118 Case C-235/00 (*CSC*), [2001] ECR I- 10237.

119 See Case C-327/94 (*Jürgen Dudda*), [1996] ECR I-4595, on sound-engineering for artistic or entertainment events.

120 See Case C-452/03 (*RAL*), [2005] ECR I-3947, on slot gaming machines and Case C-114/05 (*Gillan Beach*), [2006] ECR I-2427, on organising a boat show.

121 Case C-568/17 (*Geelen*), ECLI:EU:C:2019:388.

carried out its supplies from its place of business where it organises the interactive sessions relating to the erotic show performed by the models and, provides customers with the opportunity to view those sessions on the internet. This ruling was fed by the fact that the supplier and customers were all located in the Netherlands. With this judgment the ECJ however has opened up the opportunity for providers of this kind of activities to establish themselves in a country with a beneficial or no VAT regime.

Article 55 RVD states that the place of supply of restaurant and catering services is the place where those services are physically carried out. However, this rule should not apply to the supply of restaurant or catering services on board ships, aircrafts or trains during a passenger transport service as it would be very difficult to determine where the service is physically carried out and consumed. Instead, such services should, in line with on-board supplies of goods, be taxed at the place of departure of the passenger transport service. Article 57 RVD therefore stipulates that the place of supply of restaurant or catering services to customers physically carried out on board ships, aircrafts (plural) or trains during a passenger transport operation effected without a stopover outside the Community, between the point of departure and the point of arrival of the passenger transport operation will be the place of departure of that transport service. In the case of a return trip, the return leg is regarded as a separate transport operation.

Article 56, paragraph 2 RVD provides that other than short-term hiring, of a means of transport to a non-taxable person is subject to VAT where the customer is established, has his permanent address or usually resides. Article 24c IR allows the supplier to determine the permanent address and usual residence of its customer by way of two non-contradictory pieces of evidence, while Article 24e VIR defines what can be used as pieces of evidence. By way of derogation the place of hiring a pleasure boat to a non-taxable person, other than short-term hiring, will be the place where the pleasure boat is actually put at the disposal of the customer, where this service is actually provided by the supplier from his place of business or a fixed establishment situated in that place. Thus, the place of hiring a pleasure boat to a non-taxable person, short-term and other than short-term hiring, will in principle be the place where the pleasure boat is actually put at the disposal of the customer. In QM, the ECJ decided that by analogy with case law on the concept of the 'letting of immovable property' (Article 135(1) RVD (j) to (l), see Section 2.11. on exemptions), the term "hiring" presupposes that the owner of the means of transport confers on the person hiring that means of transport, in return for rent and for an agreed period, the right to use it and to exclude other persons from doing so.[122]

Articles 49 to 52 RVD deal with transport of goods provided to non-taxable persons. The place of supply of transport of goods on behalf of taxable persons is caught by the general rule that the place of supply is where the taxable person to whom the service is supplied has established his business.

122 C-288/19, 20 January 2021, ECLI:EU:C:2021:32.

According to Article 49 RVD, the place of supply of the service of transport of goods, other than the intra-Community transport of goods, to non-taxable persons shall be the place where the transport takes place, proportionate to the distances covered.

Article 50 RVD provides that the place of supply of the service of intra- Community transport of goods to non-taxable persons shall be the place of departure.

Article 51 RVD provides for the following definitions:

> "Intra-Community transport of goods" shall mean any transport of goods in respect of which the place of departure and the place of arrival are situated within the territories of two different Member States.
>
> "Place of departure" shall mean the place where transport of the goods actually starts, irrespective of distances covered in order to reach the place where the goods are located and "place of arrival" shall mean the place where transport of the goods actually ends.

Finally, we note that Article 52 RVD provides that Member States need not apply the tax to that part of the intra-Community transport of goods to non-taxable persons corresponding to journeys made over waters which do not form part of the territory of the Community.

Article 54 (2) RVD provides under point (a) that the place of supply of ancillary transport activities such as loading, unloading, handling and similar activities as well as (under point (b)) valuation of and work on movable tangible property to non-taxable persons shall be the place where those services are carried out.

Article 58 RVD provides that the place of supply of (a) telecommunications services (defined by Article 6a IR), (b) radio and television broadcasting services (defined by Article 6b IR) and (c) electronically supplied services (defined by Article 7 IR), in particular those referred to in Annex II, to a non-taxable person shall be the place where that person is established, has his permanent address or usually resides. In order to establish the permanent address or usual residence of the customer Article 24a and 24b (a), (b) and (c) IR provide rebuttable presumptions for certain situations, while Article 24b (d) IR as a general rule provides the opportunity to establish the permanent address or usual residence on the basis of two pieces of non-contradictory evidence. Article 24f IR describes which pieces of evidence can be used.[123] Article 24d IR provides provisions for rebuttal of the presumptions. In case electronically supplies services are provided together with the provision of accommodation in the hotel sector or in sectors with a similar function Article 31c IR states that the place of supply is where the accommodation is located. It should be noted that this is not a rebuttable presumption and the supplier must apply it. As of 1 January 2019, two simplifications have been added for suppliers of telecommunications, broadcasting and electronically provides services. As of that date suppliers that are established in only one

123 See also the non-legally binding Explanatory notes on the EU VAT changes to the place of supply of telecommunications, broadcasting and electronic services that enter into force in 2015, https://ec.europa.eu/taxation_customs/sites/taxation/files/resources/documents/taxation/vat/how_vat_works/telecom/explanatory_notes_2015_en.pdf, that explain those rules in greater detail.

EU Member State and that provide these services to customers located in other EU Member States with a turnover of no more than 10.000 euros in the current and previous year, can still charge VAT of their own country. There is an opt-out possible, which applies for at least two years. As of 1 July 2021, the turnover of intra-Community distance sales needs to be taken into account too to determine whether the 10.000 euros threshold has been exceeded. Suppliers with a turnover of no more than 100.000 euros in telecommunications, broadcasting and electronically provided services in the current and preceding year can use one piece of evidence provided that that piece of evidence originates from a person involved in the supply who is not the supplier or the customer.

According to Article 59 RVD the place of supply of the following services[124] supplied to a non-taxable person who is established or who has his permanent address or usually resides outside the Community is the place where that person is established, has his permanent address or usually resides:
(a) transfers and assignments of copyrights, patents, licences, trademarks and similar rights;
(b) advertising services;[125]
(c) the services of consultants, engineers,[126] consultancy firms, lawyers,[127] accountants and other similar services, as well as data processing and the provision of information;
(d) obligations to refrain from pursuing or exercising, in whole or in part, a business activity or a right referred to Article 59 RVD;
(e) banking, financial and insurance transactions including reinsurance, with the exception of the hire of safes;
(f) the supply of staff;
(g) the hiring out of movable tangible property, with the exception of all means of transport;
(h) the provision of access to, and of transport or transmission through, natural gas and electricity distribution systems and the provision of other directly linked services;

When the services mentioned in Article 59 RVD are supplied to non-taxable persons within the Community the main rule applies, *i.e.* the place of supply is the place where the supplier has established his business or has a fixed establishment from which the service

124 One should also keep in mind the extensive enumeration of services covered by this provision in Regulation (EU) No. 282/2011.

125 See the so-called “advertising cases”. For example, in Case C-68/92 (*Commission v. France*), [1993] ECR I-5881, the ECJ held that the French government was in breach of its obligations under Community law, in that it had applied restrictions to the definition of “advertising services” (such as the sale of goods at reduced prices, the handing-out to consumers of goods sold to the person distributing them by an advertising agency, the supply of services at reduced prices or free of charge, or the organization of a cocktail party or banquet). See also Case C-108/00 (*SPI*), [2001] ECR I-2361, on advertising services provided through the intermediary of a third party, not being a disclosed or undisclosed agent. See also Case C-1/08 (*Athesia Druck*), [2009] ECR I-1255.

126 A service such as the customisation of computer software to the specific requirements of a consumer is likely to be carried out either by engineers or by other persons trained to carry out such tasks. According to the ECJ, such a service is covered either by the services carried out by engineers or by those which are similar to the activity of an engineer. Case C-41/04 (*Levob Verzekeringen*), [2006] ECR I-9433.

127 See Case C-145/96 (*Bernd von Hoffmann*), [1997] ECR I-4857, on the services of an arbitrator.

is supplied, thus, taxable when supplied by a supplier within the Community and falling outside the scope when supplied by a supplier outside the Community.[128]

4) Effective use and enjoyment

As the tenth particular provision under the title "Prevention of double taxation or non-taxation" Article 59a RVD provides for the following override rules:[129]

> In order to prevent double taxation, non-taxation or distortion of competition Member States may, with regard to services the place of which is governed by Articles 44, 45, 56, 58 and 59:
> (a) consider the place of supply of services, if situated within their territory, as being situated outside the Community where the effective use and enjoyment of the services takes place outside the Community;
> (b) consider the place of supply of services, if situated outside the Community, as being situated within their territory where the effective use and enjoyment of the services takes place within their territory.

2.7.4 *Place of Importation*

According to Article 60 RVD, the place of importation of goods is the Member State within whose territory the goods are located when they enter the Community.

By way of derogation from Article 60, Article 61 RVD provides that where, on entry into the Community, goods which are not in free circulation are placed under one of the arrangements or situations referred to in Article 156 RVD,[130] or under temporary importation arrangements with total exemption from import duty, or under external transit arrangements, the place of importation of such goods is the Member State within whose territory the goods cease to be covered by those arrangements or situations.[131] Similarly, where, on entry into the Community, goods which are in free circulation are placed under

128 Unless taxable within the Community based on the effective use and enjoyment rules, where applied, based on Article 59a.

129 For an application of this provision, see CJEU Cases C-1/08, (*Athesia Druck*) 19 February 2009, ECLI:EU:C:2009:108) and C-593/19 (*SK telecom*), 15 April 2021, ECLI:EU:C:2021:281.

130 Those situations are:
(a) the supply of goods which are intended to be presented to customs and, where applicable, placed in temporary storage;
(b) the supply of goods which are intended to be placed in a free zone or in a free warehouse;
(c) the supply of goods which are intended to be placed under customs warehousing arrangements or inward processing arrangements;
(d) the supply of goods which are intended to be admitted into territorial waters in order to be incorporated into drilling or production platforms, for purposes of the construction, repair, maintenance, alteration or fitting-out of such platforms, or to link such drilling or production platforms to the mainland;
(e) the supply of goods which are intended to be admitted into territorial waters for the fuelling and provisioning of drilling or production platforms.

131 On the meaning of "ceasing to be covered", see Case C-371/99 (*Liberexim B.V.*) [2002] ECR I-6227.

one of the arrangements or situations referred to in Articles 276 and 277 RVD,[132] the place of importation is be the Member State within whose territory the goods cease to be covered by those arrangements or situations.

2.8 Chargeable Event and Chargeability of Tax

Pursuant to Article 62, point (1) RVD, the *chargeable event* is the occurrence by virtue of which the legal conditions necessary to charge VAT are fulfilled. *Chargeability* (Article 62, point (2) RVD) is the moment when the tax authorities become entitled to claim the tax.

The question when VAT becomes payable is closely related to the moment of the right to deduction. In a VAT based on the invoice system, the VAT mentioned on an invoice, paid *or due*, is deductible. Would the right to deduct arise earlier than the moment when VAT has been paid in by the supplier, the Revenue would have to pre-finance VAT. The best solution, therefore, was to link the moment when VAT becomes deductible to the moment the VAT becomes chargeable using the invoice as proof. Articles 63 to 65 RVD provide for some general rules; however, Article 66 RVD allows Member States to choose for certain transactions a moment when tax becomes chargeable which they think to fit best, see further below.

2.8.1 Goods and services

Pursuant to Article 63 RVD as a main rule, the chargeable event occurs and the tax becomes chargeable when the goods are delivered or the services are performed.[133] In case of a single purpose vouchers the supply takes place each time the voucher is transferred. For multiple purpose vouchers the supply takes place upon the redemption of the voucher (see section 2.6.5). Supplies which give rise to successive statements of account or payments are

132 Article 276 RVD provides:
Where dispatch or transport of the goods referred to in Article 274 [the importation of goods in free circulation which enter the Community from a third territory forming part of the customs territory of the Community] ends at a place situated outside the Member State of their entry into the Community, they shall circulate in the Community under the internal Community transit procedure laid down by the Community customs provisions in force, in so far as they have been the subject of a declaration placing them under that procedure on their entry into the Community.
Article 277 RVD provides:
Where, on their entry into the Community, the goods referred to in Article 274 [the importation of goods in free circulation which enter the Community from a third territory forming part of the customs territory of the Community] are in one of the situations which would entitle them, if they were imported within the meaning of the first paragraph of Article 30, to be covered by one of the arrangements or situations referred to in Article 156, or by a temporary importation arrangement with full exemption from import duties, Member States shall take the measures necessary to ensure that the goods may remain in the Community under the same conditions as those laid down for the application of those arrangements or situations.

133 With regard to interim payments, see Case C-10/92 (*Balocchi*), [1993] ECR I-5105. In Case C-188/09 (*Profaktor*), [2010] ECR I- 07639, the Court held that that the common system of VAT does not preclude a Member State from imposing a temporary restriction on the extent of the right of taxable persons who have not complied with a formal requirement to keep accounting records of their sales to deduct input tax paid, on condition that the sanction thus provided for complies with the principle of proportionality.

regarded as having been completed at the time when the periods to which the statements or payments pertain expire (Article 64(1) RVD).

When a payment on account is made before a supply the VAT becomes chargeable on receipt of the payment (Article 65 RVD),[134] unless the payment is a deposit which may be forfeited.[135] It must be borne in mind that it is the supplies of goods or services which are subject to VAT, rather than payments made by way of consideration for such supplies. *A fortiori*, payments on account of supplies of goods or services that have not yet been clearly identified cannot be subject to VAT.[136]

Hire/purchase and the sale of goods on deferred terms are explicitly excluded from this periodical chargeability. According to Article 14(2)(b) RVD in those cases the actual handing-over of the goods is treated as the supply and not the payment of the final instalment. Thus, at the moment of the actual handing-over of the goods in addition to the first instalment, VAT must be charged on all (future) instalments, excluding the interest element provided stated and agreed on separately.[137]

On 16 December 2008, the Council adopted Directive 2008/117/EC and a Regulation stepping up the fight against evasion of VAT. These legislative acts are intended to ensure that information on cross-border transactions is collected and exchanged between Member States more quickly, to enable more rapid detection of cases of fraud, and in particular of "VAT carousels". A prerequisite of this exchange of information is a common understanding regarding the chargeable event and chargeability of the supply of cross border services. Continuous cross-border supplied services which are deemed to be supplied where the customer is established and which are subject to the reverse charge under Article 196 RVD[138] *must* be regarded as being completed on expiry of each calendar year. For other continuous supplied services Member States *may* provide that continuous supplies of goods and services which take place during a period of time shall be regarded as being completed at least at intervals of 1 year, so that then the chargeable event is deemed to occur and the tax becomes chargeable.

With regard to continuous supplies Article 64, paragraph 2 RVD provides that continuous intra-Community supplies of goods are deemed to be completed on expiry of each calendar month. The Community legislator did not find it necessary to introduce uniform rules with regard to the chargeability in the event of domestic transactions. According to Article 66 RVD, Member States may provide that the tax shall become chargeable on a later date

134 Where rates are changed Member States may effect adjustments, see Article 95 RVD.

135 See Case C-277/05 (*Société thermale d'Eugénie-les-Bains*), [2007] ECR I-6415.

136 Prepayments whereby lump sums are paid for goods referred to in general terms in a list which may be altered at any time by agreement between the buyer and the seller and from which the buyer may possibly select articles, on the basis of an agreement which he may unilaterally resile from at any time, thereupon recovering the unused balance of the prepayments, do not fall within the scope of this provision. Case C-419/02 (*BUPA Hospitals*), [2006] ECR I-1609.

137 See Case C-281/91 (*Muys en De Winter's Bouw- en Aannemingsbedrijf BV*), [1993] ECR I-5405.

138 Under the rules regarding the place of supply of services applicable from 1 January 2010 as a main rule services supplied to a taxable person are deemed to take place where the customer is established (Article 44 RVD) and subject to the reverse charge (Article 196 RVD).

than that of the chargeable event (see Article 95 RVD when in the meanwhile rates have changed), for certain transactions or for certain categories of taxable person either:
(a) no later than the issue of the invoice; or
(b) no later than receipt of the price;[139] or
(c) where an invoice is not issued, or is issued late, within a specified period from the date of the chargeable event.

The derogations provided for in Article 66 (1) RVD shall not, however, apply to supplies of services in respect of which VAT is payable by the customer pursuant to Article 196 RVD or (deemed) intra-Community supplies.

Member States must follow the main rule with regard to services which are deemed to be supplied where the customer is established and which are subject to the reverse charge under Article 196 RVD (see section 2.13.1), *i.e.* the chargeable event occurs *and* the tax becomes chargeable when the services are performed. Thus, VAT on intra- Community supplied services becomes chargeable when a supply is made (Article 63 RVD), deemed to be made (new Article 64(1) RVD) or on receipt of the prepayment (Article 65 RVD).

Article 67 RVD provides that where, in accordance with the conditions laid down in Article 138 RVD, goods dispatched or transported to a Member State other than that in which dispatch or transport of the goods begins are supplied VAT- exempt or where goods are transferred VAT-exempt to another Member State by a taxable person for the purposes of his business, VAT becomes chargeable at the moment the invoice is issued or ultimately on the 15th day of the month following that in which the chargeable event occurs if the invoice has not been raised at that moment.

The Directive on invoicing rules disallows any derogation with regard to the chargeable event and chargeability of intra-Community supplies of goods as laid down in Article 67 RVD. It added the following paragraph to Article 67 RVD:

> Article 64(1), the third subparagraph of Article 64(2) and Article 65 shall not apply with respect to the supplies and transfers of goods referred to in the first paragraph.

It seems to us that the prohibition to treat VAT as becoming chargeable where a payment is to be made on account before the goods are intra-Community supplied for reasons of consistency should have been extended to intra-Community supplies of services. Be this as it may, based on the adopted provisions, with regard to intra- Community supplies giving rise to successive statements of account or successive payments Member State may not regard the supply of goods as being completed on expiry of the periods to which such statements of account or payments relate (as dealt with in Article 64(1)RVD) nor, in certain cases, the continuous supply of goods over a period of time as being completed at least at intervals of one year (as dealt with in Article 64(2) third paragraph RVD). Also, where a payment is

139 According to Article 167a adopted by the Directive on invoice rules Member States may provide within an optional scheme that the right of deduction of a taxable person whose VAT solely becomes chargeable in accordance with Article 66(b) be postponed until the VAT on the goods or services supplied to him has been paid to his supplier.

to be made on account before the goods are (intra-Community) supplied, VAT may not be treated as becoming chargeable on receipt of the payment and on the amount received (as dealt with in Article 65 RVD). And the derogations (of Article 66 RVD) that VAT becomes chargeable, no later than the time the invoice is issued, no later than the time the payment is received or where an invoice is not issued, or is issued late, within a specified period from the date of the chargeable event may not be applied to intra-Community supplies of goods (and services covered by Article 196 RVD). The VAT becomes chargeable on issue of the invoice, or on expiry of the time limit referred to in the first paragraph of Article 222 RVD (*i.e.* on the fifteenth day of the month following that in which the chargeable event occurs) if no invoice has been issued by that time.

As of 1 July 2021, Article 66a RVD provides for a special rule for the moment VAT becomes chargeable in case a platform is liable for payment of VAT under Article 14a RVD (see section 2.6.1). In that case VAT becomes chargeable at the time when the payment has been accepted. Under Article 41a VIR the time the payment has been accepted means the time when the payment confirmation, the payment authorisation message or a commitment for payment from the customer is received by or on behalf of the supplier selling goods through the electronic interface, regardless of when the actual payment of money is made, whichever is the earliest.

2.8.2 Intra-community acquisitions

Article 68 RVD provides that the chargeable event occurs when the intra- Community acquisition of goods is made. The intra-Community acquisition of goods shall be regarded as being made when the supply of similar goods is regarded as being effected within the territory of the relevant Member State.

The tax becomes chargeable on issuance of the invoice or, at the latest, on the 15th day of the month following that during which the acquisition took place (Article 69 RVD).

In order to be able to match intra-Community supplies (see Article 67 RVD) with acquisitions, Member States are not free to apply derogations.

2.8.3 Imports

As regards imported goods, Article 70 RVD provides that the VAT becomes chargeable when goods are imported. Article 71 RVD links the rules of the chargeable event and the chargeability with those of customs duties (on the question of the moment when the customs debt is incurred, see Chapter 1, section 1.4.1.).[140]

140 See Case C-166/94 (*Pezzullo Molini*) [1996] ECR I-331.

2.9 Taxable Amount

Title VII of the RVD distinguishes between the taxable amount regarding supplies of goods or services, intra-Community acquisitions of goods, importation of goods and miscellaneous subjects.

In VAT, not an objective but a subjective value is applied, since it is the actual private expenditure which VAT aims to tax. VAT rates are expressed as a percentage of the taxable amount, which in Article 73 RVD is defined as everything which constitutes consideration,[141] obtained or to be obtained by the supplier from the purchaser, the customer or a third party, including subsidies directly linked to the price of such supplies.[142] Separate provisions deal with self-supplies, *i.e.* private/ non-business use,[143] transfers to other Member States and internal supplies: in general the purchase price or the cost price is applicable (Articles 74, 75 and 77 RVD); obviously in these situations objective elements must be applied. In the case of a self-supply of services a fully objective value is applied, *i.e.* the objective market value (Article 76 RVD).

Pursuant to Article 79 RVD, the taxable amount includes:
(a) taxes, duties, levies and charges, excluding VAT itself;
(b) incidental expenses such as commission, packing, transport and insurance cost charged by the supplier to the purchaser or customer.

Based on Article 79 RVD the taxable amount does not include the following factors:
(a) price reductions by way of discount for early payment;
(b) price discounts and rebates granted to the customer and obtained by him at the time of the supply;
(c) amounts received by a taxable person from the customer, as repayment of expenditure incurred in the name and on behalf of the customer, and entered in his books in a suspense account (the so-called disbursements).[144]

With regard to price discounts the ECJ frequently has been asked to explain the rules regarding so-called promotion schemes. According to the ECJ the value of vouchers is

---

141 See, *ex multis*, Case 154/80 (*Aardappelenbewaarplaats*), [1981] ECR 0445. In Case C-277/05 (*Société thermale d'Eugénie-Les-Bains*), the ECJ held that a sum paid as a deposit, in the context of a contract relating to the supply of hotel services which is subject to value added tax, is to be regarded, where the client exercises the cancellation option available to him and that sum is retained by the hotelier, as a fixed cancellation charge paid as compensation for the loss suffered as a result of client default and which has no direct connection with the supply of any service for consideration and, as such, is not subject to that tax. Advocate General Maduro was of the opinion that such deposits must be regarded, where the purchaser makes use of the cancellation option available to him and those sums are retained by the vendor, as remuneration for the reservation service and, as such, subject to value added tax.

142 It is not necessary for the subsidy to correspond exactly to the diminution in the price of the goods supplied, it being sufficient if the relationship between the diminution in price and the subsidy, which may be at a flat rate, is significant. Case C-184/00 (*Office des produits Wallons*), [2002] ECR I-9115.

143 See Case C-72/05 (*Household Wollny*), [2006] ECR I-8297.

144 See, *inter alia*, Case C-98/05 (*De Danske Bilimportører*), [2006] ECR I-4945.

not their face value, but the cash received for the vouchers which may be at a discounted price, even when the vouchers can be redeemed for goods at face value.[145] In case of a non-monetary consideration provided by a customer in the form of a service to a taxable person, for which the customer receives a good free of charge the value of the good must be decided subjectively, *i.e.* the price the taxable person paid for the item in question.[146] For example, Elida Gibbs (manufacturer of toiletries) issued vouchers entitling customers to discounts on the purchase of its products. It also operated a sales promotion scheme, entitling customers who purchased and returned three of its toothpaste cartons to a refund. It claimed a repayment of output tax which it had previously accounted for, contending that the reimbursement of this money constituted a retrospective discount which reduced the consideration for its supplies The Commissioners rejected the claim on the basis that there was no direct link between the sale of the toothpaste by the retailer and the reimbursement of the money by the manufacturer. The ECJ held that the amounts refunded by the manufacturer had to be deducted from the original selling price in computing the taxable amount.[147] In another case Chaussures Bally appealed against assessments charging output tax, contending that, where customers made payment by credit card, the amount which the credit card company retained as commission should be excluded in computing the consideration on which VAT was chargeable. The ECJ rejected this contention, holding that in a credit card transaction, the commission retained by the credit card company must be included in the consideration which was chargeable to VAT.[148]

In *Koninklijke Ahold*, in answer to two questions from the Netherlands Hoge Raad, the ECJ ruled essentially that, provided that the principles of fiscal neutrality and proportionality are observed, it is for Member States to regulate the rounding of amounts of VAT, and Community law does not oblige them to allow taxable persons to round the amount down for each item supplied.[149]

Article 80 RVD, introduces an optional rule which enables Member States to revalue certain supplies and therefore to a large extent doing away with the subjective value under the European VAT. The rule can only be applied when the parties are connected. In addition to the requirement of close relationship, revaluation of a supply is only allowed in three circumstances:

145 See, *inter alia*, Case C-126/88 (*Boots Co Ltd*), [1990] ECR I-1235.
146 See, *inter alia*, Case C-33/93 (*Empire Stores Ltd*), [1994] ECR I-2329.
147 See, *inter alia*, Case C-317/94 (*Elida Gibbs*), [1996] ECR I-5339.
148 Case C-18/92 (*Chaussures Bally*), [1993] ECR I-2871.
149 Case C-484/06 (*Koninklijke Ahold*), [2008] ECR I-5097. In Case C-302/07 (*J D Wetherspoon*), [2009] ECR I-1467, the ECJ added to this that where prices are fixed exclusive of VAT, the rounding occurs before the customer pays the consideration for the supply. The amount of tax collected by the taxable person from his customer and the amount subsequently paid by the taxable person to the State are identical, irrespective of the method of rounding applied. By contrast, where VAT is included in the price of goods or services, the systematic rounding down at a lower level than the periodic VAT return would result in the taxable person collecting from his customer the amount of the VAT actually due whilst systematically paying to the State a lower amount, retaining the difference for his own benefit. According to the ECJ that result would be contrary to the principle that VAT is collected by taxable persons at each stage of the production or distribution process on behalf of the tax authorities, to which those taxable persons are required to pay it.

(1) in the case of an undervaluation where VAT has been charged and the recipient of the supply is not entitled to a full right of deduction of VAT; or

(2) in the case of undervaluation where the supply is exempt where VAT has not been charged, the revaluation is applicable where the supplier is not entitled to a full right of deduction of VAT; and

(3) in the case of an overvaluation where VAT has been charged and the supplier is not entitled to a full right of deduction of VAT.

The rule in relation to overvalued supplies is aimed at businesses who do not have full right of deduction, and who inflate their taxable supplies to a fully taxable business connected to them. The recipient is able to recover input tax in full, but by increasing the value the supplier manages to shift the balance between the value of taxable and non- taxable supplies that they are making in order to engineer an increase in the proportion of deductible VAT. This manipulation of the pro-rata can also be achieved by reducing the value of an exempt supply to decrease the exempt turnover relative to the value of their taxable supplies and thus increase their recovery rate.

In these situations the RVD allows for revaluation of the supplies to the open market value (OMV) as defined in Article 72 RVD.[150]

Article 83 RVD stipulates that in respect of the *intra-Community acquisition of goods*, the taxable amount shall be established on the basis of the same factors as are used to determine the taxable amount for the supply of the same goods within the territory of the Member State concerned. In the case of the transactions, to be treated as intra-Community acquisitions of goods, referred to in Article 21 RVD (*i.e.* the application by a taxable person, for the purposes of his business, of goods dispatched or transported by or on behalf of that taxable person from another Member State) and Article 22 RVD (*i.e.* the application by armed NATO forces), the taxable amount is the purchase price of the goods or of similar goods or, in the absence of a purchase price, the cost price, determined at the time of the supply.

Article 84 RVD instructs Member States to take the measures necessary to ensure that the excise duty due from or paid by the person making the intra- Community acquisition of a product subject to excise duty is included in the taxable amount in accordance with point (a) of the first paragraph of Article 78, prescribing that the taxable amount shall include taxes, duties, levies and charges, excluding the VAT itself.

---

150 "For the purposes of this Directive, "open market value" shall mean the full amount that, in order to obtain the goods or services in question at that time, a customer at the same marketing stage at which the supply of goods or services takes place, would have to pay, under conditions of fair competition, to a supplier at arm's length within the territory of the Member State in which the supply is subject to tax. Where no comparable supply of goods or services can be ascertained, "open market value" shall mean the following:

(1) in respect of goods, an amount that is not less than the purchase price of the goods or of similar goods or, in the absence of a purchase price, the cost price, determined at the time of supply;

(2) in respect of services, an amount that is not less than the full cost to the taxable person of providing the service.".

Where, after the intra-Community acquisition of goods has been made, the person acquiring the goods obtains a refund of the excise duty paid in the Member State in which dispatch or transport of the goods began, the taxable amount must be reduced accordingly in the Member State in the territory of which the acquisition was made.

In respect of the *importation of goods*, the taxable amount is the value for customs purposes, determined in accordance with the Community provisions in force (Article 85 RVD. On customs valuation rules, see Chapter 1, section 1.4.2.3.).[151] Article 86 RVD indicates what must be included in the taxable amount, *inter alia*, incidental expenses, such as commission, packaging, transport and insurance costs, incurred up to the first place of destination within the territory of the importing Member State. To avoid double taxation incidental expenses that are included in the taxable amount for importation are subject to an exemption with the right to deduct VAT under Article 144 RVD.

According to Article 88 RVD, where goods temporarily exported from the Community are re-imported after having undergone, outside the Community, repair, processing, adaptation, making-up or re-working, Member States must take steps to ensure that the tax treatment of the goods for VAT purposes is the same as that which would have been applied had the repair, processing, adaptation, making-up or re-working been carried out within their territory.

According to Article 90 RVD, in the case of cancellation, refusal or total or partial non-payment or where the price is reduced after the supply takes place, the taxable amount shall be reduced accordingly under conditions which are to be determined by the Member States.[152] However, in the case of total or partial non- payment, Member States may derogate from this adjustment rule.[153] Member States can however not exclude any reduction of the taxable amount. The neutrality and proportionality principle must be taken into account. In that respect the ECJ ruled that a Member State may not make the reduction of the VAT taxable amount in the event of total or partial non-payment subject to the condition that insolvency proceedings have been unsuccessful when such proceedings may last longer than ten years.[154]

As regards returnable packing costs, Article 92 RVD (provides that Member States may take one of the following measures:

---

151 See, *inter alia*, Case C-491/04 (*D&A*), [2006] ECR I-2129, regarding the delivery of goods by a company established in Jersey and services supplied in the United Kingdom.

152 See, *inter alia*, Case C-330/95 (*Goldsmiths (Jewellers)*), [1997] ECR I-3801.

153 In Case C-489/09 (*Vandoorne NV*), [2011] ECR I-00225, the Court held that Articles 11.C(1) and 27(1) and (5) of the Sixth Directive (now respectively Arts. 90, 395 and 394 RVD) must be interpreted as not precluding national legislation which, by providing, for the purposes of simplifying the procedure for charging VAT and of combating tax evasion or avoidance in regard to manufactured tobacco, for the levying of that tax by means of tax labels, in a single charge and at source, from the manufacturer or importer of those products, excludes intermediate suppliers operating at a subsequent stage in the supply chain from the right to obtain reimbursement of VAT in the event of non-payment by the purchaser of the price for those products.

154 Case C-246/16 (*Di Maura*), ECLI:EU:C:2017:887.

(a) exclude them from the taxable amount and take the measures necessary to ensure that this amount is adjusted if the packing material is not returned; or
(b) include them in the taxable amount and take the measures necessary to ensure that this amount is adjusted if the packing material is in fact returned.

For multiple purpose vouchers (see section 2.6.5) Article 73a RVD stipulates that the taxable amount is the consideration paid for the voucher or, in the absence of information on that consideration (for example when the person who issued the voucher is different from the person to whom the voucher is redeemed), the monetary value indicated on the multi-purpose voucher itself or in the related documentation.

2.10 Rates

In accordance with 93 RVD, the rate applicable to taxable transactions is that in force at the time of the chargeable event (see section 2.8 above). However, in the following situations, the rate applicable shall be that in force when VAT becomes chargeable:
(a) in the cases referred to in Articles 65 and 66 RVD, *i.e.* where a payment is to be made on account before the goods or services are supplied or where Member States have provided that VAT is to become chargeable, in respect of certain transactions or certain categories of taxable person no later than the time the invoice is issued, the payment is received or within a specified period;
(b) in the case of an intra-Community acquisition of goods, i.e. on issuance of the invoice or, at the latest, on the 15th day of the month following that during which the acquisition took place;
(c) in the cases, concerning the importation of goods, referred to in the second subparagraph of Article 71(1) and in Article 71(2) RVD, *i.e.* when the provisions in force governing customs duties are applied.

Article 94 RVD stipulates that the rate applicable to the intra-Community acquisition of goods is that applied to the supply of like goods within the territory of the Member State and Article 96 RVD provides that the standard rate of value added tax must be fixed by each Member State as a percentage of the taxable amount and must be the same for the supply of goods and for the supply of services.

Article 97 RVD prescribes that the Member States must apply a standard rate which may not be less than 15%.[155] Member States may also apply either one or two reduced rates (Article 98 RVD). The reduced rates may only apply to supplies of the categories of goods and services specified in Annex III. The reduced rates do not apply to the electronically supplied services, except those mentioned under point (6) of Annex III (i.e. electronic publications).[156] When applying the reduced rates to categories of goods, Member States may use the CN to establish the precise coverage of the category concerned. According to

155 This provision used to be subject to periodical renewal. With the adoption of Council Directive 2018/912, it has now become permanent.

156 Before the adoption of Council Directive Directive (EU) 2018/1713 amending Directive 2006/112/EC as regards rates of value added tax applied to books, newspapers and periodicals, no reduced rates could apply to any electronically supplied services was total.

Article 99 RVD, the reduced rates must be fixed as a percentage of the taxable amount, which may not be less than 5%. Each reduced rate must be so fixed that the amount of VAT resulting from its application is such that the VAT deductible under Articles 167 to 171 and Articles 173 to 177 can normally[157] be deducted in full.

The ECJ decided that in the case of a single supply comprised of two distinct elements, one principal, the other ancillary, which, if they were supplied separately, would be subject to different rates of value added tax, must be taxed solely at the rate of value added tax applicable to that single supply, that rate being determined according to the principal element, even if the price of each element forming the full price paid by a consumer in order to be able to receive that supply can be identified.[158]

Under the title "Particular provisions", Article 102 RVD provides that Member States after consultation of the VAT Committee may apply a reduced rate to the supply of natural gas, of electricity or of district heating.

Article 103 RVD provides that Member States may provide that the reduced rate, or one of the reduced rates which they apply, is also to apply to the importation of works of art, collectors' items and antiques.[159] The consequence of the application of the reduced rate upon importation is that, presumably, the VAT burden on imported goods and domestically purchased goods based on the margin scheme is equalised (it should be noted that a taxable dealer who imports goods at a reduced rate may opt to apply the margin scheme, see section 2.14.4). The reduced rate may also be applied to the supply of works of art, on an occasional basis, by a taxable person other than a taxable dealer, where the works of art have been imported by the taxable person himself, or where they have been supplied to him by their creator or his successors in title, or where they have entitled him to full deduction of VAT.

It should be noted that according to the ECJ the categories of goods and services mentioned in Annex III RVD should be interpreted narrowly, because they are exceptions to the main rule.[160] At the same time, in several decisions the ECJ has recalled that while that it is for the Member States to determine more precisely the supplies of goods and services included in the categories in Annex III to the VAT Directive to which the reduced rate apply in their jurisdictions,[161] they have to comply with the principle of fiscal neutrality whereby similar (from the perspective of the customer) supplies should be subject to a similar tax treatment. This means that when implementing reduced rates into their national legislation, they may not apply different rates to what consumers would consider to be similar supplies. For example the ECJ decided in a case concerning Polish legislation applying a reduced VAT rate to fresh pastry goods and cakes with a best before date that did not exceed 45

157 Obviously, in cases of initial investments or when only export supplies are made this is not possible.
158 Case C-463/16, (*Stadion Amsterdam*), [2006], ECLI:EU:C:2018:22.
159 In this context see Case C-305/03 (*Commission v. UK*), [2006] ECR I-1213, on the sale by auction of works of art imported under the arrangements for temporary importation.
160 Case C-331/19 (*X*), ECLI:EU:C:2020:786.
161 Case C-219/13, (*K*), [2014], EU:C:2014:2207; C-573/15, (*Oxycure*),[2017], ECLI:EU:C:2017:189.

days, that the referring court should verify whether, from the viewpoint of the average consumer, products with a longer conservation period do not have similar characteristics and do not meet the same needs, the test being whether their use is comparable, and where the differences between them do not have a significant influence on the decision of the average consumer to use one or other of those goods or services[162] (while an average consumer is likely to consider immediate consumption and long conservation pastries differently, the question may indeed be raised whether the same consumer would consider long conservation pastries differently, depending on whether the best before date is 45 days or more).[163]

On January 18th of 2018, the European Commission made a proposal to introduce more flexibility for Member States to change the VAT rates they apply to different products. This proposal will be discussed in section 2.17.1.

2.11 Exemptions

The Title "Exemptions" starts with a general provision, Article 131 RVD, stipulating that the exemptions provided for in this Title apply without prejudice to other Community provisions and in accordance with conditions which the Member States "shall lay down" for the purposes of ensuring the correct and straightforward application of those exemptions and of preventing any possible evasion, avoidance or abuse.[164]

A distinction is then made between exemptions without the right to deduction (Articles 132 to 137 RVD) and exemptions with the right to deduction, which is in fact zero-rating. These are exemptions related to cross-border transactions (Articles 138 to 166 RVD).

2.11.1 Exemptions without the Right to Deduction

There are two lists of exemptions without the right to deduction: one concerning activities exempt in the public interest and one concerning other exempt activities. Taxable persons can only opt for taxation in specified transactions relating to immovable property and financial services (Article 137(1)(a) RVD), provided the Member State where the transactions are performed has introduced the right to opt. Under certain conditions, Member States are allowed to continue to tax some activities which are exempt under the Directive (Annex X, Part A RVD), to continue to exempt some taxable activities (Annex X, Part B RVD) or to grant taxable persons the option to choose for taxation or exemption (Article 391 RVD).

Since exemptions without the right to deduction are exceptions to the principle that supplies of goods and services should be subject to VAT, they should be interpreted strictly.[165]

162 C-499/16, (*AZ*), [2017], ECLI:EU:C:2017:846.

163 The ECJ should provide clarification about the concept of "average consumer" in a case currently pending: Phantasialand, C-406/20.

164 See, *inter alia*, Case 8/81 (*Becker*) [1982] ECR 00053 in which the ECJ held that the "conditions" referred to are intended to ensure the correct and straightforward application of the exemptions. A Member State may not rely, as against a taxpayer who is able to show that his tax position actually falls within one of the categories of exemption laid down in the Directive, upon its failure to adopt the very provisions which are intended to facilitate the application of that exemption.

165 C-2/95, (*SDC*); [2002], ECLI:EU:C:1997:278*SDC*, C-141/00 (*Kügler*), [2002] ECR I-6833.

This means that the Member States may not tax transactions exempt under the RVD and, the other way around, may not exempt more transactions than listed there.

The ECJ confirmed that exemptions constitute independent concepts of Community law whose purpose is to avoid divergences in the application of the VAT system from one Member State to another.[166] In an abundant body of case law, the ECJ has thus defined the scope of the exemptions. The ECJ also clarified that, on the one hand the scope of the exemptions should be interpreted in the light of their objective and that, when implementing the exemptions, the Member States must comply with the principle of fiscal neutrality.

Activities in the public interest

The following supplies are exempt "in the public interest" (i.e. to not impose a tax obstacle to their purchase) under Article 132 RVD:

1. The supply by the public postal services of services other than passenger transport and telecommunications services, and the supply of goods incidental thereto are exempt from VAT (Article 132(1)(a) RVD).[167]
2. Hospital and medical care and closely related activities undertaken by bodies governed by public law or, under social conditions comparable with those applicable to bodies governed by public law, by hospitals, centres for medical treatment or diagnosis and other duly recognised establishments of a similar nature are exempt from VAT (132(1)(b) RVD).[168]
3. The provision of medical care in the exercise of the medical and paramedical professions as defined by the Member State concerned (Article 132(1)(c) RVD).
   On the exemption of health care services under Article 132 (1) (b) to (c) RVD the ECJ has, for example, clarified that:
   - Exempt medical activities cover activities consisting in providing care to persons by diagnosing and treating a disease or any other health disorder,[169] excluding for example biological tests meant to establish the genetic affinity of individuals[170] or aesthetic surgery. The scope is not as narrow as it may look at first sight as, taking into account the objective of the exemption (ie. affordable health care), the ECJ confirmed that conducting medical examinations of individuals for employers or insurance companies, the taking of blood or other bodily samples to test for the presence of viruses, infections or other diseases on behalf of employers or insurers, or the certification of medical fitness, for example, as to fitness to travel, are covered by the exemption provided those services are intended principally to protect the health of the person concerned.[171] The exemption also covers the accommodation

166 See for example Case C-76/99, (Commission v. France), [2001], ECLI:EU: C:2001:12.

167 See Case 107/84 (*Commission v. Germany*), [1985] ECR 2655, on services carried out on behalf of the postal authority by other undertakings. In Case C-357/ 07 (*TNT Post*), [2009] ECR I-3025, the ECJ held that the exemption applies to the supply by the public postal services acting as such – that is, in their capacity as an operator who undertakes to provide all or part of the universal postal service in a Member State – of services other than passenger transport and telecommunications services, and the supply of goods incidental thereto. It does not apply to supplies of services or of goods incidental thereto for which the terms have been individually negotiated.

168 This does not include the services of veterinary surgeons, see Case 122/87 (*Commission* v. *Italy*), [1988] ECR 2685.

169 Cases C-307/01, (*d'Ambrumenil*), [2003], ECLI:EU:C:2003:627.

170 Case C-384/98, (*D.W.*), [2000], ECLI:EU:C:2000:444.

171 Cases C-307/01, (*d'Ambrumenil*), [2003], ECLI:EU:C:2003:627.

and the provision of meals to patients, and even to people accompanying in-patients if those supplies are essential to achieve the therapeutic objectives sought by the hospital and medical care.[172]

- The concepts of "medical care" in Article 132(1)(b) RVD and of "the provision of medical care" in Article 132(1)(c) RVD are both intended to cover services that have as their aim the diagnosis, treatment and, in so far as possible, cure of diseases or health disorders.[173] The difference is that the previous covers services supplied in a hospital environment while the latter covers services provided outside such a framework, both at the private address of the person providing the care and at the patient's home or at any other place.[174]
- Services provided by telephone, consisting of giving advice regarding health and illnesses, are covered by the exemption provided that they have a therapeutic purpose.[175]
- Services exempt under Article 132(1)c) must be performed in the context of a medical or paramedical profession as defined by the Member States which means that they have a discretionary power to determine what are the required professional qualifications. However, on the one hand, in view of its objective the exemption may only apply to the provision of medical care of sufficiently high quality.[176] On the other hand, the principle of fiscal neutrality principle, which commands that similar supplies be subject to a similar VAT treatment, implies that the exemption may not be too restrictive.[177]
- A nutrition monitoring service provided in a sports facility does not fall under the scope of the exemption when there is no indication that it is provided for purposes of prevention, diagnosis, treatment of a condition or restoration of health, and accordingly with a therapeutic purpose.[178]

4. Supplies of human organs, blood and milk (Article 132(1)(d) RVD).[179] Note that Article 140(a) RVD exempts also the importation of goods the supply of which is in all circumstances exempt.

---

172 Joined Cases C-394/04 and C-395/04, (*Diagnostiko & Therapeftiko Kentro Athinon-Ygeia AE*), [2005] ECLI:EU:C:2005:734.

173 Case C-106/05 (*L.u.P*), [2006], ECR I-5123; C-262/08 (*CopyGene*), [2010] ECR I-5053. With regard to stem cells see Cases C-262/08 (*CopyGene A/S*), [2010] ECR I- 05053, C-86/09 (*Future Health Technologies*), [2010] ECR I- 05215, and C-156/09 (*Verigen Transplantation Service*), [2010] ECR I- 11733.

174 C-106/05 (*L.u.P.*), EU:C:2006:380, C-334/14, (*De Fruytier*), [2010], EU: C:2015:437; 353/85 (*Commission v. UK*), [1988] ECR 0817, and Case 122/87 (*Commission v. Italy*), [1988] ECR 2685.

175 Case C-48/19, (*X*), [2020], ECLI:EU:C:2020:169.

176 Cases C-443/04 and C-444/04, (*Solleveld and van den Hout-van Eijnsbergen*), EU:C:2006:257, and C-597/17, (*Belgisch Syndicaat van Chiropraxie and Others*), EU: C:2019:544.

177 Cases C-443/04 and C-444/04, (*Solleveld and van den Hout-van Eijnsbergen*), EU:C:2006:257; C-597/17, (*Belgisch Syndicaat van Chiropraxie and Others*), EU: C:2019:544; C-48/19, (*X*), [2020], ECLI:EU:C:2020:169.

178 C-581/19, (*Frenetikexito*), [2021], ECLI:EU:C:2021:167.

179 This does not apply to the activity of transporting, in a self-employed capacity, human organs and samples for hospitals and laboratories. See Case C-237/09 (*Nathalie De Fruytier*), [2010] ECR I- 04985.

5. Services supplied by dental technicians in their professional capacity and dental prostheses supplied by dentists and dental technicians (Article 132(1)(e) RVD).[180]
6. The supply of services by independent groups of persons who carry on an activity which is exempt from VAT or in relation to which they are not taxable persons, for the purpose of rendering to their members the services directly necessary for the exercise of that activity, where those groups merely claim from their members exact reimbursement of their share of the joint expenses, provided that such exemption is not likely to cause distortion of competition (Article 132(1)(f) RVD).[181]

   In 2017 the ECJ decided that the exemption of services provided by independent groups of persons for their members cannot apply to the supply of services which do not contribute directly to the exercise of activities in the public interest referred to in Article 132(1) RVD.[182] This decision was hard news for the financial sector who often made use of the exemption. Several Member States had to change their legislation to comply with the ECJ interpretation.

   In 2020, the ECJ also decided that the exemption does not apply in the case of supplies made by an independent group of persons to a VAT group if not all the members of that VAT group are members of that independent group of persons.[183]
7. The supply of services and of goods closely linked to welfare and social security work, including those supplied by old people's homes, by bodies governed by public law or by other bodies recognised by the Member State concerned as being devoted to social well-being (Article 132(1)(g) RVD.[184]
8. The supply of services and of goods closely linked to the protection of children and young persons by bodies governed by public law or by other organisations recognised by the Member State concerned as being devoted to social well- being (Article 132(1)(h) RVD, ex Article 13A(1)(h) – which referred to *organisations recognised as charitable*).[185]

180 See Case C-240/05 (*Eurodental*), [2006] ECR I-11479: a transaction which is exempt from VAT within the territory of a Member State under Article 13A(1)(e) of the Sixth Directive (now Article 132 (1)(e) RVD) does not give rise to the right to deduct input VAT pursuant to Article 17(3)(b) of that Directive (now Article 169(b) RVD), even when it is an intra-Community transaction, and regardless of the system of VAT applicable in the Member State of destination. See also Case C-401/05 (*VDP Dental Laboratories*), [2006] ECR I-12121.

181 The grant of VAT exemption must (only) be refused if there is a *genuine risk* that the exemption may by itself, immediately or in the future, give rise to distortions of competition. Case C-8/01 (*Assurandør-Societetet, acting on behalf of Taksatorringen*), [2003] ECR I-13711.

182 C-326/15, (DNB Banka), [2017], ECLI:EU:C:2017:719; C-605/15, (Aviva), [2017], ECLI:EU:C:2017:718 and C-616/15, (Commission v. Germany), [2017], ECLI:EU:C:2017:721.

183 C-77/19 (*Kaplan International Colleges UK Ltd*), [2020], ECLI:EU: C:2020:934.

184 Ex Article 13A(1)(g), in which reference was made to "other organisations recognised as charitable"). With regard to the concept of "charitable", see Case C- 498/03 (*Kingscrest*), [2005] ECR I-4427.

185 With regard to the concept of "charitable", see Case C-498/03 (*Kingscrest*), [2005] ECR I-4427. See Case C-415/04 (*Stichting Kinderopvang Enschedé*), [2006] ECR I-1385. See also Case C-434/05 (*Horizon College*), [2007] ECR I-4793. In Case C-79/09 (*Commission v the Netherlands*), [2010] ECR I- 00040*, the Court dismissed the Commission's submission that, by granting exemption from VAT for the making available of personnel in the socio-cultural sector, the health sector and the education sector to so-called Euregios and for promotion of work mobility, the Kingdom of the Netherlands had failed to fulfil its obligations under Article 2(1)(c), Article 24(1) and Article 132 RVD.

The ECJ further decided that these exemptions that only apply to supplies made by "bodies governed by public law or by other organisations recognised by the Member State concerned as being devoted to social well-being" are in principle applicable to legal and natural persons and potentially to both private and public entities.[186] The absence of a profit purpose, the fact that an entity does not benefit from public funding and/or does not have commit to cap its prices are not, in themselves, reasons to refuse the application of the exemption, although these elements have to be taken into account to determine the social character of the services rendered.[187]

9. The provision of children's or young people's education, school or university education, vocational training or retraining, including the supply of services and of goods closely related thereto, by bodies governed by public law having such as their aim or by other organisations recognised by the Member State concerned as having similar objects (Article 132(1)(i) RVD).
The ECJ clarified that the concept of "school or university education" for the purposes of the VAT system "refers generally to an integrated system for the transfer of knowledge and skills covering a wide and diversified set of subjects, and to the furthering and development of that knowledge and those skills by the pupils and students in the course of their progress and their specialisation in the various constituent stages of that system".[188] It further clarified that the exemption is not limited "solely to education which leads to examinations for the purpose of obtaining qualifications or which provides training for the purpose of carrying out a professional or trade activity, but includes other activities which are taught in schools or universities in order to develop pupils' or students' knowledge and skills, provided that those activities are not purely recreational".[189] The exemption of the closely related services is designed to ensure that access to the benefit of university education is not hindered by the increased cost of providing it that would follow if it, or the supply of services and goods closely related to it, were subject to VAT.[190]
10. Tuition given privately by teachers and covering school or university education (Article 132(1)(j) RVD).[191]
11. The supply of staff by religious or philosophical institutions for the purpose of the activities referred to in points (b), (g), (h) and (i) and with a view to spiritual welfare (Article 132(1)(k) RVD).
12. The supply of services, and the supply of goods closely linked thereto, to their members in their common interest in return for a subscription fixed in accordance with their

---

186 In Case C-453/93 (*Bulthuis-Griffioen*), [1995] ECR I-2341, the Court held that Article 13A(1)(g) expressly refers to the concept of "body" or "organization"; the exemption may be claimed only by legal persons. However, in Case C-216/97 (*Gregg & Gregg*), [1999] ECR I-4947, the ECJ held that The terms "establishment" and "organisation" are in principle sufficiently broad to include natural persons as well and that the legislator did not intend to confine the exemptions referred to in that provision to the activities carried on by legal persons, but meant to extend the scope of those exemptions to activities carried on by individuals.

187 C-335/14, (*Jardins de Jouvence*), ECLI:EU:C:2016:36; C-211/18, (*Idealmed*), ECLI:EU:C:2020:168.

188 C-449/17, (*A & G Fahrschul-Akademie GmbH*), [2019], ECLI:EU:C:2019:202.

189 C-473/08, (*Eulitz*), [2007], EU:C:2010:47.

190 Case C-287/00 (*Commission* v. *Germany*), [2002] ECR I-5811. See also Case C- 445/05 (*Werner Haderer*), [2007] ECR I-4841.

191 On this, see Case C-445/05 (*Werner Haderer*), [2007] ECR I-4841.

rules by non-profit-making organisations with aims of a political, trade union, religious, patriotic, philosophical, philanthropic or civic nature, provided that this exemption is not likely to cause distortion of competition (Article 132(1)(l) RVD).[192]

13. The supply of certain services closely linked to sport or physical education by non-profit-making organisations to persons taking part in sport or physical education (Article 132(1)(m) RVD).[193]
    A particularity of this exemption is that it concerns *certain services* linked to sport or physical education. The ECJ confirmed that this wording means that the Member States do not have to exempt all services related to sport and physical education but have a discretionary power in that respect. However, they still have to comply with the principle of fiscal neutrality.[194] The ECJ also decided that the wording of the provision is not unconditional and sufficiently precise and therefore does not have direct effect, hence may not be relied on in front of a national court in the absence of transposition that provision.[195]
14. The supply of certain cultural services, and the supply of goods closely linked thereto, by bodies governed by public law or by other cultural bodies recognised by the Member State concerned (Article 132(1)(n) RVD).[196]
    Here also the exemption only covers certain services and therefore the Member States do not have to exempt all cultural services (and there is no direct effect).[197] The ECJ explains the margin of manoeuver left to the Member States in the case of sport and cultural services by the fact that in both cases, and in contrast with other supplies covered by Article 132(1), the services have a recreational and entertainment nature.[198]

---

192 With regard to the concept of trade unions, see Case C-149/97 (*Institute of the Motor Industry*), [1998] ECR I-7053.

193 In Case C-124/96 (*Commission v. Spain*), [1998] ECR I-2501, Advocate- General La Pergola observed the following: "I need scarcely point out that the Spanish government's argument to the effect that Member States are free to determine the services which may benefit from an exemption since Article 13(A)(1) (m) provides only that "certain services" are exempt cannot be accepted. I do not believe that the Community legislature intended to confer such a wide discretion on Member States. The term in question ("certain") doubtless constitutes an unfortunate formulation of the provision, but it does not have the scope attributed to it in the Spanish government's defence; it simply means that not all services are to be exempt but merely those which, as the provision states, are "supplied by non-profit- making organisations". Moreover, since the latter constitutes the aim which justifies the grant of the exemption, the rule in question must in any event – in so far as it lays down the services to be exempt – be capable of pursuing that aim." In Case C- 253/07 (*Canterbury Hockey Club, Canterbury Ladies Hockey Club*), [2008] ECR I- 7821, the Court held that to be eligible for that exemption, the services must, in accordance with Article 13A(1)(m) and the first indent of Article 13A (2)(b) of the Sixth Directive (now Article 134, point (a) RVD), be supplied by a non-profit- making organization and they must be closely linked and essential to sport, since the true beneficiaries of those services are the persons taking part in sport. By contrast, supplies of services which do not meet those criteria, particularly those linked to sports clubs and to their operation such as, for example, advice about marketing and obtaining sponsors, cannot benefit from that exemption.

194 See for example C-495/12, (*Bridport and West Dorset Golf Club Limited*), [2013], ECLI:EU:C:2013:861, in which the Court decided that a Member State legislation may not limit the exemption by reference to whether the services of granting a right to play golf are made to a member of the non-profit-making organisation.

195 C-488/18, (*Golfclub Schloss Igling eV*), [2020], ECLI:EU:C:2020:1013.

196 Case C-144/00 (*Matthias Hoffmann*), [2003] ECR I-2921.

197 C-592/15, (*British Film Institute*), [2003], ECLI:EU:C:2017:117.

198 C-488/18, (*Golfclub Schloss Igling eV*), [2020], ECLI:EU:C:2020:1013.

15. The supply of services and goods, by organisations whose activities are exempt pursuant to points (b), (g), (h), (i), (l), (m) and (n), in connection with fund- raising events organised exclusively for their own benefit, is exempt provided that exemption is not likely to cause distortion of competition. For the purposes of point (o), Member States may introduce any restrictions necessary, in particular as regards the number of events or the amount of receipts which give entitlement to exemption (Article 132(1)(o) and (2) RVD).
16. The supply of transport services for sick or injured persons in vehicles specially designed for the purpose, by duly authorised bodies (Article 132 (1)(a) RVD).
17. The activities, other than those of a commercial nature, carried out by public radio and television bodies (Article 132(1)(a) RVD).

Article 133 lists four optional conditions which Member States may impose on the granting of the exemptions under Article 132 (1) (b), (g), (h), (i), (l), (m) and (n) RVD *to bodies other than those governed by public law.* The condition set out in point (a) is that the bodies in question "must not systematically aim to make a profit, and any surpluses nevertheless arising must not be distributed, but must be assigned to the continuance or improvement of the services supplied".[199] The condition set out in point (b) is that the bodies in question "must be managed and administered on an essentially voluntary basis by persons who have no direct or indirect interest, either themselves or through intermediaries, in the results of the activities concerned". The condition under (c) is that those bodies must charge prices which are approved by the public authorities or which do not exceed such approved prices or, in respect of those services not subject to approval, prices lower than those charged for similar services by commercial enterprises subject to VAT. The fourth condition under (d) is that the exemptions must not be likely to cause distortion of competition to the disadvantage of commercial enterprises subject to VAT.

Article 134 RVD states that the supply of goods or services will not be exempt under Article 132 (1) (b), (g), (h), (i), (l), (m) and (n) RVD in case the supply is not essential to the exempt transactions or where the basic purpose of the supply is to obtain additional income for the body in question through transactions which are in direct competition with those of commercial enterprises subject to VAT. This provision deals with exemptions that state that *closely related activities* are exempt. In the *Horizon college* case[200] the ECJ ruled that an activity of the hiring out of staff by one educational body to another is closely related to education if the placement of that staff is of a nature and quality such that, without recourse to such a service, there could be no assurance that the education provided by the host establishment and the education from which its students benefit, would have an equivalent value.

199 See Case C-174/00 (*Kennemer Golf & Country Club*), [2002] ECR I-3293 and Case C-267/00 (*London Zoological Society*), [2002] ECR I-3353.
200 Case C-434/05 (*Horizon college*), ECLI:EU:C:2007:343.

Other activities[201]

Under the heading "exemptions for other activities", Articles 135 to 137 RVD deal with the following exemptions:

1. Insurance and reinsurance transactions, including related services performed by insurance brokers and insurance agents (Article 135(1)(a) RVD).

The exemption of "insurance transactions" covers situations in which "the insurer undertakes, in return for prior payment of a premium, to provide the insured, in the event of materialisation of the risk covered, with the service agreed when the contract was concluded".[202] There must be a (direct or indirect)[203] contractual relationship between the provider of the insurance service and the insured party. The road assistance services that a body undertakes to provide to its members, in return for the payment by those members of a fixed annual subscription, should the risk of breakdown or accident covered by that body materialise, typically fall within the definition of "insurance transactions".[204] In contrast, the exemption does not apply in the case of a transfer for consideration of a portfolio of life reinsurance contracts which took place between a transferor company and another company (because this transaction lacks the characteristics of an insurance transaction or a reinsurance transaction).[205] The ECJ also decided that "back office" activities, consisting in rendering services, for payment, to an insurance company are not covered by the exemption.[206] In *United Biscuit*, the ECJ decided that its case law in the matter of insurance law is not relevant to define the scope of the exemption applicable to insurance transactions for VAT.[207]

201 Although exemptions "in the public interest" are listed under Article 132 RVD, it may be argued that exempting the "other transactions" listed under Article 135 to 137 RVD may also have a social objective (i.e. no tax obstacle to the acquisition of some goods or services). Yet, the main reason usually invoked to explain the exemption of transactions listed under Article 135 to 137 RVD is of a technical nature, in particular the difficulty to determine the taxable amount in these transactions or the absence of value added in the transactions. Concerning the "financial transactions" the technical argument is regularly challenged. The Commission has tried to propose the removal of the exemption for these services, without success so far.

202 Case C-349/96, (*CPP*), [1999]; C-240/99 (*Skandia*), [2001] ECR I-1951; and C-8/01 (*Taksatorringen*), [2003] ECR I-13711.

203 In Case C-124/07 (*J.C.M. Beheer BV*), [2008] ECR I-2101 the ECJ decided that the fact that an insurance broker or agent does not have a direct relationship with the parties to the insurance or reinsurance contract in the conclusion of which he has been instrumental, but merely an indirect relationship with them through the intermediary of another taxable person who is, himself, in a direct relationship with one of those parties, and to whom that insurance broker or agent is contractually bound does not prevent the service provided by the latter from being exempt from VAT under that provision.

204 Case C-13/06 (*Commission v. Greece*), [2006] ECR I-11563.

205 Case C-242/08 (*Swiss Re Germany Holding GmbH*), [2009] ECR I-10099.

206 C-472/03 (*Arthur Andersen*), [2005] ECR I-1719. See also Case C-240/99 (*Forsäkringsaktiebolaget Skandia*), [2001] ECR I-1951, concerning the outsourcing to an insurance company of the administration of the entire business of a wholly owned insurance subsidiary.

207 C-235/19, (*United Biscuits*), [2020], ECLI:EU:C:2020:801.

2. The following (financial) transactions (Article 135(1)(b) to (g) RVD):208

(b) the granting and the negotiation of credit and the management of credit by the person granting it;

This exemption also applies to services provided by a taxable person who analyses the financial situation of clients canvassed by him with a view to obtaining credit for them (to granted by a third party creditor).[209] Importantly, the quality of the supplier does not matter (the supplier does not need to be a financial institution, what matters is the nature of the service).[210]
As also clarified by the ECJ, *negotiation* (as used in several parts of Article 135(1) RVD): "refers to the activity of an intermediary who does not occupy the position of any party to a contract relating to a financial product, and whose activity amounts to something other than the provision of contractual services typically undertaken by the parties to such contracts. Negotiation is a service rendered to, and remunerated by, a contractual party as a distinct act of mediation. It may consist, amongst other things, in pointing out suitable opportunities for the conclusion of such a contract, making contact with another party or negotiating, in the name of and on behalf of a client, the detail of the payments to be made by either side. The purpose of negotiation is therefore to do all that is necessary in order for two parties to enter into a contract, without the negotiator having any interest of his own in the terms of the contract".[211]

(c) the negotiation of or any dealings in credit guarantees or any other security for money and the management of credit guarantees by the person who is granting the credit;[212]

(d) transactions, including negotiation, concerning deposit and current accounts, payments, transfers, debts, cheques and other negotiable instruments, but excluding debt collection;

Transactions concerning *transfers* must have the effect of transferring funds and entail changes of a legal and financial character.[213] The exemption is again not subject to the condition that the transactions be made by a certain type of institution or legal person, where the transactions in question relate to the sphere of financial transactions.[214]

The mere fact that a service is performed entirely by electronic means does not in itself prevent the exemption from applying. However, if the service entails only technical and

---

208 In Case C-281/91 (*Muys en De Winter's Bouw- en Aannemingsbedrijf BV*), [1993] ECR I-5405, the ECJ held where payment was deferred until delivery of the goods or services, interest was not in fact consideration for a separate supply of credit but was part of the taxable consideration for the supply.
209 In Case C-453/05 (*Volker Ludwig*), [2007] ECR I-5083.
210 C-281/91 (*Muys en De Winter's Bouw- en Aannemingsbedrijf BV*), [1993] ECR I-5405.
211 C-235/00, (*CSC Financial Services Ltd*), [2007], ECLI:EU:C:2001:696.
212 In Case C-455/05 (*Velvet & Steel Immobilien und Handels GmbH*), [2007] ECR I-3225, the ECJ held that this provision must be interpreted as meaning that the concept of "Übernahme von Verbindlichkeiten" (assumption of obligations) excludes from the scope of that provision obligations which are non-pecuniary, such as the obligation to renovate a property.
213 C-2/95, (*SDC*), [2007], ECLI:EU:C:1997:278; C-350/10, (*Nordea Pankki Suomi*), EU:C:2011:532; C-607/14, (*Bookit*), ECLI:EU:C:2016:355.
214 C-175/09 (*Axa UK*), [2016], EU:C:2010:646.

electronic assistance to the person performing the essential, specific functions for the transactions, it does qualify for the exemption[215] (e.g. services consisting in making financial information available to banks and other users are not covered).[216]

On debt collection, the ECJ confirmed that true factoring (whereby a business which purchases debts, assuming the risk of the debtors' default, and, in return, invoices its clients in respect of commission) pursues a taxable economic activity (not covered by an exemption).[217] In contrast, a taxable person who purchases, at his own risk, defaulted debts at a price below their face value (but the price reflects the actual economic value of the debts at the time of the purchase), does not make a supply of services for consideration and does not carry out an economic activity for the purpose of the VAT Directive (out of scope, no VAT).[218]

(e) transactions, including negotiation, concerning currency, bank notes and coins used as legal tender, with the exception of collectors' items, that is to say, gold, silver or other metal coins or bank notes which are not normally used as legal tender or coins of numismatic interest;

Portfolio management may fall into the scope of this exemption. Concerning this type of service, the ECJ decided that it consists of a combination of a service of analysing and monitoring the assets of client investors, on the one hand, and of a service of actually purchasing and selling securities on the other. They are both indispensable in carrying out the service as a whole, with the result that it is not possible to take the view that one must be regarded as the principal service and the other as the ancillary service. This services cannot benefit from the exemption.[219]

As confirmed by the ECJ, currency transactions are taxable only when effected in return for payment of a commission or specific fees would allow a trader to avoid taxation if he sought to be remunerated for his services by providing for a spread between the proposed transaction rates rather than by charging such sums.[220] The ECJ also held that, where no fees or commission were calculated with regard to certain specific transactions, the taxable amount was "the net result of the transactions of the supplier of the services over a given period of time".

(f) transactions, including negotiation but not management or safekeeping, in shares, interests in companies or associations, debentures and other securities, but excluding documents establishing title to goods, and the rights or securities referred to in Article 15(2) RVD;

This exemption for example covers services supplied by a credit institution, for consideration, in the form of an underwriting guarantee to a company wishing to issue shares, where

215 C-2/95, (SDC), [2007], ECLI:EU:C:1997:278.
216 See Cases C-276/09 (*Everything Everywhere Ltd*), [2010] ECR I- 12359; C- 607/14, (*Bookit*), [2016], ECLI:EU:C:2016:355 and C-42/18, (*Cardpoint*), [2019], ECLI:EU:C:2019:822.
217 Case C-305/01 (*MKG-Kraftfahrzeuge-Factory*), [2003] ECR I-6729.
218 C-93/10 (*GFKL*), [2011] ECR I-0000.
219 C-44/11, (*Deutsche Bank*), [1998], ECLI:EU:C:2012:484.
220 Case C-172/96 (*First National Bank of Chicago*), [1998] ECR I-4387.

under that guarantee the credit institution undertakes to acquire any shares which are not subscribed within the period for share subscription.[221]

(g) the management of special investment funds as defined by Member States.[222]

The concept of "management of special investment funds" is not defined. The ECJ stated that the transactions covered by that exemption are those which are specific to the business of undertakings for collective investment.[223] In such "funds", many investments are pooled and spread over a range of securities which can be managed effectively in order to optimise results, and in which individual investments may be relatively modest. Such funds manage their investments in their own name and on their own behalf, while each investor owns a share of the fund but not the fund's investments as such.[224] Pension funds that carry out a Defined Contribution arrangement (fixed premium, but no fixed pensions) can also be regarded as special investmenet funds,[225] while pension funds carrying out Defined Benefit arrangements (fixed pensions) cannot.[226]

In *Blackrock* the ECJ decided that a single supply of management services, provided by a software platform belonging to a third-party supplier for the benefit of a fund management company, which manages both special investment funds and other funds, does not fall within the exemption. The ECJ found that the services rendered should be considered as a single supply and in view of the fact that some of the services would be used also for funds other than those covered by the exemption, the exemption should be denied as a whole (the suggestion to use a *pro rata* was also rejected).[227] In Joined cases K and DBKAG, the ECJ decided that the provision of services by third parties to management companies of special investment funds, such as tax-related responsibilities consisting in ensuring that the income received from the fund by the unit-holders is taxed in accordance with national law and the grant of a right to use software which is used exclusively to carry out calculations which are essential for risk management and performance measurement, fall within the scope of the exemption provided for in that provision if they are intrinsically connected to the management of such funds and if they are provided exclusively for the purpose of managing such funds, even if those services are not outsourced in their entirety.[228]

As noted above, Article 137(1)(a) RVD allows the Member States to allow taxpayers a right of option to tax for all supplies listed under Article 135(1)(b) to (g) RVD.

221 Case C-540/09 (*Skandinaviska Enskilda Banken AB Momsgrupp*), [2010] ECR I- 01509.
222 On the concept of management, see Case C-08/03 (*BBL*), [2004] ECR I-10157 and Case C-169/04 (*Abbey National*), [2006] ECR I-4027. On closed-ended investment funds, see Case C-363/05 (*1*) (*J.P. Morgan Fleming Claverhouse Investment Trust plc 2 and The Association of Investment Trust Companies*), *[2007] ECR I-5517.*
223 Case C-169/04 *Abbey National* [2006] ECR I-4027.
224 C-44/11, (*Deutsche Bank*), [1998], ECLI:EU:C:2012:484.
225 Case C-424/11 *(Wheels)*, ECLI:EU:C:2013:144.
226 Case C-464/12 *(ATP Pension Service)*, ECLI:EU:C:2014:139.
227 C-231/19, (*BlackRock Investment Management (UK)* Ltd), [2020], ECLI:EU: C:2020:513.
228 Joined Cases C-58/20 and C-59/20 *(K, DBKAG)*, [2021], ECLI:EU: C:2021:491.

3. The supply at face value of postage stamps valid for use for postal services within their respective territory, fiscal stamps and other similar stamps (Article 135(1)(h) RVD).

4. Betting, lotteries and other forms of gambling, ie. games of chance with money stakes. It is however within the discretion of each Member State to determine, observing the principle of fiscal neutrality,[229] the "conditions and limitations" of such an exemption (Article 135 (1), (i) RVD).

5. The following transactions concerning immovable property (Article 135(1) RVD (j) to (l) RVD:

- the supply of a building or parts thereof, and of the land on which it stands, other than the supply, before first occupation, of a building or parts of a building and the land on which it stands (Article 135(1) (j) RVD);

In other words, the supply of *new* buildings and the land on which it stands are not covered by the exemption. As clarified by the ECJ, the *ratio legis* of the exemption is the relative lack of added value generated by the sale of an old building (therefore, new constructions should not be covered by the exemption).[230] The ECJ also clarified that VAT Directive makes it possible to tax supplies of buildings that have been converted, since a conversion adds value to the building concerned, in the same way as the initial construction does.[231]

The wording *first occupation* is more flexible than *new* and Article 12 (2) RVD second indent even provides that the Member States may apply another criteria, such as the period elapsing between the date of completion of the building and the date of first supply, or the period elapsing between the date of first occupation and the date of subsequent supply, provided that these periods do not exceed five and two years respectively.

- the supply of land which has not been built on, with the exception of building land defined by Article 12 (1) (b) RVD.[232] (Article 135(1) (k) RVD).

229 See Case C-259/10, (*The Rank Group*), [2011], ECLI:EU:C:2011:719.

230 C-326/99, *(Goed Wonen)*, [2001], EU:C:2001:506.

231 C-308/16, (*Kozuba Premium Selection sp. z o.o*)., [2017], ECLI:EU:C:2017:869. See also C-326/11, (*J.J. Komen en Zonen Beheer Heerhugowaard BV*), [2012], ECLI: EU:C:2012:461; C-71/18, (*KPC Herning*), [2019], ECLI:EU:C:2019:660.

232 This exemption does not cover the supply of land still occupied by a dilapidated building that is to be demolished and replaced by a new building and whose demolition, paid for by the vendor, had already begun before the actual supply took place. For value added tax purposes, such supply and such demolition form a single transaction, given that, taken as a whole, the aim of the transactions was not to supply the existing building and the land it stands on but land that has not been built on, regardless of how far demolition of the old building had progressed at the moment the land was actually supplied. Case C-461/08 (*Don Bosco Onroerend Goed BV*), [2009] ECR I-11079 and C-71/18 (*KPC Herning*), ECLI:EU: C:2019:660.

- the leasing or letting of immovable property233 (Article 135(1)(l) RVD), excluding:
  (1) the provision of accommodation, as defined in the laws of the Member States, in the hotel sector or in sectors with a similar function, including the provision of accommodation in holiday camps or on sites developed for use as camping sites;
  (2) the letting of premises and sites for parking vehicles;[234]
  (3) lettings of permanently installed equipment and machinery;
  (4) hire of safes (see Article 135(2) RVD).

Member States may apply further exclusions to the scope of this exemption. Also, based on Article 137(1), points (b), (c) and (d) RVD Member States may allow taxable persons a right of option for taxation.[235]

In a number of cases, the ECJ has defined the concept of the letting of immovable property for the purpose of this exemption as: "the conferring by a landlord on a tenant, for an agreed period and in return for rent, of the right to occupy that property as if that person

233 The ECJ has dealt with immovable property and VAT in more than 25 cases. By way of example we refer to the following cases. Case 50/87 (*Commission* v. *France*), [1988] ECR 4797. Under French law undertakings which lease buildings for an annual return of less than one fifteenth of the value of the property, in respect of which VAT is chargeable, were only allowed to deduct a fraction of the VAT charged on the purchase or construction of the property by those undertakings. The value of the property was defined as the taxable amount of the property for the purposes of VAT less the value of the land and financing costs. The Court held that this measure was incompatible with the principle of full and immediate deduction and that the original right to deduction can only be limited in so far as permitted by the Directive. In Case C-326/99 (*Stichting "Goed Wonen"*), [2001] ECR I-6831, the ECJ held that, although the leasing of immovable property is in principle covered by the concept of economic activity within the meaning of now Article 9 of the Directive, it is normally a relatively passive activity, not generating any significant added value. Like sales of new buildings following their first supply to a final consumer, which marks the end of the production process, the leasing of immovable property must therefore in principle be exempt from taxation, without prejudice to the right to opt for taxation which the Member States may grant to taxable persons. Consequently, observance of the principle of the neutrality of VAT and the requirement for a consistent application of the provisions of the VAT Directive, in particular the proper, simple and uniform application of the exemptions provided for, entail treating the grant of a right such as the usufructuary right in question in the case at issue like leasing and letting, for the purposes of the application of now Article 135(1)(l) and 137(1) RVD. Treating such a form of use of immovable property as letting prevents any abusive creation of a right to deduct input tax on immovable property, which is an aim expressly provided for by the exemptions of the Directive. In Case C-572/07 (*Tellmer Property*), [2009] ECR I-4983, the ECJ held that, for the purposes of applying Article 135(1)(k), the letting of immovable property and the cleaning service of the common parts of the latter must be regarded as independent, mutually divisible operations, so that the said service does not fall within that provision.

234 In Case 173/88 (*Henriksen*), [1989] ECR 2763, the ECJ held that Article 13B(b) of the Sixth Directive (now Article 135(1)(l)) must be interpreted as meaning that the phrase "premises and sites for parking vehicles" covers the letting of all places designed to be used for parking vehicles, including closed garages, but that such lettings cannot be excluded from the exemption in favour of the "leasing or letting of immovable property" if they are closely linked to lettings of immovable property for another purpose which are themselves exempt from VAT and that Member States may not exempt from VAT lettings of premises and sites for parking which are not covered by the exemption provided for in that provision, that is to say, those which are not closely linked to lettings of immovable property for another purpose which are themselves exempt from VAT.

235 See, *inter alia*, Case C-223/03 (*University of Huddersfield*), [2006] ECR I-1751, and Case C-269/03 (*Kirchberg*), [2004] ECR I-8067.

were the owner and to exclude any other person from enjoyment of such a right".[236, 237] The exclusiveness of the right to enjoy the property is thus key to be in scope of the exemption. The ECJ also confirmed that it is the passive nature of the leasing or letting of immovable property that justifies the exemption.[238]

Article 136 RVD provides that Member States must also exempt the following transactions:

(a) the supply of goods used solely for an activity exempt under Articles 132 (public interest activities), 135 (other activities), 371, 375, 376, 377, 378(2), 379(2) and 380 to 390 RVD (exemptions as derogations for Member States which were members of the Community on 1 January 1978 and for States which acceded to the Community after 1 January 1978), if those goods have not given rise to deductibility;
(b) the supply of goods on the acquisition or application of which VAT was not deductible, pursuant to Article 176 RVD (which is the standstill clause based on which, pending the entry into force of the provisions regarding expenditure in respect of which VAT is not be deductible, Member States may retain all the exclusions provided for under their national laws at 1 January 1979 or, in the case of the Member States which acceded to the Community after that date, on the date of their accession).

2.11.2 *Exemptions Relating to Intra-Community Transactions*

Under the Title "Exemptions for intra-Community transactions", Articles 138 to 142 RVD deal with exemptions related to the intra-Community supply of goods, exemptions for intra-Community acquisitions of goods and exemptions for certain transport services.

Exemption of intra-Community supplies

Article 138 paragraph 1 RVD instructs Member States to exempt the supply of goods dispatched or transported to a destination outside their respective territory but within the Community, when the following conditions are met:

a) the goods are supplied to another taxable person or to a non-taxable legal person acting as such in a Member State other than the Member State in which the dispatch or transport began.
b) the recipient is identified for VAT purposes in a Member State other than the Member State in which the dispatch or transport began and has indicated this VAT number to the supplier (the ECJ clarified that the recipient may be resident and identified in the Member State from which the goods are dispatched or transported if that taxable person uses the VAT identification number of another Member State for that specific transaction).[239]

This exemption is the flip side of the intra-Community acquisition. The current VAT system exempts the supply in the Member State of dispatch, while the customer must report an intra-Community acquisition in the Member State of arrival. It should be noted

236 C-326/99 (*"Goed Wonen"*), [2001], EU:C:2001:506, C-451/06, (*Walderdorff*), [2007], EU:C:2007:761.
237 See application of this definition by analogy to the concept of hiring of a means of transport in C-288/19, (*QM*), 20 January 2021, ECLI:EU:C:2021:32.
238 C-278/18, (*Sequeira Mesquita*), [2019], ECLI:EU:C:2019:160.
239 C-580/16, (*Firma Hans Bühler KG*), ECLI:EU:C:2018:261.

though that only certain parties are required to report intra-Community acquisitions (see section 2.6.2), notably taxable persons.

Article 45a IR indicates the situation in which it will be presumed that goods have been dispatched or transported from a Member State to a destination outside its territory but within the Community for the application of Article 138 RVD. These rules imply inter alia that the vendor be in possession of certain documents that prove the shipment. The presumption may be rebutted by the tax administration in situations also governed by Article 45a IR. These rules are mandatory for the Member States (meaning that they have to acknowledge that the proof of the shipment or transport of the goods has been provided when the conditions are satisfied and may not add other conditions).[240] Member States may however also accept other means of evidence.

Moreover, Article 138 (1a) RVD provides that in order to benefit from the exemption provided under Article 138 RVD, the supplier must submit recapitulative statements (an obligation foreseen under Articles 262 and 263 RVD) and the statements must include all the information required under Article 264 RVD (including the VAT number of the two parties to the transaction).

Based on Article 138, paragraph 2, RVD, Member States must also exempt:
(a) the supply of new means of transport (section 2.6.6), dispatched or transported to the customer at a destination outside their respective territory but within the Community, by or on behalf of the vendor or the customer, for taxable persons or non-taxable legal persons whose intra-Community acquisitions of goods are not subject to VAT pursuant to Article 3(1) RVD, or for any other non-taxable person;
(b) the supply of products subject to excise duty, dispatched or transported to a destination outside their respective territory but within the Community, to the customer, by or on behalf of the vendor or the customer, for taxable persons or non-taxable legal persons whose intra-Community acquisitions of goods other than products subject to excise duty are not subject to VAT pursuant to Article 3 (1) RVD, where those products have been dispatched or transported in accordance with Article 7(4) and (5) (*i.e.* under cover of an accompanying document) or Article 16 of Directive 92/12/EEC (*i.e.* the consignee being a registered trader without authorised warehousekeeper status), now Articles 17 to 31 of Directive 2008/118/EC see section 3.2.4 below;
(c) the supply of goods, consisting in a transfer to another Member State, *i.e.* a fictitious intra-Community supply, which would have been entitled to exemption under paragraph 1 and points (a) and (b) if it had been made on behalf of another taxable person.

To be noted that even if the UK has become a third country and Northern Ireland is now part of the UK's VAT system, EU VAT rules continue to apply to goods (not services) moving to, from and within Northern Ireland.[241]

240 Before the adoption of Article 45aIR taxable persons were often faced with difficulties to prove the expedition of the goods. See for example Case C-184/05 (*Twoh*), [2007] ECR I-7879.

241 Withdrawal Agreement. Protocol on Ireland/Northern Ireland. In practice the supplier making an exempt intra-CE supply of goods transported to Northern Ireland must ask his customer for a VAT number with a prefix starting with "XI" (and not "UK").

The exemption for intra-Community supplies is one of the ingredients for – sometimes massive – carrousel fraud the EU has to deal with. We explain this further in section 2.12.9.1.

Exemption of intra-Community acquisitions
Article 140 RVD provides that Member States must exempt the following transactions:
(a) the intra-Community acquisition of goods the supply of which by taxable persons would in all circumstances be exempt within their respective territory;
(b) the intra-Community acquisition of goods the importation of which would in all circumstances be exempt under points (a), (b), (c) and (e) to (l) of Article 143;
(c) the intra-Community acquisition of goods where, pursuant the refund Directives (see 2.12.1.1) Directive, referred to in Articles 170 and 171 RVD, the person acquiring the goods would in all circumstances be entitled to full reimbursement of the VAT due.

Article 141 RVD deals with the simplified triangulation (see section 2.7.2 above), providing that each Member State must take specific measures to ensure that VAT is not charged on the intra-Community acquisition of goods within its territory, made in accordance with Article 40 RVD.

2.11.3 Exemptions on Importation

Exemptions applicable to importation include:
a) the final importation of goods the supply of which by a taxable person within the country would (in all circumstances) be exempt (Article 143(1)(a) RVD);
b) the "final importation of goods", covering various situations including the importation of goods by consumers transferring their normal place of residence to the EU or by travellers in their luggage (Article 143(1) (b) and (c) RVD);
c) the importation of goods where the VAT is to be declared via the I-OSS (see section 2.14.6.4) (Article 143(1) (ca) RVD);
d) the importation of goods when the importation is followed by an exempt intra- Community supply by the person that is liable for the import VAT. Several conditions (listed under Article 143(2) RVD) must be satisfied (including the VAT number of the person making the acquisition and the proof of expedition of the goods). This exemption is regularly used by fraudsters.[242] The ECJ confirmed that the exemption cannot be denied to the importer in a situation where there is no evidence to support the conclusion that the importer knew or ought to have known that the supply subsequent to the import entailed tax evasion on the part of those making the intra-Community acquisition;[243]
e) reimportation of goods exempt from customs duties (Article 143(e) RVD);
f) importations under diplomatic or consular arrangements, by the EU or international bodies (Article 143(f) to (i) RVD);
g) importation into ports, by sea fishing companies, of their catches (unprocessed and before their supply) (Article 143(j) RVD);
h) importation of gold by central banks (Article 143(k) RVD);

242 ECA, *Tackling Intra-Community VAT Fraud: More Action Needed*, available at: https://www.eca.europa.eu/Lists/ECADocuments/SR15_24/SR_VAT_FRAUD_EN.pdf.
243 C-531/17 (*Vetsch*), [2019], ECLI:EU:C:2019:114.

i) importation of gas through a natural gas system or connected to such a system, of electricity and or heat or cooling energy through networks (Article 143(1) RVD).

The supply of services in connection with the importation of goods is also exempt, but must be included in the taxable amount (Article 144 RVD).

2.11.4 Exemptions on Exportation

Based on Article 146 RVD, the supply of goods exported from the Community is exempt.[244] The exemption applies on the condition that the traveller is not established within the Community, the goods are transported to a destination outside the Community before the end of the third month following that in which the supply was made, and the total value of the supply, including VAT, is more than the equivalent in national currency of EUR 175 (Article 147 RVD).[245]

According to Article 146(1) (b) RVD, Member States must exempt the supply of goods dispatched or transported to a destination outside the Community by or on behalf of a purchaser not established within the territory of the country, with the exception of goods transported by the purchaser himself for the equipping, fuelling and provisioning of pleasure boats and private aircraft or any other means of transport for private use.

Furthermore, Article 146(1)(c) to (e) RVD exempts respectively the supply of goods to approved bodies which export them out of the Community as part of their humanitarian, charitable or teaching activities outside the Community, the supply of services consisting in work on movable property acquired or imported for the purpose of undergoing such work within the Community, and dispatched or transported out of the Community by the supplier, by the customer if not established within their respective territory or on behalf of either of them, the supply of services, including transport and ancillary transactions, but excluding the supply of services exempt in accordance with Articles 132 and 135, where these are directly connected with the exportation or importation of goods.

2.11.5 Exemptions Related to International Transport

In accordance with Article 148 RVD the Member States must exempt the following transactions:

244 Even when the export is illegal, see Case C-111/92 (*Lange*), [1993] ECR I- 4677.

245 According to the ECJ in Case C-271/06 (*Netto Supermarkt*), [2008] ECR I-771, any sharing of the risk between the supplier and the tax authorities following fraud committed by a third party, must be compatible with the principle of proportionality. That will not be the case if a tax regime imposes the entire responsibility for the payment of VAT on suppliers, regardless of whether or not they were involved in the fraud committed by the purchaser. It would clearly be disproportionate to hold a taxable person liable for the shortfall in tax caused by fraudulent acts of third parties over which he has no influence whatsoever. On the other hand, it is not contrary to EU law to require the supplier to take every step which could reasonably be required of him to satisfy himself that the transaction which he is effecting does not result in his participation in tax evasion. Accordingly, the fact that the supplier acted in good faith, that he took every reasonable measure in his power and that his participation in fraud is excluded are important points in deciding whether that supplier can be obliged to account for the VAT after the event.

(a) the supply of goods for the fuelling and provisioning of vessels used for navigation on the high seas and carrying passengers for reward or used for the purpose of commercial, industrial or fishing activities, or for rescue or assistance at sea, or for inshore fishing, with the exception, in the case of vessels used for inshore fishing, of ships' provisions;[246]
(b) the supply of goods for the fuelling and provisioning of fighting ships, falling within the combined nomenclature (CN) code 8906 10 00, leaving their territory and bound for ports or anchorages outside the Member State concerned;
(c) the supply, modification, repair, maintenance, chartering and hiring of the vessels referred to in point (a), and the supply, hiring, repair and maintenance of equipment, including fishing equipment, incorporated or used therein;[247]
(d) the supply of services other than those referred to in point (c), to meet the direct needs of the vessels referred to in point (a) or of their cargoes;
(e) the supply of goods for the fuelling and provisioning of aircraft used by airlines operating for reward chiefly on international routes;[248]
(f) the supply, modification, repair, maintenance, chartering and hiring of the aircraft referred to in point (e), and the supply, hiring, repair and maintenance of equipment incorporated or used therein;
(g) the supply of services, other than those referred to in point (f), to meet the direct needs of the aircraft referred to in point (e) or of their cargoes.

2.11.6 *Exemptions Relating to Certain Transactions Treated as Exports*

Article 151 RVD provides for an exemption of the supply of goods or services under diplomatic and consular arrangements, to international bodies recognised as such by the public authorities of the host Member State, and to members of such bodies, within the limits and under the conditions laid down by the international conventions establishing the bodies or by headquarters agreements.

2.11.7 *Exemptions for the Supply of Services by Intermediaries*

Under a separate heading, Article 153 RVD provides for the exemption of the supply of services by intermediaries, acting in the name and on behalf of another person, where they take part in the transactions referred to under exemptions of exportation, exemptions related to international transport and exemptions relating to certain transactions treated as exports or of transactions carried out outside the Community. The exemption does not apply to travel agents who, in the name and on behalf of travelers, supply services which are carried out in other Member States.

246 See Case C-185/89 (*Velker*), [1990] ECR I-2561, on (according to the ECJ not exempt) supplies effected at previous stages in the commercial chain on condition that the goods are ultimately used for the fuelling and provisioning of vessels.
247 See Joined Cases C-181/04, C-182/04 and C-183/04 (*Elmeka*), [2006] ECR I- 8167.
248 Case C-382/02 (*Cimber Air A/S*), [2004] ECR I-8379.

2.11.8 Exemptions for Transactions Relating to International Trade

Articles 154 to 163 RVD deal with customs warehouses,[249] warehouses other than customs warehouses and similar arrangements and Articles 164 and 165 RVD with transactions exempt with a view to export and in the framework of trade between the Member States. "Warehouses other than customs warehouses", in the case of products subject to excise duty, mean the places defined as tax warehouses by Article 4(11) of Directive 2008/118/EC[250] and, in the case of products not subject to excise duty, means the places defined as such by the Member States (Article 154 RVD).

Article 155 RVD provides that Member States may, after consulting the VAT Committee (see section 2.16.2), take special measures designed to exempt all or some of the transactions referred to in Articles 154 to 163 RVD, provided that those measures are not aimed at final use or consumption and that the amount of VAT due on cessation of the arrangements or situations referred to in Articles 154 to 163 corresponds to the amount of tax which would have been due had each of those transactions been taxed within their territory.[251]

Member States may exempt the following transactions, see Article 156(1) RVD (and the supply of services relating to the supply of goods, see Article 159 RVD):
(a) the supply of goods which are intended to be presented to customs and, where applicable, placed in temporary storage (see Chapter 1, section 1.5.1.4. above);
(b) the supply of goods which are intended to be placed in a free zone or in a free warehouse (see Chapter 1 section 1.4.1.3. above);
(c) the supply of goods which are intended to be placed under customs warehousing arrangements (see Chapter 1 section 1.4.1.3. above) or inward processing arrangements (see Chapter 1 section 1.4.4.5. above);
(d) the supply of goods which are intended to be admitted into territorial waters in order to be incorporated into drilling or production platforms, for purposes of the construction, repair, maintenance, alteration or fitting-out of such platforms, or to link such drilling or production platforms to the mainland;
(e) the supply of goods which are intended to be admitted into territorial waters for the fuelling and provisioning of drilling or production platforms.

Article 160 RVD provides that Member States may exempt the supply of goods or services carried out in the locations referred to in Article 156(1) RVD, where one of the situations specified therein still applies within their territory.

Furthermore, Member States may exempt the importation of goods which are intended to be placed under warehousing arrangements other than customs warehousing and the supply of goods as well as the supply of services relating to the supply of goods which are intended to be placed, within their territory, under warehousing arrangements other than customs warehousing (Articles 157, 159 and 160 RVD). However, Member States may not provide for warehousing arrangements other than customs warehousing for goods

249 With regard to cross-border warehouses see section 1.5.4.3 above.
250 New article 3(11) of Recast General Arrangement Directive (see Chapter 3.2).
251 See on this provision Case C-305/03 (*Commission v. UK*), [2006] ECR I-1213.

which are not subject to excise duty where those goods are intended to be supplied at the retail stage. By way of derogation from this prohibition, according to Article 158, Member States may provide for warehousing arrangements other than customs warehousing in the following cases:

(a) where the goods are intended for tax-free shops, for the purposes of the supply of goods to be carried in the personal luggage of travellers taking flights or sea crossings to third territories or third countries, where that (export) supply is exempt pursuant to point (b) of Article 146(1) RVD, see section 2.11.4 above;
(b) where the goods are intended for taxable persons, for the purposes of carrying out supplies to travellers on board an aircraft or a ship in the course of a flight or sea crossing where the place of arrival is situated outside the Community;
(c) where the goods are intended for taxable persons, for the purposes of carrying out supplies to diplomats and NATO forces which are exempt from VAT pursuant to Article 151; see section 2.11.6 below.

Where Member States exercise the option of an exemption in respect of transactions effected in customs warehouses, they must take the measures necessary to provide for warehousing arrangements other than customs warehousing under which the exemption may be applied to the same transactions when they concern goods listed in Annex V and are carried out in warehouses other than customs warehouses. These goods are: tin, copper, zinc, nickel, aluminium, lead, indium, cereals, certain oil seeds and nuts, grains and seeds, coffee not roasted, tea, cocoa beans, raw sugar, rubber, wool, chemicals in bulk, mineral oils, silver, platinum, potatoes and certain vegetable oils and fats. It should be noted that gold is not included in the Annex.

Article 161 RVD allows Member States to exempt the supply of imported goods (and of services relating thereto) while they remain covered by arrangements for temporary importation with total exemption from import duty or by external transit arrangements and the supply of goods coming from a third territory (and of services relating thereto) covered by the internal Community transit procedure (see Chapter 1, section 1.5.4.2). It should be noted that in case a Member States has refrained from implementing this exemption the supply of those goods while located in that territory even if they are under those customs arrangements.[252] It should also be noted that if a Member State has implemented the exemption there may still be obligations to file VAT returns to report the exempt supply.

The supplies of goods which are intended to be placed, within the territory of another Member State, under other warehousing arrangements follow, in principle, the rules on intra-Community supplies. This seems to be correct from the perspective of a Member State which does not apply warehousing arrangements other than customs warehousing. However, when the goods arrive in a Member State which applies the other warehouse arrangements, the intra-Community acquisition would result in a treatment different from an (exempt) domestic supply of goods intended to be placed under the warehousing arrangements. Therefore, Article 162 RVD provides that the intra-Community acquisition should benefit from the same treatment as the domestic supply.

252 Case C-165/11 (*Profitube*), ECLI:EU:C:2012:692.

Finally, Article 163 RVD provides that if the goods cease to be covered by the arrangements or situations referred to above, thus giving rise to importation, the Member State of importation must take the measures necessary to prevent double taxation.

The following provision in Article 164 RVD presumably aims at preventing taxable persons from being permanently in a refund position. Member States may, after consulting the VAT Committee (see section 2.16.2), exempt intra-Community acquisitions of goods made by the taxable person, and imports for and supplies of goods to the taxable person, with a view to their exportation from the Community as they are or after processing and supplies of services linked with the export business of the taxable person carried out by, or intended for, a taxable person up to an amount equal to the value of the exports carried out by that person during the preceding 12 months. Where Member States exercise the option of this exemption regarding exportation they must, also after consulting the VAT Committee, apply that exemption to transactions relating to exempt intra-Community supplies (Article 138 RVD) carried out by the taxable person, up to an amount equal to the value of the supplies carried out by that person, in accordance with the same conditions, during the preceding 12 months.

2.12 Deductions

2.12.1 Preliminary remarks

VAT as a neutral tax

The essence of the European VAT is the deduction of input tax by non- consumers. Under the RVD a taxable person has the right to deduct from the tax for which he is liable in respect of his supplies, the tax invoiced to him on goods or services supplied to him, or (intra-Community) acquired or imported by him (Article 168 RVD; see also Article 1(2) RVD outlining the key features of the EU VAT system as discussed in Section 2.2 above). This right arises at the moment when the deductible tax becomes chargeable (Article 167 RVD, see section 2.8 above). Member States may, however, decide that the excess must be carried forward to the following tax period when deductions exceed the amount due (Article 183 RVD).[253]

Private and mixed use

The right to deduction or refund of the VAT is restricted to goods and services used for the purposes of taxable transactions (Article 168 RVD), including taxable transactions in another country, if the transactions would be eligible for deduction of tax had they occurred in the territory of the home country (Article 169 RVD). Accordingly, no deduction is permitted for goods and services used for exempt transactions based on Article 132 RVD or for non-business purposes. A trader who uses goods and services supplied for both taxed transactions and for exempt purposes may consequently deduct only the (proportion of the) tax that is attributable to the former transactions (Article 173 RVD).

253 See Case C-107/10 (*Enel Maritsa Iztok*), [2011] ECR I- 03873.

The RVD provides for apportionment methods (the so-called "pro-rata calculation") to determine the deductible proportion (Article 174 RVD). The main rule is that the deductible proportion is made up of a fraction having as numerator the total amount of turnover, exclusive of VAT, attributable to transactions in respect of which VAT is deductible, and as denominator the total amount of turnover, exclusive of VAT, per year. If a taxable person uses goods or services both for his business (economic) activities and for non-business (non-economic) activities he can deduct the VAT to the extent that he uses the goods and services for business purposes (note that VAT deduction for business purposes may be limited because of the use for exempt supplies). The ECJ noted that the RVD does not include rules relating to the methods or criteria which the Member States are required to apply when adopting provisions permitting the apportionment of input VAT paid according to whether the relevant expenditure relates to economic activities or to non-economic activities. According to the ECJ, in those circumstances, and so that taxpayers can make the necessary calculations, it is for the Member States to establish methods and criteria appropriate to that aim and consistent with the principles underlying the common system of VAT. The ECJ referred to the *Wollny* case in which it held that, where the RVD does not contain the guidance necessary for such precise calculations, the Member States are required to exercise that power, having regard to the aims and broad logic of the RVD. In particular, the measures which the Member States are required to adopt in that regard must comply with the principle of fiscal neutrality on which the common system of VAT is based. Accordingly, the Member States must exercise their discretion in such a way as to ensure that deduction is made only for that part of the VAT proportional to the amount relating to transactions giving rise to the right to deduct. They must therefore ensure that the calculation of the proportion of economic activities to non-economic activities objectively reflects the part of the input expenditure actually to be attributed, respectively, to those two types of activity and, on that basis, provide for a method of calculation which objectively reflects the part of the input expenditure actually to be attributed, respectively, to those two types of activity. The ECJ added to this that, when exercising that discretion, the Member States have the right to apply, as necessary,

- an investment formula or
- a transaction formula or
- any other appropriate formula,

without being required to restrict themselves to only one of those methods.[254] In case specific rules for this calculation are absent in a Member States' VAT legislation a full deduction of VAT is not allowed. According to the ECJ, the lack of technical rules in the applicable tax legislation that are ancillary to an essential element of the tax does not inherently constitute a breach of the principle of fiscal legality as a general principle of EU law.[255]

Furthermore, the RVD provides various rules governing the right to deduct, such as the holding of an invoice drawn up in accordance with the applicable rules or the holding of an import document (Article 178(e) RVD).

254 Case C-437/06 *(Securenta)*, [2008] ECR I-01597.
255 Case C-566/17 (*Zwifzek Gmin Zagáybia Miedziowego w Polkowicach)*, ECLI: EU:C:2019:390.

Refunds

The Thirteenth Directive and Directive 2008/9/EC are based on Article 171 RVD. Based on these Directives taxable persons established in another Member State (Directive 2008/9/EC) or established outside the Community (Thirteenth Directive)[256] are entitled to a refund of VAT. Taxable persons are not entitled to such a refund when they perform taxable activities within a territory for which they have to register. When they have to register and report the (output) VAT on a periodical return, the (input) VAT can be deducted from the VAT due. VAT is not refunded to taxable persons who perform in the Member State of establishment exclusively exempt transactions.[257]

Is VAT really neutral?

Judgments by the ECJ on the subject of taxable status (non-taxable status of holding companies and the distinction between the economic activity involved in portfolio management on behalf of a third party and management by a company of its own "private" portfolio)[258] have the effect of reducing the scope of the concept of economic activity and consequently the scope of the VAT, and this is inevitably leading to distortions of competition. All these ECJ judgments hinge on whether certain financial transactions (collection of dividends arising from financial holdings, issue of shares or securing of a bank loan with a view to raising extra capital for a company, transfer of shares, investment of surplus cash by a taxable person, sale of company's securities on the stock exchange, etc.) are deemed to fall outside the scope of the tax or are regarded as falling within the scope of the tax, but exempt.

It follows that the provisions of the VAT Directive currently in force do not always ensure that the system of taxation is sufficiently neutral. In the *BLP* case, for example, the ECJ explicitly stated that if, instead of raising extra capital by selling shares, BLP had taken out a bank loan, the VAT charged on the services of a financial adviser consulted for the purposes of concluding the loan would have been fully deductible, while VAT on the advisory services regarding the sale of shares was not deductible.[259] The result is that different methods of financing a company's activities lead to different tax treatment, which is in complete contradiction with the principle of neutrality which the tax should observe.

The rules on deduction are discussed in more detail below.

---

256 See Case C-73/06 (*Planzer*) [2007] ECR I-05655. The term business for the purposes of Article 1(1) of the Thirteenth Directive refers to the place where the essential decisions concerning the general management of that company are adopted and where the functions of its central administration are carried out. Case C-582/08 (*Commission v United Kingdom of Great Britain and Northern Ireland*), [2010] ECR I- 07195, concerns the right of persons established outside the EU, providing financial and insurance services to customers who are likewise outside the EU, to deduct or refund input VAT on goods and services obtained in the EU. The UK submitted that its legislation complies with the express wording of Article 2(1) of the Thirteenth VAT Directive, and that it has therefore not infringed EU law. The Court of Justice dismissed the action.

257 Case C-302/93 (*Debouche*), [1996] ECR I-4495. With regard to partial exemption in the Member State of establishment, see Case C-136/99 (*Societé Monte Dei Paschi Di Siena*), [2000] ECR I-6109.

258 See Cases C-60/90 (*Polysar*), [1991] ECR I-3111, C-142/99 (*Floridienne SA en Berginvest SA*), [2000] ECR I-9567, C-102/00 (*Welthgrove*), [2001] ECR I-5679 and C- 16/00 (*Cibo*), [2001] ECR I-6663.

259 Case C-4/94 (*BLP*), [1995] ECR I-0983.

2.12.2 Origin and Scope of Right of Deduction

Under the Title "Origin and Scope of the Right of Deduction", Article 167 RVD provides in the first place that the right to deduct arises at the time when the deductible tax becomes chargeable. We refer to section 2.8 with regard to the chargeability of VAT.

Article 168(a) RVD provides that in so far as the goods and services are used for the purposes of the taxed transactions[260] of a taxable person, the taxable person is entitled, in the Member State in which he carries out these transactions, to deduct from the VAT which he is liable to pay the VAT due or paid in that Member State in respect of supplies to him of goods or services, carried out or to be carried out by another taxable person. The deductible VAT referred to in this provision is not only the VAT charged (invoiced) by the supplier but also VAT which the taxable person entitled to deduction is obliged to pay based on the reverse charge mechanism. With regard to the rules governing the exercise of the right of deduction, see section 2.12.5 below.

Article 168(b) RVD provides that, in so far as the goods and services are used for the purposes of the taxed transactions of a taxable person, the taxable person is entitled, in the Member State in which he carries out these transactions, to deduct from the VAT which he is liable to pay the VAT due in respect of transactions treated as supplies of goods or services pursuant to Articles 18(a) and 27. Articles 18 (a) and 27 RVD refer to so-called internal supplies. Member States may deem the application of goods or services internally produced as a taxable supply when the taxable person cannot or cannot fully deduct the VAT if he would have purchased the goods or services from a third party. By treating this application as a taxable supply, distortion of competition can be prevented since from a VAT perspective it would have been cheaper, for example, to purchase materials and to produce or manufacture a final product, since only VAT on the materials is not deductible while the labour element escapes VAT. Where a Member State applies these rules the VAT on the materials is deductible, based on Article 168(a), because the materials are used for the purposes of his taxed transactions, *i.e.* an internal supply. Article 168 (b) covers the situation in which the taxable person is partially entitled to deduction.

Article 168(c) RVD provides that in so far as the goods and services are used for the purposes of the taxed transactions of a taxable person, the taxable person is entitled, in the Member State in which he carries out these transactions, to deduct from the VAT which he is liable to pay the VAT due in respect of intra-Community acquisitions of goods pursuant to Article 2(1)(b)(i). Since the VAT due is also deductible, *i.e.* it need not to have been paid in order to be deductible the VAT due *and* deductible can be mentioned on the same VAT return. In case a taxable person makes an intra-Community acquisition of goods under Article 41 RVD (*i.e.* he acquires the goods using a VAT identification number granted to him by an EU Member State other than the EU Member State of arrival of the goods) he

260 According to AG Jacobs in Case C-408/98 (*Abbey National*), ECLI:EU: C:2000:207 what matters is whether the taxed input is a cost component of a taxable output, not whether the most-closely linked transaction is itself taxable. The question to be asked is not what is the transaction with which the cost component has the most direct and immediate link but whether there is a sufficiently direct and immediate link with a taxable economic activity.

is not allowed to deduct the VAT. Instead, the taxable amount must be reduced when the taxable person can duly prove that he has reported the intra-Community acquisition in the EU Member State of arrival (see also section 2.7.2).[261]

Article 168(d) RVD provides that, in so far as the goods and services are used for the purposes of the taxed transactions of a taxable person, the taxable person is entitled, in the Member State in which he carries out these transactions, to deduct from the VAT which he is liable to pay the VAT due in respect of transactions treated as intra-Community acquisitions in accordance with Articles 21 and 22, *i.e.* the deemed intra-Community acquisitions.

Article 168(e) RVD provides that in so far as the goods and services are used for the purposes of the taxed transactions of a taxable person, the taxable person is entitled, in the Member State in which he carries out these transactions, to deduct from the VAT which he is liable to pay the VAT due or paid in respect of the importation of goods into that Member State. He must hold an import document specifying him as consignee or importer and stating or permitting the calculation of the amount of tax due. (See section 2.13.3 below.) Import VAT cannot be deducted by a carrier that is neither the importer nor the owner of the goods unless value of the imported goods is incorporated either in the cost of particular output transactions or in the cost of goods or services supplied by the taxable person as part of his economic activities.[262]

Article 169 RVD provides that in addition Member States must grant every taxable person the right to the deduction of the VAT referred to in Article 168 in so far as the goods and services are used for the purposes to be mentioned below. It should be noted that Article 169 RVD no longer refers to the right of deduction *or refund*, as Article 17(3) of the Sixth Directive did.

Article 169(a) RVD provides that a taxable person has the right to the deduction of VAT in so far as the goods and services are used for the purposes of transactions relating to the (economic) activities referred to in the second subparagraph of Article 9(1) RVD, carried out outside the Member State in which that tax is due or paid, in respect of which VAT would be deductible if they had been carried out within that Member State.

Article 169(b) RVD provides that a taxable person has the right to the deduction or refund of VAT in so far as the goods and services are used for the purposes of transactions which are exempt pursuant to Articles 138, 142, 144, Articles 146 to 149, Articles 151, 152, 153 or 156, Article 157(1)(b), Articles 158 to 161 or Article 164 RVD, dealing respectively with exemptions related to the intra-Community supply of goods, exemptions for certain transport services, exemptions on importation, exemptions related to international transport, exemptions relating to certain transactions treated as exports, exemptions for the supply of services by intermediaries and exemptions for transactions relating to international trade. All these supplies have in common that they are exempt with the right to deduction, often referred to as zero-rated.

261 Cases C-536/08 and C-539/08 (X and Facet), [2010] ECR I-03581.
262 Case C-187/14 *(DSV Road)*, ECLI:EU:C:2015:421.

Article 169(c) RVD provides that a taxable person has the right to the deduction or refund of VAT in so far as the goods and services are used for the purposes of any of the transactions exempt pursuant points (a) to (f) of Article 135(1) RVD, where the customer is established outside the Community or where those transactions relate directly to goods to be exported out of the Community. (It should be noted that the place of supply of these services when supplied to taxable persons or to non- taxable persons outside the Community is where the recipient is established – see Articles 44 and 59(1)(e) RVD. Under Article 168(a) RVD, the input tax regarding these activities would not have been deductible or refundable because such supplies are exempt (without the right to deduction) if rendered within a Member State.)

It must be derived, *a contrario*, from Articles 168 to 170 RVD that no deduction is allowed when exempt activities are performed. When determining whether VAT can be deducted a direct and immediate link between the costs and either particular output transactions or a direct and immediate link with the economic activity of the taxable person as a whole must be established. In case of a direct and immediate link between costs and a particular output transaction the full amount of VAT can be deducted in case that transaction gives rise to a right to deduct VAT. Instead, if the particular output transaction does not give rise to a right to deduct VAT, the VAT cannot be deducted at all. In case a direct and immediate link can be established between the costs and the economic activity of the taxable person as a whole a proportional deduction applies (section 2.12.4). The criterion of the direct and immediate link was addressed by the ECJ in the ***Midland Bank*** case.[263] Midland Bank is the representative of a group of companies, including the merchant bank Samuel Montagu, which supplies both taxed and exempt services. In 1987 Samuel Montagu had acted as a merchant bank for Quadrex, a US company. Because of a failed acquisition of shares a series of legal proceedings was started where Samual Montagu was sued for damages. The solicitors Clifford Chance supplied legal services to Samuel Montagu and were entrusted with all the work connected with this dispute and the litigation arising from it. Clifford Chance invoiced Samuel Montagu for its fees for 1988 to 1995. Midland claimed the right to deduct the entire amount of VAT paid on the legal fees invoiced by the solicitors. The ECJ observes that the right to deduct the VAT charged on goods or services presupposes that the expenditure incurred in obtaining them was part of the cost components of the taxable transactions. Such expenditure must therefore be part of the costs of the output transactions which utilise the goods and services acquired. That is why those cost components must generally have arisen before the taxable person carried out the taxable transactions to which they relate. Although the expenditure incurred in order to obtain the legal services is the consequence of the output transaction (the services provided as a merchant bank for Quadrex), it is not generally part of the cost components of the output transaction. Such services do therefore not have any direct and immediate link with the output transaction. On the other hand, the costs of those services are part of the taxable person's general costs and are, as such, components of the price of an undertaking's products. Such services therefore do have a direct and immediate link with the taxable person's business as a whole, so that VAT is, deductible only in part. It should be noted that the ECJ is not always consistent in labelling costs as direct costs (linked to a particular

263 Case C-98/98 (*Midland Bank*), [2000] ECR I-04177.

output transaction) or general costs (linked to the business as a whole) using the criterion of whether the goods and services purchased are cost components. For comparison we refer to the *Volkswagen Financial Services* case[264] and *University of Cambridge* case.[265]

The ECJ has in a number of cases ruled on the deduction of VAT in a situation where a third party benefits from costs made. In the *Iberdrola* case[266] Iberdrola purchased several parcels of land in a holiday village in order to construct buildings containing approximately 300 apartments for seasonal use. Iberdrola entered into a contract with the municipality of Tsarevo for the reconstruction of a pump station owned by the municipality by means of construction or improvement works on that pump station and commissioned those works from a third party company. Following completion of the works, the buildings which Iberdrola planned to construct in the holiday village could be connected to the pump station. The costs indicated on the invoice for the reconstruction of the pump station were listed in Iberdrola's accounts as "deferred expenditure", as expenditure for the acquisition of tangible fixed assets, and in its profit and loss account as stocks for 2009 and 2010. According to the expert, there is a link between the supplies indicated on the invoice and the goods and services which Iberdrola must supply after the construction of the authorized buildings on its parcels of land. The Bulgarian tax authority took the view that Iberdrola could not deduct input VAT. According to the ECJ in the appraisal of the question as to whether, in circumstances such as those at issue in these proceedings, Iberdrola has the right to deduct input VAT for the reconstruction of the waste-water pump station, it is necessary to determine whether there is a direct and immediate link between, on the one hand, that reconstruction service and, on the other hand, a taxed output transaction by Iberdrola or that undertaking's economic activity. It is clear from the order for reference that, without the reconstruction of that pump station, it would have been impossible to connect the buildings which Iberdrola planned to build to that pump station, with the result that that reconstruction was essential for completing that project and that, consequently, in the absence of such reconstruction, Iberdrola would not have been able to carry out its economic activity. The fact that the municipality of Tsarevo also benefits from the construction service cannot justify the right to deduct corresponding to that service being denied to Iberdrola if the existence of such a direct and immediate link is established. By contrast, if the reconstruction works relating to that pump station exceeded the needs created solely by the buildings constructed by Iberdrola, the existence of a direct and immediate link between that service and the taxed output transaction by Iberdrola, consisting of the construction of those buildings, would be partially broken and a right to deduct would thus have to be recognised in respect of Iberdrola only for the input VAT levied on the part of the costs incurred for the reconstruction of the pump station which was objectively necessary to allow Iberdrola to carry out its taxed transactions. The ECJ repeated these observations in the *Middeldeutsche Hartstein-Industrie* case[267] adding that there is no supply against a benefit in kind (i.e. the granting of permits) or a deemed supply either, under the circumstances in that case (i.e. the extension of a municipal road

264 Case C-153/17, ECLI:EU:C:2018:845.

265 Case C-316/18, ECLI:EU:C:2019:559. Other approaches can also be found in case C-435/05 (*Investrand*), [2007] ECR I-01315 and C-104/12 (*Wolfram Becker*), ECLI:EU:C:2013:99.

266 Case C-132/16, ECLI:EU:C:2017:683.

267 Case C-528/19, ECLI:EU:C:2020:712.

for the exploitation of a limestone quarry). In the *Vos Aannemingen* case[268] the ECJ however observed that in a situation where a taxable person made costs for the sale of both the land (owned by a third party) and a building upon that land, the VAT could only be deducted to the extent the costs were linked to the sale of the building. It should be observed though that in this particular case the ECJ based its judgement on the hypothesis of the referring judge that the costs do not form part of general overheads but are attributable to particular output transactions, some of which are carried out by the taxable person and others by a third party. The ECJ also ruled that the fact that it is possible for the taxable person to pass on to the third party a part of the expenditure so incurred constitutes one of the elements, along with all of the other circumstances in which the transactions concerned occurred, which the referring court must consider for the purposes of determining the scope of the taxable person's right to deduct value added tax.

2.12.3 Refunds

Articles 170 and 171 RVD provide for the refund to taxable persons of VAT on goods and services purchased in a Member State where they are not established or on import goods into such a Member State.

VAT must be refunded to taxable persons who are not established within the territory of the country but who are established in another Member State in accordance with the detailed implementing rules laid down in Directive 2008/9/ EC laying down detailed rules for the refund of value added tax, provided for in Directive 2006/112/EC, to taxable persons not established in the Member State of refund but established in another Member State. From 1 January 2010, the Eighth Directive procedure for reimbursement of VAT incurred by EU businesses in Member States where they are not established is a fully electronic procedure. Businesses will be paid interest if Member States are late making refunds.

The refund of VAT to taxable persons who are not established in the territory of the Community must be effected in accordance with the detailed implementing rules laid down in Directive 86/560/EEC, *i.e.* the Thirteenth Directive.[269]

The taxable persons referred to in Article 1 of the Directive 2008/9/EC or of the Thirteenth Directive are also considered for the purposes of applying Directive 2008/9/EC or the Thirteenth Directive as taxable persons who are not established in the country when, inside the territory of the country, they have only carried out supplies of goods and services to a person who has been designated as the person liable to pay the tax in accordance with Article 194, 195, 196, 197 or 199, *i.e.* when the reverse charge applies or must be applied. Directive 2008/9/EC or the Thirteenth Directive do not apply to intra-Community supplies

268 Case C-405/19 (*Vos Aannemingen*), ECLI:EU:C:2020:785.

269 In Case C-335/05 (*Rizeni Letoveho Provozu UR SP*), [2007] ECR I-4307, the ECJ held Article 2(2) of the Thirteenth Directive allowing Member States to make the refunds conditional upon the granting by third states of comparable advantages regarding turnover taxes must be interpreted as meaning that the "third States" referred to in that provision include all third states and that that provision is without prejudice to the ability and the responsibility of the Member States to comply with their obligations under international agreements such as the General Agreement on Trade in Services.

of goods which are, or may be, exempt under Article 138 RVD when the goods supplied are dispatched or transported by the acquirer or for his account, neither to export supplies when the goods supplied are dispatched or transported by the exporter or for his account. In other words, when the taxable person makes an intra-Community supply, or should have made one or when the taxable person makes an export supply, or should have made one, Directive 2008/9/EC or the Thirteenth Directive do not apply, but the VAT incurred on the purchase should be deducted or refunded based on the VAT returns which the taxable person should submit.[270] In case a taxable person reports VAT on B2C-services or distance sales under the One Stop Shop System (see section 2.14.6.2-2.14.6.4) it cannot deduct VAT in VAT returns filed under that system. While that taxable person needs to report VAT on supplies in other EU Member States it is still eligible for a refund request under Directive 2008/9/EC or the Thirteenth Directive.

Article 172 RVD deals with the refund regarding the occasional intra-Community supply of new means of transport (section 2.6.6), providing that any person who is regarded as a taxable person by reason of the fact that he makes an exempt intra- Community supply, on an occasional basis, of a new means of transport (that is in accordance with the conditions specified in Article 138(1) and (2)(a) RVD) is entitled, in the Member State in which the supply takes place, to deduct the VAT included in the purchase price or paid in respect of the importation or the intra-Community acquisition of this means of transport, up to an amount not exceeding the amount of VAT for which he would be liable if the supply were not exempt. A right of deduction arises and may be exercised only at the time of supply of the new means of transport.

Article 171a RVD provides that Member States may, instead of granting a refund of VAT pursuant to the Thirteenth Directive or Directive 2008/9/ EC on those supplies of goods or services to a taxable person in respect of which the taxable person is liable to pay the tax based on the reverse charge (in accordance with Articles 194 to 197 or Article 199 RVD), allow deduction of this tax pursuant to the procedure laid down in Article 168 RVD. The existing restrictions pursuant to Article 2(2), *i.e.* reciprocity, and Article 4(2) of the Thirteenth Directive, *i.e.* exclusion of certain expenditure or the making of refunds subject to additional conditions, may be retained. To that end, Member States may exclude the taxable person who is liable to pay the tax from the refund procedure pursuant to the Thirteenth Directives or Directive 2008/9/EC.

Presumably, this provision is to prevent the rare situation in which the VAT which the taxable person became liable to pay based on the reverse charge mechanism in another Member State than where he has the seat of his economic activity will be subject to the

270 This provision, presumably, prevents over-the-counter sales to disappear in the "grey circuit" in another Member State, while nevertheless a refund is claimed in the Member State of purchase.

refund procedure,[271] instead deduction may be allowed (by that other Member State) based on Article 168 RVD, *i.e.* the refundable VAT can be claimed in a regular VAT return rather than via the refund procedure for a non-established person. Once the right has been granted to deduct the VAT based on the normal procedure (*i.e.* via a VAT return rather than an electronic request for a refund) Member States may exclude the taxable person from the refund procedure altogether.

2.12.4 *Proportional Deduction*

According to Article 173 RVD, in the case of goods or services used by a taxable person both for transactions in respect of which VAT is deductible pursuant to Articles 168, 169 and 170 RVD, and for transactions in respect of which VAT is not deductible, only such proportion of the VAT that can be apportioned to the former transactions shall be deductible. This proportion must be determined, in accordance with Articles 174 and 175 RVD, for all the transactions carried out by the taxable person.

Article 174 RVD provides that the deductible proportion must be made up of a fraction comprising the following amounts:
(a) as numerator, the total amount, exclusive of VAT, of turnover per year attributable to transactions in respect of which VAT is deductible pursuant to Articles 168 and 169;
(b) as denominator, the total amount, exclusive of VAT, of turnover per year attributable to transactions included in the numerator and to transactions in respect of which VAT is not deductible.

By way of derogation from the provisions above, there must be excluded from the calculation of the deductible proportion, the amount of turnover attributable to supplies of capital goods used by the taxable person for the purposes of his business, the amount of turnover attributable to incidental real estate and financial transactions and the amount of turnover attributable to the financial transactions specified in points (b) to (g) of Article 135(1) RVD in so far as those transactions are incidental.[272] Where Member States exercise the option under Article 191 RVD not to require adjustment in respect of capital goods they may include disposals of capital goods in the calculation of the deductible proportion. The Member States may also include in the denominator the amount of subsidies, other than those specified in Article 73 RVD. In our view this provision does not make sense in a VAT.

271 For example a taxable person established in Member State A receives services for its fixed establishment (see the second sentence in Article 44: "However, if those services are provided to a fixed establishment of the taxable person in a place other than the place where he has established his business, the place of supply of those services shall be the place where the fixed establishment is located") in Member State B, where the services supplied by the fixed establishment are subject to the reverse charge *e.g.* based on Article 196 RVD. Article 3 of Directive 2008/9/EC stipulates that Directive 2008/9/EC shall apply to any taxable person not established in the Member State of refund who meets, inter alia, the condition that during the refund period, he has not supplied any goods or services deemed to have been supplied in the Member State of refund, with the exception of the supply of goods and services to a person who is liable for payment of VAT, *i.e.* the reverse charge mechanism, in accordance with Articles 194 to 197 and Article 199 RVD.

272 On this provision, see CJEU 8 July 2021, C-695/19 (*Radio Popular*), ECLI: EU:C:2021:549.

Article 173(2) RVD provides that Member States may take the following measures as regards the deductible proportion and deviating from Article 173 (1) RVD:

(a) authorise the taxable person to determine a proportion for each sector of his business, provided that separate accounts are kept for each sector;
(b) require the taxable person to determine a proportion for each sector of his business and to keep separate accounts for each sector;[273]
(c) authorise or require the taxable person to make the deduction on the basis of the use made of all or part of the goods and services;
(d) authorise or require the taxable person to make the deduction in accordance with the rule laid down in the first subparagraph of paragraph 1, in respect of all goods and services used for all transactions referred to therein;
(e) provide that, where the VAT which is not deductible by the taxable person is insignificant, it is to be treated as nil.

EU Member States are allowed to apply for the purposes of calculating the proportion of input value added tax deductible for a given operation, such as the construction of a mixed-use building, to give precedence, as the key to allocation, to an allocation key other than that based on turnover, on the condition that the method used guarantees a more precise determination of the deductible proportion.[274] The method however need not be the most precise possible.[275]

According to Article 175 RVD, the proportion must be determined on an annual basis, fixed as a percentage and rounded up to a figure not exceeding the next unit. The provisional proportion for a year must be that calculated on the basis of the preceding year's transactions. In the absence of any such transactions to refer to, or where they were insignificant in amount, the deductible proportion must be estimated provisionally, under supervision of the tax authorities, by the taxable person from his own forecasts.[276]

Deductions made on the basis of such provisional proportion must be adjusted (*i. e.* recalculated) when the final proportion is fixed during the next year (see section 2.12.6).

As regards the situation of a head office and a fixed establishment established in two different EU Member States it must be noted that when costs are incurred by the fixed establishment while a direct and immediate link can be established between the costs and the economic activity of the head office as a whole the VAT is only deductible to the extent the activities of the head office give rise to a right to deduct VAT both from the perspective of the VAT legislation of the EU Member State of the head office and the VAT legislation of the EU Member State of the fixed establishment (double test). In case there is a direct and immediate link between the costs and the economic activities of both the

273 In the case of sectorial allocation Article 175(1) RVD) does not permit Member States to require that the proportion deductible be rounded up to a figure other than the next highest whole number where that proportion is determined in accordance with Article 173(2) of the Directive. Case C-488/07 (*Royal Bank of Scotland Group*), [2008] ECR I-10409.

274 Case C-511/10 (*BLC Baumarkt*), ECLI:EU:C:2012:689.

275 Case C-332/14 (*Wolfgang und Dr. Wilfried Rey Grundstücksgemeinschaft GbR*), ECLI:EU:C:2016:417.

276 However, Member States may retain their rules in force at 1 January 1979 or, in the case of the Member States which acceded to the Community after that date, at the date of their accession.

head office and fixed establishment the deductible proportion must be calculated taking into account the turnover of both the head office and the fixed establishment, where the turnover of the head office is only taken into account in the numerator in so far the turnover gives rise to a right to deduct VAT pursuant to the VAT legislation of both the EU Member State of the head office and the fixed establishment (double test).[277] In a situation where no direct and immediate link between costs made by a French head office and its foreign (EU and non-EU) fixed establishments could be established the ECJ ruled that the VAT was deductible only to the extent the turnover of the French head office gave rise to a right to deduct VAT.[278]

2.12.5 Rules Governing the Exercise of the Right of Deduction

Articles 178 to 180 RVD identify the rules governing the exercise of the right to deduct.

As we have seen in section 2.12.1 above, according to Article 168(a) RVD, in so far as the goods and services are used for the purposes of the taxed transactions of a taxable person, the taxable person is entitled, in the Member State in which he carries out these transactions, to deduct from the VAT which he is liable to pay the VAT due or paid in that Member State in respect of supplies to him of goods or services, carried out or to be carried out by another taxable person. To exercise his right of deduction, the taxable person must, according to Article 178(a), hold an invoice[279] drawn up in accordance with Articles 220 to 236 and Articles 238, 239 and 240 RVD (see section 2.13.8 below). From the *Senatex*[280] and *Barlis 06* case[281] however it becomes clear that the neutrality of VAT requires deduction of input VAT to be allowed if the substantive requirements are satisfied, even if the taxable persons have failed to comply with some formal conditions. Accordingly, in case of an invoice that is not complying with all invoice requirements VAT can still be deducted. A taxable person can substantiate with additional information that the substantive conditions for VAT deduction are met. In *Vfdan*[282] the ECJ even ruled that VAT can be deducted without an invoice when the taxable person can demonstrate his right to deduct VAT with other evidence of the amount of input VAT he has paid.

To exercise his right of deduction, the taxable person must, according to Article 178(f) RVD, when he is required to pay the tax as a customer or purchaser where the reverse charge applies (*i.e.* where Articles 194 to 197 or Article 199 RVD apply, see section 2.13.1 below), comply with the formalities laid down by each Member State.

Article 179 RVD describes the method of deduction as follows:

> The taxable person shall make the deduction by subtracting from the total amount of VAT due for a given tax period the total amount of VAT in respect of which, during the same period,

277 Case C-165/17 (*Morgan Stanley*), ECLI:EU:C:2019:58.
278 Case C-388/11 (*Le Crédit Lyonnais*), ECLI:EU:C:2013:541.
279 See Case C-90/02 (*Gerhard Bockemühl*), [2004] ECR I-3303, Case C-152/02 (*Terra Baubedarf*), [2004] ECR I-5583 and Case C-25/03 (*Hans U. Hundt-Eßwein*), [2005] ECR I-3123.
280 Case C-518/14 (*Barlis*), ECLI:EU:C:2016:691.
281 Case C-516/14 (*Senatex*), ECLI:EU:C:2016:690.
282 Case C-664/16 (*Vadan*), ECLI:EU:C:2018:933.

> the right of deduction has arisen and is exercised in accordance with Article 178. However, Member States may require that taxable persons who carry out occasional transactions, as defined in Article 12, exercise their right of deduction only at the time of supply.

With regard to occasional intra-Community supplies of new means of transport (section 2.6.6), deduction at the moment of the supply is provided for in Article 172 RVD.[283]

VAT can however not be deducted in case VAT is due only under Article 203 RVD because a taxable person has mentioned it on the invoice (i.e. incorrectly charged VAT) as held by the ECJ in the *Genius Holding* case.[284] The ECJ held that unlike the situation in *Genius Holding*, in the joined cases *Schmeink and Strobel*[285] the risk of any loss in tax revenues has been completely eliminated in sufficient time either because the issuer of the invoice has retrieved and destroyed the invoice before its recipient used it or because, although the invoice has been used, the issuer of the invoice has settled the amount shown separately on the invoice. In that situation the principle of the neutrality of VAT requires that VAT which has been improperly invoiced can be adjusted without such adjustment being made conditional by the Member States upon the issuer of the relevant invoice having acted in good faith.

In *Ecotrade* a company established in Italy received shipping services from operators established elsewhere, who did not charge VAT on their invoices. It mistakenly believed those services to be exempt and did not include them in its VAT accounts.[286] It should in fact, under the reverse charge mechanism, have declared itself liable for input VAT on the supplies, which it should then have deducted from its output tax. That would have involved two accounting entries, cancelling each other out, so that no payment would have been due to the tax authority. It none the less achieved the same result by not declaring or deducting any input tax but paying output tax in full. Discovering the error, the tax authority sought to recover the undeclared input tax, on the basis of its right under national law to reassess VAT returns made in the four preceding years, but refused to allow any deduction which had not been claimed in the return for the second year following that in which the right to deduct arose, again on the basis of a limitation period under national law. The ECJ observed that it is not apparent from the orders for reference, nor indeed was it alleged before it, that Ecotrade's misapprehension of its accounting obligations was the result of bad faith or evasion. The ECJ added that in any event, the good faith of a taxable person is relevant for the answer to be given to the national court *only in so far as there is, on account of the conduct of that taxable person, a risk of a loss of tax revenues for the Member State concerned.* However, a misapprehension of accounting obligations, such as that at issue, cannot be regarded as giving rise to a risk of loss of tax revenues, since, in the context of the application of the reverse charge procedure, no tax is due in principle to the Exchequer. For those reasons, such misapprehension also cannot be treated as a

---

283 See also Article 320(2) RVD with regard to the right to deduction only at the moment of the supply when a taxable dealer opts to apply the normal VAT arrangements.
284 Case C-342/87 (*Genius Holding*), [1989] ECR 4227.
285 Case C-454/98 (*Schmeink and Strobel*), [2000] ECR I-6973.
286 Joined Cases C-95/07 and C-96/07 (*Ecotrade*), [2008] ECR I-3457.

transaction designed to evade tax or as a misuse of Community rules, since it was not intended to obtain a tax advantage to which there was no entitlement.

According to Article 168(e) RVD, in so far as the goods and services are used for the purposes of the taxed transactions of a taxable person, the taxable person is entitled, in the Member State in which he carries out these transactions, to deduct from the VAT which he is liable to pay the VAT due or paid in respect of the importation of goods into that Member State. To exercise his right of deduction, the taxable person must, according to Article 178(e), hold an import document specifying him as consignee or importer and stating or permitting the calculation of the amount of tax due.

Article 168(b) and (d) RVD provides that, in so far as the goods and services are used for the purposes of the taxed transactions of a taxable person, the taxable person is entitled, in the Member State in which he carries out these transactions, to deduct from the VAT which he is liable to pay the VAT due in respect of transactions treated as supplies of goods or services pursuant to Articles 18(a) and 27 RVD and in respect of transactions treated as intra-Community acquisitions in accordance with Articles 21 and 22 RVD. To exercise his right of deduction, the taxable person must, according to Article 178(b) and (d) RVD, comply with the formalities laid down by each Member State.

Article 168(c) RVD provides that, in so far as the goods and services are used for the purposes of the taxed transactions of a taxable person, the taxable person is entitled, in the Member State in which he carries out these transactions, to deduct from the VAT which he is liable to pay the VAT due in respect of intra-Community acquisitions of goods pursuant to Article 2(1)(b)(i) RVD. To exercise his right of deduction, the taxable person must, according to Article 178(e), set out in the VAT return provided for in Article 250 RVD all the information needed for the amount of the VAT due on his intra-Community acquisitions of goods to be calculated and he must hold an invoice drawn up in accordance with Articles 220 to 236 RVD.

According to Articles 180 and 181 RVD, Member States may authorise a taxable person to make a deduction which he has not made in accordance with the provisions mentioned above and authorise a taxable person who does not hold an invoice drawn up in accordance with Articles 220 to 236 RVD to make the deduction referred to in Article 168(c) in respect of his intra-Community acquisitions of goods. It is up to the Member States to determine the conditions and detailed rules for applying Articles 180 and 181 RVD.

Where, for a given tax period, the amount of deductions exceeds the amount of VAT due, the Member States have a choice either to make a refund or to carry the excess forward to the following period (Article 183 RVD).[287]

Finally, Article 184 RVD provides that where for a given tax period the amount of authorised deductions exceeds the amount of tax due, the Member States may, in accordance with

287 See, *inter alia*, Case C-286/94 (*Garage Molenheide*), [1997] ECR I-7281, regarding the principle of proportionality.

conditions which they shall determine, either make a refund or carry the excess forward to the following period. However, Member States may refuse to refund or carry forward if the amount of the excess is insignificant.[288]

2.12.6 *Adjustment of Deductions*

The basic principle of a consumption-type value added tax is contained in the VAT Directive. A taxable person may deduct (immediately and fully) the tax on investment or capital goods. If there were no rules governing a change occurring in the deductible proportion during the lifetime of an investment (or capital) good, the initial deduction might lead to an unjustified advantage or disadvantage for the taxable person. Provisions, therefore, are made for a limited period during which the original deduction can be adjusted if it turns out to be excessive or inadequate. In the words of the ECJ:

> "The adjustment is an integral part of the VAT deduction scheme established by the VAT Directive and is intended to enhance the precision of VAT deductions so as to ensure tax neutrality, which is a fundamental principle of the common system of VAT put in place by the EU legislature in the field (..). In accordance with that principle, transactions effected at an earlier stage continue to give rise to the right to deduct only to the extent that they are used to make supplies subject to VAT. The VAT Directive thus aims to establish a close and direct relationship between the right to deduct input VAT and the use of the goods and services concerned for taxable output transactions".[289]

First of all the RVD provides that the initial deduction should be adjusted where that deduction was higher or lower than that to which the taxable person was entitled or where after the return is made some change occurs in the factors used to determine the amount to be deducted, in particular where purchases are cancelled or price reductions are obtained. Recalculations need not be made in cases of transactions remaining totally or partially unpaid and of destruction, loss or theft of property duly proved or confirmed, nor in the case of applications for the purpose of making gifts of small value and giving samples. However, Member States may require recalculation in cases of transactions remaining totally or partially unpaid and of theft (Article 185 RVD). Article 186 RVD expressly makes Member States responsible for defining the conditions for such adjustments.[290]

Furthermore, the Directive provides for a 5-year adjustment period for capital goods, deemed to correspond to the normal depreciation period. Each year one fifth of the tax paid on the capital good when it was purchased is to be adjusted in proportion to the actual use (Article 187(1) RVD).[291] Member States may provide that the adjustment period starts

288 In Case C-78/00 (*Commission v. Italy*), [2001] ECR I-8195, the ECJ held that by providing that the category of taxable persons whose tax position for 1992 was in credit be belatedly issued with Government bonds instead of refunds of the excess VAT, the Italian Republic had failed to fulfil its obligations under Articles 17 and 18 of the Sixth Directive (now Articles 167 to 183 RVD).

289 Case C-791/18 (*Stichting Schoonzicht*), [2020], ECLI:EU:C:2020:731, para 26. Reference is made to Cases C-255/02 (*Halifax and Others*), EU:C:2006:121; C-532/16, (*SEB bankas*) EU:C:2018:228; C-234/11 (*TETS Haskovo*), EU:C:2012:644.

290 Case C-791/18 (*Stichting Schoonzicht*), [2020], ECLI:EU:C:2020:731, para 28.

291 See, *ex multis*, Joined Cases C-487/01 and C-7/02 (*Leusden* (C-487/01) and *Holin* (C-7/02), [2004] ECR I-5337, Case C-500/13 (*Gmina Miydzyzdroje*), ECLI: EU:C:2014:1750 and Case C-791/18 (*Stichting Schoonzicht*), ECLI:EU:C:2020:731.

from the time at which the goods are first used (Article 187 (1) second sentence RVD). Member States retained discretion to extend this period up to 20 years for immovable property (Article 187 (1) third sentence RVD).[292]

It is further provided that, in the case of a supply during the period of adjustment, capital goods must be regarded as if they had still been applied only for business use by the taxable person until expiry of the adjustment period. Such business activities are presumed to be fully taxable where the supply of the goods is taxed; they are presumed to be fully exempt where the supply is exempt (Article 188 RVD).[293] Thus, in the former case full deduction is allowed for the remaining time of the adjustment period (of the VAT that can be allocated to this period) and in the latter case no deduction is allowed at all, often resulting in an obligation to reimburse partially the deducted tax.

In *Gmina Miydzyzdroje*[294] the ECJ confirmed that Article 187 RVD precludes a domestic legislation permitting the adjustment of deductions concerning capital goods over a period of less than five years (and therefore also precludes any system of one-off adjustment), In *Stichting Schoonzicht*,[295] the ECJ clarified that Article 187 RVD does not preclude domestic capital goods adjustment schemes from providing that, in the year the goods in question are first used, where that year is also the first adjustment year, the total amount of the initial deduction for those capital goods is adjusted in a single step (i.e. a one-off adjustment), if, when first used, it becomes apparent that that deduction deviates from the deduction which the taxable person was entitled to apply on the basis of the actual use of those goods. This one-off adjustment does not preclude subsequent adjustment within the 5 years adjustment period if a change of use again occurs.

Article 191 RVD allows Member States under certain conditions not to require adjustment in respect of capital goods. If they do so, they may include disposal of capital goods in the calculation of the deductible proportion of the pro rata (see section 2.12.4 above).

Articles 187 and 188 RVD lay down some specific rules for adjustment of deductions of input VAT on capital goods. Article 189 RVD stipulates that Member States may define the concept of capital goods.[296] Under Article 190 RVD Member States can also apply the adjustment rules for capital goods on services that have characteristics similar to those normally attributed to capital goods.

292 The following formula can be applied:

$$\frac{\text{Total input tax incurred}}{\text{Number of years}} \times (a - b) = \text{adjustment},$$

where a = deduction entitlement in year of purchase, and b = deduction entitlement in current year.

293 See for the situation where taxation and exemption coincide, Case C-63/04 (*Centralan*), [2005] ECR I-11087.

294 Case C-500/13 (*Gmina Miydzyzdroje*) EU:C:2014:1750.

295 Case C-791/18 (*Stichting Schoonzicht*), [2020], ECLI:EU:C:2020:731.

296 See also Case 51/76 (*VNO*), [1977] ECR 0113.

2.12.7 Private Use

It is settled case-law of the ECJ that a taxable person may choose whether or not to integrate into his business, for the purposes of applying the VAT rules, part of an asset which is given over to his private use.[297] If the taxable person chooses to treat capital goods used both for business and private purposes as business goods, the VAT due as input tax on the acquisition of those goods is in principle wholly and immediately deductible.[298]

It follows from Articles 26 and 75 RVD that the use of capital goods for the private use of a taxable person or of his staff or for purposes other than those of his business, where the input VAT paid on such goods is wholly or partly deductible, is treated as a supply of services for consideration and is taxed on the basis of the cost of providing the services.

Accordingly, where a taxable person chooses to treat an entire building as forming part of the assets of his business and subsequently uses part of that building for private purposes, on the one hand, he is entitled to deduct the input VAT paid on all construction costs relating to that building and, on the other, he is subject to the corresponding obligation to pay VAT on the amount of expenditure incurred for such use.

Including all mixed-use goods in the company's assets and liabilities generally offers cash flow benefits. When goods change from non-business to the business sphere the RVD does not provide for a correction mechanism. Thus, the inclusion in the company's assets also prevents the loss of the right of deduction in so far goods are first allocated to private use and later used for business purposes. Furthermore, the result of including mixed-use goods in the company's assets and liabilities may be that there will be untaxed end use, because the adjustment period provided for in Article 187 of the Directive is likely to correct to a limited extent only the deduction of input tax made when the building was constructed.

Since 1 January 2011 Article 168a RVD provides that when immovable property intended to be used simultaneously for business and non-business purposes, the initial deduction is *limited to the actual use* of the property for transactions that give rise to a right of deduction when the tax becomes chargeable. This applies to VAT related not only to acquisitions of immovable property, but also to services such as construction, renovation or substantial transformations that, in economic terms, can be placed on the same level as the acquisition or construction of immovable property. Simple repairs or improvements are, however, excluded from the scope of the measure. Thus, for cases of "mixed" use, it will not be possible to deduct immediately all input VAT in case of immovable property. Given this limitation of the deduction for the taxable person, an adjustment system has been set up to take into account changes between business and non-business use of the immovable property concerned for a duration that corresponds to the current adjustment period for immovable property acquired as capital goods. The new system applies to both increases and reductions in business use. This system replaces the tax on non-business

297 See, *ex multis*, Case C-291/92 (*Armbrecht*), Case C-415/98 (*Bakcsi*), and Case C-269/00 (*Wolfgang Seeling*) [2003] ECRI-4101.

298 See, inter alia, Case C-97/90 (*Lennartz*), paragraph 26, [1991] ECR I-3795 and *Bakcsi*, cited above, paragraph 25.

use (Article 26 RVD) during the adjustment period and sets up an adjustment system for taxable persons in the event of an increase in business use relating to transactions giving rise to a right of deduction. This adjustment system is applied in parallel to the existing adjustment system. For movable property the former rules still apply today. In case mixed-used goods are fully attributed to the business assets VAT is fully deductible (assuming the business does not provide exempt supplies) and the use for private purposes is subject to VAT under Article 26 RVD. Article 168a (2) RVD however allows EU Member States to apply the rules for immovable property to movable property, as specified by the Member State, too. Article 176 RVD contains a stand-still provision allowing EU Member States to apply restrictions as regards the right to deduct VAT they already had in place before 1979 or upon their accession to the EU. This may cover expenditure that is not of a "strictly business nature", but also business expenditure.[299]

Article 26 and 75 RVD also apply to services for purposes other than those of the business of the taxable person. In the *Vereniging Noordelijke Land- en Tuinbouw Organisatie* (VNLTO) case[300] the ECJ made clear that transactions outside the scope of the system of VAT, in that particular case activities in the general interest, may not be considered to be carried out for "purposes other than" those of the business within the meaning of Article 26 RVD. The activities of VNLTO where, according to the ECJ, not to be considered as non-business transactions, given that they constitute the main corporate purpose of that association. The result of this judgement is that where non-economic activities are carried out by a taxable person that person is allowed to attribute the assets used for both an economic and non- economic activity fully to its business assets. It can however only deduct the VAT to the extent that a property is used for its economic activities (and this applies to both immovable and movable property). The *Gmina Ryjewo* case[301] however shows that if such a taxable person uses a property at a later stage more or exclusively for its economic activities the adjustment rules can be applied if the property is part of the business assets. This can even be applied if the property originally was only used for non-economic activities. This requires the taxable person to have acquired the goods as a taxable person which can be demonstrated by the fact that that person did not exclude the possibility that the property could be used, at least in part, for economic purposes in a later stage.

2.12.8 Deductions and Shares and Dividends

The ECJ has ruled on numerous occasions about the VAT status of and deductibility of VAT for holding companies. The first landmark case is the *Polysar* case (see also section 2.5). In this case the ECJ assimilated the position of a holding company with that of a private person. The dividend yielded by the holding is merely the result of ownership of the property (no economic "activity" is involved).[302] To this the ECJ added its famous sentence in paragraph 14:

---

299 Case C-225/18 (*Grupa Lotos*), ECLI:EU:C:2019:349.
300 Case C-515/07 (*VNLTO*), [2009] ECR I-839.
301 Case C-140/17 (*Gmina Ryjewo*), ECLI:EU:C:2018:595.
302 In Case C-80/95 (*Harnas & Helm*), [1997] ECR I-745, the ECJ held that there is no reason to treat bondholding differently from shareholding.

... it is otherwise where the holding is accompanied by direct or indirect involvement in the management of the companies ... .

Like public authorities, we believe that activities of companies cannot and should not fall outside the scope of VAT in the sense that they do not serve a wider business purpose. Final consumers of any good or service are necessarily physical persons. Any goods or services acquired by legal persons have to be viewed as inputs to the activities in which they are engaged. Moreover, all of the activities of legal persons should be viewed as ultimately leading to a supply of some sort. Presumably this would require a change of the RVD. (Still, we are not sure whether the ECJ would decide in exactly the same way if the questions raised in *Polysar* would have been asked for the first time now. If we see it correctly the ECJ is more and more looking at the economic reality; see for example the *DFDS* and *EMU Tobacco* cases.[303] From that perspective the question whether the holding of shares should be treated in any case as a taxable activity – *i.e.* for wider business purposes – when a pure holding company belongs to a worldwide group which outwardly appears under a single name could be answered positively.)

In the *Wellcome Trust* case the ECJ argued that if the holding of shares falls beyond the scope of VAT equally the sale of these shares falls beyond the scope. In paragraph 35 the ECJ mentions two exceptions: 1) "where such transactions are effected as part of a commercial share-dealing activity" and 2) "in order to secure a direct or indirect involvement in the management of companies by a holding company", the latter referring to *Polysar*.

To these exceptions to assimilation another exception was added in the *Régie dauphinoise* case. Basically, the ECJ said that in this case the receipt of interest does not arise simply from ownership of the asset (as in the case with dividends in *Polysar*), since Régie acts as a taxable person, because – and this is exception 3 – the receipt of interest constitutes "the direct, permanent and necessary extension of the taxable activity" of Régie,[304] which for that reason cannot be qualified as incidental!

Next are the judgments in *Floridienne*[305] and *Cibo*[306] and the ECJ Order in Case C-102/00 (*Welthgrove*).[307] The *Floridienne* case, and the *Welthgrove* case turn on the question: What did the ECJ mean in paragraph 14 of the Polysar case: "it is otherwise where the holding is accompanied by direct or indirect involvement"? What is otherwise? Does this involvement make the holding company a taxable person by definition?

In *Floridienne* the ECJ held that the payment of dividends is not consideration for the management services. The ECJ also further explained what involvement in the management as stated in paragraph 14 of the Polysar case means. Involvement in the management entails

303 Case C-260/95 (*DFDS A/S*), Case C-296/95 (*EMU Tabac* and Others), [1997] ECR I-1005. See also Case C-73/06 (*Planzer*), in which the ECJ noted: "taking account of the economic reality constitutes a fundamental criterion for applying the common system of VAT".

304 The so-called "extension theory".

305 Case C-142/99 (*Floridienne SA*), [2000] ECR I-9567.

306 Case C-16/00 (*Cibo*), [2001] ECR I-6663.

307 Case C-102/00 (*Welthgrove*), [2001] ECR I-5679.

carrying out transactions which are subject to VAT, such as the supply by Floridienne and Berginvest of administrative, accounting and information technology services to their subsidiaries. A holding company must therefore provide services against a separate consideration (not dividend) to qualify as taxable person and deduct the input tax. Later in the *Marle Participations* case[308] the ECJ made clear that involvement in the management can be any type of service as long as it is made on a continuing basis and is carried out for consideration. In the joined cases *Larentia + Minerva* and *Marenhave Schifffahrt*[309] the ECJ made clear that in case a holding company is involved in the management its position as a shareholder does not restrict the right to deduct VAT. VAT can however not be deducted in case the services that constitute the management are exempt from VAT without a right to deduct VAT. If a holding company however has subsidiaries in which management it is involved, and subsidiaries in which it is not, VAT deduction on general costs will be limited because the holding company caries out both economic (holding shares in subsidiaries in which management it is involved) and non-economic (holding shares in subsidiaries in which management it is not involved) activities.

Acquisition of shares

The ECJ has, up till now, ruled in four cases about the deductibility of VAT in a situation where a holding company acquired shares in a subsidiary where it was clear from objective facts that the holding company pursued to provide services on a continuing basis and against consideration towards that subsidiary. In the first case, *Cibo Participations,*[310] the ECJ ruled that in that particular situation the costs made for acquiring the shares in the subsidiary are general costs, thus resulting in a proportional deduction if the holding company provides both taxed and exempt supplies and a full deduction of VAT, as was the case for Cibo, in a situation where the holding company has only taxed turnover (similarly there will be no deduction if the holding company only has exempt turnover). The ECJ ruling in Cibo Participations was reaffirmed by the ECJ in the cases *Marle Participations*[311] and *Sonaecom.*[312] In the *Sonaecom* case the ECJ made it clear though that in a situation where a holding company also has subsidiaries where it is not involved in the management, the VAT deduction may be limited because of that non-economic activity. In the *Ryanair* case[313] the ECJ however ruled differently. Ryanair, an aviation company, pursued to acquire all the shares in another airline. It however failed to do so. According to the ECJ the VAT on costs made for acquiring the shares, even though the takeover failed, was deductible. In paragraph 31 the ECJ in that respect stated:

> "In the present case, it is apparent from the file before the Court that the services at issue were provided to Ryanair when it intended, by the planned acquisition of shares in the target company, to pursue an economic activity consisting in providing to that company management services subject to VAT. Thus, it appears that, first, Ryanair acted as a taxable person at the time it incurred the expenditure linked to the services at issue. By doing so, Ryanair thus benefits, in principle, from the right to deduct VAT paid on the services at issue

308 Case C-320/17 (*Marle Participations*), ECLI:EU:C:2018:537.
309 Case C-108/14 and C-109/14 (*Larentia + Minerva* and *Marenhave Schifffahrt*), ECLI:EU:C:2015:496.
310 Case C-16/00 (*Cibo Participations*), [2001] ECR I-6663.
311 Case C-320/17 (*Marle Participations*), ECLI:EU:C:2018:537.
312 Case C-42/19 (*Sonaecom*), ECLI:EU:C:2020:913.
313 Case C-249/17 (*Ryanair*), ECLI:EU:C:2018:834.

> immediately, even if, ultimately, that economic activity, which was to give rise to taxable transactions, was not carried out and, accordingly, did not give rise to such transactions. Second, as regards the conditions for the exercise of the right to deduct and more specifically the scope of that right, the expenditure incurred for the purpose of the acquisition of the shares of the target company must be regarded as being attributable to the performance of that economic activity which consisted in carrying out transactions giving rise to a right to deduct. On that basis, that expenditure has a direct and immediate link with that economic activity as a whole and, consequently, is part of its general costs. It follows that the corresponding VAT gives rise to the right to deduction in full".

Different from the other three cases the ECJ sees a direct and immediate link between the acquisition costs and the intended economic activity: involvement in the management of the subsidiary that Ryanair intended to acquire. In our view this may be due to the fact that Ryanair, next to holding the shares in the target company, carries out an airline. It seems that in such a situation the ECJ sees cause to distinguish two separate economic activities, the airline activities and the holding activities, and attribute costs to those activities.

Issue of shares and Bonds

The *Kretztechnik*[314] case deals with the issue of shares. Kretztechnik AG is an Austrian public limited company whose objects are the development and sale of all types of electro-medical appliances, in particular ultrasound apparatus for medical and technical purposes, and other medical appliances. Sales of its products are subject to VAT, and it is therefore entitled to deduct input tax on supplies of goods or services which it acquires for the purposes of making those sales.

In January 2000, Kretztechnik decided to increase its issued share capital by 25%, by issuing 2.5 million bearer shares at an issue price of EUR 1.00 per share. For that purpose, the company was listed on the Neues Markt stock exchange in Frankfurt, Germany, from 23 March 2000. In order to obtain that listing, it had to pay for certain services, on which it was charged VAT. In its VAT assessment for that year, the tax authority refused Kretztechnik's deduction of the input tax on costs involved in the company's admission to the German stock market, on the ground that the share transactions for the purposes of which those costs had been incurred were exempt from tax. Kretztechnik challenged that assessment before the Unabhängiger Finanzsenat, an independent tribunal with jurisdiction in tax and customs matters. In its challenge, Kretztechnik, relying on Article 17(2) of the Sixth Directive, submitted that input tax could be deducted in so far as the services in respect of which it was charged were used ultimately for the purposes of its taxable transactions.

Referring to its decision in *KapHag*[315] that a partnership which admits a partner in consideration of payment of a contribution in cash does not provide to that partner a supply of services for consideration within the meaning of Article 2(1) of the Sixth Directive (now Article 2 (1) RVD), the ECJ drew the same conclusion regarding the issue of shares for the purpose of raising capital. A company that issues new shares is increasing its assets by acquiring additional capital, whilst granting the new shareholders a right of ownership of part of the capital thus increased. From the issuing company's point of view, the aim is to

314 Case C-465/03 (*Kretztechnik AG*), [2005] ECR I-4357.
315 Case C-442/01 (*Kaphag*), ECR [2003] I-06851.

raise capital and not to provide services. As far as the shareholder is concerned, payment of the sums necessary for the increase of capital is not a payment of consideration but an investment or an employment of capital. The ECJ concluded that a share issue does not constitute a supply of goods or of services for consideration within the meaning of Article 2(1) of the Sixth Directive (now Article 2(1) RVD). Therefore, such a transaction, whether or not carried out in connection with admission of the company concerned to a stock exchange, does not fall within the scope of that Directive.

As to the question whether Article 17(1) and (2) of the Sixth Directive (now Articles 167 and 168 RVD) confers a right to deduction of input VAT paid on supplies linked with a share issue, the ECJ referred to its case-law, in which it has been decided that "the right of deduction is an integral part of the VAT scheme and in principle may not be limited. It must be exercised immediately in respect of all the taxes charged on transactions relating to inputs. The deduction system is meant to relieve the trader entirely of the burden of the VAT payable or paid in the course of all his economic activities. The common system of VAT consequently ensures complete neutrality of taxation of all economic activities, whatever their purpose or results, provided that they are themselves subject in principle to VAT". According to the ECJ, it is clear from the last-mentioned condition that, for VAT to be deductible, the input transactions must have a direct and immediate link with the output transactions giving rise to a right of deduction. Thus, the right to deduct VAT charged on the acquisition of input goods or services presupposes that the expenditure incurred in acquiring them was a component of the cost of the output transactions that gave rise to the right to deduct. In this case, in view of the fact that, first, a share issue is an operation not falling within the scope of the Sixth Directive and, second, that operation was carried out by Kretztechnik in order to increase its capital for the benefit of its economic activity in general, it must according to the ECJ be considered that the costs of the supplies acquired by that company in connection with the operation concerned form part of its overheads and are therefore, as such, component parts of the price of its products. Those supplies have a direct and immediate link with the whole economic activity of the taxable person.[316]

The ECJ held that, under Article 17(1) and (2) of the Sixth Directive (now Articles 167 and 168 RVD), Kretztechnik is entitled to deduct all the VAT charged on the expenses incurred by that company for the various supplies which it acquired in the context of the share issue carried out by it, provided, however, that all the transactions carried out by that company in the context of its economic activity constitute taxed transactions. A taxable person who effects both transactions in respect of which VAT is deductible and transactions in respect of which it is not may, under the first subparagraph of Article 17(5) of the Sixth Directive (now Article 173 RVD), deduct only that proportion of the VAT which is attributable to the former transactions.

In the *Securenta* case[317] also the ECJ dealt with the issue of shares, but that case had a different outcome. With regard to expenditure connected with the issue of shares or

316 For the lack of a direct and immediate link, see Case C-435/05 (*Investrand B. V.*) [2007] ECR I-01315 further below.
317 C-437/06 (*Securenta*), [2008] ECR I-01597.

atypical silent partnerships, the ECJ referred to its case-law and recalled that, in order for the input VAT paid in respect of such a transaction to give rise to a right to deduct, the expenditure incurred in that regard must be a component of the cost of the output transactions that gave rise to the right to deduct.[318] It recalled that in those circumstances, the input VAT paid in relation to the expenditure connected with the issue of shares or atypical silent partnerships can give rise to the right to deduct only if the capital thus acquired was used in connection with the economic activities of the person concerned. The ECJ then focused on the case at hand and noted that the expenditure connected with supplies of services carried out in the context of the issue of shares and financial holdings was not solely attributable to downstream economic activities carried out by Securenta and was not therefore among the elements which, alone, go to make up the cost of the transactions relating to those activities. The ECJ added to this that, if that had been the case, the supplies of services concerned would have had a direct and immediate link with the taxpayer's economic activities (referring to *Abbey National*,[319] paragraphs 35 and 36, and *Cibo Participations*, paragraph 33). However, it is apparent to the ECJ from the documents before it that the costs incurred by Securenta for the financial transactions at issue in the main proceedings were, at least in part, for the performance of non-economic activities.

If we understand it correctly the expenditure connected with Securenta's issue of shares and atypical silent partnerships is to be treated partially as costs forming part of the overheads and partially as costs forming part of operations not falling within the scope of the VAT Directive, see the ECJ' conclusion that the costs incurred by Securenta for the financial transactions at issue in the main proceedings were, *at least in part*, for the performance of non-economic activities.

In the *Sonaecom* case[320] the ECJ ruled on the deductibility of VAT on costs made for the issue of bonds. In that particular case Sonaecom issued the bonds to acquire a new subsidiary for which it intended to provide management services. However the acquisition failed and Sonaecom used the money raised to provide a loan to its parent company. According to the ECJ the actual use of the money is decisive for the answer to the question whether VAT can be deducted on the acquisition cost. Because the actual use is the provision of the loan which is exempt from VAT without a right to deduct VAT Sonaecom could not deduct the VAT on the costs made for issuing the bonds.

Disposal of shares

The *SKF* case is the first case that deals with the VAT consequences of a disposal of shares. The Swedish share company AB SKF is the parent company of an industrial group which carries on activities in a number of countries. It takes an active part in the management of its subsidiaries and supplies to them, for a consideration, services, including management, administration and marketing policy. Those services are invoiced to the subsidiaries and SKF is liable for VAT on them.[321] SKF intended to restructure the group and, in that connection,

318 See Case C-408/98 (*Abbey National*), [2001] ECR I-01361 paragraph 28; Case C-16/00 (*Cibo*), [2001] ECR I-06663 paragraph 31; and Case C-435/05 (*Investrand*), [2007] ECR I-01315 paragraph 23.

319 Case C-408/98 (*Abbey National*), [2001] ECR I-1361.

320 Case C-42/19 (*Sonaecom*), ECLI:EU:C:2020:913.

321 Case C-29/08 (*AB SKF*), [2009] ECR I-10413.

to dispose of the business of its subsidiary by transferring all the shares in the latter. In addition, SKF would dispose of its 26.5% shareholding in the controlled company, which was in the past wholly owned and to which SKF also supplied, as the parent company, services subject to VAT. The reason for those disposals was to obtain funds to finance other activities of the group. In order to carry out those disposals, SKF envisaged requiring supplies of services in the area of valuation of shares, assistance with negotiations and specialised legal advice for the drafting of the contracts. Those supplies of services would be subject to VAT. In its decision the ECJ observed that in the present case SKF, as the parent company of an industrial group, was involved in the management of the subsidiary and the controlled company by supplying to them, for consideration, a variety of administrative, accounting and marketing services, in respect of which it was liable to pay VAT. By the disposal of all of its shares in the subsidiary and in the controlled company, SKF brought to an end its holdings in those companies. According to the ECJ, that disposal, carried out in order to enable the parent company to restructure a group of companies, can be regarded as a transaction that consists in obtaining income on a continuing basis from activities which go beyond the compass of the simple sale of shares. That transaction has a direct link with the organisation of the activity carried out by the group and constitutes accordingly the *direct, permanent and necessary extension of the taxable activity* of the taxable person. Such a transaction consequently comes within the scope of VAT. At this place we note that such a direct, permanent and necessary extension of the taxable activity excludes the possibility of treating the sale of shares as incidental.

The ECJ then turned to the nature of the transaction at issue and the argument of the Commission that it should be regarded as equivalent to a transfer of a totality of assets or part thereof. The ECJ recalled that it has interpreted the concept of a "transfer … of a totality of assets or part thereof" (TOGC: transfer of a going concern) as covering the transfer of a business or an independent part of an undertaking, including tangible elements and, as the case may be, intangible elements which, together, constitute an undertaking or a part of an undertaking capable of carrying on an independent economic activity, but that it does not cover the simple transfer of assets, such as the sale of a stock of products. In the present case, it was not possible, on the basis of the case-file submitted, to determine whether the effect of the sale of shares in the subsidiary and in the controlled company was the total or partial disposal of the assets of the undertakings concerned. The ECJ observed that in any event, even if the concept of a TOGC could be applied to a transaction such as that at issue, a matter which it is for the national court to determine, the Kingdom of Sweden has chosen to exercise the option of treating the transfer of a totality of assets as not coming within the scope of the Sixth Directive. That being the case, a disposal of shares which amounts to a transfer of a totality of assets does not constitute an economic activity subject to VAT. We note that if the transfer by SKF is treated as TOGC, SKF should be entitled to full deduction following the treatment of its general costs. Later in the X case[322] the ECJ clarified its judgement in the SKF case in this respect. According to the ECJ the disposal to a single person of all the shares in a company by all the shareholders of that company cannot be regarded as equivalent to a TOGC. A disposal of shares in our

322 Case C-651/11 (*X*), ECLI:EU:C:2013:346.

view can only be regarded within the scope of the rules for a TOGC in case they are part of a disposal of several assets constituting a business.

The ECJ further ruled on the question whether a disposal of shares such as that at issue, in the event that it comes within the scope of VAT, must be exempt from VAT that a sale of shares changing the legal and financial position of the parties to the transaction, in so far as it comes within the scope of VAT, is covered by the exemption. The ECJ concluded that a disposal of shares such as that at issue must be exempt from VAT pursuant to both Article 13B(d)(5) of the Sixth Directive and Article 135(1)(f) RVD. At this place we note that the exemption could result in non- deduction while treatment as a TOGC or as a supply outside the scope of VAT as advocated by SKF should result in full deduction following the treatment of SKF's general costs.

The ECJ stated that there is a right to deduct input VAT in respect of services carried out in connection with financial transactions *if the capital acquired by means of those transactions is used in connection with the economic activities of the person concerned.* Furthermore, the costs associated with input services have a direct and immediate link to the taxable person's economic activities in circumstances where they are solely *attributable to downstream economic activities* and consequently are among the cost components of transactions within the scope of those activities.[323]

From the later *C&D Foods* case[324] it becomes clear that the objective of the disposal of shares is important to determine whether a holding company is acting in a capacity of taxable person. C&D Foods Acquisition ApS made costs for the disposal of shares by its wholly owned subsidiary. It intended to use the money thus raised to repay a loan to its main creditor. Even though C&D Foods Acquisition ApS was a holding company that was actively involved in the management of its subsidiary the ECJ ruled that it did not act as a taxable person when disposing of the shares. In order for a share disposal transaction to be able to come within the scope of VAT, the direct and exclusive reason for that transaction must, in principle, be the taxable economic activity of the parent company in question, or that transaction must constitute the direct, permanent and necessary extension of that activity. That is the case where that transaction is carried out with a view to allocating the proceeds of that sale directly to the taxable economic activity of the parent company in question or to the economic activity carried out by the group of which it is the parent company.

Summary

The law as it stands seems to be as follows. A pure holding company is not a taxable person. A holding company involved in the management of its subsidiaries is a taxable person when it receives consideration (dividends or interest on loans arising from reinvested dividends are not to be treated as consideration). Involvement in management can be any service that is provided on a continuing basis and against consideration.

323 C-437/06 (*Securenta*), ECLI:EU:C:2008:166, paragraphs 28 and 29.
324 Case C-502/17 (*C&D Foods*), ECLI:EU:C:2018:888.

The purchase of shares by a management holding company is not directly linked to its transactions outside the scope of VAT, or to a subsequent transaction of which the costs related to the purchase of the shares form a cost component. There is a direct and immediate relation with the totality of business activities; thus, the *pro rata*, if applicable, is to be applied to these costs. In situations where, next to holding activities, the company also carries out other economic activities there may be reason to attribute the costs solely to the holding activities.

If, however, expenditure connected with supplies carried out in the context of the issue of shares and financial participations cannot solely be attributed to downstream economic activities (*i.e.* with the totality of business activity) VAT deduction related to the performance of non-economic activities is to be excluded in a pre-*pro-rata*.

The same applies, *mutatis mutandis*, with regard to the sale of shares by a management holding company that is already a taxable person. When there is a direct and immediate relation with the totality of business activities deduction on costs incurred follows the deduction of general costs unless costs are likely to be incorporated in the price of the shares sold, then and to that extent there is no deduction.

2.12.9 *Fraud and abusive practices*

2.12.9.1 *Fraud*

A combination of the exemption for intra-Community supplies and the right to deduct VAT without that deduction being dependent on whether the counterparty has actually remitted the VAT to the tax authorities is a cause for carrousel fraud the EU has to deal with. In its simplest form (also called "missing trader fraud") a carrousel fraud includes three parties established in two different EU Member States. A, established in Member State 1 supplies goods to B in Member State 2, that subsequently supplies those goods to C in Member State 2. The A-B supply is subject to the exemption for intra-Community supplies, while B must report VAT on an intra-Community acquisition in Member State 2, which he can deduct in the same VAT return. The B-C supply is subject to VAT in Member State 2. B collects the VAT from C, who deducts the VAT, but B does not remit it to the tax authorities. If C supplies the goods to A, the carrousel is complete and the same process can be repeated over and over again in a short period of time, after which B disappears, before being discovered by the tax authorities.

Do transactions forming part of a carousel fraud by definition not qualify as economic activities (which means they could escape the application of VAT)? That is the question answered in the cases of Optigen, Fulcrum and Bond House Systems.[325] According to the UK tax authorities, first, as regards the purchases, by Optigen, Fulcrum and Bond House Systems, they received no supplies used or to be used for VAT purposes, so that the amounts of VAT purportedly paid in respect of those purchases were not input tax.

325 Joined Cases C-354/03 (*Optigen*), C-355/03 (*Fulcrum*) and C-484/03 (*Bond House Systems*), [2006] ECR I-0483.

Also, for the purposes of VAT, the relevant sales were not supplies made in the course of a business and do not therefore give any entitlement to a refund. Finally, the purchases and the sales, judged objectively, were devoid of economic substance and were not part of any economic activity. Accordingly, the purchases were not supplies used or to be used for the purposes of any economic activity and the sales were not supplies made in the course of economic activity for the purposes of VAT. According to the ECJ, transactions such as those at issue, which are not themselves vitiated by VAT fraud, constitute supplies of goods or services effected by a taxable person acting as such and an economic activity within the meaning of Articles 2(1), 9(1) and 14(1) RVD where they fulfil the objective criteria on which the definitions of those terms are based, regardless of the intention of a trader other than the taxable person concerned involved in the same chain of supply and/or the possible fraudulent nature of another transaction in the chain, prior or subsequent to the transaction carried out by that taxable person, of which that taxable person had no knowledge and no means of knowledge. The right to deduct input VAT of a taxable person who carries out such transactions cannot be affected by the fact that in the chain of supply of which those transactions form part another prior or subsequent transaction is vitiated by VAT fraud, without that taxable person knowing or having any means of knowing. In the situation where a taxable person however knew or should have known of the fraud the ECJ held that there is no economic activity or taxable supply and the right to deduct VAT can be refused to that taxable person.[326]

The exemption for intra-Community supplies may also be denied in the case of fraud. In *R*[327] the taxable person (of Portuguese nationality) was manager of a German company trading in luxury cars. Since 2002 he sold cars to Portugal while concealing the true identity of the real purchasers and invoicing to fictitious purchasers. By doing so R could demand higher prices. The fictitious purchasers were also included in the European Sales Listing to avoid identification of the real purchasers under the VIES. The real purchasers sold the cars to private individuals without paying VAT due on the intra-Community acquisitions. R claimed that the intra-Community supplies of the cars were exempt. The German tax administration refused to apply the zero rate since R enabled the evasion of VAT in Portugal. According to the ECJ, in circumstances such as those at issue, the Member State of departure of the intra-Community supply *may refuse to apply the exemption* pursuant to its powers under the first part of the sentence in Article 28c(A) of the Sixth Directive (now Articles 131 and 138(1) RVD) and for the purpose of ensuring the correct and straightforward application of the exemptions and of preventing any evasion, avoidance or abuse. With regard to particular cases in which there are genuine reasons to assume that the intra-Community acquisition corresponding to the supply at issue might escape payment of the VAT in the destination Member State, notwithstanding the mutual assistance of and administrative cooperation between the tax authorities of the Member States concerned, the Member State of departure is, in principle, required to refuse to grant the exemption to the supplier of the goods *and to require that supplier to pay the tax subsequently* in order to ensure that

326 Case C-439/04 and C-440/04 (*(joined cases Kittel and Recolta)*, ECLI:EU: C:2006:446. Similarly the right to apply the exemption for intra-Community supplies can be refused, Case C-285/09 (*R.*), ECLI:EU:C:2010:742.

327 Case C-285/09 (*Criminal proceedings against R*), [2010] ECR I- 12605.

the transaction in question does not escape taxation altogether. Before that, in *Collee*,[328] the ECJ had decided that the first subparagraph of Article 28c(A)(a) of the Sixth Directive (now Article 138 RVD) must be interpreted as precluding the refusal by the tax authority of a Member State to allow an intra-Community supply – which actually took place – to be exempt from VAT solely on the ground that the evidence of such a supply was not produced in good time. When examining the right of exemption from VAT in relation to such a supply, the referring court should take into account the fact that the taxable person initially knowingly concealed the fact that an intra-Community supply had occurred only if there is a risk of a loss in tax revenues and that risk has not been wholly eliminated by the taxable person in question.

In *Vetsch*,[329] the Austrian tax authorities had revoked the exemption granted to an Austrian company who imported goods from Switzerland that were subsequently subject to an exempt intra-Community supply with an acquisition taxable in Bulgaria (importation followed by exempt intra-Community supplies benefit from an exemption under Article 143(1)(d) RVD, see section 2.11 above). The tax administration justified their decision by the fact that the VAT had not been paid upon acquisition in Bulgaria. Like in other cases on fraud discussed above, the ECJ confirmed that the exemption upon importation could not be denied in a situation where the VAT was not paid in a subsequent supply and there was "no evidence to support the conclusion that the importer knew or ought to have known that that subsequent transaction entailed tax evasion on the part of the recipient".

2.12.9.2 Abusive practices

When VAT is not deductible (typically in the case of exemptions without a right to deduct VAT and in B2C transaction) taxable persons might artificially try to create a right to deduct VAT. In *Halifax*[330] the ECJ defined the contours of the concept of "abusive practices" in VAT.

In this decision it started by confirming that:

> "Where the taxable person chooses one of two transactions, the Sixth Directive does not require him to choose the one which involves paying the highest amount of VAT. On the contrary, as the Advocate General observed (...), taxpayers may choose to structure their business so as to limit their tax liability".

It then ruled that:

> "in the sphere of VAT, an abusive practice can be found to exist only if, first, the transactions concerned, notwithstanding formal application of the conditions laid down by the relevant provisions of the Sixth Directive and the national legislation transposing it, result in the accrual of a tax advantage the grant of which would be contrary to the purpose of those provisions. Second, it must also be apparent from a number of objective factors that the essential aim of the transactions concerned is to obtain a tax advantage".

328 Case C-146/05 (*Collée*), [2007] ECR I-7861.
329 Case 531/17 (*Vetsch Int. Transporte GmbH*), [2018], ECLI:EU:C:2019:114.
330 Case C-255/02 (*Halifax*), [2006] ECR I-1609.

Concerning the first element (purpose of the legislation) the ECJ observed that to allow taxable persons to deduct all input VAT even though, *in the context of their normal commercial operations*, no transactions conforming to the RVD or to the national legislation transposing it would have enabled them to deduct such VAT, or would have allowed them to deduct only part of it, would be contrary to the principle of tax neutrality, on which the deduction rules of the Directive are based.

In Part services[331] the ECJ further clarified that there *can* be a finding of an abusive practice when the accrual of a tax advantage constitutes the principal aim of the transaction or transactions at issue. This implies, first, that there is *not automatically* an abusive practice when the accrual of a tax advantage constitutes the principal aim of a transaction and, second, that the tax advantage does not need to be the sole aim of the transaction(s). In *Emsland Stärke*,[332] the ECJ decided that the national court may take account of the purely artificial nature of those transactions and the links of a legal, economic and/or personal nature between the operators involved in the scheme for reduction of the tax burden.

Again concerning the purpose of the legislation (first element above), in *Weald Leasing*[333] the ECJ decided that the tax advantage accruing from an undertaking's recourse to asset leasing transactions instead of the outright purchase of those assets, does not constitute a tax advantage the grant of which would be contrary to the purpose of the harmonized VAT legislation and of the national legislation transposing it.[334] The fact that the undertaking does not engage in leasing transactions in the context of its normal commercial operations is irrelevant in that regard.

---

331 Case C-425/06 (*Part Service*), [2008] ECR I-897. According to the ECJ, the transactions at issue had the following (abusive) characteristics:
- the two companies taking part in the leasing transaction are part of the same group;
- the service supplied by the leasing company is subject to a division, the financing element is entrusted to another company to be split into a credit service, an insurance service and a brokerage service;
- the service of the leasing company is therefore reduced to a service for renting a vehicle;
- the lease payments made by the customer are of an amount which is only slightly higher than the purchase cost of the vehicle;
- that service, considered in isolation, therefore seems to be economically unprofitable, so that the viability of the business cannot be ensured solely by means of contracts concluded with the customers;
- the leasing company receives the consideration of the leasing transaction only through the cumulative lease payments made by the customer and the amounts transferred from the other company of the same group.

332 *Case C-110/99* (*Emsland-Stärke*), [2000] ECR I-11569.

333 Case C-103/09 (*Weald Leasing Limited*), [2010] ECR I-13589.

334 Provided that the contractual terms of those transactions, particularly those concerned with setting the level of rentals, correspond to arm's length terms and that the involvement of an intermediate third party company in those transactions is not such as to preclude the application of those provisions, a matter which it is for the national court to determine. If certain contractual terms of the leasing transactions at issue and/or the intervention of an intermediate third party company in those transactions, constituted an abusive practice, those transactions must be redefined so as to re-establish the situation that would have prevailed in the absence of the elements of those contractual terms which were abusive and/or in the absence of the intervention of that company.

In the *Paul Newey* case[335] the ECJ ruled that the contractual arrangements normally constitute a factor to be taken into consideration when the supplier and the recipient in a "supply of services transaction" have to be identified. It is however possible that those contractual terms do not wholly reflect the economic and commercial reality of the transactions. In that situation the economic reality will have to be taken into account. That is in particular the case if those contractual terms constitute a purely artificial arrangement which does not correspond with the economic and commercial reality of the transactions.[336]

On the question how should abusive practices be sanctioned, in *Halifax* the ECJ clarified that a finding of abusive practice must not lead to a penalty, for which a clear and unambiguous legal basis would be necessary, but rather to an obligation to repay, simply as a consequence of that finding, which rendered undue all or part of the deductions of input VAT.[337] From this the ECJ concluded that transactions involved in an abusive practice *must be redefined so as to re-establish the situation that would have prevailed in the absence of the transactions constituting that abusive practice.*

In *Cussens* the ECJ decided that the prohibition of abusive practices qualifies as a general principle of EU law that can directly be invoked against an individual (in that case it was to refuse the benefit of an exemption) irrespective of the absence of national measure giving effect to this principle in the domestic legal order, without it being contrary to the principles of legal certainty and of the protection of legitimate expectations.[338]

2.13 Obligations of Taxable Persons and Certain Non-Taxable Persons

Under the title "Obligations of Taxable Persons and Certain Non-Taxable Persons" the Recast VAT Directive in Title XI deals with the obligation to pay, identification, invoicing, accounting, recapitulative statements, miscellaneous provisions and obligations relating to certain importations and exportations.

2.13.1 Obligation to Pay

On 17 October 2000, the European Council adopted Directive 2000/65/EC abolishing the obligation of European traders under the VAT system to appoint a fiscal representative in Member States in which they are not established. The Directive provides that the appointment of a tax representative may no longer be an obligation but an option for European businesses carrying out taxable transactions in another Member State. However, Member States are allowed to retain the possibility of deciding that the recipient of a supply may be held liable for payment of the VAT (reverse charge mechanism).

335 Case C-653/11 (*Paul Newey*), ECLI:EU:C:2013:409.
336 For a further reflection on the criterion of economic reality the authors refer to: A.J. van Doesum en F.J.G. Nellen, "Economic Reality in EU VAT", EC Tax Review volume 29, issue 5, 2020.
337 Compare however case C-158/08 (*Pometon*), ECLI:EU:C:2009:349, para. 29 where the ECJ ruled that an importer who improperly brings himself within the inward processing procedure and benefits from it by artificially creating the conditions required for its application is obliged to pay the duties on the products concerned, without prejudice, where appropriate, to administrative, civil or criminal sanctions provided for by national law.
338 Case C-251/16 (*Cussens and others*), 2017, ECLI:EU:C:2017:881.

(1) Persons Liable for Payment of VAT to the Tax Authorities
As a general principle, or main rule (without explicitly stating this), Article 193 RVD provides that VAT is payable by any taxable person carrying out a taxable supply of goods or services, except where it is payable by another person in the cases referred to in Articles 194 to 199 and Article 202.

As mentioned in section 2.7.3 under the main rule for the place of supply B2B- services are taxed in the country of the recipient. Article 196 RVD provides for a reverse charge mechanism in case the supplier of the service is not established in the recipient's Member State. Under the reverse charge rule the recipient instead of the supplier will be obliged to report the VAT due on the service. This reverse charge rule is mandatory for EU Member States to implement in their national legislation. A similar mandatory provision applies for the supply of gas, electricity, heating and cold (Article 195 RVD. Under Article 194 RVD) Member States have the option to implement a reverse charge rule for other supplies of goods or services in a situation where the supplier is not established in the EU Member State where the supply is taxed.

Article 192a RVD provides that for the section of the Directive dealing with persons liable for payment of VAT, a taxable person who has a fixed establishment within the territory of the Member State where the tax is due shall be regarded as a taxable person who is not established within that Member State (*i.e.* there is no force d'attraction) when the following conditions are met:

(a) he makes a taxable supply of goods or of services within the territory of that Member State;
(b) an establishment which the supplier has within the territory of that Member State does not intervene in that supply *i.e.* the technical or human resources of the establishment are in no way used by him for the fulfilment of that supply.[339]

Article 53 (2) IR defines the concept of intervention and states that:

> Where a taxable person has a fixed establishment within the territory of the Member State where the VAT is due, that establishment shall be considered as not intervening in the supply of goods or services within the meaning of point (b) of Article 192a of Directive 2006/112/EC, unless the technical and human resources of that fixed establishment are used by him for transactions inherent in the fulfilment of the taxable supply of those goods or services made within that Member State, before or during this fulfilment.
>
> Where the resources of the fixed establishment are only used for administrative support tasks such as accounting, invoicing and collection of debt-claims, they shall not be regarded as being used for the fulfilment of the supply of goods or services.
>
> However, if an invoice is issued under the VAT identification number attributed by the Member State of the fixed establishment, that fixed establishment shall be regarded as having intervened in the supply of goods or services made in that Member State unless there is proof to the contrary.

339 For a recent application of this provision, see CJEU 3 June 2021, C-931/19 (*Titanium*), ECLI:EU:C:2021:446. The case concerns the lease of immovable property by a company not established in the Member State of taxation.

Article 197(1) RVD provides for the reverse charge in cases of triangulation, *i.e.* where business A established in Member State A sells goods to business B established in Member State B[340] which in turn sells the goods to business C established in Member State C; the goods are directly transported from Member State A to Member State C and business C (or a non-taxable legal person C) is then designated as the person liable for payment of the VAT, *i.e.* the VAT that B should have charged to C had B been registered in Member State C, see also section 2.7.2.

Article 197(2) RVD allows Member States to derogate from the provision above where the taxable person (B) who is not established in the country (C) has appointed a fiscal representative in that country, *i.e.* in Member State C. As we will see below, appointing a fiscal representative is an option for businesses established in the EU and possibly compulsory for businesses established outside the EU.

Article 198(1) RVD provides that where specific transactions relating to investment gold between a taxable person who is a member of a regulated gold bullion market and another taxable person who is not a member of that market are taxed pursuant to Article 352 RVD, Member States must designate the customer as the person liable for payment of VAT. (Article 352 RVD provides that a Member State may apply VAT to specific transactions relating to investment gold which take place in that Member State between taxable persons who are members of a gold bullion market regulated by the Member State concerned or between such a taxable person and another taxable person who is not a member of that market.) If the customer who is not a member of the regulated gold bullion market is a taxable person required to be identified for VAT purposes in the Member State in which the tax is due solely in respect of the transactions referred to in Article 352, the vendor must fulfil the tax obligations on behalf of the customer, in accordance with the law of that Member State.

According to Article 198(2) RVD, where gold material or semi-manufactured products of a purity of 325/1000 or greater, or investment gold as defined in Article 344(1) is supplied by a taxable person exercising one of the options for taxation under Articles 348, 349 and 350, *i.e.* by persons who produce investment gold or transform gold into investment gold, by persons who, in the course of their economic activity, normally supply gold for industrial purposes and by agents who act in the name and on behalf of those persons, Member States may designate the customer as the person liable for payment of VAT.

Article 199 RVD allows Member States to provide that the person liable for payment of VAT is the taxable person to whom any of the following supplies are made:

(a) the supply of construction work, including repair, cleaning, maintenance, alteration and demolition services in relation to immovable property, as well as the handing-over of construction works regarded as a supply of goods pursuant to Article 14(3);

(b) the supply of staff engaged in activities covered by point (a);

340 If B is registered or has appointed a representative in Member State A, the simplified rules do not apply in certain Member States.

(c) the supply of immovable property, as referred to in Article 135(1)(j) and (k), *i.e.* the supply of a building or parts thereof, and of the land on which it stands, other than the supply referred to in point (a) of Article 12(1) and the supply of land which has not been built on other than the supply of building land as referred to in point (b) of Article 12(1) where the supplier has opted for taxation of the supply pursuant to Article 137;
(d) the supply of used material, used material which cannot be reused in the same state, scrap, industrial and non-industrial waste, recyclable waste, part processed waste and certain goods and services, as listed in Annex VI;[341]
(e) the supply of goods provided as security by one taxable person to another in execution of that security;
(f) the supply of goods following the cession of a reservation of ownership to an assignee and the exercising of this right by the assignee;
(g) the supply of immovable property sold by a judgment debtor in a compulsory sale procedure.[342]

When applying the option provided for above, Member States may specify the supplies of goods and services covered, and the categories of suppliers or recipients to whom these measures may apply. On 29 September 2009, the Commission presented its Proposal for a Directive amending the Recast VAT Directive 2006/112/EC as regards an optional and temporary application of the reverse charge mechanism in relation to supplies of certain goods and services susceptible to fraud.[343]

The purpose of Article 199a RVD is to allow the temporary application of the reverse charge mechanism to combat existing fraud in relation to trade involving certain fraud-sensitive goods and services, *i.e.* mobile telephones, integrated circuits, carbon emission certificates and telecommunication services.

On 23 July 2013 the Council adopted the quick reaction mechanism (Directive 2013/42/EU), which is now listed in Article 199b RVD. The quick reaction mechanism allows Member States to request the European Commission to derogate from the provisions of the VAT Directive applying a reverse charge rule in case of sudden and massive forms of VAT fraud. After the European Commission has received all information necessary, it will respond within a period of one month.

On 20 December 2018 the Council on the initiative of the Czech Republic adopted Directive 2018/2057/EU[344] providing the opportunity for EU Member States that deal with a high level of VAT fraud to implement a general reverse charge mechanism (*i.e.* apply the reverse charge rule on all local supplies in that EU Member State that exceed a threshold of 17.500 euro per transaction) under strict conditions and with approval of the Council. Up till now there is not one EU Member State that has requested for application of the general reverse charge rule, not even the Czech Republic, and it is not expected that one of the

341 Relevant case law: C-550/14 (*Envirotec Denmark*), ECLI:EU:C:2016:354.
342 Relevant case law: C-125/12 (*Promociones y Construcciones BJ 200*), ECLI:EU: C:2013:392, C-499/13 (*Macikowski*), ECLI:EU:C:2015:201 and C-564/15 (*Farkas*), ECLI:EU:C:2017:302.
343 COM(2009) 511 final.
344 OJ L 329, 27.12.2018, p. 3–7.

EU Member States will request it. The general reverse charge mechanism can be applied until 30 June 2022 only.

Article 200 RVD provides that any person effecting a taxable intra-Community acquisition of goods is liable to pay VAT.

Based on Article 201 RVD, on importation, VAT is payable by any person or persons designated or recognized as liable by the Member State of importation.

Article 202 RVD stipulates that VAT is payable by any person who causes goods to cease to be covered by the arrangements or situations listed in Articles 156, 157, 158, 160 and 161 RVD (regarding the exemptions for transactions relating to international trade).

Finally, Article 203 RVD provides that VAT is payable by any person who enters the VAT on an invoice.[345]

Member States may not prescribe a tax representative for businesses established within the EU. Article 204 RVD introduces the option for a foreign taxpayer to appoint a tax representative, unless a tax representative must (at the choice of the Member State involved) be appointed, *i.e.* by persons established or having their seat in a third country where no legal instruments exist relating to mutual assistance.[346]

A common provision, Article 205 RVD (ex Article 21(3) Sixth Directive), allows Member States to provide that someone other than the person liable for payment is held jointly and severally liable for payment of the VAT.

(2) Payment Arrangements

Under the heading "Payment Arrangements" the VAT Directive contains the not unimportant provision (Article 206 RVD) that any taxable person liable for payment of VAT must pay the net amount of the VAT when submitting the VAT return. Member States may, however, set a different date for payment of that amount or may require interim payments to be made.

Articles 207 to 209 RVD provide that Member States must take the measures necessary to ensure that persons who are regarded as liable for payment of VAT instead of a taxable person not established in their respective territory, persons held to be jointly and severally liable, the customer for investment gold as the person liable and non- taxable legal persons who are liable for payment of VAT due in respect of intra- Community acquisitions of goods, comply with the payment obligations.

345 See Joined Cases C-78 to 80/02 (*Marie Karageorgou*), [2003] ECR I-13295.

346 In Case C-249/05 (*Commission v. Finland*), [2006] ECR I-80*, the ECJ held that, by imposing an obligation to appoint a tax representative on taxable persons not established in the country who carry out taxable transactions in Finland and are established in another Member State or in the territory of a third country with which a convention has been concluded concerning mutual assistance Finland has failed to fulfil its obligations under Articles 21 and 22 of the Sixth Directive.

Furthermore, Article 210 RVD instructs Member States to adopt arrangements for payment of VAT on intra-Community acquisitions of new means of transport and on intra-Community acquisitions of products subject to excise duty, as referred to in Article 2(1)(b)(iii) RVD.

The Member States are authorized in Article 211 RVD to lay down rules for the making of declarations and payments, which are generally provisions copied from the rules applicable to customs declarations. However, Member States may provide that the VAT payable on importation of goods by taxable persons or persons liable to tax need not be paid at the time of importation, on condition that the tax is mentioned as such in the normal periodic VAT return. This system is generally referred to as the postponed accounting system (PAS).[347] It should be noted that Article 143(d) RVD (as amended by Directive 2009/69/EC) exempts imports when the goods are subsequently (exempt) intra-Community supplied by the importer, thus to a large extent neutralizing the advantages of importing via a Member State applying the postponed accounting system (PAS) vis-à-vis the Member States not doing so.

Finally, with regard to payment obligations Article 212 RVD provides that Member States may release taxable persons from payment of the VAT due where the amount is insignificant.

2.13.2 Identification

Article 213 RVD prescribes that every taxable person must state when his activity as a taxable person commences, changes or ceases. Member States must allow, and may require, the statement to be made by electronic means.

It follows from the additional provisions regarding identification numbers and the provision that Member States must adopt arrangements for declaration and subsequent payment (in the case of intra-Community acquisitions of new means of transport) that not every individual necessarily has to register when such acquisition occurs. However, acquisitions above the threshold of EUR 10,000 by flat-rate scheme farmers, taxable persons not entitled to deduction and non-taxable legal persons (or because they have opted for taxation) trigger the obligation to register since in such cases they effect (taxable) intra-Community acquisitions of goods (Article 213(2) RVD).

Article 214 RVD obliges the Member States to identify, by an individual identification number, having a prefix by which the Member State of issue may be identified (see Article 215 RVD), every taxable person, except in cases of occasional transactions or occasional supplies of new means of transport (section 2.6.6), but including certain categories of taxable persons when their purchases exceed the minimum threshold of EUR 10,000 or they have opted to be taxed on intra-Community acquisitions.

347 Case 42/83 (*Denkavit*), [1984] ECR 2649, in which the ECJ held that differences in time limits prescribed by national legislation regarding the taxation of imports and taxation of domestic transactions may, in certain circumstances, constitute an infringement of now Article 110 TFEU. Nevertheless, tax periods which serve as a basis for calculating the net tax position of each taxable person under the internal system need not, as Community legislation stands at present, be taken into consideration in the comparison of the periods for payment.

Directive 2008/8/EC added to Article 214 that the Member States must identify by means of an individual number every taxable person who within their respective territory *receives* services for which he is liable to pay VAT pursuant to Article 196 and every taxable person, established within their respective territory, who *supplies* services within the territory of another Member State for which VAT is payable solely by the recipient pursuant to Article 196 RVD.

2.13.3 Invoicing

The European VAT is a consumption type of value added tax based on the so- called subtractive/indirect method of calculating the added value, also referred to as the credit or invoice method of deduction.[348] In contrast to another method of calculating the added value – the subtractive/direct method[349] – in the credit method the invoice plays a pivotal role. An invoice has three functions: it contains information as to which VAT regime is applicable, it enables the tax authorities to carry out controls, and it enables customers to prove, if necessary, their right to deduction. The invoice has been dubbed the "admission ticket to deduction".[350]

On 20 December 2001, the Council adopted Directive 2001/115/EC amending the Sixth Directive with a view to simplifying, modernizing and harmonizing the conditions laid down for invoicing in respect of VAT.[351] This Directive has been transposed in the RVD in Articles 217 to 250. On 13 July 2010, the Council adopted Directive 2010/45/ EU amending Directive 2006/112/EU on the common system of value added tax as regards the rules on invoicing (hereinafter referred to as the Directive on invoicing rules).[352] The adopted changes are applicable from 1 January 2013.

Below the rules based on the Directive on invoicing rules are dealt with distinguishing between:
- issuance and contents of an invoice;
- paper invoices and electronic invoices; and
- storage of invoices.

Issuance and Contents of an Invoice
The Directive on invoicing rules aims at creating a set of harmonised rules for Business to Business (B2B) invoices with the consequence that a taxable person issuing an invoice from where he is identified for VAT will have legal certainty that the invoice is valid throughout the EU. For Business to Consumer (B2C) supplies the applicable rules remained as the place of taxation but with greater harmonisation and transparency for business. The Directive attempts to balance the needs of Member States to control the tax, and the need to reduce

348 In which the value added is calculated as follows (*t* is the tax rate): *t* (output) – *t* (input).
349 In which the total sales minus the total purchases equal the added value inclusive the tax: *t* (output – input): what in French is called the *base sur base* method.
350 See AG Sir Gordon Slynn in Case 123/87 (*Jeunehomme*), [1988] ECR 4517.
351 O.J. 2002, L 15, p. 24.
352 O.J. 2010, L 189, p. 1. On 5 October 2011, the Commission published not legally binding "Explanatory Notes" on the VAT invoicing rules, intended to serve as a guidance tool that can be used to clarify the application of the VAT invoicing rules.

administrative burdens. According to the Commission, transparency for business can be achieved by requiring Member States to make available on a website detailed information regarding invoicing rules for B2C supplies.

Issue of Invoices
According to the current Article 220 RVD, an invoice must be issued in respect of:
(1) Supplies of goods or services to another taxable person or to a non-taxable legal person;
(2) Supplies of goods subject to the distance selling rules of Article 33 and article 33 (a) as of 1 July 2021 (as of 1 July 20201 the obligation to issue invoices is dropped when the supplier uses the One Stop Shop (see section 2.14.6.3));
(3) Exempt intra-Community supplies of goods referred to in Article 138;
(4) Any payment on account made before one of the supplies of goods referred to in points (1), (2) and (3) was carried out;
(5) Any payment on account by another taxable person or non-taxable legal person before the provision of services was completed.

It should be noted that with regard to supplies of goods subject to the distance selling rules of Article 33 and exempt intra-Community supplies of goods referred to in Article 138 simplified invoices are not allowed, see further in this section below.

Member State where the Rules Are Applicable
As a main rule the invoicing rules of the EU Member State in which the supply of goods or services is deemed to be made apply. There are however three situations in which the Recast VAT Directive provides for different rules:

1. In case the supplier is not established in the EU Member State where the supply of goods or services is deemed to be made and the person liable for the payment of VAT is the person to whom the goods or services are supplied. In that situation the invoicing rules of the EU Member State of the supplier apply. In case of self-billing (the customer issues the invoice) we return to the main rule and the invoicing rules of the EU Member State where the supply is deemed to be made apply.
2. In case the supply is not subject to VAT in the EU the invoicing rules of the EU Member State of the supplier apply as well.
3. As of 1 January 2019 when the supplier reports supplies via the One Stop Shop (see section 2.14.6.2-2.14.6.4). the invoicing rules of its EU Member State of establishment or identification (if it is not established in the EU and has no EU intermediary) apply.

As Article 219a(2) RVD pursuant to its wording is not applicable in case of suppliers not established within the EU, it remains to be seen what the (detrimental) consequences are for the customer being liable for VAT.

It seems to us that if the supplier which issues the invoice is established in a third country, the applicable rules are those in paragraph 1.

With regard to self billing the principle for the applicable law is that the rules of the Member State apply where the self billing customer to whom the supply in question is made is established if the customer is liable to pay the tax.

Simplified Invoices

As a way of reducing burdens on business, the Recast VAT Directive allows Member States to release taxable persons from the requirement to issue invoices for certain exempt supplies (see Article 221, paragraph 2). Member States vary in their approach to this option: some make full use of it, others apply it restrictively and others do not apply it at all. Consequently businesses are often faced with selective exceptions to the general rule, and hence a greater administrative burden.

In order to harmonise the rules, it was proposed that for exempt B2B supplies an invoice be required in all cases, but that this need only be a simplified invoice where the customer is in the same Member State as the supplier and the supplier does not have a right to deduction at the preceding stage. Apparently the Member States could not agree on this uniform approach. They may require a full invoice or a simplified invoice or they may release an exempt taxable person from issuing an invoice altogether!

Based on Article 220a RVD Member States *must* allow taxable persons to issue a simplified invoice where the taxable amount of the supply of goods or services is less than EUR 100, where the invoice issued is a document or message treated as an invoice pursuant to Article 219 (providing that any document or message that amends and refers specifically and unambiguously to the initial invoice must be treated as an invoice) and where the taxable person uses the exemption for small businesses of Article 284 RVD (see section 2.14.1)

According to Article 220a(2) RVD a simplified invoice may not be allowed with regard to supplies of goods subject to the distance selling rules and intra-Community supplies of goods and services.

According to Article 221 RVD, Member States may impose on taxable persons an obligation to issue an invoice in respect of supplies of goods or services made in their territory, other than those referred to in Article 220 RVD. Member States may, in respect of those invoices, impose fewer obligations than for "full" invoices. Member States may even release taxable persons from the obligation to issue an invoice in respect of supplies of goods or services which they have made in their territory and which are exempt, with or without deductibility of the VAT.

According to Article 221(2) RVD Member States *may* impose on taxable persons who have established their business in their territory or who have a fixed establishment in their territory from which the supply is made, an obligation to issue a full or simplified invoice in respect of supplies of insurance and financial services exempt under points (a) to (g) of Article 135(1) RVD which those taxable persons have made in their territory or outside the Community.

Finally, Article 221(3) RVD allows Member States to release taxable persons from the obligation to issue a full or a simplified invoice (laid down in Article 220(1) or in Article 220a) in respect of supplies of goods or services which they have made in their territory and which are exempt, with or without deductibility of the VAT paid in the preceding stage, pursuant to Articles 110 (dealing with zero rating) as well as 111 (dealing with zero rating by Finland and Sweden), Article 125(1) (dealing with zero rating by Cyprus), Article 127 (dealing with zero rating by Malta), Article 128(1) (dealing with zero rating by Poland), Article 132 (exemption for certain activities in the public interest), points (h) to (l) of Article 135(1) (exemption for the supply of stamps, for betting, for the supply of buildings, building land and for leasing of real estate), Articles 136 (technical exemption), 371 (exemptions Annex X, Part B), 375 (certain exemptions Annex X, Part B Greece), 376 and 377 (certain exemptions Annex X, Part B Spain and Portugal), Article 378(2) (certain exemptions Annex X, Part B Austria), Article 379(2) (certain exemptions Annex X, Part B Finland)) and Articles 380 to 390c (certain exemptions Annex X, Part B latest 14 new Member States).

Time when an Invoice Must Be Issued

Article 222 RVD allows Member States to decide the time limit for issuing an invoice. This naturally creates different rules across the EU and the possibility for different tax points. Where the tax becomes chargeable on cross-border supplies of services, this has already given rise to an amendment of the rules to create a common tax point (see section 2.8 above) in order to ensure accurate exchange of information on recapitulative statements for services.

With the aim of creating a common date on which tax becomes chargeable on intra-Community supplies of goods and cross-border supplies of services subject to the reverse charge procedure it is important that the invoice is issued in time to provide proof of these supplies. The Directive on invoicing rules therefore lays down that taxable persons must issue an invoice at the latest by 15 calendar days in the month following that in which the chargeable event occurred. In this way both the supplier and customer have sufficient time to record the supply in the same tax period.

Article 222 RVD provides:

For supplies of goods carried out in accordance with the conditions specified in Article 138 RVD or for supplies of services for which VAT is payable by the customer pursuant to Article 196 RVD, an invoice shall be issued no later than on the fifteenth day of the month following that in which the chargeable event occurs. For other supplies of goods or services Member States may impose time limits on taxable persons for the issue of invoices. This rule means that companies will be obliged to issue their invoices no later than the 15th day of the month following that in which the chargeable event occurs for intra-Community supplies of goods or for supplies of services to customers in other Member States. Business may also issue the invoice earlier if they wish. To reduce the burden on business it was deemed to be sufficient to stipulate an obligatory time limit only for intra-Community supplies to improve control possibilities with the help of recapitulative statements. The Member States may impose time limits for domestic supplies that are different than the time limit for intra-community supplies.

Summary Invoices

Article 223 RVD allows Member States to lay down conditions for summary invoices, resulting in different sets of conditions in different Member States. It provides that:

> Member States shall allow taxable persons to issue summary invoices which detail several separate supplies of goods or services provided that VAT on the supplies mentioned in the summary invoice becomes chargeable during the same calendar month.

To this provision is added that Member States may allow summary invoices to include supplies for which VAT has become chargeable during a period of time longer than one calendar month, *without prejudice to Article 222*, meaning that only intra-Community supplies of goods or services may be included of another month as long as the summary invoice is issued no later than on the fifteenth day of the month following that in which the chargeable event occurred.

Self-Billing

Under the current rules (see Article 220 RVD), an invoice can be issued by the supplier, by the customer, or by a third party on behalf of the supplier. For commercial reasons it is important to keep these options. According to Article 224 RVD, invoices may be drawn up by the customer in respect of the supply to him, by a taxable person, of goods or services, if there is a prior agreement between the two parties and provided that a procedure exists for the acceptance of each invoice by the taxable person supplying the goods or services. It is up to the Member States in whose territory the goods or services are supplied to determine the terms and conditions of such prior agreements and of the acceptance procedures between the taxable person and the customer. Member States may impose further and specific conditions (see Article 225 RVD) on taxable persons supplying goods or services in their territory concerning the issue of invoices by the customer. They may, in particular, require that such invoices be issued in the name and on behalf of the taxable person. These conditions must always be the same wherever the customer is established.

Thus, for self-billing (invoices issued by the customer), the conditions applicable vary between the Member States. The Directive on invoicing rules aims to withdraw to a large extent the Member States' option of imposing conditions on self-billed invoices so as to achieve a more harmonised set of rules across the EU. At the same time, in order to facilitate control of self-billed invoices, the customer is required to enter the words "self- billed invoice' on the invoice so that the supplier and tax authorities are aware of the issuer. The customer's VAT number is also required on the invoice.

Article 224 RVD provides that invoices may be drawn up by the customer in respect of the supply to him, by a taxable person, of goods or services, where there is a prior agreement between the two parties and provided that a procedure exists for the acceptance of each invoice by the taxable person supplying the goods or services. In principle, the only condition Member States may impose is that they may require that such invoices be issued in the name and on behalf of the taxable person. However, pursuant to Article 225 RVD, Member States may impose specific conditions on taxable persons in cases where the third party, or the customer, who issues invoices is established in a country with which no legal instrument exists relating to mutual assistance.

Outsourcing to Third Parties outside the EU
Based on Article 225 RVD, Member States may impose specific conditions on taxable persons supplying goods or services in their territory in cases where the third party, or the customer, who issues invoices is established in a country with which no legal instrument exists relating to mutual assistance. Article 235 RVD provides that Member States may lay down specific conditions for invoices issued by electronic means in respect of goods or services supplied in their territory from a country with which no legal instrument exists relating to mutual assistance.

According to the Commission, in general, both business and Member States take the view that imposing specific conditions on third parties outside the EU issuing invoices on behalf of taxable persons making supplies in the EU is unnecessary. The Council did not change Articles 225 and 235 RVD.

Invoice Details
According to the Commission, in general the details required on an invoice cause fewer problems for business. The details listed in Article 226 RVD seem to meet the needs of tax authorities without being too burdensome for business. However, what is noticeable is that when Member States require invoices to be issued for certain supplies, typically B2C, there is a corresponding disparity between the contents of the invoices as Member States can opt to require fewer details. However, this does not often have the intended burden reduction benefits because of the cost to businesses of setting up and adjusting billing systems to the different rules.

The Directive on invoicing rules aims to create two categories of invoices: full VAT invoices and simplified VAT invoices but fails to prescribe common rules when the different categories must be applied allowing Member States to differentiate in many circumstances. Member States will not be allowed to require different types of invoices falling between a full VAT invoice and a simplified VAT invoice. Businesses, of course, will still be free to add other details on the invoice.

Content of a Full VAT Invoice
An invoice is generally required to be issued for VAT purposes to evidence the VAT due to be paid to the Treasury and to allow the customer to exercise a right of deduction. The importance of the invoice in cases where a right to deduct can be exercised is clearly greater than where only VAT is due from the supplier.

With this in mind the Directive on invoicing rules aims to create a two tier system of invoicing. Firstly there is a full VAT invoice which is a compulsory invoice containing an extensive set of details for B2B supplies when there is the likelihood that the customer will be exercising a right to deduction, the supplier has a right of deduction at the preceding stage or for a cross border supply. Secondly, there is the option, or in certain cases the requirement, for a simplified invoice.

The requirements for a full VAT invoice can be found in Article 226 RVD, where we can differentiate between requirements applying to all invoices and requirements applying in certain situations.

The general requirements (for all invoices are):
1. the date of issue;
2. a sequential number, based on one or more series, which uniquely identifies the invoice;
3. the VAT identification number referred to in Article 214 under which the taxable person supplied the goods or services;
4. the full name and address of the taxable person and of the customer;
5. the quantity and nature of the goods supplied or the extent and nature of the services rendered;
6. the date on which the supply of goods or services was made or completed or the date on which the payment on account referred to in points (4) and (5) of Article 220 was made, in so far as that date can be determined and differs from the date of issue of the invoice;
7. the taxable amount per rate or exemption, the unit price exclusive of VAT and any discounts or rebates if they are not included in the unit price;
8. the VAT rate applied;
9. the VAT amount payable, except where a special arrangement is applied under which, in accordance with this Directive, such a detail is excluded;

The requirements applying to certain situations are:
1. the customer's VAT identification number, as referred to in Article 214, under which the customer received a supply of goods or services in respect of which he is liable for payment of VAT, or received a supply of goods as referred to in Article 138;
2. where the VAT becomes chargeable at the time when the payment is received in accordance with Article 66(b) and the right of deduction arises at the time the deductible tax becomes chargeable, the mention "Cash accounting';
3. where the customer receiving a supply issues the invoice instead of the supplier, the mention "Self-billing';
4. in the case of an exemption, reference to the applicable provision of this Directive, or to the corresponding national provision, or any other reference indicating that the supply of goods or services is exempt;
5. where the customer is liable for the payment of the VAT, the mention "Reverse charge';
6. in the case of the supply of a new means of transport made in accordance with the conditions specified in Article 138(1) and (2)(a), the characteristics as identified in point (b) of Article 2(2);
7. where the margin scheme for travel agents is applied, the mention "Margin scheme – Travel agents';
8. where one of the special arrangements applicable to second-hand goods, works of art, collectors' items and antiques is applied, the mention "Margin scheme – Second-hand goods'; "Margin scheme – Works of art' or "Margin scheme – Collector's items and antiques' respectively;
9. where the person liable for payment of VAT is a tax representative for the purposes of Article 204, the VAT identification number, referred to in Article 214, of that tax representative, together with his full name and address.

Article 227 RVD provides that Member States may require taxable persons established in their territory and supplying goods or services there to indicate the VAT identification number, referred to in Article 214, of the customer in cases other than those referred to in point (4) of Article 226.

Article 230 RVD provides:

> The amounts which appear on the invoice may be expressed in any currency, provided that the amount of VAT payable or to be adjusted is expressed in the national currency of the Member State, using the conversion rate mechanism provided for in Article 91.

According to Article 91(1) RVD, where information for determining the taxable amount on importation is expressed in a currency other than that of the Member State where assessment takes place, the exchange rate must be determined in accordance with the Community provisions governing the calculation of the value for customs purposes. Article 91(2) first paragraph RVD provides that where the factors used to determine the taxable amount of a transaction other than the importation of goods are expressed in a currency other than that of the Member State in which assessment takes place, the exchange rate applicable shall be the latest selling rate recorded, at the time VAT becomes chargeable, on the most representative exchange market or markets of the Member State concerned, or a rate determined by reference to that or those markets, in accordance with the rules laid down by that Member State.

The Directive on invoice rules replaced in Article 91(2) RVD, the second subparagraph and prescribes that Member States must accept the use of the latest exchange rate published by the European Central Bank at the time the tax becomes chargeable. Conversion between currencies other than the Euro shall be made by using the euro exchange rate of each currency. Member States may require that they be notified of the exercise of this option by the taxable person.

Content of a Simplified VAT Invoice

Member States must allow a simplified invoice (Article 220a RVD) or may allow the use of a simplified invoice (Article 221(1) and (2) RVD), see this section above. Article 226b RVD provides:

> As regards simplified invoices issued pursuant to Articles 220a and 221(1) and (2), Member States shall require at least the following details:
> (a) the date of issue;
> (b) identification of the taxable person supplying the goods or services;
> (c) identification of the type of goods or services supplied;
> (d) the VAT amount payable or the information needed to calculate it;
> (e) where the invoice issued is a document or message treated as an invoice pursuant to Article 219, specific and unambiguous reference to that initial invoice and the specific details which are being amended.
>
> They may not require details on invoices other than those referred to in Articles 226, 227 and 230.

It should be noted that in the Proposal on invoicing rules reference was made to "only the following details are required on simplified invoices"; apparently Member States are now allowed to require additional details as long as they stay within the limits of the details required for a full invoice (Article 226) or permitted under Article 227 with regard to the requirement of mentioning a VAT identification number in other cases than intra-Community transactions or permitted under Article 230 with regard to currency.

Article 220a (2) RVD disallows the use of simplified invoices for intra-Community supplies and distance selling.

Paper Invoices and Electronic Invoices
The Directive on invoicing rules requires that paper invoices and e-invoices should be treated equally (Article 218 RVD). Therefore, neither the Directive nor any of the Member States can make the use of any particular e-invoicing technology, such as EDI or electronic signatures, compulsory (see however derogations below under Article 395 RVD).

The principle for both electronic and paper invoicing is that the authenticity of the origin, the integrity of the content and the legibility of the invoice shall be ensured from the point in time of issuance until the end of the period for storage of the invoice. Any business control can be used to establish reliable audit trails linking invoices and supplies.

In case business controls are not appropriate, technology can also meet the aforementioned requirements when issuing electronic invoices. Examples of technologies that are mentioned in the Directive are EDI and advanced electronic signatures based on a qualified certificate and created by a secure signature creation device (*i.e.* qualified signatures).

Prior to switching from paper to electronic invoicing, the recipient is still required to accept electronic invoices. Electronic invoices are defined as invoices which have been issued and received in electronic format (Article 217 RVD).

Storage of Invoices
Article 244 RVD provides that every taxable person must ensure that copies of the invoices issued by himself, or by his customer or, in his name and on his behalf, by a third party, and all the invoices which he has received, are stored.

Article 245 RVD provides that the taxable person may decide the place of storage of all invoices provided that he makes the invoices or information stored in accordance with Article 244 available to the competent authorities without undue delay whenever they so request. Member States may require taxable persons established in their territory to notify them of the place of storage, if it is outside their territory. Member States may also require taxable persons established in their territory to store within that territory invoices issued by themselves or by their customers or, in their name and on their behalf, by a third party, as well as all the invoices that they have received, when the storage is not by electronic means guaranteeing full on-line access to the data concerned.

Article 247 RVD allows each Member State to determine the period throughout which taxable persons must ensure the storage of invoices.

2.13.4 Accounting

Articles 242 RVD provides for the following general obligation:

> Every taxable person shall keep accounts in sufficient detail for VAT to be applied and its application checked by the tax authorities.

Article 242a RVD as of 1 July 2021 lays down certain accounting provisions for electronic interfaces that facilitate supplies of goods and services. Article 54b IR defines the term facilitates, while Article 54c provides the details for the accounting obligations.

Article 243 RVD introduces special obligations (*inter alia* keeping a register) with regard to temporary intra-Community movements of goods providing that every taxable person must keep a register of the goods dispatched or transported, by that person or on his behalf, to a destination outside the territory of the Member State of departure but within the Community for the purposes of transactions consisting in work on those goods or their temporary use as referred to in points (f), (g) and (h) of Article 17(2) (*i.e.* the supply of a service performed for the taxable person and consisting of work on the goods in question physically carried out within the territory of the Member State in which dispatch or transport of the goods ends, the temporary use of the goods within the territory of the Member State in which dispatch or transport of the goods ends, for the purposes of the supply of services, the temporary use of the goods, for a period not exceeding 24 months, within the territory of another Member State). Furthermore, every taxable person must keep accounts in sufficient detail to enable the identification of goods dispatched to him from another Member State, by or on behalf of a taxable person identified for VAT purposes in that other Member State, and used for services consisting in valuations of those goods or work on those goods. A taxable person applying the call-off- stock-arrangement (Article 17a RVD) will need to keep a register as well (Article 243(3) RVD).

2.13.5 Returns

Returns must be submitted by a deadline, not later than 2 months after the end of the tax period. The tax period may be fixed at 1 or 2 months or a quarter or at different periods provided they do not exceed 1 year, Article 252 RVD. In addition to the information necessary to calculate the tax payable or refundable (Article 250 RVD), the Directive provides that the return must also set out the following information (Article 251 RVD):

(a) the total value, exclusive of VAT, of the (intra-Community) supplies of goods referred to in Article 138 in respect of which VAT has become chargeable during this tax period;

(b) the total value, exclusive of VAT, of the (distance selling) supplies of goods referred to in Articles 33 and 36 carried out within the territory of another Member State, in respect of which VAT has become chargeable during this tax period, where the place where dispatch or transport of the goods began is situated in the Member State in which the return must be submitted;

(c) the total value, exclusive of VAT, of the intra-Community acquisitions of goods, or transactions treated as such, pursuant to Article 21 or 22, made in the Member State in which the return must be submitted and in respect of which VAT has become chargeable during this tax period;

(d) the total value, exclusive of VAT, of the (distance selling) supplies of goods referred to in Articles 33 and 36 RVD carried out in the Member State in which the return must be submitted and in respect of which VAT has become chargeable during this tax period, where the place where dispatch or transport of the goods began is situated within the territory of another Member State;

(e) the total value, exclusive of VAT, of the supplies of goods carried out in the Member State in which the return must be submitted and in respect of which the taxable person has been designated, in accordance with Article 197, as liable for payment of VAT and in respect of which VAT has become chargeable during this tax period.

Member States must allow, and may require, the VAT return to be submitted by electronic means (Article 250 (2) RVD). It should be noted that some EU Member States apply real time reporting or SAF-T[353] in addition to VAT returns and it is expected that this is an important part of the future of VAT where these reporting obligations may ultimately replace traditional VAT returns.

2.13.6 Recapitulative Statements

With effect from 1993, every taxable person identified for VAT purposes must submit a recapitulative statement of the persons acquiring goods identified for VAT purposes to whom he has performed intra-Community supplies of goods – the so- called "European Sales List". The recapitulative statement must be drawn up for each calendar quarter within a period and in accordance with procedures to be determined by the Member States.

Article 262 RVD amended by Directive 2008/8/EC obliges suppliers of services (other than those that are exempt from VAT) to taxable persons, who are required to account for the VAT under the reverse charge mechanism pursuant to Article 196, to include those taxable persons and non-taxable legal persons identified for VAT purposes in their recapitulative statement.

From 1 January 2010 the recapitulative statement must in principle be drawn up for each calendar month within a period not exceeding one month and in accordance with procedures to be determined by the Member States. Member States will nevertheless be able to authorize operators with less than EUR 50,000 (excluding VAT) per quarter for cross-border supplies of goods and all service providers to continue to submit recapitulative statements on a quarterly basis, Article 263 RVD. Member States may in particular require the taxable persons who carry out intra- Community supplies of both goods and services to submit the recapitulative statement on a monthly basis when their combined supplies exceed EUR 50,000 in respect of a current quarter.

The recapitulative statement must set out (Article 264 RVD):

353 OECD (2005) ' Guidance on Tax Compliance for Business and Accounting Software', May 2005, p. 6 and OECD (2010) "Guidance for the Standard Audit File – Tax Version 2.0', April 2010.

(a) the VAT identification number of the taxable person in the Member State in which the recapitulative statement must be submitted and under which he has carried out the (exempt intra-Community) supply of goods in accordance with the conditions specified in Article 138(1) and under which he effected taxable supplies of services in accordance with the conditions laid down in Article 44 RVD;
(b) the VAT identification number of the person acquiring the goods or receiving the services in a Member State other than that in which the recapitulative statement must be submitted and under which the goods or services were supplied to him;
(c) the VAT identification number of the taxable person in the Member State in which the recapitulative statement must be submitted and under which he has carried out a transfer to another Member State, as referred to in Article 138(2)(c) RVD, and the number by means of which he is identified in the Member State in which the dispatch or transport ended;
(d) for each person who acquired goods or received services, the total value of the supplies of goods and the total value of the supplies of services carried out by the taxable person;
(e) in respect of supplies of goods consisting in transfers to another Member State, as referred to in Article 138(2)(c) RVD, the total value of the supplies, *i.e.* the purchase or cost price determined in accordance with Article 76 RVD;
(f) the amounts of adjustments made pursuant to Article 90 RVD, *i.e.* in the case of cancellation, refusal or total or partial non-payment.

2.13.7 Other Provisions

The Member States can release certain taxable persons from some or all obligations discussed in sections 2.13.2-2.13.6. Article 273 RVD allows Member States to impose other obligations which they deem necessary to ensure the correct collection of VAT and to prevent evasion. The obligations are subject to the requirement of equal treatment as between domestic transactions and transactions carried out between Member States. The obligations may not, in trade between Member States, give rise to formalities connected with the crossing of the EU's internal frontiers. Article 273 RVD cannot be relied upon in order to impose additional invoicing obligations over and above those laid down in Chapter 3 (discussed in section 2.13.3).

2.13.8 Obligations in Respect of Imports

Articles 275, 276 and 277 RVD apply to the importation of goods in free circulation which enter the Community from a third territory forming part of the customs territory of the Community. The formalities relating to the importation of the goods in free circulation which enter the Community from a third territory forming part of the customs territory of the Community are the same as those laid down by the Community customs provisions in force for the importation of goods into the customs territory of the Community (Article 275 RVD).

Article 276 RVD provides that where dispatch or transport of the goods referred to above ends at a place situated outside the Member State of their entry into the Community, they shall circulate in the Community under the internal Community transit procedure laid down by the Community customs provisions in force, in so far as they have been the subject of a declaration placing them under that procedure on their entry into the Community.

Where, on their entry into the Community, the goods in free circulation which enter the Community from a third territory forming part of the customs territory of the Community are in one of the situations which would entitle them, if they were imported, to be covered by one of the arrangements or situations referred to in Article 156 RVD (*i.e.* goods which are intended to be presented to Customs and, where applicable, placed in temporary storage, goods which are intended to be placed in a free zone or in a free warehouse, goods which are intended to be placed under customs warehousing arrangements or inward processing arrangements, goods which are intended to be admitted into territorial waters in order to be incorporated into drilling or production platforms and goods which are intended to be admitted into territorial waters for the fuelling and provisioning of drilling or production platforms), or by a temporary importation arrangement with full exemption from import duties, Member States must take the measures necessary to ensure that the goods may remain in the Community under the same conditions as those laid down for the application of those arrangements or situations (Article 277 RVD).

Articles 279 and 280 RVD apply to the exportation of goods in free circulation which are dispatched or transported from a Member State to a third territory forming part of the customs territory of the Community.

Article 279 RVD provides that the formalities relating to the exportation of the goods in free circulation which are dispatched or transported from a Member State to a third territory forming part of the customs territory of the Community are the same as those laid down by the Community customs provisions in force for the exportation of goods from the customs territory of the Community.

In the case of goods which are temporarily exported from the Community, in order to be reimported, Member States must take the measures necessary to ensure that, on reimportation into the Community, such goods may be covered by the same provisions as would have applied if they had been temporarily exported from the customs territory of the Community (Article 280 RVD).

2.14 Special Schemes

The VAT Directive provides for special schemes for small undertakings, farmers, travel agents, second-hand goods, investment gold and special schemes for reporting and remitting VAT on B2C services and distance sales by non-established businesses. Since 1 July 2021 a special arrangement exists for the reporting and remitting of import VAT.

2.14.1 Small and Medium-Sized Enterprises

The special scheme for small undertakings (Arts. 281 to 295 RVD) provisionally allows Member States to use simplified procedures such as flat-rate schemes for charging and collecting the tax, but also requires that the tax cannot be reduced. The intention of this provision is apparently to reduce the compliance burden on small enterprises[354] and not to reduce the amount of tax, as is the intention of reduced rates or exemptions.

Member States are permitted to exempt taxable persons with an annual turnover[355] not exceeding varying thresholds as mentioned in Articles 284 to 287 RVD (this is an exemption without the right to deduct VAT). Any small business that is eligible for the exemption under the special scheme can opt to apply the normal VAT rules or simplified procedure (Article 290 RVD). This sales-related exemption (in this case the exemption is not linked to the nature of the supplies but to the turnover on an annual basis) clearly results in both administrative simplification and a tax reduction. Since annual turnover is not necessarily the best indicator of the size nor of the ability of a business to bear the burden of maintaining records, the scheme for small businesses is unsatisfactory in a number of respects, especially in relation to the neutrality of the basis of taxation and the budgeting problems caused thereby. A key issue is also that the scheme cannot be applied by businesses established in other EU Member States. According to the CJEU this restricts the freedom to provide services, but this restriction is justified because of guaranteeing the effectiveness of fiscal supervision in order to combat fraud, tax evasion and possible abuse and the objective of the scheme for small undertakings, which is to support the competitiveness of such undertakings.[356]

As of 1 January 2025, the special scheme for SMEs will be amended.[357] The main aspects of these amendments are the cross-border application of the scheme and the possibility for Member States to set thresholds per sector.

2.14.2 Farmers

The second special scheme is restricted to the agricultural sector,[358] because farmers are considered to be another group that may be burdened by the keeping of detailed records necessary for a VAT return (Articles 295 to 305 RVD). Unlike the vast majority of small businesses, the administrative problems of farmers, so it was believed, cannot be solved by exempting them up to a certain level of turnover. In contrast to most small businesses, which sell to final consumers, farmers sell primarily to manufacturers, wholesalers and other taxable persons. An exemption would consequently lead to accumulation of taxes, *i.e.* of the non-deducted input tax. In order to avoid this and to ensure tax neutrality, the Directive offers a special scheme – the common flat-rate scheme – in which the following

354 See Case C-128/05 (*Commission v. Austria*), [2006] ECR I-9265.
355 The scheme does not apply to supplies of goods and services effected by a taxable person who is not established in the territory of the country. See Case C-97/ 09 (*Ingrid Schmelz*), [2010] ECR I- 10465.
356 Case C-97/09 (*Schmelz*), [2010] ECR I-10465.
357 Council Directive (EU) 2020/285 of 18 February 2020 amending Directive 2006/112/EC on the common system of value added tax as regards the special scheme for small enterprises and Regulation (EU) No 904/2010 as regards the administrative cooperation and exchange of information for the purpose of monitoring the correct application of the special scheme for small enterprises, OJ L 62, 2.3.2020, p. 13–23.
358 See Case C-43/04 (*Stadt Sundern*), [2005] ECR I-4491and Case C-321/02 (*Detlev Harbs*), [2004] ECR I-7101.

mechanism is applied: supplies by a farmer under the special scheme are exempt, but the farmer is compensated with a flat rate to offset the value added tax charged to him on inputs. The compensation, which either is paid to the farmer or can be deducted by the customers (in effect the deduction which would otherwise be available to farmers is passed forward to their customers) is calculated as a percentage fixed by the Member State and applied to the farmer's turnover. Since the States themselves calculate the charge on inputs, it is not unlikely that the desired neutrality of the tax base is impaired and budgetary difficulties are caused. In our view, the scheme for small undertakings is preferable, notwithstanding the (slight) accumulation of tax.

2.14.3 Travel Agents

Also travel agents enjoy a special VAT scheme (in Articles 306 to 310 RVD). The problem with travel agents is that they usually purchase services for their customers in their own name. Without special provisions the traveller would have to pay VAT on the amount he pays to the travel agents, which results in taxation where the travel agent is established. The special scheme for travel agents provides that the taxable amount is the travel agent's margin, *i.e.* the difference between the total amount paid by the traveller, exclusive of VAT, and the actual cost to the travel agent of the purchased services. The travel agent cannot deduct the VAT on the services purchased (Article 310 RVD). The result is that these purchased services are taxed where they are actually enjoyed and the service of the agent where he is established.

According to Article 306 RVD, the special scheme for travel agents applies to transactions of travel agents (including tour operators) where the travel agents deal with travellers in their own name and use the supplies and services of other taxable persons in the provision of travel facilities. The special scheme does not apply to travel agents who are acting only as intermediaries.

The rules mentioned above are not always easy to apply.[359] A travel agent must distinguish between supplies he makes, without involvement of third parties (in principle taxed according to the normal rules, with the right to deduction), supplies he makes as intermediary (either, based on a fiction, with full deduction, or when relating to travel insurances, without deduction) and supplies made under the margin scheme (no deduction or refund with regard to services bought from third parties, while the margin is only subject to VAT in so far as relating to travel services within the Community). Furthermore it should be noted that not all Member States apply the special scheme for travel agents. Based on Article 370 RVD juncto Annex X, Part A, point (4), Member States may continue to subject the services of travel agents and those of travel agents acting in the name and on account of the traveller to tax, for journeys outside the Community. Based on Article 371 RVD juncto Annex X, Part B, point (13), Member States may continue to exempt the services of travel

359 See, *inter alia*, Case C-163/91 (*Van Ginkel*), [1992] ECR I-5723, Joined Cases C-308/96 and C-94/97 (*Howden Court Hotel*), [1998] ECR I-6229, Case C-149/01 (*First Choice Holidays plc*), [2003] ECR I-6289 and Case C-31/10 (*MINERVA Kulturreisen GmbH*), [2010] ECR I- 12889, C-422/17 (*Skarpa Travel*), ECLI:EU: C:2018:1029 and C-552/17 (*Alpenchalets Resorts*) ECLI:EU:C:2018:1032.

agents and those of travel agents acting in the name and on account of the traveller, for journeys within the Community.

2.14.4 Second-Hand Goods, Works of Art, Collectors' Items and Antiques

Article 32 of the original Sixth Directive provided that the Council, acting unanimously on a proposal from the Commission, must adopt before 31 December 1977 a Community taxation system to be applied to used goods, works of art, antiques and collectors' items. After many years during which the Council failed to do so, notwithstanding various proposals of the Commission, finally, in 1994 the Council adopted Directive 94/5/EC of 14 February 1994 "Supplementing the Common System of Value Added Tax and Amending Directive 77/388/EEC – Special Arrangements Applicable to Second-Hand Goods, Works of Art, Collectors' Items and Antiques". The purpose of this scheme is to prevent double taxation and the distortion of competition between taxable persons when products return from the consumer sphere to the productive sphere.[360]

In the RVD the "second-hand goods regime" is covered by Articles 311 to 343 RVD. Article 311 RVD starts with definitions; *inter alia*, "second-hand goods" are defined as tangible movable property that is suitable for further use as it is or after repair, other than works of art, collectors' items or antiques and other than precious metals or precious stones as defined by the Member States.[361] From this definition it may be derived that the special scheme for second-hand goods is not applicable to immovable property and that second-hand goods are by definition used goods, since they must be suitable for "further" use. According to Article 313 RVD, in respect of supplies of second-hand goods, works of art, collectors' items and antiques effected by taxable dealers (not to be confused with taxable dealers in energy products, see section 2.7.1), Member States must apply special arrangements for taxing the profit margin made by the taxable dealer, referred to as the "margin scheme" (see Article 314 RVD). A taxable dealer is any taxable person who, in the course of his economic activity and with a view to resale, purchases, or applies for the purposes of his business, or imports, second-hand goods, works of art, collectors' items or antiques, whether that taxable person is acting for himself or on behalf of another person pursuant to a contract under which commission is payable on purchase or sale. A taxable dealer does not have to sell the acquired good immediately, but can first use it for another activity. As the CJEU pointed out in the *Jyske Finans* case[362] there is a taxable dealer in case of sale and leaseback undertakings where a taxable person purchases second-hand cars and subsequently leases them to their previous owners, when the resale after the leasing period ends forms part of the normal business of that taxable person and the intention to resell is present at the moment of purchase, even when the reselling is secondary in comparison with the leasing. A taxable dealer may apply the normal VAT arrangements (see Articles 319 en 320 RVD) which choice can be made for each individual supply. Pursuant to Article 333 RVD Member States may determine to apply the margin scheme or a scheme providing for a special taxable amount in cases of supplies of second-hand goods, works of

360 51th recital to the preamble of Directive 2006/112/EC.

361 See Case C-320/02 (*Förvaltnings AB Stenholmen*), [2004] ECR I-3509 and Case C-280/04 (*Jyske Finans*), [2005] ECR I-10683.

362 Case C-668/15 (*Jyske Finans*), ECLI:EU:C:2017:278.

art, collectors' items or antiques effected by an organiser of sales by public auction, acting in his own name, pursuant to a contract under which commission is payable on the sale of those goods by public auction.

2.14.5 Investment Gold

On 12 October 1998, the Council adopted Directive 98/80/EC introducing a special scheme for investment gold which provides for an exemption of investment gold (Article 344-356 RVD). Member States must also exempt services of so-called disclosed agents (acting in the name and for the account of another) when they intervene in the supply of investment gold for their principal. The exemption from VAT on investment gold transactions is an exemption with the right to limited deduction. Certain operators may opt for normal taxation with *full* deduction. The scheme introduces a common standard of minimum obligations in accounting and documentation, as the different types of use of gold may well open windows to VAT fraud. Furthermore, in order to prevent tax fraud the reverse charge mechanism is applied. There are special simplifications for transactions carried out on a bullion market regulated by a Member State.

2.14.6 Special schemes for reporting and remitting VAT by non-established businesses

2.14.6.1 Introduction

Since 1 July 2003 special schemes are in place for taxable persons that need to pay VAT in several EU Member States where they are not established that allow for a single VAT return and payment in one EU Member State. These schemes have been gradually extended, the latest extension entered into application on 1 July 2021.

On 1 July 2003 the first special scheme was applied allowing non-EU-businesses to file a single VAT return for VAT due on electronically provided services to non-taxable persons in the EU. This scheme accompanied the change in the place of supply rules where services by these suppliers established outside the EU to EU non-taxable persons were subject to VAT in the EU Member State of the customer as of that date.

In 2015 the scheme has been extended to cover all B2C telecommunication, broadcasting and electronically provided services of both EU and non-EU suppliers. This extension again accompanied a change in the place of supply rules.

As of 1 July 2021 the schemes were extended to cover all other B2C services, EU distance sales and in certain cases domestic B2C supplies of goods. The current scheme consists of three different schemes: the non-Union scheme (section 2.14.6.2), the Union scheme (section 2.14.6.3) and the Import One Stop Shop or I-OSS (section 2.14.6.4). Since 1 July 2021 a special arrangement exists for the reporting and remitting of import VAT. Because of its relation to the I-OSS, this scheme will be addressed in section 2.14.6.5.

2.14.6.2 Non-Union scheme

Under the non-Union scheme (Article 358a-369 RVD) taxable persons without an establishment in the EU can report VAT due on B2C supplies of services to non- taxable persons in the EU. Distance sales of goods cannot be reported through this scheme. Instead the Union scheme (section 2.14.6.3) in case of EU distance sales or the I-OSS (section 2.14.6.4) in case of distance sales of goods from third countries or third territories must be applied.

Under the non-Union scheme the supplier chooses a Member State to register, the Member State of Identification, where he files quarterly VAT returns (Article 364 RVD) in which he reports all VAT due on B2C services in the EU Member States, the Member States of Consumption. The supplier also pays the VAT to the Member State of Identification (Article 367 RVD) that distributes this VAT to the Member States of Consumption.

The non-Union scheme is an optional scheme for which the alternative is a VAT registration in all EU Member States where the supplier needs to remit VAT. It is not possible to deduct VAT in the VAT return filed under the non-Union scheme (Article 368 RVD). Instead the supplier will need to file for a refund request under the Thirteenth Directive or – in case he also has supplies that he cannot report under the non-Union scheme or any of the other special schemes or in case he hasn't used these other special schemes – deduct the VAT in a regular VAT return. It should however be noted that once opted for the non-Union scheme the supplier will be required to report all VAT on B2C services to EU non-taxable persons under the non-Union scheme. The option to use the non-Union scheme cannot be applied per Member State. Suppliers that make use of the non-Union scheme will be required to keep a record of information on the supplies reported under the non-Union scheme for ten years (Article 369 RVD).

2.14.6.3 The Union scheme

Under the Union scheme (Article 369a-369k RVD) three type of supplies can be reported:
1. EU distance sales (section 2.7.1) by EU and non-EU suppliers
2. Local sales in case of an electronic interface that is liable for the payment of VAT under Article 14a RVD (section 2.6).
3. B2C supplies of services by EU suppliers that are not established in the Member State where the service is subject to VAT (Article 369b RVD). Non-EU suppliers use the non-Union scheme (section 2.14.6.2) for reporting these B2C services.

The Union scheme can be used by three types of taxable persons:
1. Taxable persons with their main establishment in the EU. Their Member State of Identification is the Member State of their main establishment.
2. Taxable persons with their main establishment outside the EU, but one or more fixed establishments within the EU. Their Member State of Identification is the Member State of the fixed establishment – and in case they have a fixed establishment in more than one EU Member State, one of those Member States by choice.
3. Taxable persons without an establishment within the EU. Their Member State of Identification is the Member State where the transport or dispatch of the EU distance

sales starts. In case the supplier has stock in more than one EU Member State one of those EU Member States by choice (Article 369a (2) RVD).

Like under the non-Union scheme the supplier files quarterly VAT returns of all VAT due in the EU Member States on supplies covered by the scheme in the Member State of Identification (Article 369g RVD). The supplier makes a payment of the VAT amount to the Member State of Identification too, which distributes the VAT to the other Member States (Article 369j RVD). It should be noted that VAT due on B2C services subject to VAT in a Member State where the supplier is established (main or fixed establishment) cannot be reported under the Union scheme. Instead this VAT will be reported in a local VAT return.

Like the non-Union scheme the Union scheme is optional and no VAT can be deducted under the scheme (Article 369k RVD). Instead a refund request must be filed under Directive 2008/9/EC (EU suppliers) or the Thirteenth Directive (non- EU suppliers) or in case the supplier has the obligation to report VAT in a Member State on supplies that are not covered by the scheme, deduct the VAT in a local VAT return. The inability to deduct VAT can be a reason why the supplier chooses not to use the Union scheme, but it should be noted that if the supplier opts to use the scheme it will need to report all supplies that are eligible to be reported under the scheme through that scheme. It is not possible to use the scheme to report VAT in one EU Member State, but not in the other. Suppliers that make use of the Union scheme are required to keep a record of information on the supplies reported under the scheme for a period of ten years (Article 369k RVD).

2.14.6.4 Import One Stop Shop (I-OSS)

Like the non-Union and Union scheme the I-OSS (Article 369l-369x RVD) or "Special scheme for distance sales of goods imported from third territories or third countries', is a One Stop Shop system that allows a taxable person to report the VAT due on supplies in all 27 EU Member States through a single VAT return. The I-OSS however only applies to distance sales of goods from third countries or third territories with an intrinsic value of no more than 150 euros (excise goods are excluded, Article 369l RVD). With these type of supplies there are two taxable events for VAT: a supply of goods and an import of goods. If a supplier opts to use the I-OSS the import will be exempt from VAT (Article 143 (1) (ca) RVD) and the supplier will be required to report VAT in the Member State of arrival of the goods on the supply of those goods. This can be done through one single VAT return under the I-OSS.

The I-OSS can be used by EU and non-EU suppliers. EU suppliers must register for the scheme in the Member State of their main establishment or in case their main establishment is located outside the EU, but they have one or more fixed establishments in the EU in the EU Member State of the fixed establishment or in case of fixed establishments in multiple Member States in one of those Member States by choice. Non-EU suppliers must appoint an EU representative to make use of the scheme. The non-EU supplier will register for the scheme in the EU Member State of the representative, where the representative will file I-OSS returns on its behalf. An exception applies for non-EU suppliers established in a country with which the EU has concluded an agreement on mutual assistance similar in scope to Council Directive 2010/24/EU and Regulation (EU) No 904/2010 (currently only

Norway), who can use the scheme without appointing an EU representative and register for the scheme in a Member State of choice. This however only applies in case of distance sales of goods from that third country (Article 369m RVD). If the supplier supplies goods from other non-EU countries it will need an EU representative to report these sales under I-OSS.

The VAT returns must be filed monthly in the Member State of Identification (Article 369s RVD). VAT is due in the month in which the payment is accepted (Article 369n RVD).[363] The supplier also makes the payment to the Member State of Identification (Article 369v RVD), which will distribute the VAT to the other EU Member States. The scheme is optional and VAT cannot be deducted under the scheme (Article 369w RVD). Instead the supplier must file for a refund request under Directive 2008/9/EC (EU suppliers) or the Thirteenth Directive (non-EU suppliers) or in case the supplier has a local VAT registration because of other supplies VAT must be deducted in that local VAT return. It should be noted that in case the supplier opts to use the scheme he should report all VAT on supplies eligible under the scheme. He cannot report some of these supplies under the scheme, but not other supplies, e.g. because he wants to deduct VAT in a certain Member State through a local VAT return. Suppliers that make use of the I-OSS are required to keep a records of transactions covered by the scheme for a period of ten years. An intermediary shall keep records for each of the taxable persons he represents (Article 369x RVD).

Finally it should be noted that the vulnerability of the scheme has been pointed out in the literature.[364] Because the exemption upon importation is granted upon demonstration of a special VAT number attributed to the supplier under the scheme, but goods can be imported by or in the name of another person the supplier will need to share this number with other parties who can (later) misuse it, because only the validity of the number is checked by Customs, not whether the number belongs to the supplier who has supplied the goods to the customer. Especially when electronic interfaces are liable for the VAT payment of supplies to consumers (see section 2.6) misuse can take place.

2.14.6.5 The special arrangement for declaration and payment of import VAT

If the supplier opts not to use the I-OSS (section 2.14.6.4) VAT will need to be paid upon import of distance sales of goods from third countries or third territories. It is up to the Member State to appoint the person liable for the payment of import VAT under Article 201 RVD. Under the special arrangement (Article 369y-369zb RVD), that only applies to goods with an intrinsic value of no more than 150 euros and excluding excise goods (Article 369y RVD), the declaration of import VAT can be made each month (Article 369zb (1) RVD) with a postponement of the payment until the mid of the next month following the month in which the import VAT was collected. Under the special arrangement that will be applied by postal and courier companies, it is the person that presents the goods to Customs that remits the VAT under the special arrangement and collects it from the person for whom the goods are destined. It is that latter person that is liable for the import VAT (Article 369z RVD). It is an optional scheme and Member States may provide that the standard rate of

363 Article 61b VIR defines the concept of acceptance of the payment.
364 Marie Lamensch, "Rendering Platforms Liable to Collect and Pay VAT on B2C Imports: A Silver bullet?', International VAT Monitor, March/April 2018.

VAT applicable in the Member State of importation is applicable when using this special arrangement even when goods are subject to a reduced VAT rate (Article 369za RVD). However the person for whom the goods are destined can refuse the use of the standard rate in which case the special arrangement cannot be used. The persons making use of the special arrangement must keep records of the transactions covered by the special arrangement for a period of time to be determined by the Member State of importation (Article 369zb RVD).

2.15 Derogations

Title XIII of the Recast VAT Directive deals with derogations applying until the adoption of definitive arrangements and with derogations subject to authorisation, distinguishing between simplification measures and measures to prevent tax evasion or avoidance and international agreements.

2.15.1 Derogations Applying until the Adoption of Definitive Arrangements

Under de heading "Derogations Applying until the Adoption of Definitive Arrangements" a distinction is made between derogations for States which were members of the Community on 1 January 1978 and those for States which acceded to the Community after 1 January 1978. Article 370 RVD allows Member States which, at 1 January 1978, taxed the transactions listed in Annex X, Part A to continue to tax those transactions. According to Article 371 RVD, Member States which, at 1 January 1978, exempt the transactions listed in Annex X, Part B may continue to exempt those transactions, in accordance with the conditions applying in the Member State concerned on that date.[365]

According to Article 372 RVD, Member States which, at 1 January 1978, applied provisions derogating from the principle of immediate deduction laid down in the first paragraph of Article 179 RVD may continue to apply those provisions. In practice this means that the taxable person may exercise his right to deduct in a subsequent period. The ECJ decided that a limitation period of 2 years was long enough to reasonably allow a taxable person to exercise his right to deduct,[366] provided first, that the limitation period applies in the same way to analogous rights in tax matters founded on domestic law and to those founded on EU law (principle of equivalence) and, second, that it does not in practice render impossible or excessively difficult the exercise of the right to deduct (principle of effectiveness).[367] In *Biosafe*,[368] a taxable person was confronted with a request for additional payment by one of its suppliers because the latter had initially wrongly charged a reduced rate of VAT. The taxable person refused to pay (even if the supplier had sent a rectifying invoice) because this additional VAT, whose payment would arise more than 4 years after it had become chargeable, would not have been deductible anymore due to expiry of the limitation period.

365 See, *inter alia*, Case C-136/97 (*Norbury Developments Ltd*), [1999] ECR I-2491, Case C-36/99 (*Idéal Tourisme*), [2000] ECR I-6049 and Case C-267/99 (*Urbing*), [2001] ECR I-7467.
366 C-332/15, (*Astone*), [2016], ECLI:EU:C:2016:614.
367 C-95/07 and C-96/07 (*Ecotrade*), [2009], EU:C:2008:267, C-284/11, (*EMS- Bulgaria Transport*), [2012], EU:C:2012:458).
368 Case C-8/17 (Biosafe), [2018], ECLI:EU:C:2018:249.

The ECJ ruled that such a denial of the exercise of the right to deduct in a case where a rectifying invoice is only sent after the expiry of a limitation period is not compliant with the RVD and the principle of neutrality.

Article 373 RVD allows Member States which, at 1 January 1978, applied provisions derogating from Article 28 (the undisclosed agent regarding services) or from point (c) of the first paragraph of Article 79 (regarding suspense accounts) to continue to apply those provisions.

According to Article 374 RVD, by way of derogation from Articles 169 (regarding deduction when economic activities are carried out outside the territory) and 309, Member States which, at 1 January 1978, exempt, without deductibility of the VAT paid at the preceding stage, the services of travel agents, as referred to in Article 309, may continue to exempt those services. That derogation applies also in respect of travel agents acting in the name and on behalf of the traveller.

With regard to the derogations for States which acceded to the Community after 1 January 1978 Articles 375 to 390b RVD sum up the derogations granted to Greece, Spain, Portugal, Austria, Finland, Sweden, the Czech Republic, Estonia, Cyprus, Lithuania, Hungary, Poland, Slovenia, Slovakia and Croatia with, where applicable, the agreed (and later extended) time limits.

Article 391 RVD provides that the Member States which exempt the transactions based on the derogations referred to in Articles 371, 375, 376 or 377, Article 378 (2), Article 379(2) or Articles 380 to 390 may grant taxable persons the right to opt for taxation of those transactions.

Based on Article 392 RVD Member States are allowed to provide that, in respect of the supply of buildings and building land purchased for the purpose of resale by a taxable person for whom the VAT on the purchase was not deductible, the taxable amount shall be the difference between the selling price and the purchase price.

Finally, Article 393 RVD stipulates that, with a view to facilitating the transition to the definitive arrangements (referred to in Article 402 RVD), the Council, on the basis of a report from the Commission, must review the situation with regard to the derogations provided for above and that it must decide whether any or all of those derogations is to be abolished. To this is added that, by way of definitive arrangements, passenger transport shall be taxed in the Member State of departure for that part of the journey taking place within the Community, in accordance with the detailed rules to be laid down by the Council.

2.15.2 Derogations Subject to Authorisation

According to Article 394 RVD, Member States which, at 1 January 1977, applied special measures to simplify the procedure for collecting VAT or to prevent certain forms of tax evasion or avoidance to retain them, provided that they have notified the Commission accordingly before 1 January 1978 and that such simplification measures do not, except to a negligible extent, affect the overall amount of the tax revenue of the Member State collected at the stage of final consumption.[369]

In accordance with Article 395 (1) RVD the Council, acting unanimously on a proposal from the Commission, may authorise any Member State to introduce special measures for derogation from the provisions of this Directive, in order to simplify the procedure for collecting VAT or to prevent certain forms of tax evasion or avoidance.[370] Measures intended to simplify the procedure for collecting VAT may not, except to a negligible extent, affect the overall amount of the tax revenue of the Member State collected at the stage of final consumption.[371] Article 395(2) RVD organises the different steps of the procedure which must, in any event, be completed within 8 months of receipt of the application by the Commission. This provision can be relied on by the Member States in situations not covered by Article 199 to 199c RVD (see section 2.13.1).

2.16 Miscellaneous

Under the title "Miscellaneous" Articles 397 to 401 RVD deal with implementing measures, the VAT Committee (see section 2.16.2), conversion rates and other taxes, duties and charges not characterised as VAT.

2.16.1 Implementing Measures

In accordance with Article 397 RVD: "The Council, acting unanimously on a proposal from the Commission, shall adopt the measures necessary to implement this Directive".

On 17 October 2005, the Council adopted Regulation (EC) No. 1777/2005 laying down implementing measures for Directive 77/388/EEC on the common system of value added tax.[372] Following the adoption of the Recast, on 15 March 2011, the Council adopted implementing Regulation (EU) No. 282/2011 laying down implementing measures for Directive 2006/112/EC on the common system of value added tax (IR). The IR has been amended several times ever since.[373] As highlighted in Recital 2 of the IR: "Directive 2006/112/EC contains rules on value added tax (VAT) which, in some cases, are subject to interpretation by the Member States. The adoption of common provisions implementing Directive 2006/112/EC should ensure that application of the VAT system complies more fully with the objective of the internal market, in cases where divergences in application have arisen or may arise which

369 See Case C-494/04 (*Heintz van Landewyck*), [2006] ECR I-5381.

370 Based on Article 396 RVD the Council, acting unanimously on a proposal from the Commission, may authorise any Member State to conclude with a third country or an international body an agreement which may contain derogations from this Directive. The procedure is identical to the one mentioned in Article 395.

371 See, *inter alia*, Case C-17/01 (*Walter Sudholz*), [2004] ECR I-4243.

372 The background of this Regulation is Directive 2004/7/EC as regards conferment of implementing powers (see section 2.16.1 above) which make it possible that the measures necessary for the implementation of existing VAT Directive provisions are adopted by the Council, acting unanimously on a proposal from the Commission.

373 The complete list of amendments is updated in the consolidated version of the IR available on the European Commission website, at: https://eur-lex.europa.eu/legalcontent/EN/TXT/?uri=CELEX%3A02011R0282-20200101.

are incompatible with the proper functioning of such internal market. These implementing measures are legally binding only from the date of the entry into force of this Regulation and are without prejudice to the validity of the legislation and interpretation previously adopted by the Member States".

The IR more specifically lays down measures for the implementation of certain provisions of Titles I to V, and VII to XII of the RVD.

2.16.2 VAT Committee

Article 398 RVD provides for the setting up of an advisory committee composed of representatives of the Member States and of the Commission with a view to promote the uniform application of the provisions of the VAT Directive.[374] This so-called "VAT Committee" examines questions raised by either the Commission or the Member States and may issue guidelines "*Where the issue is of general interest and the conclusions of the Committee are supported by a clear majority consisting of nineteen Member States or more*".[375] More precisely, a guideline is adopted "unanimously" in the case of positive vote by (unsurprisingly) 27 Member States, is adopted "almost unanimously" in the case of positive vote by 26 to 24 Member States, and is adopted "with a large majority" in the case of positive vote by 23 to 18 Member States.[376] It is not possible to know which Member State voted against or in favour of a guideline. The VAT Committee has been set up in 1977, but its guidelines have only been published since 2012 (including all guidelines adopted since 1977). "In recent cases the ECJ decided that, although not binding, VAT Committee guidelines constitute an aid in interpreting the VAT Directive".[377]

Certain provisions of the RVD also *require* that the VAT Committee be consulted or notified before certain measures are applied; see Articles 11 RVD (single taxable person), 27 RVD (internal supplies of services), 80 RVD (objective valuation), 155 RVD (special exemptions linked to international goods traffic), 164 (exemption supply to exporter), 177 RVD (cyclical economic reasons),[378] 191 RVD (non-application of adjustment rules), 199 RVD (reverse charge) a, 238 (exceptions to invoice requirements), 281 RVD (simplified procedures for

374 Article 398 of the VAT Directive reads as follows: "*1. An advisory committee on value added tax, called "the VAT Committee', is set up. 2. The V A T Committee shall consist of representatives of the Member States and of the Commission. The chairman of the Committee shall be a representative of the Commission. Secretarial services for the Committee shall be provided by the Commission. 3. The VAT Committee shall adopt its own rules of procedure. 4. In addition to the points forming the subject of consultation pursuant to this Directive, the VAT Committee shall examine questions raised by its chairman, on his own initiative or at the request of the representative of a Member State, which concern the application of Community provisions on VAT*".

375 Article 4 of the VAT Committee rules of procedures (taxud.c.1(2013)1103950 – EN).

376 "Guidelines resulting from meetings of the VAT Committee up until 17 July 2015", p. 2, available at: http://ec.europa.eu/taxation_customs/resources/documents/taxation/vat/key_documents/vat_committee/guidelines-vat-committee-meetings_en.pdf.

377 See order of 8 October 2020, C-621/19 (*Weindel Logistik Service*) EU: C:2020:814 and 15 April 2021, C593/19 (*SK telecom*), ECLI:EU:C:2021:281.

378 Case C-409/99 (*Metropol Treuhand Wirtschafstreuhand GmbH*), [2002] ECR I- 81 See further on the issue of consultation of the VAT Committee Case C-228/05 (*Stradasfalti*) [2006] ECR I-8391 and Case C-162/07 (*Ampliscientifica*).

small undertakings), 318 RVD (globalisation of the margin scheme) and 352 RVD (disapplying the exemption for investment gold).

It is here relevant to mention other Commission's initiatives and appointed experts groups.

The Commission's explanatory notes
The Commission (more precisely the Commission's Directorate General for Taxation and Customs Union) recently started to adopt explanatory notes, a sort of administrative guidance at the EU level. These explanatory notes "*aim at providing a better understanding of the EU VAT legislation*". They are neither legally binding nor exhaustive.[379]

Explanatory notes are now available concerning the following:[380]
- Invoicing rules (2011)
- The MOSS for TBE services (2013)
- Place of supply rules for TBE services (2014).
- Auditing under the MOSS (2014)
- Place of supply rules for services connected to immovable property (2015)
- The quick fixes (call off stock arrangements, chain transactions, the exemption for intra-Community supplies of goods and the proof of transport for the purposes of that exemption (2019)
- VAT rules applicable to cross-border business-to-consumer (B2C) e-commerce activities (2020)

In the same way as VAT Committee guidelines, the Commission's explanatory notes are thus soft law of an interpretative nature that concern existing legislation. Unlike VAT Committee guidelines, they do not emanate from the legislative power but from the executive power (supranational in nature), whose role is to represent the interest of the EU as a whole (still different than private sector actors).

The VAT Expert Group
A "VAT Expert Group" ("VEG") was appointed as a follow-up to the 2011 Communication from the Commission on the future of VAT,[381] which acknowledged the need for the Commission to call upon expertise of VAT specialists in order to carry out the measures listed in this Communication.[382] The VEG is composed of organizations and individuals appointed in a personal capacity for 2 (now 3) years, from among the organizations and

379 European Commission (2014): "Explanatory notes on the EU VAT changes to the place of supply of telecommunications, broadcasting and electronic services that enter into force in 2015", available at: http://ec.europa.eu/taxation_customs/resources/ documents/taxation/vat/how_vat_works/telecom/explanatory_notes_2015_en.pdf.

380 Direct access to the documents is available at: https://ec.europa.eu/taxation_customs/business/vat/commission-guidelines_en.

381 Communication from the Commission to the European Parliament, the Council and the European Economic and Social Committee on the future of VAT: Towards a simpler, more robust and efficient VAT system tailored to the single market, COM(2011) 851 final.

382 Commission decision dated 26 June 2012 "setting up a group of experts on value added tax", 2012/C 188/02.

individuals that have responded to a call for applications.[383] Their role is to advise the Commission on the preparation of legislative acts and other policy initiatives in the field of VAT and to provide insight concerning the practical implementation of legislative acts and other EU policy initiatives.[384] They must act independently and in the public interest.[385] The Commission's representative may in addition invite outside experts to participate in the work of the group or sub-group on an *ad hoc* basis if they have a specific expertise that would benefit the group. Finally, the Commission's representative may give observer status to certain individuals or organizations.[386]

The VEG sometimes (but not lately) produces "opinions" that are, unsurprisingly, non-binding, neither on the Commission nor on the Member States. VEG Opinions are available on the following topics:[387]

- the definitive VAT regime for the taxation of intra-EU B2B supplies of goods (once in 2014 and twice in 2016).
- Cross-border rulings (2015).

VEG Opinions are thus soft law of an interpretative and/or steering nature that emanates from civil society.

The Group on the Future of VAT

The Group on the Future of VAT (GFV) is yet another expert group set up by the European Commission. It is composed of representatives of national tax administrations and is meant to provide a forum for consulting Member States on pre-legislative initiatives. Minutes of the meetings are available online.[388]

The VAT Forum

Finally, the EU VAT Forum was set up by a Commission Decision of 3 July 2012.[389] It offers a discussion platform where business and VAT authorities meet to discuss how the implementation of the VAT legislation can be improved in practice. consists of Members States' VAT authorities and of 15 organisations representing business and tax practitioners. The EU VAT Forum recently endorsed a report on how to prevent and solve double taxation dispute in VAT.[390]

383 Article 4 (6) of Commission decision of 26 June 2012 setting up a group of experts on value added tax, 2012/C 188/02.
384 Article 2 of Commission decision of 26 June 2012 setting up a group of experts on value added tax, 2012/C 188/02.
385 Article 4 (8) of Commission decision of 26 June 2012 setting up a group of experts on value added tax, 2012/C 188/02.
386 Article 5 (3) of Commission decision of 26 June 2012 setting up a group of experts on value added tax, 2012/C 188/02.
387 The text of these opinions is available at: https://ec.europa.eu/taxation_customs/business/vat/vat-expert-group_en.
388 Available at: https://circabc.europa.eu/ui/group/cb1eaff7-eedd-413d-ab88- 94f761f9773b/library/c0328c68-dd13-4969-b249-2bcf8e513cfe?p=1&n=10&sort=modified_DESC.
389 Decision 2012/C 198/05, OJ C 198 of 6 July 2012.
390 Report available at: https://ec.europa.eu/taxation_customs/sites/taxation/ files/01-2020-executive-note-eu-vat_forum.pdf.

2.16.3 Conversion Rates

The unit of account used in the original Sixth Directive was the European Unit of Account (EUA), which was replaced by the ECU and subsequently the euro. Article 399 RVD provides that, without prejudice to any other particular provisions, the equivalents in national currency of the amounts in euro specified in the RVD must be determined on the basis of the euro conversion rate applicable on 1 January 1999. Member States having acceded to the EU after that date, which have not adopted the euro as single currency, must use the euro conversion rate applicable on the date of their accession. When converting the amounts referred to in Article 399 into national currencies, Member States may adjust the amounts resulting from that conversion either upwards or downwards by up to 10% (Article 400 RVD).

2.16.4 Taxes Not to Be Characterised as Turnover Taxes

Under the title "Other Taxes, Duties and Charges" Article 401 RVD provides that a Member may maintain or introduce taxes on insurance contracts, taxes on betting and gambling, excise duties, stamp duties or, more generally, any taxes, duties or charges which cannot be characterised as turnover taxes, provided that the collecting of those taxes, duties or charges does not give rise, in trade between Member States, to formalities connected with the crossing of frontiers.

The restriction that the taxes, dues or charges mentioned in Article 401 RVD may not be classified as turnover taxes has been an especially fertile source for litigation. In more than 30 cases the ECJ has been asked to decide whether a particular tax or levy was permitted.[391] In all cases but one[392] the ECJ was of the opinion that the imposition of the tax or charge in question was not precluded.

The ECJ has held that among the essential characteristics of value added tax are the following features:[393]

- VAT applies generally to transactions relating to goods or services;
- it is proportional to the price charged by the taxable person in return for the goods and services which he has supplied;
- that tax is charged at each stage of the production and distribution process, including that of retail sale, irrespective of the number of transactions which have previously taken place;
- the amounts paid during the preceding stages of the production and distribution process are deducted from the VAT payable by a taxable person, with the result that that tax

391 See, *ex multis*, Case C-437/97 (*Evangelischer Krankenhausverein*), [2000] ECR I- 1157 and Case C-475/03 (*Banco Popolare di Cremona*), [2006] ECR I-9373 and more recently Case C-426/07 (*Dariusz Krawczyn-ski*), [2008] ECR I-6021, Case C-156/08 (*Monika Vollkommer*), [2008] ECR I-*165**, Case C-151/08 (*N.N. Renta*), [2008] ECR I-*164**, and Case C-119/08 (*Mechel Nemunas*), [2009] ECR I-*12*.

392 Case C-200/90 (*Denkavit and Poulsen* v. *Skatteministeriet*), [1992] ECR I-2217.

393 See Joined Cases C-283/06 and C-312/06 (*Kögáz a.o.*), [2007] ECR I-8463; Case C-75/18 (*Vodafone Magyarország Mobil Távközlési Zrt*), ECLI:EU: C:2020:139.

applies, at any given stage, only to the value added at that stage and the final burden of that tax rests ultimately on the consumer.

2.17 Final Provisions

The last title of the RVD contains the final provisions. It deals with transitional arrangements and transitional measures and the transposition and entry into force of the Directive.

2.17.1 Transitional Arrangements and Transitional Measures

Article 402 RVD contains the following "policy statement":

> The arrangements provided for in this Directive for the taxation of trade between Member States are transitional and shall be replaced by definitive arrangements based in principle on the taxation in the Member State of origin of the supply of goods or services.

Having concluded, upon examination of the report referred to in Article 404 RVD (see below), that the conditions for transition to the definitive arrangements are met, the Council, acting in accordance with Article 93 of the Treaty (now Article 113 TFEU), *i.e.* unanimously, is to adopt the provisions necessary for the entry into force and for the operation of the definitive arrangements. Furthermore the Council is instructed, acting in accordance with now Article 113 TFEU, to adopt Directives appropriate for the purpose of supplementing the common system of VAT and, in particular, for the progressive restriction or the abolition of derogations from that system (Article 403 RVD).

In Article 404 RVD, the Commission is instructed to present every 4 years starting from the adoption of the Recast VAT Directive, on the basis of information obtained from the Member States, a report to the European Parliament and to the Council on the operation of the common system of VAT in the Member States and, in particular, on the operation of the transitional arrangements for taxing trade between Member States. "That report shall be accompanied, where appropriate, by proposals concerning the definitive arrangements."

On October 4th of 2017, the European Commission has made a proposal for the definitive system. The main document is the "Proposal for a COUNCIL DIRECTIVE amending Directive 2006/112/EC as regards harmonising and simplifying certain rules in the value added tax system and introducing the definitive system for the taxation of trade between Member States".[394] In a nutshell the proposal is made to rescind the current system for intra-Community transactions and the breaking down of a single transaction into two taxable supplies (ie. a taxable but exempt (with a right to deduct) intra-Community supply followed by a taxable intra-Community acquisition) and to replace it with a single taxable supply: the intra-Union supply. In principle the supplier would be liable to charge, collect and remit the VAT at destination on this intra-Union supply. The declaration and

394 COM(2017) 569 final. Related proposals include: Proposal for a COUNCIL REGULATION amending Regulation (EU) No 904/2010 as regards the certified taxable person (COM(2017) 567 final), Proposal for a COUNCIL DIRECTIVE amending Directive 2006/112/EC as regards the introduction of the detailed technical measures for the operation of the definitive VAT system for the taxation of trade between Member States (COM(2018) 329 final).

payment could be made via a dedicated OSS (see section 2.14.6). In order to reduce the volume of declarations via the OSS, the Commission also proposed to apply the reverse charge system (i.e. customer becomes liable for the VAT) if the customer is a "certified taxable person", a concept to be harmonized. Four years after its submission the proposal still has not been adopted. It is unclear whether the Commission will withdraw it or if an amended version could eventually be approved. In the meantime, the Member States have adopted "quick fixes" to improve the transitional system (see section 2.6.2 about the call-off-stock-arrangement, section 2.7.1 about chain transactions and section 2.11.2 for the extra substantive conditions for an intra-Community supply (i.e. VAT identification number of the recipient and filing of a correct European Sales Listing) and the presumption of transport to another EU Member State).

Linked to the proposal for the definitive system the Commission also submitted a proposal to amend the system concerning the harmonization of VAT rates.[395] As discussed in section 2.10, the current system is based on a positive list (Annex 3 of the VAT Directive) of goods and services that may be subject to a reduced rate in the Member States. The harmonization of rates within the EU was justified by the "historical" ambition to eventually set up a harmonized VAT system based on the origin principle (in such a system, the harmonization of rates is necessary to prevent distortions of competition). Since the proposal for the definitive system confirms the application of a destination based system (in which different rates do not result in competition distortions), the Commission proposed to change the approach. The proposal is made to switch from a positive list to a negative list, laying down the supplies for which reduced rates could not apply. The minimum standard rate of 15% would be maintained but Member States would be allowed, in addition to the two reduced rates of a minimum of 5% and one 0% rate, to apply a third reduced rate of between 0% and 5%. The proposal nevertheless sets some limits to the liberty of the Member States by imposing a minimum weighted average rate of 12%. A possible "disharmonisation" of rates is a serious source of concern for businesses as it complexifies the application of VAT rules (keeping in mind that under the definitive system, suppliers would be responsible for charging a correct amount of VAT due at destination).

Articles 405 to 410 RVD deal with transitional arrangements and transitional measures applicable in the context of accession to the EU (not discussed here).

2.17.2 *Transposition and Entry into Force*

Article 411 RVD repeals the First and Sixth VAT Directives, without prejudice to the obligations of the Member States concerning the time limits, for the transposition into national law and the implementation of those Directives. (These time limits are listed in Annex XI, Part B to the RVD.) References to the repealed Directives are to be construed as references to the RVD (to be read in accordance with the correlation table in Annex XII to the RVD).

395 Proposal for a COUNCIL DIRECTIVE amending Directive 2006/112/EC as regards rates of value added tax, COM(2018) 20 final.

Article 412 RVD granted a "terme de grace" until 1 January 2008 to the Member States, instructing them to bring into force with effect from that date the laws, regulations and administrative provisions necessary to comply with the new provisions introduced by the Directive, namely the new definition of products subject to excise duty, *i.e.* including energy products, the place of supply of services by intermediaries, compulsory effective use and enjoyment rule exclusively for telecommunication services, conversion rates and Annex III, point 18 (supply of services provided in connection with street cleaning, refuse collection and waste treatment, other than the supply of such services by public bodies referred to in Article 13).

Finally, Article 413 RVD provides that the Recast VAT Directive enters into force on 1 January 2007 and Article 414 RVD contains the inevitable statement for a Directive that it is addressed to the Member States.

2.18 Final words on the ECJ case law

Since 1970 the ECJ has rendered more than 1000 decisions in the field of VAT, with more than 450 cases decided during the decade 2010-2019 only. Most of the decisions are preliminary rulings. This "inflation' of VAT cases is probably due to the difficulty 1) to apply the VAT to constantly evolving types of business models and transactions and 2) to amend the RVD or adopt clarifying rules in the IR (under the unanimity rule).

The interpretations offered by the ECJ are most welcome for businesses, national courts and tax administrations as they guarantee a consistent application of the EU VAT legislation throughout the VAT territory. However, this situation is not fully satisfactory in view of the time lapse between the moment when the question arises in one of the Member States and the moment when a decision is taken by the CJEU. It is also noteworthy that some national courts remain quite reluctant to interrogate the ECJ while others are much more active. As the taxable persons may not themselves seize the ECJ directly, this means that some questions that would deserve to be raised are not being raised, at least until another Member State or the Commission decides to raise them.

Another notable development in the ECJ VAT case law of the past decade (in addition to the sharp increase in numbers) is that the Charter of Fundamental Rights of the European Union[396] is now routinely being invoked (or at least discussed), in particular:[397]

- Article 3 (right to integrity);[398]
- Article 7 (private and family life);[399]
- Article 8 (personal data);[400]

---

396 O.J. 18.12.2000, C 364/1.

397 This case law review was compiled and presented by Ine Lejeune at the 2021 Annual Conference on CJEU case law organized by the Vienna University of Business (WU).

398 Case C-412/15 (*TMD Gesellschaft*), ECLI:EU:C:2016:738.

399 C-419/14 (*WebMindLicences*) ECLI:EU:C:2015:832; C-310/16 (*Dzivev and others*) see AG opinion (ECLI:EU:C:2018:623); C-380/16 (*Commission v. Germany*), ECLI:EU:C:2018:76; C- 469/18 (*IN and JM v. Belgische Staat*) see both judgement (ECLI:EU:C:2019:895) and AG Opinion (ECLI:EU:C:2019:597).

400 C-419/14 (*WebMindLicences*), ECLI:EU:C:2015:832; C-380/16 (*Commission v. Germany*), ECLI:EU:C:2018:76.

- Article 16 (freedom to conduct a business);[401]
- Article 17 (right to property);[402]
- Article 20 (equality before the law);[403]
- Article 21 (non-discrimination);[404]
- Article 47 (effective remedy and fair trial);[405]
- Article 48 (presumption of innocence and right of defence);[406]
- Article 49 (principle of legality and proportionality of criminal offences and penalties);[407]
- Article 50 (ne bis in idem);[408]
- Article 51 (the Charter only applies to European Union Institutions and bodies and to the Member States only when they are implementing Union law);[409] and
- Article 52 (scope and interpretation of rights and principles).[410]

---

401 C-534/16 (*BB Construct*), ECLI:EU:C:2017:820; C-152/17 (*Consorzio Italian Management, Catania Multiservizi SpA*), ECLI:EU:C:2018:264; C-446/18 (*Agrobet CZ*) see opinion AG (ECLI:EU:C:2019:1137); C-380/16 (*Commission v. Germany*), ECLI:EU:C:2018:76.

402 C-654/13 (*Delphi Hungary*), ECLI:EU:C:2014:2127; C-446/18 (*Agrobet CZ*) see AG opinion (ECLI:EU:C:2019:1137); C-246/16 (*Di Maura*) see Judgement (ECLI:EU: C:2017:887) and AG opinion (ECLI:EU:C:2017:440); C-427/10 (*Banca Antoniana Popolare Veneta SpA*) see AG Opinion (ECLI:EU:C:2011:595); C-531/17 (*Vetsch*) see AG opinion (ECLI:EU:C:2019:114).

403 Joined cases C-144/13, C-154/13 and C-160/13 (*VDP Dental*), ECLI:EU: C:2015:116; C-264/14 (*Hedqvist*), ECLI:EU:C:2015:718; C-174/11 (*Zimmerman*), ECLI:EU:C:2012:716; C-390/15 (*RPO*), ECLI:EU:C:2017:174; C-462/16 (*Boehringer Ingelheim Pharma*), ECLI:EU:C:2017:1006; C-140/17 (*Gmina Ryjewo*), ECLI:EU:C:2018:595.

404 C-390 /15 (*RPO*), ECLI:EU:C:2017:174; C-534/16 (*BB Construct*), ECLI:EU: C:2017:820; C-533/16, (*Volkswagen*), ECLI:EU:C:2018:204; C-298/16 (*Ispas*), ECLI:EU:C:2017:843.

405 C-500/10 (*Belvedere Construzioni* Srl), ECLI:EU:C:2012:186; C-610/19 (*Vikingo Fővállalkozó Kft.*), ECLI:EU:C:2020:673; C-662/13 (*Surgicare*), ECLI:EU:C:2015:89; C-543/14 (*Ordre des barreaux francophones et germanophones* e.a.), ECLI:EU:C:2016:605; C-492/08 (*European Commission vs. French Republic*), ECLI:EU:C:2010:348; C-648/16 (*Fortunata Silvia Fontana*) see AG opinion (ECLI:EU:C:2018:213); C-133/18 (*Sea Chefs Cruise Services GmbH*) see AG opinion (ECLI:EU:C:2019:37); C-310/16 (*Dzivev and others*) 2019, ECLI:EU:C:2019:30; C-469/18 (*IN and JM v. Belgische Staat*) see Judgement (ECLI:EU:C:2019:895) and AG Opinion (ECLI:EU:C:2019:597); C-13/18 (*Sole Mizo*) see AG Opinion (ECLI:EU:C:2020:292).

406 C-648/16 (*Fortunata Silvia Fontana*) see AG opinion (ECLI:EU:C:2018:213).

407 C-105/14 (*Tarrico and others*), ECLI:EU:C:2015:555; Joined cases C-131/13, C- 163/13 and C-164/13 (*Schoenimport "Italmoda"*), ECLI:EU:C:2014:2455; C-42/17 (*M. A.S.*), ECLI:EU:C:2017:936; C-574/15 (*Scialdone*), ECLI:EU:C:2018:295.

408 C-617/10 (*Åkerberg Fransson*), ECLI:EU:C:2013:280; C-217/15 (*Orsi*), ECLI:EU: C:2017:264; C-350/15 (*Baldetti*), decision not published; C-524/15 (*Luca Menci*), ECLI: EU:C:2018:197; C-234/17 (XC, YB, ZA), ECLI:EU:C:2018:853.

409 C-566/17 (*Związek Gmin Zagáeþia Miedziowego w Polkowicach*) see AG Opinion ECLI:EU:C:2018:995; C-469/18 (*IN and JM v. Belgische Staat*) see Judgement (ECLI:EU:C:2019:895) and AG Opinion (ECLI:EU:C:2019:597); C-446/18 (*Agrobet CZ*) see AG opinion (ECLI:EU:C:2019:1137).

410 C-105/14 (*Tarrico and others*), ECLI:EU:C:2015:555; C-355/19 (*E.Sp.z o.o Sp. K*), see AG Opinion (ECLI:EU:C:2020:746); C-380/16 (*Commission v. Germany*), ECLI:EU:C:2018:76.

CHAPTER 3

Excises and Energy Taxation

Update and elaboration by Ilona van den Eijnde

3.1 Introduction

Article 17 EC Treaty provided that the rules on the elimination of customs duties between the Member States also apply to customs duties of a fiscal nature. Normally customs duties are meant to protect national products, *i.e.* they are discriminatory by nature. Duties of a fiscal nature are purely meant to raise revenue and not to protect simply because domestically the product subject to the duty is not produced. According to Article 17 Member States retained the right to substitute for these duties an internal tax which complies with Article 95 EC Treaty. The present Article 30 TFEU, prohibiting customs duties on imports and exports and charges having equivalent effect between Member States, extends this prohibition to customs duties of a fiscal nature. Any internal tax on a product not produced locally must comply with the rules of Article 110 TFEU (formerly Article 95 EC Treaty), *i.e.* no internal tax may be imposed, directly or indirectly, on the products of other Member States in excess of that imposed on similar domestic products, and indirect protection to other products is also forbidden. The case law of the ECJ on this prohibition of discrimination is very extensive.

The *OutuKompu* case[1] deals with rate differentiations and energy. In Finland, based on ecological considerations, excise is levied on certain sources of energy. For electricity a different rate is applied, depending on the method of production by nuclear or waterpower. OutuKompu imported electricity from Sweden, and on this importation an average duty applied. According to OutuKompu this levy was prohibited based on Articles 9 and 12 EC Treaty, today Articles 28 and 30 TFEU (charges having equivalent effect), and in the alternative the tax was discriminatory under Article 95 EC Treaty (now Article 110 TFEU). Preliminary questions were directed to the ECJ. The Court observed that it has consistently held that provisions relating to charges having equivalent effect and those relating to discriminatory internal taxation cannot be applied together. A charge which forms part of system of internal dues cannot be characterized as a forbidden pecuniary charge whatever its designation and mode of application, which is imposed unilaterally on goods by reason of the fact that they cross a frontier. Article 95 EC Treaty allows a tax system which differentiates between certain products even when they are similar. The rule of non-discrimination is however violated when objective criteria are not applied or objectives are pursued incompatible with the Treaty. Protection of the environment constitutes one of the essential objectives of the Community; however, Article 95 EC Treaty is infringed where the taxation on the import

1 Case C-213/96 (*OutuKompu Oy*), [1998] ECR I-1777.

product and that on a similar domestic product is calculated in a different manner, and that was the case. The Finnish government raised the objection that it is difficult to determine the method of production of imported electricity. Practical difficulties according to the ECJ do not justify the application of a discriminatory tax. (Furthermore the importer was not even given the opportunity of demonstrating the method of production.) The ECJ held that although Article 95 EC Treaty does not require Member States to abolish differences which are objectively justified and which national legislation establishes between internal taxes on domestic products, it is otherwise where such abolition is the only way of avoiding direct or indirect discrimination against the imported products.

Articles 17 and 95 EC Treaty and later Articles 25 and 90 EC (now Articles 30 and 110 TFEU) lead us to the harmonization of excises.

As early[2] as 1972, a draft framework[3] directive on excise duties and indirect taxes other than VAT levied directly or indirectly on the consumption of products[4] envisaged the progressive harmonization of excise duties and taxes on goods. With effect from 1 January 1974 the Member States should apply a harmonized system of excise duties to mineral oils, manufactured tobacco, alcohol, beer, and wine. All other duties and taxes on goods other than turnover tax were to be discontinued, with the exception of those which did not require border controls or tax adjustments. Any proposed changes in the rates of existing duties were to be subject to a consultation procedure. The Council was to retain the power to introduce harmonized taxes on other products.[5] This proposed framework Directive was never adopted.

Following the White Paper of 1985,[6] the Commission put forward a new proposal for a framework directive in 1990, along with its proposals on structures of duty on the main dutiable products;[7] it was intended in particular to permit the abolition of frontier controls on the completion of the Single Market.

The proposal was adopted and resulted in three sets of Community rules:[8]
(1) Council Directive 92/12/EEC of 25 February 1992 on the general arrangements for products subject to excise duty and the holding, movement and monitoring of such

2 See also the proposal of 1967 for a Regulation in section 3.6.
3 On drafting excise laws, see also 'Excises', by Ben Terra in *Tax Law Design and Drafting*, editor Victor Thuronyi, IMF 1996, pp. 246–264. See in general with regard to excises: The World Bank Policy research working paper 1251, John Due, *Excise Taxes*.
4 O.J. 1972, C 43, p. 23.
5 A further draft decision called for the establishment of an excise committee which was to be consulted by the Commission before the adoption of implementing measures in relation to the harmonization of excise duties. Proposal for a Council Decision establishing a Committee on Excise Duties, O.J. 1972, C 43, p. 42.
6 COM(96) 328 final.
7 O.J. 1990, C 322, p. 1.
8 It is admitted that it is based on a new concept of "general and flexible harmonization" or on the "smallest common denominator". See E. Stubbe, Die harmonisierung der besonderen Verbrauchssteueren in der Europäischen Gemeinschaft', *ZfZV* 1993, p. 170.

products.[9] This Directive, known as the "horizontal Directive", prescribed that products subject to excise duty moving under duty-suspension arrangements between the territories of the Member States must be accompanied by a document (the so-called AAD) drawn up by the consignor.[10] From 1 April 2010, this Directive is replaced by Directive 2008/118/EC, see further below.

(2) Three Directives on the harmonization of the structures of the excises which are subject of the general arrangements procedure, namely mineral oils,[11] alcohol and alcoholic beverages,[12] and manufactured tobacco[13] hereinafter referred to as the "structure Directives". The directive on manufactured tobacco was replaced in 1995 by Directive 95/59/EEC.[14] On 21 June 2011, the Council adopted Directive 2011/64/EU on the structure and rates of excise duty applied to manufactured tobacco. Directives 92/79/EEC, 92/80/EEC and 95/59/EEC are codified by assembling them in a single act.[15]

(3) Four Directives on the approximation of rates of duties applicable to the above mentioned excises, hereinafter referred to as the "Directives on rates" Directive 92/82/EEC[16] (mineral oils), Directive 92/84/EEC[17] (alcohol and alcoholic beverages), Directive 92/79/EEC[18] (cigarettes) and Directive 92/80/ EEC[19] (manufactured tobacco other than cigarettes). On 21 June 2011, the Council adopted Directive 2011/64/EU on the structure and rates of excise duty applied to manufactured tobacco. Directives 92/79/EEC, 92/80/ EEC 95/59/ EEC are codified by assembling them in a single act.

On 27 October 2003, the Council adopted Directive 2003/96/EC which restructures the Community framework for the taxation of energy products and electricity.[20] The Directive repeals Directives 92/81/EEC and 92/82/EEC and replaces the excise on mineral oils by taxation on energy products and electricity. For this taxation there is no longer a separate structure and rates directive. See further section 3.8 below.

---

9 O.J. 1992, L 76, p. 1, as amended by Directive 92/108/EEC of 14 December 1992, O.J. 1992. L 390, p. 124, Directive 94/74/EC, O.J. 1994, L 365, p. 46, Directive 96/99/EC O.J. 1997, L 008, p. 12, Directive 2000/44/EC, O.J. 2000, L 161, p. 82, Directive 2000/47/EC, O.J. 2000, L 197, p. 73 and by Council Regulation (EC) No. 807/2003, O.J. 2003, L 122, p. 36 in Annex III, point 45.

10 Regulation (EEC) No. 2719/92 of 11 September 1992 O.J. 1992, L 276, p. 1 provides for the details on this document. The document was changed by Regulation (EEC) No. 2225/93 of 27 July 1993 O.J. 1993, L 198, p. 5 and Regulation (EC) No.1792/2006 of 23 October 2006, O.J. 2006, L 362, p. 1 and the Acts of accession O.J., repealed by Regulation(EC) No. 684/2009, see section 3.3 below.

11 Directive 92/81/EEC of 19 October 1993 O.J. 1992, L 316, p. 12, as amended by Directive 94/74/ EC (see above).

12 Directive 92/83/EEC, O.J. 1992, L 316, p. 21.

13 Directive 92/78/EEC, O.J. 1992, L 316, p. 5 and Directive 92/79/EEC O.J. 1992, L 316, p. 8, as amended by Directive 2010/10/EU O.J. 2010, L 50, p. 1.

14 Directive 95/59/EC, O.J. 1994, L 291, p. 40, as amended by Directive 1999/81/ EC, O.J. 1999, L 211, p. 47, by Directive 2002/10/EC, O.J. 2002, L 46, p. 26 and Directive 2010/12/EU O.J. 2010, L 50, p. 1.

15 Directive 2011/64/EU, O.J. 2011, L 176, p. 24.

16 Directive 92/82/EEC, O.J.1992, L 316, p. 19, as amended by Directive 94/74/ EC (see above).

17 Directive 92/84/EEC, O.J. 1992, L 316, p. 29 as amended by Directive 2003/ 117/EC, O.J. 2003, L 33, p. 49.

18 Directive 92/79/EEC, O.J. 1992, L 316, p. 8, as amended by Directive 1999/ 81/EC, O.J. 1999, L 211, p. 47, Directive 2002/10/EC, O.J. 2002, L 46, p. 26 and Directive 2010/ 10/EU O.J. 2010, L 50, p. 1.

19 Directive 92/80/EEC, O.J. 1992, L 316, p. 10, as amended by Directive 1999/ 81/EC, O.J. 1999, L 211, p. 47, Directive 2002/10/EC, O.J. 2002, L 46, p. 26 and Directive 2010/ 10/EU O.J. 2010, L 50, p. 1.

20 Directive 2003/96/EC of 27 October 2003, O.J. 2003, L 283, p. 51.

The provisions contained in Directive 92/12/EEC needed to be reviewed to take into account the introduction of the Excise Movement and Control System (hereinafter: EMCS).

The EMCS has been put into place following Decision No. 1152/2003/EC of the European Parliament and of the Council of 16 June 2003 on computerising the movement and surveillance of excisable products.[21]

As a result, notably, the provisions relating to movements under suspension of excise duty needed to be adapted so as to allow such movements to be covered by procedures under this new system. Changes to this effect provide a simplified and paperless environment for trade, while permitting more integrated, faster and risk oriented control approaches for excise authorities (cf. third and fourth recital of Decision No. 1152/2003/EC). In the interest of clarity, Decision No. 1152/2003/EC was recast by Decision (EU) 2020/263 of the European Parliament and of the Council of 15 January 2020.[22]

Apart from these new provisions, other amendments of the rules set out in Directive 92/12/EEC were considered to be necessary such as:

- to update the language used in the directive, taking into account new legislative standards;
- to recast the text enhancing the logical structure and to take out those provisions which have lost relevance over time;
- to take account of legal developments and new legal concepts;
- to simplify and modernise the excise procedures, with the aim of reducing excise obligations for traders, in particular for traders carrying out cross-border business, without compromising excise controls.

On 16 December 2008, the Council adopted Directive 2008/118/EC concerning the general arrangements for excise duty (hereinafter the General Arrangements Directive)[23] adapting the excise duty arrangements based on Directive 92/12/EEC (which it replaces from 1 April 2010) and permitting the introduction of a computerised excise duty monitoring system (ECMS). The General Arrangements Directive was recast by Council Directive (EU) 2020/262 of 19 December 2019.[24] Directive 2008/118/EC is repealed with effect from 13 February 2023. Member States have until 31 December 2021 to comply with the Recast General Arrangements Directive.[25]

On 24 July 2009, Commission Regulation (EC) No. 684/2009 was adopted implementing the General Arrangements Directive as regards the computerised procedures for the movement

21 O.J. 2003, L 162, p. 5.
22 O.J. 2020, L 58, p. 43.
23 Council Directive 2008/118/EC of 16 December 2008 concerning the general arrangements for excise duty and repealing Directive 92/12/EEC, O.J. 2009, L 9, p. 12, as amended by Directive 2010/10/EU, O.J. 2010, L 50, p. 1.
24 O.J. 2020, L. 58, p. 4.
25 Where Directive 2008/118/EC is different from Directive 2020/262, the differences will be addressed and discussed separately in this chapter. Where no (significant) differences apply, reference will be made to the Recast General Arrangements Directive, i.e., Directive 2020/262.

of excise goods under suspension of excise duty.[26] Since the movement of excise goods under suspension of excise duty is to take place under cover of an electronic administrative document and since the computerised system is intended to allow movements of excise goods under suspension of excise duty to be followed and monitored, it was necessary to establish the structure and content of the electronic messages to be used on such movements.

In particular, as movements are to take place under cover of an electronic administrative document (e-AD), the structure and content of the messages constituting that document had to be laid down. It was also necessary to determine the structure and content of the messages constituting the so-called report of receipt and the report of export.

Under the Recast General Arrangements Directive, an electronic administrative document may be cancelled, the destination of the goods may be changed and a movement of excise goods may be split. It was therefore necessary to determine the structure and content of messages concerning the cancellation of the electronic administrative document, a change of destination and the splitting of a movement, and to lay down the rules and procedures which apply in relation to exchanges of messages concerning such cancellation, change of destination and splitting. Furthermore it was necessary to lay down the structure of the paper documents referred to in Article 26 and 27 of the Recast General Arrangements Directive which are to be used when the computerised system is unavailable. See further section 3.3 below.

3.2 The Recast General Arrangements Directive

Directive 2020/262 concerning the general arrangements for excise duty consists of 8 Chapters:

(I) General provisions; (II) General procedural provisions; (III) Production, processing, holding and storage; (IV) Movement of excise goods under suspension of excise duty; (V) Movement and taxation of excise goods after release for consumption; (VI) Miscellaneous; (VII) Exercise of the delegation and committee procedure; and (VIII) Reporting and transitional and final provisions.

The main provisions of the Directive are discussed below.

3.2.1 General Provisions

Under the Title "General Provisions", Chapter I of the Recast General Arrangements Directive deals with the scope of the Directive (see section 3.2.1.1), and the territorial application (see section 3.2.1.3) and it provides for a series of definitions, that will be dealt with under the subjects to which they relate. Article 2 of Directive 2008/118/EC, concerning the chargeable event, was moved to Chapter II under Directive 2020/262/EU.

26 O.J. 2009, L 197, p. 24.

3.2.1.1 Scope

Definition of excise goods
According to Article 1, defining the scope, the Recast General Arrangements Directive lays down the arrangements in relation to excise duty which is levied directly or indirectly on the consumption of excise goods.

The Recast General Arrangements Directive applies at Union level to:
- energy products (originally mineral oils, see sections 3.4 and 3.8 below),
- alcohol and alcoholic beverages (see section 3.5 below),
- manufactured tobacco (see section 3.6 below),

referred to as excise goods.

Article 1(1) of the Recast General Arrangements Directive defines the nature of the excise duty as being a tax levied directly or indirectly[27] on the consumption of excise goods. The definition of the different excise goods (which is necessary to identify exactly which goods are subjected to the provisions of the Directive), the structure of the excise duty to be applied (*e.g.* per hl; per degree alcohol; per 1000 pieces, etc.), the scope of possible exemptions, as well as the minimum rates of duty that Member States have to respect, are set out in the specific Directives referred to in Article 1(1).[28]

Other indirect taxes on excise goods
According to Article 1(2) of the Recast General Arrangements Directive, Member States may levy other indirect taxes on excise goods for specific purposes, provided that those taxes comply with the Community tax rules applicable for excise duty or value added tax as far as determination of the tax base, calculation of the tax, chargeability and monitoring of the tax are concerned, but not including the provisions on exemptions. Thus, Member States may add, for specific policy (*e.g.* environmental) purposes, other indirect taxes to the excise goods. (See also the preamble point (4) reciting that excise goods may be subject to other indirect taxes for specific purposes but that in such cases and in order not to jeopardise the useful effect of Community rules relating to indirect taxes, Member States should comply with certain essential elements of those rules.)

Under Directive 92/12/EEC similar provisions to Article 1(2) and 1(3) of the General Arrangements Directive, but less clearly formulated, applied as can be seen in the following case law, to the extent dated before the introduction of Directive 2008/118 and Directive 2020/262.

The *EKW* case[29] is rather instructive with regard to the provision that Member States may subject excise products to other (non-general) indirect taxes. A dispute between, *inter alia*,

27 The fact that that the tax is also levied directly (see Articles 8 and 32 of the Directive) does not deprive the excise duties of their legal character of "specific *indirect* taxes on consumption". See Article 1(2) allowing Member States to levy "other indirect taxes" and, in general, Article 113 TFEU which prescribes the Council to adopt, provisions for the harmonisation of legislation concerning turnover taxes, excise duties and "other forms of indirect taxation".

28 See section 3.1 above.

29 Case C-437/97 (*Evangelischer Krankenhausverein Wien (EKW)*), [2000] ECR I- 1157.

the Evangelischer Krankenhausverein Wien (Protestant Hospital Society, Vienna; "the EKW") and the Tax Appeals Commission, Vienna, concerned the requirement to pay a municipal duty on beverages and ice cream (beverage duty). The EKW operates a hospital cafeteria.

The first question asked to the ECJ was whether Article 33 of the Sixth VAT Directive (now Article 401 of the VAT Directive) precluded the retention of the beverage duty. In line with its settled case law the ECJ observed that the duty applies only to a limited category of goods and therefore does not have the essential characteristics of VAT.

The second question was whether Article 3(2) or (3) of horizontal Directive 92/ 12/ EEC precluded the retention of the beverage duty.

The ECJ drew a distinction between the duty on non-alcoholic products and alcoholic beverages. According to the Court, Article 3(3) of Directive 92/12/EEC (now Article 1(3) of Directive 2008/118/EC) allows a duty on non-alcoholic beverages and ice cream. With regard to alcoholic beverages the ECJ observed that Article 3(2) of Directive 92/12/EEC requires (as now Article 1(2) of Directive 2008/118/EC likewise requires) one or more specific purposes to levy an additional tax and that such a tax must comply with the tax rules applicable for excise duty and VAT[30] as far as the tax base, calculation of the tax, and chargeability and monitoring of the tax are concerned.

The Austrian arguments regarding the specific purposes were: reinforcement of the municipalities' tax autonomy, offsetting the substantial costs of tourism and protection of public health. According to the ECJ, a purely budgetary objective cannot constitute a specific purpose in the sense contemplated by Article 3(2) of Directive 92/12/EEC. There is also no connection with tourist infrastructure since the duty is also levied in areas where there is little or no tourism. Since in Austria direct sales of wine are exempt it must be questionable whether the duty is intended to discourage the consumption of alcoholic beverages and to protect public health.

With regard to the question whether the beverage duty complied with the tax rules applicable to excise duty *and* VAT, the ECJ observed that the language versions of Article 3(2) of Directive 92/12/EEC diverged, as some versions refer to excise duty *or* VAT. For that reason not all rules should be complied with, it is sufficient that the beverage duty accords with the general scheme of the taxation techniques structured by Community legislation. However, the duty did not accord with the general scheme of excise duties on alcoholic beverages since an ad valorem duty was applied and not a specific duty. Furthermore, chargeability occurred only at the stage of sale to the consumer and not at the time of release for consumption (see section 3.2.2.1 below). Nor did the duty accord with the general scheme of VAT since it is not charged at each stage of production and distribution nor can any deduction be made for input tax. The beverage duty on alcoholic beverages was, thus, precluded by Article 3(2) of Directive 92/12/EEC.

30 Note that the present Article 1(2) of Directive 2008/118/EC refers to rules applicable to excises *or* VAT.

In an infringement procedure against France[31] the Commission challenged the French "social security" contribution on alcoholic beverages. The Commission admitted that the contribution pursued a specific purpose but that its scope and tax base were not compatible with the structure of excise duties on alcohol and alcoholic beverages.

The ECJ again pointed out the differences in the authentic languages of Article 3 (2) of Directive 92/12/EEC. In some languages the compliance with VAT *and* excise rules was required in others VAT *or* excise rules. It concluded that it was not possible to comply with all rules.

The ECJ noted in point 24 of its judgment that VAT and excise duty have a number of incompatible characteristics. VAT is proportional to the price of the goods on which it is charged, whereas excise duty is primarily calculated on the volume of the product. Further, VAT is levied at each stage of the production and distribution process (input tax paid on the occasion of the previous transaction being in principle deductible), whereas excise duty becomes payable when the products subject to it are made available for consumption (without any similar deduction mechanism coming into operation). Finally, VAT is characterised by its general nature, whereas excise duty is imposed only on specified products. Consequently, if Article 3(2) of the horizontal excise Directive were to be construed as requiring Member States to comply simultaneously with the tax rules governing those two categories of charges, it would be laying down a condition that is impossible to satisfy.

The French charges do not apply to the category of alcoholic beverages in full, this is not required by Article 3(2) of Directive 92/12/EEC according to the ECJ. That the amount of the social security contribution is proportionate to the quantity of beverage irrespective of its alcohol content, which the Commission criticized, is according to the ECJ consistent with the general scheme of tax rules applicable for excise duty purposes. The Court consequently found that the charges were allowed.

In order to assess whether a (supplementing) national tax on excise goods is permitted, it is necessary to first determine whether it falls within the scope of Article 1(2) of the General Arrangements Directive (see case *IRCCS – Fondazione Santa Lucia*[32]). In the *Promociones Olivia Park* case,[33] the Spanish taxation of electricity is under review. The Spanish regime is based on the gross income of taxpayers involved in the production and incorporation of electricity into the system. The rate is equal for each taxpayer and does not progress based on pollution levels and there is no exemption in place or subsidy provided for the use of renewable sources of energy. The referring court considers that this tax may be contrary to EU law as it has no specific purpose, it has no connection with the environmental objective and does not differentiate according to environmental impact. The ECJ ruled that this Spanish tax is not an indirect tax that is levied directly or indirectly on the consumption of electricity, and therefore does not fall within the scope of Article 1(2) of the General Arrangements Directive. Whether the national tax is acceptable is then further reviewed

31 Case C-434/97 (*Commission v. France*), [2000] ECR I-1129.
32 Case C-189/15 (IRCCS – Fondazione Santa Lucia), [2017] ECLI:EU:2017:17.
33 Case C-220/19 (*Promociones Oliva Park*), [2021] ECLI:EU:C:2021:163.

on the basis of the Renewable Energy Directive[34] and the Directive on the Internal Market for Electricity.[35]

In the *Statoil Fuel* case,[36] the ECJ ruled with respect to a sales tax that was collected by Estonia in order to promote public transport and thus reduce the density of road traffic and its adverse impact on the environment. The revenue of the tax was earmarked for the city of Tallinn to improve the quality of public transport and at the same time penalise the consumption of certain goods and services. The Court ruled that the predetermined allocation of the revenue to finance general expenditure that is incumbent upon the public authority is not regarded as pursuing a specific purpose. In absence of a predetermined allocation, the tax can be regarded as pursuing a specific purpose in case it is designed in such a way as to guide the behaviour of taxpayers in a direction which facilitates the achievement of the specific purpose, which in the case at issue, the Court ruled that such was not the case. In absence of a specific purpose, as such, the tax was not permitted under Directive 2008/118/EC.

The *Messer* case[37] concerns the French public electricity service tax (CSPE), which has an objective to ensure the supply of electricity throughout the national territory in the general public interest. The first question asked to the ECJ was whether this CSPE qualifies as 'another indirect tax' in light of Article 3(2) of Directive 92/12/EEC, now Article 1(2) of Directive 2020/262/EU, provided that France had not (yet) instated a harmonised excise duty on electricity. The Court ruled that, even in lieu of a harmonised excise duty on electricity, the CSPE should indeed be assessed as another indirect tax for specific purposes.

The second question relates to the two cumulative conditions to be met for another indirect tax to be allowed. Firstly, the tax must have a specific purpose and secondly, it complies with the tax rules applicable for excise duty or VAT purposes as far as determination of the tax base, calculation of the tax, chargeability and monitoring of the tax are concerned. With respect to the first condition, the Court ruled in line with the abovementioned *Statoil Fuel* case, that the predetermined allocation of revenue from a tax is merely a matter of internal organization of the budget of a Member State and can therefore not, in itself, constitute a sufficient condition. As such, financing the costs of the National Energy Ombudsman and the Equalisation Fund do not pursue any specific purpose other than a budgetary purpose. Furthermore, objectives of territorial and social cohesion, namely the implementation of a geographical price-balancing mechanism and a reduction of the price of electricity for low-income households, are objectives that are normally met from State budgets and equally do not pursue a specific purpose. In the third place, the CSPE pursued an environmental objective, by way of encouraging the production of electricity from renewable sources and cogeneration by contributing to its financing. Only that environmental objective indeed

34 Directive 2009/28/EC, O.J. 2009, L 140, p. 16, as amended by Council Directive 2013/18/EU, O.J. 2013, L 158, p. 230 and Directive 2015/1513, O.J. 2015, L 239, p 1.

35 Directive 2019/944, O.J. 2019, L 158, p. 125.

36 Case C-553/13 (Statoil Fuel), [2015] ECLI:EU:C:2015:149. See also for similar facts and circumstances Case C-82/12 (*Transportes Jordi Besora*), [2014] ECLI:EU: C:2014:108.

37 Case C-103/17 (*Messer France*), [2018] ECLI:EU:C:2018:587.

pursues a specific purpose. The CSPE furthermore complied with the tax rules applicable for excise duty purposes.

As a result and answering the third question, taxable persons concerned are entitled to partial reimbursement in proportion to the overall expenditure financed by the CSPE which did not relate to a specific purpose. The *Braathens* case[38] deals with Article 8(1)(b) of Directive 92/81/EEC on the harmonization of the structures of excise duties on mineral oils (see section 3.4 below) which prescribes an exemption of excise on mineral oils supplied for use as fuel for the purpose of air navigation other than private pleasure flying. (Now Article 14(1)(b) of Directive 2003/96/EC, see section 3.8.3.1 below.) In Sweden an environmental tax was levied on mineral oils supplied for domestic flights. The tax was calculated based on data supplied by the Swedish Civil Aviation Authority regarding the fuel consumption and emissions of hydrocarbons and nitric oxide from the type of aircraft used on an average flight. According to Braathens the environmental tax violated Article 3(2) of Directive 92/12/EEC. According to the Swedish tax authorities this is not a tax on fuel consumption, but an environmental tax on polluting emissions.

According to the ECJ, there is a direct and inseverable link between fuel consumption and the polluting substances. To allow the Member States to levy another indirect tax on products which must be exempt would render Article 8(1)(b) entirely ineffective.

The Swedish tax authorities also argued that the provision in question does not have direct effect since the Directive allows Member States a varying degree of latitude in implementing certain of its provisions. Referring to the *Becker* case,[39] the ECJ held that individuals may not for that reason be denied the right to rely on any provisions which, owing to their particular subject-matter, are capable of being severed from the general body of provisions and applied as such. The Court ruled that the Swedish levy was not compatible with Article 8(1) of Directive 92/12/EEC. (See now under the Recast General Arrangements Directive Article 1(2) expressly providing that Member States may levy other indirect taxes on excise goods for specific purposes, provided that those taxes comply with the Community tax rules applicable for excise duty or value added tax as far as determination of the tax base, calculation of the tax, chargeability and monitoring of the tax are concerned, *but not including the provisions on exemptions.*)

Taxes on products other than excise goods and on the supply of services

Notwithstanding the "harmonization" of the excises, based on Article 1(3) Member States retain the right to maintain or even introduce taxes levied on products other than excise

38 Case C-346/97 (*Braathens*), [1999] ECR I-3419.
39 Case 8/81 (*Ursula Becker*), [1982] ECR 0053.

goods and on the supply of services,[40] including those relating to excise goods, which cannot be characterised as turnover taxes.[41]

In contrast to Article 1(2), Article 1(3) does not require that taxes on products other than excise goods or on the supply of services are levied for specific purposes. However, the levying of such taxes on products other than excise goods or on the supply of services may not, in trade between Member States, give rise to formalities connected with the crossing of frontiers (see also point (5) in the preamble).

The *Ottmar Hermann* case[42] deals with the provision that Member States are allowed to levy taxes on the supply of services which cannot be characterized as turnover taxes, including those relating to products subject to excise duty. The City of Frankfurt am Main levied until 1 January 2000 a local beverage tax on the supply of alcoholic beverages for immediate consumption on the premises. Volkswirt Weinschänken GmbH operated a restaurant in the City of Frankfurt am Main. For the third quarter of 1995, it was liable to pay the sum of DEM 9,135,35 (approximately EUR 4,670) in beverage tax. Taking the view that that tax infringed, *inter alia*, the provisions of horizontal Directive 92/12/EEC, that company challenged, before the Verwaltungsgericht Frankfurt am Main (Administrative Court, Frankfurt am Main), the notice of assessment of 7 November 1995. In its judgment of 14 May 2002, that court annulled the notice.

Stadt Frankfurt am Main brought an appeal against that judgment before the Hessischer Verwaltungsgerichtshof (Higher Administrative Court, Hesse). It explained that the tax does not apply to the supply of goods but to transactions for the supply of services and argued that under the second paragraph of Article 3(3) of Directive 92/12/EEC, Member States are to remain free to levy taxes such as the tax on beverages under discussion.

The Hessischer Verwaltungsgerichtshof asked the ECJ whether the beverage tax should be seen as another indirect tax on products subject to excise duty for the purposes of Article 3(1) and (2) of Directive 92/12/EEC (now Article 1(2) of the Recast General Arrangements Directive) or as a tax on the supply of services relating to products subject to excise

40 Different from Article 3(3) of Directive 92/12/EEC, Article 1(3) of Directive 2020/262/EU provides that the supply of services may include those relating to excise goods based on the *Ottmar Hermann* case, see this section further below. See also Case C-2/09 (*Petar Dimitrov Kalinchev*), [2010] ECR I- 04939, in which the ECJ ruled that the first subparagraph of Article 3(3) of Directive 92/12/EEC does not apply to a case such as the main proceedings and cannot therefore preclude a Member State from laying down provisions levying excise duty on the introduction of used motor vehicles into its territory, if that duty is not directly payable on the second-hand purchase of such vehicles which are already in the country and on which excise duty has already been paid on first introduction into the territory of the Member State, provided that such a system does not give rise to border-crossing formalities in trade between Member States.

41 See also Article 401 of the RVD providing:
"Without prejudice to other provisions of Community law, this Directive shall not prevent a Member State from maintaining or introducing taxes on insurance contracts, taxes on betting and gambling, excise duties, stamp duties or, more generally, any taxes, duties or charges which cannot be characterised as turnover taxes, provided that the collecting of those taxes, duties or charges does not give rise, in trade between Member States, to formalities connected with the crossing of frontiers."

42 Case C-491/03 (*Ottmar Hermann*), [2005] ECR I-2025.

duty within the meaning of the second subparagraph of Article 3(3) of Directive 92/12/EEC (now Article 1(3)(b) of the Recast General Arrangements Directive) and if it is a tax on the supply of services whether such a tax must also be for "specific purposes", as laid down in Article 3(2) of the Directive.

On 10 March 2005, the ECJ decided the case. As a preliminary point, the ECJ noted that Article 3(2) of Directive 92/12/EEC lays down strict requirements for indirect taxes imposed by Member States in the case of products subject to excise duty, such as alcoholic beverages. That provision states that indirect taxes, other than excise duty, must have 'specific purposes', namely purposes other than purely budgetary purposes (see for example Case C-437/97 (*EKW*), reported above in this section), and that they must also comply with 'the tax rules applicable for excise duty or VAT purposes as far as determination of the tax base, calculation of the tax, chargeability and monitoring of the tax are concerned'. Under Article 3(3) of Directive 92/12/EEC, Member States are to retain the right to introduce or maintain taxes which are levied on products not subject to excise tax (first subparagraph) or taxes 'which cannot be characterised as turnover taxes' levied on 'the supply of services ..., including those relating to products subject to excise duty' (second subparagraph).

As to whether the beverage tax relates to products subject to excise duty for the purposes of Article 3(2) of Directive 92/12/EEC or to the supply of services relating to such products within the meaning of the second subparagraph of Article 3(3), the ECJ pointed out that in the case of the beverage tax under discussion the chargeable event is the supply for consideration of alcoholic beverages for immediate consumption on the premises. Unlike in *EKW*, which dealt with a tax levied on the supply for consideration of alcoholic beverages, the chargeable event in the case at hand is not the mere supply of such beverages but, on the contrary, refers to a transaction involving a supply of services.

According to the ECJ, in order to determine whether the beverage tax imposed applies to products subject to excise duty for the purposes of Article 3(2) of Directive 92/12/EEC or, rather, to the services supplied in relation to such products for the purposes of the second subparagraph of Article 3(3), regard must be had to the predominant feature of the transaction on which it is imposed (see, by analogy, the *Faaborg-Gelting Linien* case in this section further below). The ECJ observed that where the marketing of a product is always accompanied by a minimal supply of services (such as the displaying of the products on shelves, the issuing of an invoice, etc.), only services other than those which necessarily accompany the marketing of a product may be taken into account in assessing the part played by the supply of services within the whole of a complex transaction also involving the supply of a product.

According to the ECJ, it is not possible to state generally that, for all the operations falling within the scope of the beverage tax, the feature relating to the supply of services will always predominate, but in the case of Volkswirt Weinschänken the ECJ came to the following assessment. It operates a restaurant in which it serves prepared dishes and beverages. The supply of alcoholic beverages to customers in a catering context is accompanied by a series of services other than the operations which are necessarily connected with the marketing of such products. Those services consist in placing an infrastructure at the customer's disposal, including a dining room with furniture and appurtenances (cloakrooms, toilets, etc.), providing the customer with advice and explanations concerning the beverages served, serving them to him in a suitable container, serving at table and, finally, clearing the tables and cleaning after the food and drink have been consumed. A supply of alcoholic beverages in a catering context is characterised by an array of features and acts, of which the supply of the product itself is only one component and in which services predominate.

Consequently, the beverage tax must be regarded as a tax levied on the supply of services 'relating to products subject to excise duty' within the meaning of the second subparagraph of Article 3(3) of Directive 92/12/EEC. The ECJ also held that the tax cannot be 'characterised as [a] turnover tax ...' within the meaning of that provision since it applies only to a defined category of products, namely alcoholic beverages.[43]

As to the second question, whether a tax on the supply of services within the meaning of the second subparagraph of Article 3(3) of Directive 92/12/EEC is subject to the condition that it be for a specific purpose as referred to in Article 3(2), the ECJ recalled that, under the first subparagraph of Article 3(3) of Directive 92/ 12/EEC, Member States are to retain the right to introduce or maintain indirect taxes levied on products not subject to excise duty 'provided, however, that those taxes do not give rise to border-crossing formalities in trade between Member States'. The second subparagraph of that same paragraph provides that 'subject to the same proviso', Member States are also to retain the right to levy taxes on the 'supply of services which cannot be characterised as turnover taxes, including those relating to products subject to excise duty'. According to the ECJ, the right referred to in the second subparagraph of Article 3(3) of Directive 92/12/EEC is subject only to the proviso contained in the first subparagraph, namely that such 'taxes do not give rise to border-crossing formalities in trade between Member States'. The directive therefore does not require taxes falling within the scope of Article 3(3) to comply with the condition laid down in Article 3(2), namely that they be for a specific purpose.

Recast General Arrangements Directive incorporates this judgment. Article 1(2) concerns levies which must be levied for specific purposes while Article 1(3) concerns taxes on a) products other than excise products and b) services; both subject (only) to the limitation that the taxes do not give rise to formalities in trade between the Member States.

In the Joined Cases *Elecdey Carcelen*,[44] the Court ruled that Article 1(2) of the Recast General Arrangement Directive only refers to indirect taxes, which are levied directly or indirectly on the consumption of 'excise goods', such as those listed in Article 1(1) of the Directive. The levy at issue in the main proceedings applies to wind turbines designed to produce electricity and as such, does not tax the consumption of energy products or

43 See, *ex multis*, Case 252/86 (*Bergandi*), [1988] ECR 1343, Case C-437/97 (*Evangelischer Krankenhausverein*), [2000] ECR I-1157 and Case C-475/03 (*Banco Popolare di Cremona*), [2006] ECR I-9373 and most recently Case C-426/07 (*Dariusz Krawczy/ski*), [2008] ECR I-6021, Case C-156/08 (*Monika Vollkommer*), [2008] ECR I-165*, Case C-151/08 (*N.N. Renta*), [2008] ECR I-164*, and, Case C-119/08 (*Mechel Nemunas*), [2009] ECR I-12*.

44 Joined Cases C-215/16 (*Elecdey Carcelen*), C-216/16 (*Energias Eolicas de Cuenca*), C-220-16 (*Iberenova Promociones*) and C-221/16 (*Iberdrola Renovables Castilla La Mancha*), [2017] ECLI:EU:C:2017:705.

electricity. Whether the levy has an environmental objective should be reviewed as a matter of national law.

The *Faaborg-Gelting Linien* case[45] referred to above involved taxable transactions under the Sixth VAT Directive (now Recast). Instead of breaking the taxable transaction down into its various particles in order to tax them separately, the ECJ applied the principle of 'the unity of the supply'. Based on this principle the ECJ comes to the conclusion in the *Ottmar Hermann* case at hand that a beverage tax which is not explicitly levied on the supply but refers to a transaction involving a supply of services is a tax on services.

We have our serious doubts whether the drafters of the horizontal Directive 92/12/ EEC had in mind that additional taxes on the supply of excise goods were only permitted when for a specific purpose, but that this requirement could be circumvented by an absorption theory which makes identical supplies of excised goods disappear in a cluster of services. These doubts no longer apply to Directive 2008/ 118/EC which clearly states that Member States may levy taxes on the supply of services, *including those relating to excise goods,* which cannot be characterised as turnover taxes.

Both the excise and VAT systems contain prohibitions against introducing other indirect taxes than those complying with the conditions laid down in the VAT Directive and the Recast General Arrangements Directive. It is clear from the case law on the prohibition of other indirect taxes with the character of the VAT in Article 401 of the VAT Directive that a specific tax is not prohibited. As seen above, according to Article 1(2) and (3) of the Recast General Arrangements Directive, Member States may levy other indirect taxes on excise goods for specific purposes, provided that they conform to the applicable EU rules.

These EU rules are subject to preliminary questions in *e.g.* the *Kernkraftwerke Lippe-Ems* case,[46] more specifically Article 107(1) of the TFEU (State Aid) and the Euratom Treaty.

3.2.1.2 Application of the Union Customs Code to excise goods

Article 2(1) and 2(2) of Recast General Arrangements Directive provide that the formalities relating to importation or exportation laid down by the Union customs provisions in force shall apply *mutatis mutandis* to the importation from or exportation to the territories referred to in Article 4(2) which form part of the customs territory of the Union but fall outside the territorial scope of the Recast General Arrangements Directive (see section 3.2.1.3 below). These formalities already apply to excise goods by virtue of Articles 275 and 279 of Directive 2006/112/EC on the common system of VAT. However, to clarify these situations, these provisions are included in Directive 2020/262/EU as well.

According to Article 275 of the VAT Directive (see Chapter 2, section 2.13.8), the formalities relating to the importation of the goods referred to in Article 274, *i.e.* goods in free circulation which enter the Community from a third territory forming part of the customs

45 Case C-231/94 (*Faaborg-Gelting Linien*), [1996] ECR 2395.
46 Case C-5/14 (Kernkraftwerke Lippe-Ems), [2015] ECLI:EU:2015:354.

territory of the Community, must be the same as those laid down by the Community customs provisions in force for the importation of goods into the customs territory of the Community. Article 279 of the VAT Directive provides that the formalities relating to the exportation of the goods referred to in Article 278, *i.e.* goods in free circulation which are dispatched or transported from a Member State to a third territory forming part of the customs territory of the Community from the territory of the Community, must be the same as those laid down by the Community customs provisions in force for the exportation of goods from the customs territory of the Community.

In order to avoid duplication of procedures, Article 2(4) provides that for excise goods under a customs suspensive procedure or arrangements (see section 1.5.2), the provisions laid down in the Directive on the production, processing, holding and storage as well as the movement under suspension of excise duty do not apply.

On the question whether "illegal supplies" should be subject to EU harmonized taxes (VAT and excise duties), in the *Salumets* case[47] the ECJ held that, in contrast to narcotic drugs, ethyl alcohol can be lawfully marketed and introduced into economic channels. The circumstances in which the goods were imported in the present case cannot alter that assessment. An intrinsically lawful product such as ethyl alcohol may not be equaled with a narcotic drug for reasons connected with its origin, quality or purity. The principal of fiscal neutrality prevents any general distinction between lawful and unlawful transactions. In the *BAT* case the Court held that also the illegal importation and supply of manufactured tobacco, which are not prohibited by their very nature or because of their special characteristics, are admittedly subject to taxation, since those goods are capable of being lawfully marketed and introduced into economic channels.[48]

3.2.1.3 *Territorial Application*

Articles 4 and 5[49] provide where the Recast General Arrangements Directive and the specific excise Directives apply. To enhance clarity, the structure of these provisions has been aligned to the structure used in Articles 6 and 7 of the VAT Directive. The minor differences from the VAT Directive with respect to the special territories are outlined below.

According to Article 4(1), the Recast General Arrangements Directive and the Directives on specific excise goods, referred to in Article 1, apply to the territory of the Union, *i.e.* the territory of the Member State to which the Treaty is applicable, in accordance with Article 349 and 355 of the TFEU, with the exception of third territories.[50]

47 Case C-455/98 (*Salumets*), [2000] ECR I-4993.
48 Case C-435/03 (*British American Tobacco*), [2005] ECR I-7077, point 38.
49 Due to reorganization and renumbering of the recast, these are Article 5 and 6 of Directive 2008/118/EC.
50 According to Article 3:
"(2) 'territory of a Member State' means the territory of each Member State to which the Treaty is applicable, in accordance with Article 349 and 355 of the TFEU, with the exception of third territories;
(3) 'territory of the Union' means the territories of the Member States".

Based on Article 4(2) of the Recast General Arrangements Directive, they do not apply to the following territories forming part of the customs territory of the Union:
(a) the Canary Islands;
(b) the French territories referred to in Article 349 and 355(1) TFEU;[51]
(c) the Åland Islands;
(d) the Channel Islands.

In comparison with Directive 92/12/EEC, the Proposal for Directive 2008/118/ EC added Gibraltar to the list of territories in Article 5 (territories not forming part of the customs territory of the Community to which the Directive and the specific excise Directives do not apply). This was "in order to remove any doubt as to whether, in view of the Act of Accession of the UK, the Community provisions on excise duty apply to Gibraltar as well". Eventually Gibraltar was not listed. Due to the fact that the Recast General Arrangements Directive refers to the territory of the Union, any changes in the territory of the Union furthermore directly apply to the excise territory as well, including but not limited to the withdrawal of the United Kingdom from the European Union on 31 January 2020.[52]

Article 2(1) and (2) of the Recast General Arrangements Directive provides that the formalities laid down by the Union customs provisions for the entry of goods into the customs territory of the Union shall apply *mutatis mutandis* to the *entry* of excise goods into the Union from a territory[53] referred to in Article 4(2).

The formalities laid down by the Union customs provisions for the *exit* of goods from the customs territory of the Union apply *mutatis mutandis* to the exit of excise goods from the Union to a territory referred to in Article 4(2).

However, by way of derogation, Finland is authorised, for movements of excise goods between its territory and the Åland Islands (the "third" territories referred to in Article 4(2)(c)), to apply the same procedures as those applied for such movements on its territory (and not as between its territory and third territories), see Article 2(3) of the Recast General Arrangements Directive.

According to Article 4(3) of the Recast General Arrangements Directive and the Directives on specific excise goods do not apply to the territories within the scope of Article 355(3)

51 It concerns Guadeloupe, French Guiana, Martinique, Réunion, Saint-Barthélemy and Saint-Martin.

52 See Council Decision (EU) 2020/135 of 30 January 2020 on the conclusion of the Agreement on the withdrawal of the United Kingdom of Great Britain and Northern Ireland from the European Union and the European Atomic Energy Community, O.J. 2020, L 29, p. 1. Northern Ireland remains part of the excise territory of the EU.

53 According to Article 3(4):
"'third territories' means the territories referred to in Article 4(2) and (3)".

TFEU,[54] nor to the following other territories[55] not forming part of the customs territory of the Union:
(a) the Island of Heligoland;
(b) the territory of Büsingen;
(c) Ceuta;
(d) Melilla;
(e) Livigno.

Based on Article 4(4), Spain may give notice, by means of a declaration, that the General Arrangements Directive and the Directives referred to in Article 1 shall apply to the Canary Islands – subject to measures to adapt to their extreme remoteness – in respect of all or some of the excise goods referred to in Article 1, as from the first day of the second month following deposit of such declaration.

The words "subject to measures to adjust to their extreme remoteness" have been added in Article 4(4) concerning the Canary Islands, aligning as such this paragraph to Article 4(5) concerning the French overseas territories.

Article 4(5) allows France to give notice, by means of a declaration, that the Recast General Arrangements Directive and the Directives referred to in Article 1 apply to the French territories – subject to measures to adapt to their extreme remoteness – in respect of all or some of the excise goods referred to in Article 1, as from the first day of the second month following deposit of such declaration.

We note that the French and Spanish possibilities to include within the territorial scope of the Recast General Arrangements Directive certain territories is not present with regard to determining the territorial scope of the VAT Directive. Pursuant to Article 8 of the VAT Directive if the Commission considers that the provisions laid down in Article 6 of the VAT Directive (dealing with the territories forming part of the customs territory to which the VAT Directive does not apply and territories not forming part of the customs territory to which the VAT Directive does not apply) and Article 7 of the VAT Directive (dealing with the Principality of Monaco and the United Kingdom Sovereign Base Areas of Akrotiri

54 Providing:
"3. The provisions of the Treaties shall apply to the European territories for whose external relations a Member State is responsible."

55 Up to 31 December 2019, the territories excluded from the excise regime also included Campione d'Italia and the Italian waters of Lake Lugano. These were removed from exclusion, and therefore included in the excise (and customs) territory of the EU, as of 1 January 2020 by way of Council Directive (EU) 2019/475 of 18 February 2019 amending Directives 2006/112 and 2008/118/EC as regards the inclusion of the Italian municipality of Campione d'Italia and the Italian waters of Lake Lugano in the customs territory of the Union and in the territorial application of Directive 2008/118/EC, O.J. 2019, L 83, p. 42. Based on the Explanatory Memorandum underlying the proposal for this amendment, the geographic location of the two territories has historically justified their exclusion from the EU customs territory, but Italy considered the exclusion to be no longer necessary. To date, the territories continue to be excluded from the EU VAT territory, applying a local indirect taxation in line with Swiss value added tax to ensure a level playing field (see Chapter 2, section 2.2.).

and Dhekelia)[56] are no longer justified, particularly in terms of fair competition or own resources, it must present appropriate proposals to the Council.

According to Article 4(6) of the Recast General Arrangements Directive, the provisions of the Directive shall not prevent Greece from maintaining the specific status granted to Mount Athos as guaranteed by Article 105 of the Greek Constitution.

In view of the conventions and treaties concluded with France, Italy, Cyprus and the United Kingdom respectively,[57] Article 5(1) of the Recast General Arrangements Directive provides that the Principality of Monaco, San Marino, the United Kingdom Sovereign Base Areas of Akrotiri and Dhekelia will not be regarded, for the purposes of the Directive, as third countries.

Member States must take the measures necessary to ensure that movements of excise goods originating in or intended for:
(a) the Principality of Monaco are treated as movements originating in or intended for France;
(b) San Marino are treated as movements originating in or intended for Italy;
(c) United Kingdom Sovereign Base Areas of Akrotiri and Dhekelia are treated as movements originating in or intended for Cyprus;

Different from the VAT Directive, the Member States must also take the necessary measures to ensure that transactions originating in or intended for:
- Jungholz and Mittelberg (Kleines Walsertal); are treated as transactions originating in or intended for the Federal Republic of Germany, and
- San Marino; are treated as transactions originating in or intended for the Italian Republic.

See Annex I for a comparison table between the customs territory, the VAT territory and the excise territory.

3.2.2 *Taxable event, Time and place of chargeability, Irregularities during movement under duty suspension, Reimbursement, Remission, Exemption*

Chapter II of Directive 2020/262/EU deals with the taxable event (see section 3.2.2.1), time and place chargeability (see section 3.2.2.2), reimbursement and remission (see section 3.2.2.3) and exemptions (see section 3.2.2.4).

56 The Isle of Man used to be part of that list also but has been removed as a consequence of the UK withdrawal from the EU.

57 See now Protocol relating to the sovereign base areas of the United Kingdom of Great Britain and Nortern Ireland in Cyprus as part of the new EU/UK Trade Agreement.

3.2.2.1 Taxable Event

Article 6(1)[58] of the Recast General Arrangements Directive provides that excise goods are subject to excise duty at the time of their production (including, where applicable, their extraction)[59] within, or their importation or irregular entry into, the territory of the Union.

The event production is not further defined in the Directive. According to Article 14 it is up to each Member State to determine its rules concerning the production of excise goods subject to the Recast General Arrangements Directive. The territory of the Union is defined in Article 3(3), see section 3.2.1.2 above.

Importation of excise goods is defined in Article 3(7) of the Recast General Arrangement Directive as the release for free circulation in accordance with Article 201 of the UCC.[60] Irregular entry is defined in Article 3(8) as an entry of goods into the territory of the Union, which have not been placed under release for free circulation in accordance with Article 201 of the UCC and for which a customs debt under Article 79(1) of that Regulation has been incurred, or would have been incurred if the goods had been subject to customs duty.

Under Directive 2008/118/EC, the importation of excise goods (including irregular importation), was defined as entry into the territory of the Community unless the goods are placed under a customs or excise suspensive procedure or arrangement. Despite the apparent change in the wording, this should not be considered as a change of the definition of import of excise goods. The Recast General Arrangement Directive has merely clarified the definition and perhaps simplified its maintenance, by linking it directly to the respective articles of the UCC. See section 3.2.4.4 below.

Notwithstanding this clear-cut enumeration of what triggers the taxable event in Article 6 (*i.e.* production, extraction, importation or irregular entry), the occurrence of the event does not necessarily result in chargeability of the tax. (We understand the 'chargeable event' to mean the occurrence by virtue of which the legal conditions necessary for excise duty to become chargeable are fulfilled and the duty becomes 'chargeable' when the tax authority becomes entitled under the law, at a given moment, to claim the duty from the person liable to pay, even though the payment may be deferred.) When goods are imported, the destination may be re-exportation, or goods may be placed in a free zone or under another special (customs) procedure. Reimbursement of the payment upon importation would then be necessary. If excise duty would be due immediately upon production, this would result in (high) financing costs *e.g.* when the products require time to ripen (wine) or when based on the destination principle one is entitled to a refund, *i.e.* in cases of exportation, of intra-EU supplies or of exempt (domestic) consumption. According to Article 6 of the

58 Due to reorganisation of the recast, this is Article 2 of Directive 2008/118/EC.
59 Direct extraction from the soil is covered by the word "production", as specified in Article 21(2) of Directive 2003/96/EC of 27 October 2003 restructuring the Community framework for the taxation of energy products and electricity, see section 3.8.5 below.
60 Regulation (EU) No 952/2013 of the European Parliament and of the Council of 9 October 2013 laying down the Union Customs Code, O.J. 2013, L 269, p. 1.

Directive[61] excise duty becomes chargeable at the time of *release for consumption*. This requires some further explanation.

Produced or imported excise goods may be held in a so-called tax warehouse or may be placed under a customs suspensive procedure or arrangement. A tax warehouse is a place where a natural or legal person (the so-called authorized warehousekeeper, defined in Article 3(1) as a natural or legal person authorised by the competent authorities of a Member State, in the course of his business, to produce, process, hold, store, receive or dispatch excise goods under a duty suspension arrangement in a tax warehouse),[62] subject to certain conditions laid down by the competent authorities of the Member State where the tax warehouse is located may produce, process, hold, store, receive or dispatch goods subject to excise duty without the duty becoming chargeable. This is called the "duty suspension arrangement", defined in Article 3(6) as a tax arrangement applied to the production, processing, holding, storage or movement of excise goods whereby excise duty is suspended.

Under certain conditions, this duty suspension arrangement not only applies to production, processing, holding and storage but also to the movement of excise products. Article 16 provides for the possibility to move excise goods under suspension of excise duty and enumerates the different movement destinations and various movement scenarios (see also section 3.2.4 and section 3.3 below).

Excise goods may be moved under a duty suspension arrangement within the territory of the Union, including where the goods are moved via a third country[63] or a third territory,[64] *inter alia*, from a tax warehouse to another tax warehouse, to a registered consignee, to a place where the excise goods leave the territory of the Community and from the place of importation[65] to any of the destinations just mentioned where the goods are dispatched by a registered consignor. (Art. 3(9) defines 'registered consignee' as a natural or legal person authorised by the competent authorities of the Member State of destination, in the course of his business and under the conditions fixed by those authorities, to receive excise goods moving under a duty suspension arrangement from another Member State. 'Registered consignor' means, according to Article 3(10), a natural or legal person authorised by the competent authorities of the Member State of importation, in the course of his business and under the conditions fixed by those authorities, to only dispatch excise goods under

61 Article 7 of Directive 2008/118/EC.

62 See also the Commission Recommendation (2000/789/EC) of 29 November 2000 setting out guidelines for the authorisation of warehousekeepers under Council Directive 92/12/EEC in relation to products subject to excise duty. See further section 3.2.3.

63 Defined in Article 3(5) as any State or territory to which the Treaty is not applicable.

64 Defined in Article 3(4) as the territories referred to in Article 4(2) and (3) of Directive 2020/262/EU, *i.e.* certain territories forming part of the customs territory of the Union and the territories within the scope of Article 349 TFEU and certain other territories not forming part of the customs territory of the Union. See section 3.2.1.3 below.

65 Place of importation means the place where the goods are when they are released for free circulation in accordance with Article 87 of the Union Customs Code, see the next footnote.

a duty suspension arrangement upon their release for free circulation in accordance with Article 201 of the Union Customs Code.[66])

Any departure from the duty suspension arrangement, *i.e.* release for consumption, results in chargeability of the duty (see further section 3.2.2.1 below).

'Customs suspensive procedure or arrangement' referred to above means any one of the special procedures as provided for under the Union Customs Code (UCC) relating to the customs supervision to which non-Union goods are subjected upon their entry into the customs territory of the Union, *i.e.* transit, storage, specific use or processing, more specifically any of the arrangements referred to in Article 210 of the Union Customs Code.[67] According to the preamble to Directive 2008/118/EC, point (7), since suspensive procedures under the Union Customs Code provide for adequate monitoring whilst excise goods are subject to the provisions of the Customs Code, there is no need for the separate application of an excise monitoring system for the time that the excise goods are subject to a Union customs suspensive procedure or arrangement. As a consequence however, (irregular) removal from customs supervision also leads to a chargeable event from an excise duty perspective. See the *Commission v. Hellenic Republic* case below.

3.2.2.2 *Time and Place of Chargeability*

Article 6(2), (3) and (4) of the Recast General Arrangements Directive deal with the time and the place of chargeability.

Release for Consumption

Point (7) of the preamble to the Recast General Arrangements Directive recites that since it remains necessary for the proper functioning of the internal market that the concept, and conditions for chargeability, of excise duty be the same in all Member States, it is necessary to make clear at Union level when excise goods are released for consumption and who the person liable to pay the excise duty is.

With regard to the incurrence of excise duty, Article 6(2)[68] provides that excise duty becomes chargeable at the time, and in the Member State, of release for consumption.

According to Article 6(3) 'release for consumption' means any of the following:

(a) the departure of excise goods, including irregular departure, from a duty suspension arrangement (defined in Article 3(6) as a tax arrangement applied to the production, processing, holding, storage or movement of excise goods, excise duty being suspended);

---

66 Regulation (EU) No. 952/2013, O.J. 2013, L 269, p. 1. Article 201 provides:
Release for free circulation shall confer on non-Union goods the customs status of Union goods. It shall entail the application of commercial policy measures, completion of the other formalities laid down in respect of the importation of goods and the charging of any duties legally due.

67 The following arrangements:
- external and internal transit;
- customs warehousing and free zones;
- temporary admission and end use;
- inward and outward processing.

68 Due to restructuring of the Directive, this was article 7(1) of Directive 2008/ 118/EC.

(b) the holding or storage of excise goods, including cases of irregularity, outside a duty suspension arrangement where excise duty has not been levied pursuant to the applicable provisions of Union law and national legislation;
(c) the production, including processing, of excise goods, including irregular production and processing, outside a duty suspension arrangement;
(d) the importation of excise goods, unless the excise goods are placed, immediately upon importation, under a duty suspension arrangement, or the irregular entry of excise goods, unless the customs debt was extinguished, where:
    (i) goods liable to import or export duty are confiscated or seized and simultaneously or subsequently confiscated (point e of Article 124(1) UCC);
    (ii) goods liable to import or export duty are destroyed under customs supervision or abandoned to the State (point f of Article 124(1) UCC);
    (iii) the disappearance of the goods or the non-fulfilment of obligations arising from the customs legislation results from the total destruction or irretrievable loss[69] of those goods as a result of the actual nature of the goods or unforeseeable circumstances or force majeure, or as a consequence of instruction by the customs authorities (point g of Article 124(1) UCC);
    (iv) the customs debt was incurred pursuant to Article 79 UCC[70] and evidence is provided to the satisfaction of the customs authorities that goods have not been used or consumed and have been taken out of the customs territory of the Union (point k of Article 124(1) UCC).

In case of confiscation or seizure, Member States are allowed to still impose a penalty taking into account the amount of excise debt which would have been incurred, according to the last sentence of Article 6(3)(d).

The remainder of the reasons based on which the customs debt can be extinguished, *i.e.*, points (a) to (d) and (h) to (j) of Article 124(1) UCC, do not automatically lead to the non-chargeability of an excise debt. This includes situations whereby the non-compliance leading to the customs debt had no significant effect on the correct operation of the customs procedure.

We note that the importation of excise goods is defined in Article 3(7) as the release for free circulation in accordance with Article 201 UCC. Under Directive 2008/118/EC, the chargeable event of irregular entry was not defined in (then) Article 4 of Directive 2008/118/EC. In the Recast General Arrangements Directive irregular entry is separately defined as entry of goods into the territory of the Union, which have not been placed under release

69 For the purpose of this point, goods shall be considered as irretrievably lost when they have been rendered unusable by any person.

70 A customs debt incurs on the basis of Article 79 UCC in case of non-compliance with the obligations laid down in the customs legislation concerning the introduction of non-Union goods into the customs territory of the Union, their removal from customs supervision, the movement, processing, storage, temporary storage, temporary admission or disposal of the goods, the end-use of goods, a condition governing the placing of non-Union goods under a customs procedure or the granting, by virtue of the end-use of goods, of duty exemption or a reduced rate of import duty.

for free circulation in accordance with Article 201 UCC and for which a customs debt under Article 79(1) UCC has been incurred.

In the *Commission v. Hellenic Republic* case,[71] the ECJ ruled that the definitions of and conditions for chargeability of excise duty are the same in all Member States. The infringement procedure concerns the exemption from excise duty provided by the Hellenic Republic to the fuel sold at the filling stations at the border posts of Kipoi Evrou (on the border with Turkey), Kakavia (on the border with Albania) and Evzonoi (on the border with Macedonia). These filling stations acted as tax warehouses, meaning that the storage of fuels is subject to a duty suspension arrangement. The Hellenic Republic argued that following the sale of fuel, the goods were immediately placed under a customs export arrangement and therefore no excise duty could become chargeable. The ECJ however ruled that the same has no bearing on the chargeability of excise duty, as the fueling itself constitutes as a removal of excise dutiable goods from a duty suspension arrangement and therefore as a dutiable release for consumption.

Insofar Article 6(3) leaves any doubt, it was clarified in the *Polihim-SS* case[72] that excise duty is levied on consumption and not on sale. As such, the time at which it becomes chargeable, must be very closely linked with the customer. A sale of excisable goods held in a tax warehouse does not include consumption and only leads to the release for consumption as and when the goods are physically removed from that tax warehouse.

Article 8 of the Recast General Arrangements Directive (formerly Article 9 of Directive 2008/118/EC and Article 6(2) of the horizontal Directive)[73] provides that the chargeability conditions and rate of excise duty to be applied shall be those in force on the date on which duty becomes chargeable in the Member State where release for consumption takes place. Furthermore, the provision states that excise duty shall be levied and collected and, where appropriate, reimbursed or remitted according to the procedure laid down by

71 Case C-590/16 (Commission v. Hellenic Republic), [2018] ECLI:EU:C:2018:77.

72 Case 355/14 (Polihim-SS), [2016] ECLI:EU:C:2016:403, see also section 3.8.3.1.

73 In Case C-325/99 (*Van de Water*), [2001] ECR I-2729, the ECJ stated that by ensuring, in Article 6(1) of the horizontal Directive, that the rules governing the chargeability of excise duty are the same in all the Member States, the Community legislature was clearly not seeking to harmonise the procedures for the levying and collection of duty by those States. On the contrary, in Article 6(2), it expressly left it to the Member States to determine those procedures, subject to the non-discrimination requirement. The ECJ also noted that, whilst Article 6 of the Directive does not specify the person liable to pay the duty chargeable, it follows from the scheme of the Directive, and from the ninth recital in its preamble, that the national authorities must in any event ensure that the tax debt is in fact collected. According to the ECJ, Article 6(1) of the horizontal Directive must be interpreted as meaning that the mere holding of a product subject to excise duty constitutes a release for consumption where duty has not yet been levied on that product pursuant to the applicable provisions of Community law and national legislation. Thus, Member States are free to determine the procedures for the levying and collection of excise duty, but the national authorities must ensure that the tax debt is in fact collected.

each Member State. Member States must apply the same procedures to national goods and to those from other Member States.[74]

Time of Chargeability
According to Article 6(2) of the Recast General Arrangements Directive, excise duty becomes chargeable *at the time*, and in the Member State, of release for consumption, thus, when excise goods depart from a duty suspension arrangement, or when they are held outside a duty suspension arrangement excise duties not having been levied, at the moment of production (outside a suspension arrangement) and upon importation, including irregular entry.

Article 6(4) further specifies that the time of departure from a duty suspension arrangement shall be deemed *the time of receipt*, distinguishing the following situations:
(a) When excise goods are moved under a duty suspension arrangement within the territory of the Union, including where the goods are moved via a third country or a third territory from a tax warehouse to a registered consignee (*i.e.* in the situations referred to in Article 16(1)(a)(ii), see section 3.2.4.1), the time of receipt of the excise goods by the registered consignee;
(b) When excise goods are moved under a duty suspension arrangement within the territory of the Community, including where the goods are moved via a third country or a third territory from a tax warehouse in the context of diplomatic or consular relations, of recognized international organisations and of NATO armed forces (*i.e.* in the situations referred to in Article 16(1)(a)(iv), see section 3.2.4.1 below), the time of receipt of the excise goods by the consignee;
(c) Where by the Member State of destination excise goods are allowed (in derogation from a movement from a tax warehouse to another tax warehouse or to a registered consignee or from the place of importation to prescribed destinations) to be moved under a duty suspension arrangement to a place of direct delivery situated on its territory, where that place has been designated by the authorised warehousekeeper in the Member State of destination or by the registered consignee (*i.e.* the situations referred to in Article 16(4), see section 3.2.4.1 below), the time of receipt of the excise goods at the place of direct delivery.

Article 6(5) provides that the total destruction or irretrievable loss of excise goods under a duty suspension arrangement, as a result of the actual nature of the goods, of unforeseeable

74 In Case C-230/08 (*Dansk Transport og Logistik*), [2010] ECR I- 03799, (for the facts see section 1.4.1.1) the ECJ suggested that it is likely that the goods discovered and seized are being held for commercial purposes. However, it is for the national court, which is the only court with direct knowledge of the dispute before it, to assess whether that is the case. If that is the case, it is apparent from Article 6(1) in conjunction with Article 7(1) of the horizontal Directive (now Articles 7(1) and 33 of the General Arrangements Directive) that the authorities of the Member State in which the goods which are unlawfully introduced into the Community were discovered and seized are competent to recover excise duty. In the case in the main proceedings at issue, those are the Danish authorities. If that is not the case, the first Member State into which the goods were imported, the Federal Republic of Germany in this case, remains competent to recover the excise duty pursuant to Article 6 of the horizontal Directive, even if the unlawfully introduced goods were only discovered subsequently by the authorities in another Member State.

circumstances or *force majeure*, or as a consequence of authorization by the competent authorities of the Member State, is not to be considered a release for consumption.

Goods are considered totally destroyed or irretrievably lost when they are rendered unusable as excise goods, following Article 6(6). The partial loss due to the nature of the goods that occurs during a duty suspension movement between the Member States shall not be considered a release for consumption in so far as the amount of loss falls below the common partial loss threshold for those excise goods, unless a Member State has reasonable cause to suspect fraud or irregularity. Each Member State is allowed to lay down its own rules for the treatment of partial losses under duty suspension arrangement not covered by the common partial loss threshold.

The total destruction or irretrievable loss of the excise goods in question must be proven to the satisfaction of the competent authorities of the Member State where the total destruction or irretrievable loss occurred or, when it is not possible to determine where the loss occurred, where it was detected.

This provision replaces and simplifies Article 14 of Directive 92/12/EEC which extensively dealt with losses and shortages occurring under suspension arrangements. In line with the nature of excise duty as a tax on the consumption of excise goods, the condition for the application of the rule is whether the goods placed under a suspension arrangement have been destroyed and/or can still be used and therefore effectively be released – and made available – for consumption. Compared to Directive 92/12/EEC, it no longer is necessary for the competent authorities to establish the reason for the occurrence of the shortage, in terms of fortuitous events of *force majeure*.

A further important difference with Article 14 of Directive 92/12/EEC is that, in case of intra-Union movements under suspension of excise duty, it will be for the Member State where the destruction or the loss of the goods occurs instead of the Member State of destination to decide on the application of Article 6(5).

With regard to *force majeure*, see also the *Société Pipeline Méditerranée et Rhône* case,[75] in which the ECJ ruled that the concept of *force majeure* giving rise to losses under duty suspension arrangements within the meaning of Article 14(1) of horizontal Directive 92/12/EEC implies that the loss has occurred under circumstances which are unforeseeable and unavoidable and beyond the control of the person who seeks to rely on those circumstances and the consequences of which he could not have avoided even if he had taken due care. Losses of part of products which have leaked from a pipeline due to their liquid nature and the characteristics of the ground on which they spilled which hindered their recovery cannot be regarded as inherent in the nature of the products within the meaning of Article 14(1) of Directive 92/12/EEC.

We note the different treatment of destruction and loss under VAT and under the excise provisions. Article 185(2) of the VAT Directive provides that no adjustments are to be made

---

75 Case C-314/06 (*Société Pipeline Méditerranée et Rhône*), [2007] ECR I-12273.

in the case of transactions remaining totally or partially unpaid or in the case of destruction, loss or theft of property duly proved or confirmed, or in the case of goods reserved for the purpose of making gifts of small value or of giving samples. (In the case of transactions remaining totally or partially unpaid or in the case of theft, Member States may require adjustment to be made.) Under the excise provisions the actual nature of the goods is decisive on whether destruction or loss is considered not to be a release for consumption.

The Person Liable to Pay

The horizontal Directive 92/12/EC did not provide who must pay the excise duty when it became chargeable at the time of release for consumption or when shortages were recorded. Each Member State could lay down its procedure on levying and collection of the duties, although it was understood that Member States apply the same procedures that were applied to national products. These national rules were also applicable to shortages.

Point (7) of the preamble to the Recast General Arrangements Directive recites that since it remains necessary for the proper functioning of the internal market that the concept, and conditions for chargeability, of excise duty be the same in all Member States, it is necessary to make clear at Community level when excise goods are released for consumption and *who the person liable to pay the excise duty is.*

Furthermore, point (12) recites that arrangements for the collection and reimbursement of duty have an impact on the proper functioning of the internal market and should therefore follow non-discriminatory criteria.

In relation to the departure of excise goods from a duty suspension arrangement (as referred to in Article 6(3)(a)) the person liable to pay the excise duty that has become chargeable is, according to Article 7(1)(a)(i), the authorised warehousekeeper, the registered consignee or any other person releasing the excise goods or on whose behalf the excise goods are released from the duty suspension arrangement and, in the case of irregular departure from the tax warehouse, any other person involved in that departure.

In the case of an irregularity during a movement of excise goods under a duty suspension arrangement (as defined in Article 9(1), (2) and (4), see further below) the person liable to pay the excise duty that has become chargeable is, according to Article 7(1)(a)(ii), the authorised warehousekeeper, the registered consignor or any other person who guaranteed the payment (in accordance with Article 17(1) and (3) see section 3.2.4.1 below) and any person who participated in the irregular departure and who was aware or who should reasonably have been aware of the irregular nature of the departure.

In relation to the holding of excise goods outside a duty suspension arrangement where excise duty has not been levied pursuant to the applicable provisions (as referred to in Article 6(3)(b),) the person liable to pay the excise duty that has become chargeable is, according to Article 7(1)(b) the person holding the excise goods and any other person involved in the holding of the excise goods.

In relation to the production of excise goods, including irregular production, outside a duty suspension arrangement (as referred to in Article 6(3)(c)) the person liable to pay the excise duty that has become chargeable is, according to Article 7(1) (c) the person producing the excise goods and, in the case of irregular production, any other person involved in their production.

In relation to the importation or irregular entry of excise goods (as referred to in Article 6(3)(d)) the person liable to pay the excise duty that has become chargeable is, according to Article 7(1)(d) the person who declares the excise goods or on whose behalf they are declared upon importation and, in the case of irregular entry, any other person involved in that irregular entry.

Article 7(2) provides that where several persons are liable for payment of one excise duty debt, they shall be jointly and severally liable for such debt.

According to Article 8, the chargeability conditions and rate of excise duty to be applied shall be those in force on the date on which duty becomes chargeable in the Member State where release for consumption takes place. Since arrangements for the collection and reimbursement of duty have an impact on the proper functioning of the internal market and should therefore follow non-discriminatory criteria (see point (7) of the preamble to the Recast General Arrangements Directive) Article 8 also provides that excise duty must be levied and collected and, where appropriate, reimbursed or remitted according to the procedure laid down by each Member State. Member States must apply the same procedures to national goods and to those from other Member States. (See also the *Van de Water* case above.)

In the case of irregularities, any person involved in the irregularity is liable to pay. There is a remarkable difference between VAT and excise liability rules. In principle the supplier or the recipient of transactions in VAT is the person liable to pay the tax. Under the excise regime in the case of irregularities, any person involved in the irregularity is liable to pay.

As regards joint and several liability, Article 8(2) of the Recast General Arrangements Directive provides that where several persons are liable for payment of one excise duty debt, they shall be jointly and severally liable for such debt. Article 205 of the VAT Directive merely allows Member States to provide that someone other than the person liable for payment is held jointly and severally liable for payment of the VAT.

The Place of Chargeability

According to Article 6(2) of the Recast General Arrangements Directive, excise duty becomes chargeable at the time, and *in the Member State*, of release for consumption.

According to the preamble to the Directive, point (13), in the event of an irregularity, excise duty should be due in the Member State on whose territory the irregularity has been committed which has led to the release for consumption or, if it is not possible to establish where the irregularity has been committed, it should be due in the Member State where it has been detected. Where excise goods do not arrive at their destination and no irregularity has been detected, the irregularity shall be deemed to have occurred in the Member State of dispatch.

Article 9 of the Recast General Arrangements Directive provides for rules to identify the Member State entitled to recover excise duty in case of irregularities that occurred during the movement of excise goods under suspension of excise duty. Article 9(6) defines the term "irregularity" as a situation in which a movement under suspension of excise duty of excise goods has not ended in accordance with Article 19(2), which provides that the consignee has taken delivery of the excise goods or when the goods have left the territory of the Union (see also section 3.2.4.1 below). This means that all or part of the goods concerned have not been taken for delivery of or have not been exported.

The principle laid down in Article 9(1) is that excise duty shall be due in the Member State *where the irregularity occurred.* Exceptions to this main rule apply if it is not possible to determine where the irregularity occurred, or if no irregularity was detected, but the goods have not arrived at their destination (see below). Both of these exceptions can be overruled by the main rule as and when new or additional information on irregularities becomes clear before the expiry of three years after the dispatch of the goods. According to Article 9(5), as and when it is ascertained in which Member State the irregularity actually occurred, excise duty shall be due in the Member State where the irregularity occurred. In these situations, the competent authorities of the Member State where the irregularity occurred must inform the competent authorities of the Member State where the excise duty was initially levied, which must reimburse or remit it as soon as evidence of the levying of the excise duty in the other Member State has been provided.

The main purpose of the refund procedure, and the below mentioned allocation of taxation rights, is to ensure that excise duty is levied only in one Member State and double taxation can be avoided.[76] The prevention of double taxation is however not an absolute principle on which the Recast General Arrangements Directive is based.[77] It appears to us as only the main rule can overrule both exceptions outlined below. That means that, in case following further investigations, a Member State does detect that an irregularity has taken place, *e.g.*, by retrieving duly marked goods that were stolen, but cannot establish where the irregularity took place, it appears that the Member State of dispatch, where the excise duty was initially levied, is not required by Article 9(5) to reimburse or remit this excise duty. Provided that the Member State where the irregularity was detected, would gain the right to levy excise duty at the time when the irregularity was detected, this may lead to double taxation that is not prevented by the Recast General Arrangements Directive.

Article 9(2) and (4) deal with the situation in which it is (and remains) not possible to determine where the irregularity took place. Article 9(2) provides that in that situation the release for consumption is deemed to have occurred in the Member State at the time

76 Case C-663/11 (*Scandic Distilleries*), [2013] ECLI:EU:C:2013:347. In this case, the ECJ ruled that the refund request in the Member State of departure (Romania) can be filed at any time, even before the excise goods are shipped to the Member State of consumption (Czech Republic), as long as the required documentation to support excise duty was paid in another Member State is (eventually) provided to the Member State in which the refund was requested.

77 Case C-374/06 (*BATIG*), [2007] ECR I-11271.

when and *where the irregularity was detected.*[78] The right to tax is allocated to the Member State where the irregularity was actually detected, and not where the irregularity was presumed to have taken place first, based on the detection. By way of illustration, in the *Prankl* case,[79] cigarettes are smuggled from Hungary to the United Kingdom by Mr. Prankl, upon instructions of an Austrian resident. Based on the assumption that the cigarettes were transported through Austria without coverage by a valid document to transport goods under excise duty suspension, the Zollamt Wien has imposed excise duty on Mr Prankl. The ECJ ruled in this case that neither the Member State of departure, Hungary, nor the Member State(s) of transit, Austria, are allowed to collect excise duty in case the goods are (also) discovered in the Member State of arrival (the United Kingdom), where the goods are held for commercial purposes.

According to Article 9(4) first subparagraph, where no irregularity giving rise to their release for consumption has been detected during the movement, an irregularity is deemed to have occurred *in the Member State of dispatch* and at the time when the movement began, unless, within a period of four months from the start of the movement (under cover of an electronic accompanying document in accordance with Article 19(1)), evidence is provided to the satisfaction of the competent authorities of the Member State of dispatch of the end of the movement (*i.e.* the consignee has taken delivery[80] of the excise goods or the goods have left the territory of the Union in accordance with Article 19(2)), or of the place where the irregularity occurred.

The second subparagraph of Article 9(4) of the Recast General Arrangements Directive,[81] provides that where the person who guaranteed the payment (in accordance with Article 17, see section 3.2.4.1 below) has not been, or could not have been, informed that the goods have not arrived at their destination, a period of one month from the date of communication of this information by the competent authorities of the Member State of dispatch must be granted to enable him to provide evidence of the end of the movement in accordance with

78 Article 10(3) provides that in the situations referred to in paragraphs 1 and 2, the competent authorities of the Member States where the goods have been or are deemed to have been released for consumption shall inform the competent authorities of the Member State of dispatch.

79 Case C-175/14 (*Ralph Prankl*), [2015] ECLI:EU:C:2015:142.

80 For the moment that a consignee can be considered to have taken delivery of the goods, see also the BP *Europa* case referred to in paragraph 3.2.4.1.

81 For the rules under the horizontal Directive see Case C-395/00 (*Distillerie Fratelli Cipriani SpA*), [2002] ECR I-11877.

Article 19(2) (*i.e.* the consignee has taken delivery of the excise goods or the goods have left the territory of the Union), or of the place where the irregularity occurred.[82]

3.2.2.3 *Reimbursement and Remission*

According to the preamble to the Recast General Arrangements Directive 2020/ 262/EU, point (12), arrangements for the collection and reimbursement of duty have an impact on the proper functioning of the internal market and should therefore follow non-discriminatory criteria. Point (14) adds to this that Member States should also be able, where the purpose of this Directive so allows, to reimburse excise duty paid on excise goods released for consumption.

The main difference between reimbursement and remission lies in the question whether the excise duty was already paid. Article 3(15) defines remission as the waiving of the obligation to pay an amount of excise duty that has not been paid, as opposed to reimbursement, that is defined in Article 3(16) to be the refunding of an amount of excise duty that has been paid.

Article 8 of the Recast General Arrangements Directive[83] requires excise duty to be levied and collected and, where appropriate, reimbursed or remitted according to the procedure laid down by each Member State. Member States must apply the same procedures to national goods and to those from other Member States.

Pursuant to Article 10 of the Directive, excise duty on excise goods which have been released for consumption may,[84] at the request of a person concerned, be reimbursed or remitted by the competent authorities of the Member State where those goods were released for consumption in the situations fixed by the Member States and in accordance with the

---

82 See also Case C-349/07 (*Sopropé – Organizaçies de Calçado Lda v. Fazenda Pública*), [2008] ECR I-10369, in which the Court formulated the general principle of respect for the rights of the defence as follows:
"1. With regard to recovery of a customs debt for the purpose of effecting post- clearance recovery of customs import duties, a period of 8 to 15 days allowed to an importer suspected of having committed a customs offence in which to submit its observations complies in principle with the requirements of Community law.
2. It is for the national court before which the case has been brought to ascertain, having regard to the specific circumstances of the case, whether the period actually allowed to that importer made it possible for it to be given a proper hearing by the customs authorities.
3. The national court must also ascertain whether, in the light of the period which elapsed between the time when the authorities concerned received the importer's observations and the date on which they took their decision, they can be deemed to have taken due account of the observations sent to them."

83 Due to restructuring, this is Article 9 of Directive 2008/118/EC.

84 Cf. the cases referred to in Article 37(4) (providing that the excise duty shall, upon request, be reimbursed or remitted in the Member State where the release for consumption took place where the competent authorities of the other Member State find that excise duty has become chargeable and has been collected in that Member State), Article 44(5) (providing that in the case of distance selling, the excise duty levied in the first Member State shall be reimbursed or remitted, at the vendor's request, where the vendor or his tax representative has followed the prescribed procedures), and Article 46(3) (providing that where an irregularity has been detected during a movement of excise goods excise duty shall be due from the person who guaranteed payment), as well as those provided for by the Directives referred to in Article 1 (see section 3.2.5.1 below).

conditions to be laid down by Member States for the purpose of preventing any possible evasion or abuse. Such reimbursement or remission may not give rise to exemptions other than those provided for in Article 11, *i.e.* the diplomatic exemptions,[85] see section 3.2.2.4 below, or by one of the Directives on specific excise goods.

Article 10 lays down as a general principle that it is for Member States to determine the cases and the conditions in which a reimbursement or remission of excise duty is granted. Conditions imposed must be enacted in order to prevent possible evasion or abuse.

3.2.2.4 Exemptions

According to the preamble to the Recast General Arrangements Directive 2020/ 262/EU, point (15), the rules and conditions for the deliveries which are exempt from the payment of excise duty should remain harmonised. For the exempt deliveries to organisations situated in other Member States, use should be made of an exemption certificate.

Point (17) of the preamble to the Recast General Arrangements Directive recites that the situations in which tax-free sales to travellers leaving the territory of the Community are allowed should be clearly determined with a view to avoiding evasion and abuse. Since persons travelling over land can move more frequently and more freely as compared to persons travelling by boat or aircraft, the risk of non- respect of the duty and tax free import allowances by the traveller and consequently the control burden for the customs authorities is substantially higher in the case of travel over land. It is therefore appropriate to provide that excise duty-free sales at land borders should not be allowed, as should be the case in all Member States following the expiration of the transitional period on 1 January 2017.[86]

Exemptions in the Context of Diplomatic and Consular Relations
Articles 11 and 12 of the Recast General Arrangements Directive concern the traditional exemptions in the context of diplomatic and consular relations, international organizations and NATO forces.

85 In Case C-494/04 (*Heintz van Landewijck*), [2006] ECR I-5381 deals with reimbursement of sums paid for excise stamps which went missing before being affixed to tobacco products. The ECJ found that the manufactured tobacco in respect of which the stamps were purchased may still be sold and the VAT debt, like the excise duty debt, may still arise. See also Case C-435/03 (*British American Tobacco International*), [2005] ECR I-7077.

86 Article 14(4) of Directive 2008/118/EC contained a transitional period for having duty-free shops at land borders:
"Member States which, at 1 July 2008, have tax-free shops situated elsewhere than within an airport or port may, until 1 January 2017, continue to exempt from excise duty excise goods supplies by such shops and carried away in the personal luggage of travellers to a third territory or to a third country."
At the time of writing, however, we understand that Bulgaria, Croatia, Czech Republic, Poland, Romania and Slovenia retain duty-free shops at their land borders with neighbouring countries, being both Member States such as Austria, Greece and Italy, as well as non-EU Member States, such as Moldova and Ukraine. It is unclear how these duty-free shops relate to the expiration of the abovementioned transitional period.

Consequently, Article 11 exempts from payment of excise duty excise goods where they are intended to be used in the context of diplomatic or consular relations, by international organisations recognised as such, by the armed forces of any State party to the NATO, by the armed forces of the United Kingdom stationed in Cyprus[87] or for consumption under an agreement concluded with third countries or international organisations provided that such an agreement is allowed or authorised with regard to exemption from VAT.

Member States may grant the exemption by means of a refund of excise duty. As mentioned point (15) of the preamble refers to an exemption certificate. According to Article 12 of the Recast General Arrangements Directive, excise goods moving under a duty suspension arrangement to a consignee referred to in Article 11 (see the enumeration above) must be accompanied by an exemption certificate. In a regulation the Commission has laid down the form and content of the exemption certificate.[88]

Tax-Free Shops

According to Article 13 of the Recast General Arrangements Directive a 'tax-free shop' is any establishment situated within an airport or port which fulfils the conditions laid down by the competent authorities of the Member States, to ensure that the tax free exemptions in such a way as to prevent any possible evasion, avoidance or abuse. Article 13 provides for an arrangement for tax-free shops which allows such shops situated in an airport or seaport only to supply excise goods under exemption of excise duty to travellers taking a flight or sea-crossing to a third territory or to a third country,[89] *i.e.* any passenger holding a transport document, for air or sea travel, stating that the final destination is an airport or port situated in a third territory or a third country. In principle, there are no limits as to the quantity or value of the goods that can be purchased but those quantities can be restricted by Member States to prevent any possible evasion, avoidance or abuse.

In the context of the exemptions the following question raised in the European Parliament should be mentioned:[90]

> In the light of the rise of disturbances due to drunken passengers on board aircraft and ferries, does the Commission believe that the decision to exempt goods from excise duty when consumed immediately aboard aircraft or ferries is a sensible one?

87 We note that this provision was not updated following the withdrawal of the United Kingdom from the European Union and currently still applies.

88 Commission Regulation (EC) No. 31/96 of 10 January 1996 on the excise duty exemption certificate. O.J. 1996, L 8, p. 11.

89 We note that the European Travel Retail Confederation (ETRC) in October 2020 called upon the European Commission to amend current legislation to allow EU airports to operate duty and tax free *arrivals* shops, *i.e.*, by allowing travellers arriving from a third country or third territory to purchase duty-free at the (EU) destination airport. While this is not expected to increase overall duty-free sales, it may cause duty-free sales to shift from outside the EU to within the EU, adding a new stream of revenue for airports whose revenues have been hit hard by the impact of the Covid-19 pandemic. At the time of writing we are unaware of any such proposals being reviewed or considered by the European Commission.

90 Written question No. E-3256/98 by Bill Miller (PSE) to the Commission (28 October 1998), O.J. 1999, C 142, p. 112.

Answer given by Mr Monti on behalf of the Commission:

> There has been no decision at Community level to exempt goods from excise duty when consumed immediately aboard aircraft or ferries. Under Article 23, paragraph 5, of Council Directive 92/12/EEC of 25 February 1992 on the general arrangements for products subject to excise duty and on the holding, movement and monitoring of such products, the excise treatment of goods consumed on board ferries and aircraft has been and remains entirely a matter for individual Member States.

3.2.3 Production, Processing, Holding and Storage

Chapter III of the Recast General Arrangements Directive 2020/262/EU includes very limited provisions on the production, processing, holding and storage of excise goods. It is predominantly left to the Member States to determine the rules subject to the provisions of the Directive. From Article 14(2) of the Directive, providing that production, processing and holding of products subject to excise duty, where the latter has not been paid, must take place in a tax warehouse, it could be derived that production outside a tax warehouse is not permitted. This conclusion, however, would contradict the definition of release for consumption (see section 3.2.2.2 above) which includes any (including irregular) manufacture of excise goods outside a suspension arrangement.

According to the preamble, point (18), since checks need to be carried out in production and storage facilities in order to ensure that the duty is collected, it is necessary to retain a system of warehouses, subject to authorisation by the competent authorities, for the purpose of facilitating such checks. It is also necessary to lay down requirements to be complied with by authorised warehousekeepers and traders without authorised warehousekeeper status.

Article 15 of the Directive deals with the authorization and requirements referred to above.

As a preliminary remark, we note that in order to avoid duplication of procedures, Article 2(4) provides that to excise goods that have the customs status of non-Union goods as defined in Article 5(24) UCC, Article 14 (the general provision on production, processing, holding and storage) and Article 46 (on the irregularities during the movement of excise goods) do not apply.

According to Article 15, the opening and operation of a tax warehouse (*i.e.* a place where excise goods are produced, processed, held, stored, received or dispatched under duty suspension arrangements by an authorised warehousekeeper in the course of his business, subject to certain conditions laid down by the competent authorities of the Member State where the tax warehouse is located) by an authorised warehousekeeper (*i.e.* a natural or legal person authorised by the competent authorities of a Member State, in the course of his business, to produce, process, hold, store, receive or dispatch excise goods under a duty suspension arrangement in a tax warehouse) is subject to authorisation by the competent authorities of the Member State where the tax warehouse is situated.

An authorised warehousekeeper is required to:

(a) provide, if necessary, a guarantee to cover the risk inherent in the production, processing and holding of excise goods;
(b) comply with the requirements laid down by the Member State within whose territory the tax warehouse is situated;
(c) keep, for each tax warehouse, accounts of stock and movements of excise goods;
(d) enter into his tax warehouse and enter in his accounts at the end of their movement all excise goods moving under a duty suspension arrangement, except where Article 16(4) applies, *i.e.* where excise goods are allowed to be moved under a duty suspension arrangement to a place of direct delivery situated on the territory of a Member State of destination, where that place has been designated by the authorised warehousekeeper in the Member State of destination or by the registered consignee;
(e) consent to all monitoring and stock checks.

From Article 6 of Commission Recommendation setting out guidelines for the authorisation of warehousekeepers[91] we derive that the amount of the guarantee should reflect the risk inherent in the activities of the warehousekeeper and that the amount of the guarantee should be regularly reviewed to reflect any changes in the volume of trade, the activities of the warehousekeeper or the rates of excise duties applicable in the Member States.

In order to facilitate the exchange of information necessary to verify details of goods moved under suspension of excise duty, details of all authorised warehousekeepers are kept in both national registers and a central register: the System for Exchange of Excise Data (SEED).[92]

3.2.4 *Movement of Excise Goods under a Suspension Arrangement*

Chapter IV of the Recast General Arrangements Directive 2020/262/EU makes it possible for excise goods, prior to their release for consumption, to move within the Community under suspension of excise duty. Such movement should be allowed from a tax warehouse to various destinations, in particular another tax warehouse but also to places equivalent for the purposes of the Directive. The movement of excise goods under suspension of duty is also allowed from their place of importation to those destinations. With regard to the general provisions applying to the movement of excise goods, see section 3.2.4.1. For the procedure and simplified procedures see sections 3.2.4.2 and 3.2.4.3 below. For the movement under a customs suspensive procedure or arrangement, see section 3.2.4.4. For movement under the electronic excise duty monitoring system, see section 3.3 below. At this place we note that in order to safeguard the payment of excise duty in a case of non-discharge of the excise movement, Member States should require a guarantee, which should be lodged by the authorised warehousekeeper of dispatch or the registered consignor or, if the Member State of dispatch so allows, by another person involved in the

---

91 Commission Recommendation of 29 November 2000 setting out guidelines for the authorisation of warehousekeepers under Council Directive 92/12/EEC in relation to products subject to excise duty (2000/789/EC), O.J. 2000, L 314, p. 29.

92 Commission Implementing Regulation (EU) No 612/2013 of 25 June 2013 on the operation of the register of economic operators and tax warehouses, related statistics and reporting pursuant to Council Regulation (EU) No 389/2012 on administrative cooperation in the field of excise duties, O.J. 2013, L173, p. 9.

movement, under the conditions set by the Member States. With regard to the obligations of a warehousekeeper see section 3.2.3 above and with regard to the actual use of options available to Member States under Chapter IV of the General Arrangements Directive, see the Commissions Working paper of 10 November 2009.[93]

3.2.4.1 Movement of Excise Goods; General Provisions

Article 16(1)(a) of the Recast General Arrangements Directive provides for the possibility to move excise goods under suspension of excise duty and enumerates the different movement destinations and various movement scenarios (from a tax warehouse to another tax warehouse, to a registered consignee, to a place where the excise goods leave the territory of the Community or to a consignee falling under the diplomatic exemptions referred to in Article 11(1), where the goods are dispatched from another Member State). See with regard to the time of chargeability section 3.2.2.2 above.

Paragraph 1(b) of Article 16 provides for the possibility to start the movement at the place of importation under the responsibility of a registered consignor. This only applies to situations whereby the goods are released into free circulation in accordance with Article 201 UCC, *i.e.*, it cannot apply in situations whereby the goods are entered irregularly. Article 16(2) further outlines the requirements for this movement. The declarant must provide to the Member State of importation the unique excise number identifying the registered consignor, the unique excise number identifying the consignee to whom the goods are dispatched and, if applicable, evidence that the imported goods are intended to be dispatched from the territory of the Member State of importation to the territory of another Member State. According to Article 16(3), Member States may provide that the evidence mentioned above is only required to be presented upon request. These requirements, that are new compared to Directive 2008/118/EC, do not apply when importation takes place inside a tax warehouse. They allow for the Member State of importation for customs duty purposes to be different from the Member State of importation for excise duty purposes.

It is apparent that the suspension arrangements defined in the Directive are the only ones that are allowed, *i.e.* Member States are not allowed to limit or increase the scope of the suspension arrangements as laid down in the Directive.

Paragraph 4 of Article 16 allows the movement to continue to a place of direct delivery, which is a place indicated by the tax warehousekeeper or registered consignee under his responsibility. See with regard to the time of chargeability section 3.2.2.2 above.

Article 17 of the Recast General Arrangements Directive contains the provisions concerning the guarantee to be provided to cover the risk inherent in the movement under suspension of excise duty. Article 18 provides a wide circle of persons who must be allowed to act as guarantor, so as to allow traders to better align the fiscal responsibility with the commercial responsibility of the movement. A guarantee must be provided by the authorised warehousekeeper of dispatch or the registered consignor; however, the competent authorities

93 CED 691; TAXUD/308253/2009.

of the Member State of dispatch, may allow the guarantee to be provided by the transporter or carrier, the owner of the excise goods, the consignee, or jointly by two or more of these persons and the authorised warehousekeeper of dispatch or the registered consignor.

We note that the provision better reflects modern supply chain design where the logistics supplier/transport company is more deeply involved in the supply chain, also sometimes taking (formal) ownership to goods transported.[94]

Article 18 of the Recast General Arrangements Directive contains the specific provisions concerning movements destined for a registered consignee or a temporary registered consignee receiving excise goods only occasionally. Provisions concerning chargeability and payment of duty are included in Article 6 (see section 3.2.2.2 above). Article 18 provides that a registered consignee may not produce, process, hold, store or dispatch excise goods under a duty suspension arrangement. It is clear from this that the registered consignee is only designed to facilitate the receipt of excise goods in a Member State upon immediate payment of excise duty in that Member State.

A registered consignee must comply with the following requirements:

(a) before dispatch of the excise goods, guarantee payment of excise duty under the conditions fixed by the competent authorities of the Member State of destination;

(b) at the end of the movement, enter in his accounts excise goods received under a duty suspension arrangement;

(c) consent to any check enabling the competent authorities of the Member State of destination to satisfy themselves that the goods have actually been received.

For a temporary registered consignee, *i.e.* receiving excise goods only occasionally, the authorisation is limited to a specified quantity of excise goods, a single consignor and a specified period of time. Member States may even limit the authorisation to a single movement. A temporary registered consignee is excluded from the possibility of continuing a movement under suspension (from a tax warehouse or from a place of importation) to a place of direct delivery, cf. Article 16(4) of the Recast General Arrangements Directive.

Article 19 of the Recast General Arrangements Directive defines when a movement under suspension of excise duty is deemed to begin (when the excise goods leave the tax warehouse of dispatch, or upon their release for free circulation) and end (when the consignee has taken delivery of the excise goods, when the goods have left the territory of the Union,

94 Despite, commercial responsibilities do not always match or have to match the fiscal responsibilities of a movement. In the Case 414/17 (*Arex CZ*), [2018] ECLI: EU:C:2018:1027, goods were transported from Austria to the Czech Republic while being subject to a number of chain transactions. Commercially, it was agreed that the goods were picked up by the last party in the respective chain (Arex). The goods were transported from Austria to the Czech Republic under an excise duty suspension arrangement, entered into by the Austrian suppliers, to be delivered at a company acting as registered consignee on behalf of the first Czech buyers. During that transport, ownership had however already transferred to Arex, *i.e.*, ownership transferred to Arex already at the time the goods were still located in Austria. In this example and under the provisions of Directive 2020/262/EU, the Austrian supplier, as authorised warehousekeeper, is required to set the guarantee covering the movement under suspension. The Austrian authorities may however also allow for Arex, as transporter, as the owner of the goods or as consignee, to provide for this guarantee.

or when the goods are placed under the external transit procedure). This is necessary to determine the field of application of the various rules relating to movement under suspension of excise duty. It also provides the exact moment at which the responsibility for the goods is moved to and from the person responsible for the movement under excise duty suspension.

The Recast General Arrangements Directive however does not further define 'when a consignee has taken delivery of the excise goods'. Based on the *BP Europa* case,[95] this must be understood as the actual receipt of the goods by the consignee. That is the moment when the consignee is in a position to know precisely what quantity of goods he has actually received. Should (part of) the excise goods be found missing following receipt, the movement of excise goods has ended. For the place of chargeability (see paragraph 3.2.2.2), it should first be determined whether it can be established that the goods are missing as a consequence of an irregularity (see paragraph 3.2.5.5 and Article 9(4) of the Directive). If such irregularity or the place thereof cannot be established, the excise duty is due in the Member State of dispatch, even in case only part of the goods moved under suspension eventually are missing upon arrival.

3.2.4.2 Movement of Excise Goods; Procedure

On 3 June 2003, the Council adopted a Decision[96] to computerize the system under which excise goods are moved between traders in the Union in bond under duty-suspension arrangements. The system, the Excise Movement and Controls System (EMCS), introduces a computerized message to replace the administrative documents that accompany excise goods coming from one Member State for consumption in another under duty-suspension arrangements. The computerized message links up all traders, via the relevant national administrations. The system provides Member States with real-time information about consignments underway, enabling them to plan checks and inspections in advance. It also notifies consignors immediately when goods arrive and enables them to have the guarantee covering the excise duties released faster than in the past. Computerization affects all traders involved in producing, processing, holding, storing, receiving or dispatching excise goods. More than 100,000 individuals and firms are currently using the system via the twenty-seven national administrations and the administration of the United Kingdom.[97]

The Decision was repealed and recast in 2020 by way of Decision 2020/263/ EU,[98] hereinafter referred to as the Recast Decision. The extension of the computerised system must

95 Case 64/15 (BP Europa), [2016] ECLI:EU:C:2016:62. This case may be conducted either principally or in relation to a significant number of other shipments, that were not part of the dispute in the main proceedings, considering the fact that BP Europa was charged with EUR 24.93 in the case at hand.

96 Decision No 1152/2003/EC of the European Parliament and of the Council of 16 June 2003 on computerising the movement and surveillance of excisable products. O.J. 2003, L 162, p. 5.

97 The United Kingdom continued using the EMCS system as of their withdrawal from the European Union, both for movements between Northern Ireland and EU Member States, as well as movements only with the UK or exported from the UK. Considering the special status of Northern Ireland, it appears unlikely that the UK will at some stage switch to their own, self-developed excise system.

98 Decision (EU) 2020/263 of the European Parliament and of the Council of 15 January 2020 on computerising the movement and surveillance of excise goods (recast), O.J. 2020, L58, p. 43.

be initiated as of 10 February 2021, while no targeted end date has been adopted. By February 2025 and every five years thereafter, the European Commission shall present a report to the European Parliament and the Council on the implementation and operation of the computerised system.

The preamble of the Recast General Arrangements Directive 2020/262/EU recites the following:

(27) In order to ensure a speedy collection of the necessary formalities and facilitate the supervision of movements of excise goods moved under suspension of excise duty, it is appropriate to use the computerised system under Decision (EU) 2020/263/EU of the European Parliament and of the Council for the exchange of electronic administrative documents between the persons and competent authorities concerned.

(30) It is appropriate to lay down the procedure by which economic operators inform the competent authorities of the Member States of dispatch and destination of consignments of excise goods. Due regard should be had to the situation of certain consignees not connected to the computerised system but who may receive excise goods moving under suspension of duty.

(31) In order to ensure the proper functioning of the rules relating to movement under suspension of excise duty, the conditions for the start of the movement as well as the end, and the discharge of responsibilities, should be clarified.

(32) In order to enable the competent authorities to ensure consistency between the electronic administrative document and the customs declaration for export in cases where excise goods are moved under duty suspension before being taken out of the territory of the Union, the person who declares the excise goods for export should inform the competent authorities in the Member State of export of the unique administrative reference code (ARC).

(33) In order to enable the Member State of dispatch to take appropriate action, the competent authority in the Member State of export should inform the competent authority in the Member State of dispatch of any irregularities that occur during the export or of the fact that the goods are no longer to be taken out of the territory of the Union.

(34) In order to enable the consignor to assign a new destination to the excise goods, the Member State of dispatch should inform the consignor that the goods are no longer to be taken out of the territory of the Union.

(35) In order to improve the possibility of carrying out controls during a movement of excise goods, the person accompanying the excise goods, or where there is no accompanying person, the transporter or carrier, should be able to present the unique administrative reference code (ARC), in any form, to the competent authorities to allow them to retrieve details of the excise goods.

(36) It is necessary to determine the procedures to be used in a case in which the computerised system is not available.

(37) In order to align the procedures under this Directive with those provided for in Article 335(4) of the IRUCC, and in order to simplify the recognition of alternative evidence of exit in the Member State of dispatch, a minimum list of standard alternative evidence of exit, proving that the goods have been taken out of the territory of the Union, should be established.

(43) The computerised system, which is currently used for the movement of excise goods under duty suspension, should be extended to the movement of excise goods which have been released for consumption in the territory of one Member State and are moved to the territory of another Member State in order to be delivered there for commercial purposes. The use of that computerised system will simplify the monitoring of such movements and ensure the proper functioning of the internal market.

Article 20(1) of the Recast General Arrangements Directive provides that a movement of excise goods may be considered to take place under suspension of excise duty only if it takes place under cover of an electronic administrative document (hereinafter: e-AD). Paragraph 2 provides that the e-AD shall be submitted by the consignor using the computerised system developed under the Recast Decision 2020/263/EU. Paragraphs 3 to 5 describe the various stages that the e-AD has to pass through and provides, in particular, for the assignment of a unique Administrative Reference Code (ARC) which must be available throughout the movement. Ironically, where appropriate, the competent authorities may still request a printed copy of the electronic administrative document or any other commercial document. Paragraphs 6 and 7 lay down specific provisions concerning respectively the possibility to cancel an e-AD before the start of the movement and to change the destination of the movement during it.

Article 21 of the Recast General Arrangements Directive is new compared to Directive 2008/118/EC and concerns the handling of the e-AD in case of goods being exported out of the Union. Similar to Article 16 outlined above, Article 21 facilitates the export from a different Member State than the Member State of dispatch.

Article 22 of the Recast General Arrangements Directive allows for the data for the submitted e-AD (limited to energy products) to be filled in at a later stage. This does not apply to movement of goods to a destination outside of the EU (export), as outlined above.

Article 23 of the Recast General Arrangements Directive provides that the Member States may allow the consignor to split a movement of energy products.

Articles 24 and 25 of the Recast General Arrangements Directive provide for the use of an electronic report of receipt or report of export, for proof that the excise movement has ended correctly and describe the various stages that it has to pass through.

Article 26 of the Recast General Arrangements Directive stipulates that alternative proof of the correct ending of a movement may be provided in the absence of the electronic reports referred to in the previous Articles.

Finally, Articles 27 to 29 of the Recast General Arrangements Directive lay down the procedures to be used when the computerised system is not yet available.

See further section 3.3 on the electronic system (EMCS).

3.2.4.3 *Simplified Procedures*

Point (38) of the preamble to the Recast General Arrangements Directive 2020/ 262/EU recites that Member States should be allowed to provide a special arrangement for the movement of excise goods under suspension of duty which takes place entirely on their territory, or conclude bilateral agreements with other Member States to allow simplification.

Article 30 of the Recast General Arrangements Directive allows Member States to simplify the procedures for movements which take place entirely on their territory.

Article 31 of the Directive allows for a simplification of the formalities for the movement of excise goods under suspension of excise duty, by agreement between two or more Member States for frequent and regular movements between certain economic operators. Furthermore, Article 31 allows for the possibility for the Member States to simplify the procedures for movements via fixed pipelines.

3.2.4.4 *Movement under a Customs Suspensive Procedure or Arrangement*

As mentioned earlier in order to avoid duplication of procedures, Article 2(4) of the Recast General Arrangements Directive provides that for excise goods that have the customs status of non-Union goods, the provisions laid down in the Directive on the production, processing, holding and storage as well as the movement under suspension of excise duty shall not apply. For an overview of the customs status of non-Union goods under the Union Customs Code see section 1.5.2.

3.2.5 *Movement and Taxation of Excise Goods after Release for Consumption*

Chapter V of the Recast General Arrangements Directive 2020/262/EU deals with the movement and taxation of excise goods after release for consumption.

According to point (40) of the preamble to the Recast General Arrangements Directive, where excise goods are acquired by private individuals for their own use and transported from one Member State to another by them, excise duty should be paid in the Member State in which the goods are acquired, in accordance with the principle governing the internal market. According to point (41) of the preamble, excise duty levels for tobacco products and alcoholic beverages applied by Member States vary due to a number of factors, such as fiscal and public health policy and such divergences in some cases are significant. In this context, Member States should be able to contain risks, which are facilitating tax fraud, avoidance or abuse, threatening or undermining public policy or protection of health and life of humans. Therefore Member States should be able to take appropriate and proportionate measures enabling them to determine whether excise goods transported from the territory of one Member State to the territory of another Member State by a private individual were acquired by that private individual for his or her own use, see section 3.2.5.1.

According to point (42) of the preamble to the Recast General Arrangements Directive, in cases where, following their release for consumption in a Member State, excise goods are held for commercial purposes in another Member State, excise duty is due in the second Member State. This requires a definition of the concept of 'delivered for commercial purposes', see section 3.2.5.2. According to point (44), it is appropriate to clarify also who is liable to pay the duty and when the duty is chargeable.

According to point (51) of the preamble to the Recast General Arrangements Directive, distance selling rules apply where excise goods are acquired by persons who are not authorised warehousekeepers or registered consignees and do not carry out an independent economic activity, and are dispatched or transported directly or indirectly by the vendor or on his behalf, see section 3.2.5.3.

According to point (52) of the preamble to the Recast General Arrangements Directive, in order to avoid conflicts of interest between Member States and double taxation in cases in which excise goods already released for consumption in one Member State move within the Union, provision are made for situations in which excise goods, following their release for consumption, are subject to destruction or losses (see section 3.2.5.4) or irregularities (see section 3.2.5.5).

3.2.5.1 Acquisition by Private Individuals

Article 32 of the Recast General Arrangements Directive 2020/262/EU concerns movements of goods acquired by private individuals.

It should be borne in mind that the taxation of excise products is based on the destination principle; hence the suspension arrangement makes it possible to postpone taxation until the products reach the country of destination. Only with regard to products acquired by private individuals for their own use and transported by them the principle governing the internal market applies based on which excise duty is charged in the Member State in which they are acquired. Of course "own use" has its limitations. Article 33 of the General Arrangements Directive provides that excise duty becomes chargeable when products released for consumption in a Member State are held for commercial purposes in another Member State.

In order to determine the own use of a private individual, Member States must, according to Article 32(2) of the Recast General Arrangements Directive, take account at least of the following:
(a) the commercial status of the holder of the excise goods and his reasons for holding them;
(b) the place where the excise goods are located or, if appropriate, the mode of transport used;
(c) any document relating to the excise goods;
(d) the nature of the excise goods;
(e) the quantity of the excise goods.

With regard to point (e), the Recast General Arrangements Directive provides for so-called minimum "guide levels" – solely as a form of evidence – below which quantities are not treated as held for commercial purposes, for example 800 cigarettes, 90 litres of wine including 60 litres of sparkling wine (see Article 32(3) of the Directive).

For mineral oil, the guide level is based on the form of transportation. Atypical transport, *i.e.* other than in tanks of vehicles or in appropriate reserve fuel canisters, can result in taxation in the Member State of consumption (see Article 32(4) of the Recast General Arrangements Directive).[99]

3.2.5.2 *Delivered to Another Member State for Commercial Purposes*

Articles 33 to 43 of the General Arrangements Directive 2008/118/EC concern excise goods which have already been released for consumption in one Member State and delivered for commercial purposes to another Member State.

'Delivered for commercial purposes' means the movement of excise goods that have been released for consumption in one Member State, from that Member State to another Member State and delivered either to a person other than a private individual or to a private individual if the movement is not covered by Article 32 or Article 44 of the Recast General Arrangements Directive (see section 3.2.5.1 above). Excise goods shall not be delivered for commercial purposes where they are transported by that private individual for own use.

The Directive provides that where excise goods which have already been released for consumption in one Member State are delivered for commercial purposes to another Member State, they are subject to excise duty and excise duty becomes chargeable in the Member State of destination. According to Article 33(1) of the Directive, the excise goods must move from a certified consignor (a natural or legal person authorised by the competent authorities of the Member State of importation, to only dispatch excise goods under a duty suspension arrangement upon their release for free circulation in accordance with Article 201 of the UCC in the course of the business of that person and under the conditions fixed by those authorities, as per Article 3(10)) to a certified consignee (a natural or legal person authorised by the competent authorities of the Member State of destination to receive, in the course of the business of that person and under the conditions fixed by those authorities, excise goods moving under a duty suspension arrangement from the territory of another Member State). The movement should be under cover of an electronic simplified administrative processed in accordance with Article 36 (Article 35(1) of the Directive). The movement begins when the goods leave the certified consignor's premises (or any other location in the Member State of dispatch) and ends when the certified consignee has taken delivery of the excise goods at their premises or any other location in the Member State of destination.

The person liable to pay the excise duty which becomes chargeable when the goods have been delivered, is the certified consignee (Article 34(1) of the Directive). In case one or all persons involved in the movement are not duly registered or certified, these persons all become liable to pay the excise duty (Article 34(2) of the Directive).

99 See also Case C-247/97 (*Schoonbroodt*), [1998] ECR I-8095.

Article 35 and 36 of the Directive lay down the conditions for movement of goods between the certified consignor and consignee, including movement under cover of an electronic simplified administrative document (SAD), the required guarantee and payment of excise duty in the Member State of destination. Article 35 (8) concerns the sending or receiving of excise goods only occasionally, similar to Article 18(3).

Article 37 of the Recast General Arrangements Directive prescribes that the certified consignee must submit a report of receipt through EMCS in principle no later than five working days after the end of the movement. Upon request, the excise duty paid in the Member State of dispatch must be reimbursed on the basis of this report of receipt. Considering that reference is only made to 'reimbursed' and not to 'remitted' (as was the case under Directive 2008/118/EC), we presume that it was required for the excise duty to have been paid in the Member State of dispatch for it to be reimbursed. For the difference between reimbursement and remission, we refer to section 3.2.2.3.

Article 38 and 39 of the Directive provide for fallback procedures in situations whereby the EMCS system is unavailable, both at the time of the start of the movement and at the time of the end of the movement.

Article 40 of the Recast General Arrangements Directive allows for the use of alternative proof of delivery of excise goods in absence of the report of receipt outlined above. The alternative evidence must be appropriate (the fallback document referred to in Article 39 constitutes appropriate evidence, but it doesn't seem to exclude other pieces of alternative evidence) and endorsed by the competent authorities of the Member State of destination. Once endorsed by the competent authorities of the Member State of destination, it shall also be deemed sufficient proof that the certified consignee has fulfilled the necessary formalities and has made payment of excise duty to the Member State of destination. It appears that it is not up to the Member State of dispatch to dispute the delivery or arrival (or, consequently, withhold reimbursement of excise duty paid in the Member State of dispatch), once the Member State of destination has accepted alternative evidence.

Article 41 of the Directive allows Member States to apply simplified procedures for movement of goods which occur between the territories of two or more Member States.

Article 42 of the Recast General Arrangements Directive deals with the situation where excise goods already released for consumption in a Member State are moved to a place of destination in that Member State via the territory of another Member State. Where excise goods which have already been released for consumption in one Member State are delivered within the Union for commercial purposes, they are not be regarded as delivered for those purposes until they reach the Member State of destination, provided that they are moving under cover of an electronic simplified administrative document.[100]

3.2.5.3 *Distance Selling*

Article 44 of the Recast General Arrangements Directive provides for procedures applicable to sales made by consignors who take responsibility, directly or indirectly, for the transport of excise goods to private individuals established in another Member State (so-called "distance selling").[101]

The excise duty becomes chargeable in the Member State of destination (the Member State to which excise goods are to be delivered or used in accordance with the provisions of the Directive – this definition was relocated from Article 36(1) of Directive 2008/118/EC to Article 3(14) of Directive 2020/262/EU) at the time of delivery of the excise goods. The chargeability conditions and rate of excise duty to be applied are those in force on the date on which duty becomes chargeable.

The excise duty is to be paid in accordance with the procedure laid down by the Member State of destination.

The person liable to pay the excise duty in the Member State of destination is the consignor. However, the Member State of destination may provide that the liable person shall be a tax representative, established in the Member State of destination. Furthermore

100 Case C-5/05 (*Joustra*), [2006] ECR I-11075, concerned a purchaser who himself arranges for the transport. The situation is one not of distance selling, as to be discussed in the *Man in Black* in the section 3.2.5.3 below, but of distance buying. The ECJ found that Article 7 of Directive 92/12/EEC (now Article 33 to 43 of the Recast General Arrangements Directive) is capable of applying to the case at hand since, under paragraph 2 thereof, that provision covers the situation in which products are delivered or intended for delivery in another Member State or used in another Member State for the purposes of a trader carrying out an economic activity independently. That is true of a private individual who, as in the present case, is not acting with a view to profit, since the transport of the products subject to excise duty is carried out by a trader acting on his behalf. Where excise duty is levied under Article 7 of the horizontal Directive in the Member State in which the products are being held for commercial purposes, although they have already been released for consumption in another Member State, Article 7(6) of Directive 92/12/EEC provides that the excise duty paid in that other State is to be reimbursed in accordance with Article 22(3) of Directive 92/12/EEC. We have no reason to believe that *Joustra* will be decided differently based on Directive 2020/262/EU.

101 Case C-296/95 (*The Queen* v. *Commissioners of Customs and Excise, ex parte EMU Tabac SARL, The Man in Black Ltd, John Cunningham*), [1998] ECR I-1605, deals with the question under the provisions of the horizontal Directive of whether private individuals must transport product acquired in another Member State themselves and whether by using an agent anti-avoidance provisions can be circumvented. The ECJ held that Directive 92/12/EEC 'must be interpreted as not precluding the levying of excise duty in Member State A on goods released for consumption in Member State B, where the goods were acquired from a company, X, for the use of private individuals in Member State A, through a company, Y, acting in return for payment as agent for those individuals, and where transportation of the goods from Member State B to Member State A was also arranged by company Y on behalf of those individuals and effected by a professional carrier charging for his services'. This case is still relevant under the Recast General Arrangements Directive.

Article 36 provides that excise duty levied in the first Member State must be reimbursed, at the consignor's request, where the consignor or his tax representative has followed the prescribed procedures.

We note that Article 36(6) of the General Arrangements Directive provides that Member States may lay down specific rules for applying distance selling rules to excise goods that are covered by special national distribution arrangements, presumably such as Systembolaget in Sweden.

3.2.5.4 Destruction and Losses

Article 45 of the Recast General Arrangements Directive 2020/262/EU provides for a similar treatment of the destruction or loss of excise goods transported between Member States after the release for consumption, as for the destruction or loss occurring during a movement under suspension of excise duty (discussed above in section 3.2.2.1), *i.e.* the excise duty is not chargeable.

The guarantee lodged must be released, fully or partially, upon the production of satisfactory proof.

3.2.5.5 Irregularities

As seen in section 3.2.5.4 above, Article 45 of Directive 2020/262/EU provides for a similar treatment of the destruction or loss of excise goods transported between Member States after the release for consumption, as for the destruction or loss occurring during a movement under suspension of excise duty.

Article 36 of Directive 2020/262/EU does the same concerning the treatment of irregularities on the understanding that excise duty is chargeable in the Member State where the irregularity occurred or if not detected during the movement of the goods where the irregularity was detected.[102] In this context 'irregularity' means a situation due to which a movement, or a part of a movement, of excise goods has not duly ended. In addition thereto, paragraph 5 was added under Directive 2020/262/EU, stating that any lack of registration or certification of one or all persons involved in the movement, or any lack of respect of the provisions under Article 35(1), *i.e.*, the conditions for movement, including the requirement to move goods covered under an electronic simplified administrative document (SAD), shall be deemed an irregularity too.

The excise duty is due from the person who guaranteed payment thereof and from any person who participated in the irregularity. The use of the word 'and' adverts to joint and

---

102 However, if, before the expiry of a period of three years from the date on which the excise goods were acquired, it is ascertained in which Member State the irregularity actually occurred, the main rule applies that that excise duty is chargeable in the Member State where the irregularity occurred.

several liability for both the person who guaranteed payment and every participant[103] in the irregularity.

The competent authorities of the Member State in which the excise goods were released for consumption must, upon request, reimburse or remit the excise duty where it was levied in the Member State where the irregularity occurred or was detected.

3.2.6 Miscellaneous

Chapter VI of the Recast General Arrangement Directive 2020/262/EU contains a number of miscellaneous topics that were not covered by any of the aforementioned chapters. It concerns:
- provisions around the tax markings or national identification marks of excise goods, see section 3.2.6.1;
- provisions specific to small wine producers, see section 3.2.6.2;
- (future) provisions on stores for boats and aircraft, see section 3.2.6.3; and
- provisions specific to excise goods used for the construction and maintenance of cross-border bridges, see section 3.2.6.4.

3.2.6.1 Marking

According to the preamble to the Recast General Arrangements Directive, point (53), Member States should be able to provide that goods released for consumption carry tax markings or national identification marks. The use of these markings or marks should not place any obstacle in the way of intra-Union trade.

Since the use of these markings or marks should not give rise to a double taxation burden, it should be made clear that any amount paid or guaranteed to obtain such markings or marks is to be reimbursed, remitted or released by the Member State which issued the marks if excise duty has become chargeable and has been collected in another Member State.

However, in order to prevent any abuse, Member States which issued such markings or marks should be able to make reimbursement, remittance or release conditional on the presentation of evidence that they have been removed or destroyed.

Article 47 of the Recast General Arrangements Directive allows Member States the possibility to impose on its territory the use of tax or national identification marks used for fiscal purposes.[104] The first paragraph clarifies that tax markings or identification marks may also be required when excise goods are transported to (*i.e.* enter) a Member State outside

103 According to the case C-579/18 (Comida paralela 12), [2019] ECLI:EU: C:2019:875, the use of the word 'person' does not exclude legal persons. More particularly, a legal person can be held liable for excise duty, by reason of the conduct of a natural person, where that natural person has acted on behalf of the legal person.

104 In case C-503/17 (*Commission v. United Kingdom*), [2018] ECLI:EU: C:2018:831, the ECJ clarified that it is not allowed for Member States to use a fiscal marker for fuels that are subject to excise duty at the full rate. The fiscal marking is designed to facilitate easy checks of applied exemptions or reduced rates and not to earmark fuel that was purchased in the United Kingdom.

suspension of excise duty, in the situations referred to in Articles 33(1) (delivery of goods released for consumption for commercial purposes to another Member State) and 44(1) (distance sales). Moreover, Article 47 contains a number of elements intended to clarify, in view of the judgment of the ECJ in the *BATIG* case[105] that such markings are not to give rise to a double tax burden, directly or indirectly.

As a matter of national law, Member States may lay down provisions to prevent evasion, avoidance and abuse, following Article 47(3). Such provisions are required to be at least detrimental to the objectives and principles of EU law, including but not limited the principle of proportionality. Based on the *Commission v. Portugal* case,[106] provisions in accordance with the principle of proportionality are understood to include the restriction of the sale of tobacco products bearing a particular excise marking until the end of the third month of the year following that during which the goods were released for consumption. This provision is however only necessary in case the rate of excise duty increases, in order to prevent that excessive quantities of tobacco products are released for consumption right before an increase of the excise duty rate. The provision is therefore not allowed in general, i.e. if the excise duty rate decreases or stays the same.

3.2.6.2 Small Wine Producers

In point (54) of the preamble it is considered that application of the normal requirements relating to the movement and monitoring of excise goods could put a disproportionate administrative burden on small wine producers. Therefore, Member States should be able to exempt those producers from certain requirements.

Small producers are persons producing on average less than 1 000 hl of wine per year (Article 48(3) of the Recast General Arrangements Directive).

Member States may exempt small wine producers from the requirements regarding production, processing, holding and storage (see section 3.2.3) and regarding movement of excise goods under suspension of excise duty (see section 3.2.4) and from the other requirements relating to movement and monitoring (see section 3.3 below). Where these small producers themselves carry out intra-Union transactions, they are obliged to inform

105 Case C-374/06 (*BATIG*), [2007] ECR I-11271, deals with a dispute between BATIG Gesellschaft für Beteiligungen mbH and the Hauptzollamt Bielefeld concerning the latter's refusal to reimburse the amount paid to obtain tax marks which were later affixed to cigarette packets intended for the German market but stolen in Ireland during dispatching. According to the ECJ Directive 92/12/EEC does not preclude the legislation of a Member State which excludes the reimbursement of the amount paid to obtain tax markings issued by that Member State when those markings have been affixed to products subject to excise duty before being released for consumption in that Member State, when those products have been stolen in another Member State, involving the payment of excise duties in that other Member State, and when evidence has not been furnished that the stolen products will not be marketed in the Member State which issued those markings.

106 Case C-126/15 (*Commission v. Portugal*), [2017] ECLI:EU:2017:504.

their relevant authorities and comply with the requirements laid down by Commission Delegated Regulation (EU) 2018/ 273.[107]

Where small wine producers are exempt from requirements mentioned above, the consignee is instructed to inform the competent authorities of the Member State of destination of the wine deliveries received (Article 48(2) of the Recast General Arrangements Directive).

3.2.6.3 *Stores for Boats and Aircraft*

According to point (55) of the preamble account should be taken of the fact that, with regard to excise goods used as stores for boats and aircraft, no suitable common approach has yet been found.

Until the Council has adopted Community provisions on stores (*i.e.* provisions, victuals) for boats and aircraft, Member States may maintain their national provisions concerning exemptions for such stores (Article 49 of the Recast General Arrangements Directive).

This provision has remained unchanged compared to Directive 2008/118/EC and Directive 92/12/EEC.

3.2.6.4 *Special Arrangements*

With respect to excise goods used for the construction and maintenance of cross- border bridges between Member States, point (56) of the preamble recites that those Member States should be allowed to adopt measures derogating from the normal rules and procedures applying to excise goods moving from one Member State to another, in order to reduce the administrative burden.

Member States which have concluded an Agreement on the responsibility for the construction or maintenance of a transborder bridge may adopt measures derogating from the provisions of Directive 2020/262/EU in order to simplify the procedure for collecting excise duty on the excise goods used for the construction and the maintenance of that bridge.

For the purposes of those measures, the bridge and the construction sites referred to in the Agreement must be deemed to be part of the territory of the Member State which is responsible for the construction or maintenance of the bridge in accordance with the Agreement.

107 Commission Delegated Regulation (EU) 2018/273 of 11 December 2017 supplementing Regulation (EU) No 1308/2013 of the European Parliament and of the Council as regards the scheme of authorisations for vine plantings, the vineyard register, accompanying documents and certification, the inward and outward register, compulsory declarations, notifications and publication of notified documentation, and supplementing Regulation (EU) No 1306/2013 of the European Parliament and of the Council as regards the relevant checks and penalties, amending Commission Regulations (EC) No 555/2008, (EC) No 606/2009 and (EC) No 607/2009 and repealing Commission Regulation (EC) No 436/2009 and Commission Delegated Regulation (EU) 2015/560, O.J. 2018, L058, p. 1.

We presume that the only excise goods that are eligible to be used for the construction and maintenance of cross-border bridges, are energy products (mineral oils) or electricity and that Article 50 of the Directive therefore merely applies to these goods.

3.2.7 *Exercise of the Delegation and Committee on Excise Duty*

The following Articles of the Recast General Arrangements Directive 2020/262/ EU include references to delegating acts to be adopted by the Commission:

- Article 6(10), establishing the common partial loss thresholds referred to in Article 6(7) and Article 45(2) of the Directive;
- Article 29(1), establishing the structure and content of the electronic administrative documents exchanged through EMCS (Articles 20 to 25 of the Directive) and of the fallback documents referred to in Articles 26 and 27 of the Directive;
- Article 43(1), establishing the structure and content of the electronic administrative documents exchanged through EMCS (Articles 36 and 37 of the Directive) and of the fallback documents referred to in Articles 38, 39 and 40 of the Directive.

The power to adopt these delegated acts is conferred on the Commission by way of Article 51 of the Directive. Before adopting a delegated act, the Commission is required to consult experts designated by each Member State in accordance with the principles laid down in the Interinstitutional Agreement of 13 April 2016 on Better Law-Making.[108]

Measures for the implementation of the Recast General Arrangements Directive 2020/262/ EU must be adopted in accordance with Regulation (EU) No 182/2011 of 16 February 2011 laying down the rules and general principles concerning mechanisms for control by Member States of the Commission's exercise of implementing powers.[109]

For that purpose Article 52 of the Recast General Arrangements Directive stipulates that the Commission will be assisted by the Committee on Excise Duty.

3.2.8 *Reporting and Transitional and Final Provisions*

Article 53 of the General Arrangements Directive 2020/262/EU prescribes that the Commission shall submit a report on the implementation of this Directive every five years, with the first report due three years after the application date of the Directive (18 March 2020 and 13 February 2023, depending on the Article).

By way of transitional measures, Member States are required to allow receipt of excise goods under the formalities set out in Directive 2008/118/EC until 31 December 2023 (Article 54 of Directive 2020/262/EU). See also section 3.3 below.

Article 55 of Directive 2020/262/EU stipulates that Member States must adopt and publish the required national provisions to comply with this Directive by 31 December 2021. The

108 O.J. 2016, L123, p. 1.
109 O.J. 2011, L55, p. 13.

measures with respect to receipt of excise goods as outlined in Article 54 of the Directive, are applied as of 13 February 2023.

Article 56 of the General Arrangements Directive 2020/262/EU stipulates that Directive 2018/118/EC is repealed as of 13 February 2023 which is the foreseen date of entry into application of the updated computerised system.

Other transitional measures that were included under Directive 2018/118/EC, are not included in the General Arrangements Directive 2020/262/EU. Under Directive 2018/118/EC, as of 1 January 2014, Member States were allowed to apply a quantative limit of not less than 300 items for cigarettes brought into their territory from other Member States without further payment of excise duty, if these Member States apply a lower excise duty. Bulgaria, Estonia, Greece, Latvia, Lithuania, Hungary, Poland and Romania were only allowed to apply such a restriction as and when they levy an excise duty of at least EUR 77 per 1,000 cigarettes. Due to the fact that the excise duty rates were traditionally lower in these countries compared to the average throughout the EU, these Member States were allowed a transitional period up to 31 December 2017[110] in order to raise excise duty rates to the EU agreed minimum rates as per Directive 2011/64.

3.3 The ECMS Regulation

The Recast General Arrangements Directive 2020/262/EU introduces a computerised system to ensure speedy completion of the necessary formalities and facilitate the supervision of movements of excise goods moved under suspension of excise duty, in point 27 of the preambule. This system is referred to as the Excise Movement and Control System (EMCS) under Decision 2020/263/EU.[111]

3.3.1 General Provisions

Article 20(1) of the Recast General Arrangements Directive provides that a movement of excise goods shall be considered to take place under suspension of excise duty only if it takes place under cover of an electronic administrative document (e-AD). Paragraph 2 provides that the e-AD shall be submitted by the consignor using the computerised system referred to in Article 1 of Decision (EU) 2020/263 (hereinafter referred to as 'EMCS'). The e-AD replaced the paper accompanying document prescribed in Directive 92/12/EEC. Paragraphs 3 to 5 describe the various stages that the e-AD has to pass through and provides, in particular, for the assignment of a unique Administrative Reference Code (ARC) which must be available throughout the movement (see further section 3.3.2.3 below). Paragraphs 6 and 7 lay down specific provisions concerning respectively the possibility to cancel an e-AD before the start of the movement and to change the destination of the movement during it (see sections 3.3.2.4 and 3.3.2.5 below).

110 See also the infringement procedure against Hungary with respect to this obligation; Case C-856/19 (*Commission v. Hungary*), [2021] ECLI:EU:C:2021:253.

111 Decision (EU) 2020/263 of the European Parliament and of the Council of 15 January 2020 on computerising the movement and surveillance of excise goods, O.J. 2020, L58, p. 43.

Article 21 of the General Arrangements Directive lays down the provisions for handling of the electronic administrative document for goods that are exported from the territory of the Union (see section 3.3.2.6 below).

Article 22 of the General Arrangements Directive allows for the data for the submitted e-AD (limited to energy products) to be filled in at a later stage (see section 3.3.2.5).

Article 23 of the General Arrangements Directive provides that the Member States may allow the consignor to split a movement of energy products (see section 3.3.2.7).

Articles 24 and 25 of the Directive provide for the use of an electronic 'report of receipt' or the 'report of export', for proof that the excise movement has ended correctly and describe the various stages that it has to pass through (see section 3.3.2.8).

Articles 26 and 27 of the Directive lay down the procedures to be used when EMCS is not yet available (see section 3.3.2.9).

Finally, Article 28 of the General Arrangements Directive stipulates that alternative proof of the correct ending of a movement may be provided in the absence of the electronic reports referred to in the previous Articles (see section 3.3.2.10).

3.3.2 Implementing Provisions

On 24 July 2009, the Council adopted Commission Regulation (EC) No. 684/ 2009 implementing the General Arrangements Directive as regards the computerised procedures for the movement of excise goods under suspension of excise duty (hereinafter "the ECMS Regulation").[112] Since the movement of excise goods under suspension of excise duty is to take place under cover of an electronic administrative document and since ECMS is intended to allow movements of excise goods under suspension of excise duty to be followed and monitored, it was necessary to establish the structure and content of the electronic messages to be used on such movements.

The EMCS Regulation was not (yet) recast in accordance with Article 6 of the Recast Decision 2020/263/EU. It therefore still refers to Directive 2008/118/EC and below, these references are updated to Directive 2020/262/EU insofar possible.

3.3.2.1 Subject Matter

The ECMS Regulation lays down measures concerning the following:
(a) the structure and content of the electronic messages exchanged through EMCS referred to in Article 20(2) of the Recast General Arrangements Directive for the purposes of Articles 21 to 28 of that Directive;
(b) the rules and procedures to be followed on the exchange of the electronic messages referred to in point (a);

112 O.J. 2009, L 197, p. 24.

(c) the structure of the paper documents referred to in Articles 26 and 27 of the Recast General Arrangements Directive.

3.3.2.2 *Obligations Relating to Messages Exchanged through EMCS*

With regard to the obligations relating to messages exchanged through EMCS, Article 2 of the ECMS Regulation prescribes that the structure and content of the messages exchanged for the purposes of Articles 21 to 28 of the Recast General Arrangements Directive must comply with Table I of Annex I to the ECMS Regulation.

In Annex I the data elements of the electronic messages used for the purpose of EMCS referred to in Article 20(2) of Directive 2020/262/EU are structured in data groups and, where applicable, data subgroups.

3.3.2.3 *Formalities before the Start of the Movement of Excise Goods*

Article 20(2) of the General Arrangements Directive prescribes that the consignor must submit a draft electronic administrative document to the competent authorities of the Member State of dispatch using EMCS.

Article 20(3) of the General Arrangements Directive instructs the competent authorities of the Member State of dispatch to carry out an electronic verification of the data in the draft electronic administrative document. Where these data are not valid, the consignor must be informed thereof without delay. Where these data are valid, the competent authorities of the Member State of dispatch must assign to the document a unique *administrative reference code* (ARC) and must communicate it to the consignor.

Article 3 of the ECMS Regulation dealing with formalities before the start of the movement of excise goods prescribes that the *draft electronic administrative document* submitted in accordance with Article 20(2) of the Recast General Arrangements Directive and the electronic administrative document to which an administrative reference code has been assigned in accordance with Article 20(3) must comply with the requirements set out in Table 1 of Annex I to the ECMS Regulation, which gives details of the draft electronic administrative document and electronic administrative document.

The draft electronic administrative document must be submitted *no earlier than 7 days* before the date indicated on that document as date of dispatch of the excise goods concerned.

3.3.2.4 *Cancellation of the Electronic Administrative Document*

Article 20(6) of the Recast General Arrangements Directive provides that the consignor may cancel the electronic administrative document as long as the movement has not begun under Article 19(1), which provides that the movement of excise goods under a duty suspension arrangement begins, from a tax warehouse, when the excise goods leave the tax warehouse of dispatch, and from the place of importation upon their release for free circulation.

According to Article 4(1) of the ECMS Regulation, the consignor wanting to cancel the electronic administrative document as referred to in Article 20(6) of the Recast General Arrangements Directive must complete the fields of the *draft cancellation message* and submit it to the competent authorities of the Member State of dispatch. The draft cancellation message must comply with the requirements set out in Table 2 of Annex I to the ECMS Regulation.

Article 4(2) of the ECMS Regulation instructs the competent authorities of the Member State of dispatch to carry out an electronic verification of the data in the draft cancellation message. Where those data are valid, those authorities must add the date and time of validation to the cancellation message, communicate that information to the consignor and forward the cancellation message to the competent authorities of the Member State of destination. Where those data are not valid, the consignor must be informed thereof without delay.

Upon receipt of the cancellation message, the competent authorities of the Member State of destination must, based on Article 4(3) of the ECMS Regulation, forward the *cancellation message* to the consignee where the consignee is an authorised warehousekeeper or a registered consignee (or a certified consignee).

3.3.2.5 *Handling of the Electronic Administrative Document for Goods being Exported*

Article 21(1) of the Recast General Arrangements Directive provides that the competent authorities of the Member State of dispatch shall forward the e-AD to the competent authorities of the Member State where the export declaration is lodged, if that Member State is different from the Member State of dispatch. According to paragraph 2, the declarant must provide the competent authorities of the Member State of export with the ARC indicating the excise goods referred to in the export declaration. Subsequently, the competent authorities in the Member State of export shall verify, before the release for export of the goods, whether the data of the e-AD correspond to those contained in the export declaration. Where there are any inconsistencies between the e-AD and the export declaration, the competent authorities in the Member State of export shall notify the competent authorities in the Member State of dispatch using EMCS.

Paragraph 5 stipulates that where the goods are no longer to be taken out of the customs territory of the Union, the competent authorities in the Member State of export shall notify the competent authorities in the Member State of dispatch thereof by means of EMCS as soon as they become aware that the goods will no longer be taken out of the customs territory of the Union. The competent authorities in the Member State of dispatch shall forward the notification to the consignor without delay. On receipt of the notification, the consignor shall cancel the electronic administrative document as provided for in Article 20(6) or change the destination of the goods as provided for in Article 20(7), as appropriate (see below).

3.3.2.6 *Amendment or Completion of Destination*

Article 20(7) of the Recast General Arrangements Directive provides that during the movement under a duty suspension arrangement, the consignor may, using EMCS, amend the destination to show a new destination which must be one of the following destinations (referred to in Article 16(1)(a)(i), (ii) or (iii) or, where applicable, in Article 16(4)): another tax warehouse; a registered consignee; a place where the excise goods leave the territory of the Community or, where applicable, to a place of direct delivery situated on the territory the Member State of destination, where that place has been designated by the authorised warehousekeeper in the Member State of destination or by the registered consignee (cf. section 3.2.4.2 above).

Article 22(1) of the Recast General Arrangements Directive provides that in the case of movements of energy products under a duty suspension arrangement by sea or inland waterways to a consignee who is not definitely known at the time when the consignor submits the draft e-AD referred to in Article 20(2), see section 3.3.2.3 above, the competent authorities of the Member State of dispatch may authorise the consignor to omit the data concerning the consignee in that document.

Based on Article 22(2), as soon as the data concerning the consignee are known, and at the latest at the end of the movement, the consignor must, using the amendment of destination procedure referred to in Article 20(7), transmit them to the competent authorities of the Member State of dispatch.

Article 5(1) of the ECMS Regulation instructs the consignor wanting to amend the destination as provided for in Article 20(7) of the Recast General Arrangement Directive, or to complete the destination as provided for in Article 22(2) thereof, to complete the fields of the *draft change of destination message* and submit it to the competent authorities of the Member State of dispatch. The draft change of destination message must comply with the requirements set out in Table 3 of Annex I to the ECMS Regulation.

According to Article 5(2) of the ECMS Regulation, the competent authorities of the Member State of dispatch must carry out an electronic verification of the data in the draft change of destination message. Where those data are valid, the competent authorities of the Member State of dispatch are instructed to:
(a) add the date and time of validation and a sequence number to the change of destination message and inform the consignor thereof;
(b) update the original electronic administrative document according to the information in the *change of destination message*.

If the update includes a change of Member State of destination or a change of consignee, Articles 20(4) and 21(1) of the Recast General Arrangements Directive applies in respect of the forwarding of updated electronic administrative document.

Articles 20(4) and 21(1) provide the following. According to Article 20(4) of the Recast General Arrangements Directive, where excise goods are moved under a duty suspension arrangement (as referred to in Article 16(1)(a)(i), (ii) and (iv), Article 16(1)(b) and Article 16(4)) from a tax warehouse to another tax warehouse, a registered consignee or to a diplomatic or consular consignee or an international organisation (referred to in Article 11(1), see section 3.2.2.4), where the goods are dispatched from another Member State or where excise goods are moved from the place of importation to any of the destinations referred to directly above where the goods are dispatched by a registered consignor, or, where applicable, where the goods are dispatched to a place of direct delivery situated on the territory the Member State of destination, where that place has been designated by the authorised warehousekeeper in the Member State of destination or by the registered consignee *the competent authorities of the Member State of dispatch must forward the e-AD* without delay to the competent authorities of the Member State of destination, which must forward it to the consignee where the consignee is an authorised warehousekeeper or a registered consignee. Where the excise goods are intended for an authorised warehousekeeper in the Member State of dispatch, the competent authorities of that Member State must forward the electronic administrative document directly to him.

According to Article 21(1) of the Recast General Arrangements Directive, in the case (referred to in Article 16(1)(a)(iii) and (v)) of excise goods being moved under a duty suspension arrangement to a place where the excise goods leave the territory of the Union, *the competent authorities of the Member State of dispatch must forward the e- AD* to the competent authorities of the Member State where the export declaration is lodged if that Member State is different from the Member State of dispatch.

As mentioned above, according to Article 5(2)(b) of the ECMS Regulation the competent authorities of the Member State of dispatch are instructed to update the original electronic administrative document according to the information in the change of destination message.

Article 5(3) of the ECMS Regulation provides that if the update referred to in paragraph 2(b) includes a change of Member State of destination, the competent authorities of the Member State of dispatch must forward the change of destination message to the competent authorities of the Member State of destination mentioned in the original e-AD. The latter authorities must inform the consignee mentioned in the original e-AD of the change of destination by using the "*notification of change of destination*" that should comply with the requirements set out in Table 4 of Annex I.

Article 5(4) of the ECMS Regulation provides that if the update referred to in paragraph 2(b) includes a change of the place of delivery, but not a change of the Member State of destination nor a change of the consignee, the competent authorities of the Member State of dispatch must forward the change of destination message to the competent authorities of the Member State of destination mentioned in the original e-AD. The latter authorities must forward the change of destination message to the consignee.

Article 5(5) of the ECMS Regulation provides that where the data in the draft change of destination message are not valid, the consignor must be informed thereof without delay.

According to Article 5(6) of the ECMS Regulation, if the updated e-AD includes a new consignee in the same Member State of destination as in the original e-AD, the competent authorities of that Member State must inform the consignee mentioned in the original e-AD of the change of destination using the "notification of a change of destination" that should comply with the requirements set out in Table 4 of Annex I.

3.3.2.7 *Splitting of a Movement of Energy Products*

According to Article 23 of the Recast General Arrangements Directive, the competent authorities of the Member State of dispatch may allow, under the conditions fixed by that Member State, that the consignor splits a movement of energy products under suspension of excise duty into two or more movements provided that:
1. the total quantity of excise goods does not change;
2. the splitting is carried out in the territory of a Member State which permits such a procedure;
3. the competent authorities of that Member State are informed of the place where the splitting is carried out.[113]

Article 6(1) of the ECMS Regulation provides that the consignor wanting to split the movement of excise goods as provided for in Article 23 of the Recast General Arrangements Directive must complete the fields of the *draft splitting operation message* for each destination and submit it to the competent authorities of the Member State of dispatch. The draft splitting operation message must comply with the requirements set out in Table 5 of Annex I to the ECMS Regulation.

Article 6(2) of the ECMS Regulation instructs the competent authorities of the Member State of dispatch to carry out an electronic verification of the data in the draft splitting operation messages. Where those data are valid, the competent authorities of the Member State of dispatch must:
(a) generate a new e-AD for each destination, which replaces the original e-AD;
(b) generate for the original eAD a "notification of splitting", which must comply with the requirements set out in Table 4 of Annex I to the ECMS Regulation;
(c) send the *notification of splitting* to the consignor and to the competent authorities of the Member State of destination mentioned in the original e-AD.

Article 20(3), third subparagraph, Article 20(4) and (5) and Article 21(1) of the Recast General Arrangements Directive apply in respect of each new electronic administrative document referred to in point (a). These provides the following.

According to Article 20(3), third subparagraph, where the data in the draft e-AD are valid, the competent authorities of the Member State of dispatch shall assign to the document a *unique administrative reference code* and shall communicate it to the consignor.

113 Member States must inform the Commission if they allow movements to be split on their territory and under what conditions. The Commission must transmit this information to the other Member States.

According to Article 20(4) of the Recast General Arrangements Directive, where excise goods are moved under a duty suspension arrangement (as referred to in Article 16(1)(a)(i), (ii) and (iv), Article 16(1)(b) and Article 16(4)) from a tax warehouse to another tax warehouse, to a registered consignee or to a diplomatic or consular consignee or an international organisation (referred to in Article 11(1), see section 3.2.2.4), where the goods are dispatched from another Member State or where excise goods are moved from the place of importation to any of the destinations referred to directly above where the goods are dispatched by a registered consignor, or, where applicable, where the goods are dispatched to a place of direct delivery situated on the territory the Member State of destination, where that place has been designated by the authorized warehousekeeper in the Member State of destination or by the registered consignee the competent authorities of the Member State of dispatch *must forward the electronic administrative document* without delay to the competent authorities of the Member State of destination, which must forward it to the consignee where the consignee is an authorized warehousekeeper or a registered consignee. Where the excise goods are intended for an authorized warehousekeeper in the Member State of dispatch, the competent authorities of that Member State must forward the electronic administrative document directly to him.

According to Article 21(1) of the Recast General Arrangements Directive, in the case (referred to in Article 17(1)(a)(iii) and (v)) of excise goods being moved under a duty suspension arrangement to a place where the excise goods leave the territory of the Union, the competent authorities of the Member State of dispatch *must forward the electronic administrative document* to the competent authorities of the Member State where the export declaration is lodged, if that Member State is different from the Member State of dispatch.

According to Article 20(5) of the Recast General Arrangements Directive, the consignor must provide the person accompanying the excise goods with the unique administrative reference code. It must be possible for that ARC to be presented to the competent authorities upon request throughout the movement under an excise duty suspension arrangement. Where appropriate, the competent authorities may request a printed copy of the e-AD or any other commercial document.

Furthermore, Article 6(3) of the ECMS Regulation provides that the competent authorities of the Member State of destination mentioned in the original electronic administrative document *must forward the notification of splitting* to the consignee mentioned in the original electronic administrative document where the consignee is an authorised warehousekeeper or a registered consignee.

According to Article 6(4) of the ECMS Regulation, where the data in the draft splitting operation message are not valid, the consignor must be informed thereof without delay.

3.3.2.8 Formalities at the End of the Movement of Excise Goods

According to Article 24 of the General Arrangements Directive, on receipt of excise goods at any of the destinations referred to in Article 16(1)(a)(i), (ii) or (iv) or in Article 16(4), *i.e.* of excise goods moved from a tax warehouse to another tax warehouse, a registered consignee or a diplomatic or consular consignee or an international organisation (referred to in Article 11(1), see section 3.2.2.4), where the goods are dispatched from another Member State or where excise goods are moved from the place of importation to any of the destinations referred to before where the goods are dispatched by a registered consignor, or, where applicable, where the goods are dispatched to a place of direct delivery situated on the territory the Member State of destination, where that place has been designated by the authorised warehousekeeper in the Member State of destination or by the registered consignee, the consignee must, without delay and *no later than five working days* after the end of the movement, except in cases duly justified to the satisfaction of the competent authorities, submit a report of their receipt (hereinafter the '*report of receipt*'), using EMCS.

According to Article 25 of the General Arrangements Directive, in the cases referred to in Article 16(1)(a)(iii) and, where applicable, Article 16(1)(b) of this Directive, *i.e.* movement of excise goods to a place where the excise goods leave the territory of the Union or from the place of importation to a place where the excise goods leave the territory of the Community a *report of export* must be completed by the competent authorities of the Member State of export on the basis of the endorsement drawn up by the customs office of exit as referred to in Article 329 of IRUCC[114] or by the office where the formalities applicable to the exit of excise goods from the Union to a territory forming part of the customs territory (but not the excise territory) referred to in Article 2(2) of the Directive (see section 3.2.1.3) are accomplished, certifying that the excise goods have left the territory of the Union.

Article 7 of the ECMS Regulation provides that the report of receipt submitted in accordance with Article 24 of Directive 2020/262/EU and the report of export submitted in accordance with Article 25 of that Directive, must comply with the requirements set out in Table 6 of Annex I to the ECMS Regulation.

3.3.2.9 *Fallback Procedures*

According to the preamble to the Recast General Arrangements Directive:

> (47) It is necessary to determine the procedures to be used where the computerised system is not available and a fallback document is to be used.

Article 26(1) of the Recast General Arrangements Directive provides that in derogation from Article 20(1) (prescribing that a movement of excise goods under a duty suspension arrangement may only take place under cover of an e-AD), where EMCS is unavailable in the Member State of dispatch, the consignor may start a movement of excise goods under a duty suspension arrangement provided that:

(a) the goods are accompanied by a paper document containing the same data as the draft electronic administrative document referred to in Article 20(2), see section 3.3.2.3 above;

---

114 Commission Implementing Regulation (EU) 2015/2447 of 24 November 2015 laying down detailed rules for implementing certain provisions of Regulation (EU) No 952/2013 laying down the Union Customs Code. Article 329(1) provides:
"Except where paragraphs 2 to 7 apply, the customs office of exit shall be the customs office competent for the place from where the goods leave the customs territory of the Union for a destination outside that territory."

(b) he informs the competent authorities of the Member State of dispatch before the beginning of the movement.

The Member State of dispatch may also require a copy of the document referred to in point (a), the verification of the data contained in that copy and, if the consignor is responsible for the unavailability, appropriate information on the reasons for that unavailability before the beginning of the movement.

Article 8 of the ECMS Regulation stipulates that the paper document referred to in Article 26(1)(a) of the Recast General Arrangements Directive must carry the title "*Fallback Accompanying Document for movements of excise goods under suspension of excise duty*". The data required must be displayed in the form of data elements, expressed in the same manner as in the e-AD.[115]

When the availability of EMCS is restored, the consignor must, according to Article 26 (2) submit a draft electronic administrative document, in accordance with Article 20(2), see section 3.3.2.3 above. As soon as the data in the e-AD have been validated, in accordance with Article 20(3) see section 3.3.2.3 above, that document will replace the paper document. Article 20(4) and 21(1), *i.e.* regarding the forwarding of the document and Articles 24 and 25, *i.e.* regarding the report of receipt and the report of export apply *mutatis mutandis.*

Article 26(3) prescribes that copy of the fallback document must be kept by the consignor to back up his records.

Article 26(4) provides that where EMCS is unavailable in the Member State of dispatch, the consignor must communicate the information referred to in Article 20(7), *i.e.* amending the destination, or Article 23, *i.e.* splitting of a movement of energy products, using alternative means of communication. To that end, the consignor must inform the competent authorities of the Member State of dispatch before the change of destination or splitting of the movement is initiated. Paragraphs 2 and 3 of Article 26, see above, apply *mutatis mutandis.*

Article 8(2) of the ECMS Regulation provides that the information referred to in Article 26(5) to be communicated by the consignor to the competent authorities of the Member State of dispatch must be displayed in the form of data elements, expressed in the same manner as in the change of destination message or the splitting operation message, as the case may be.[116]

According to Article 27(1) of the General Arrangements Directive, when, in the cases referred to in Article 16(1)(a)(i), (ii) and (iv), Article 16(1)(b) and Article 16(4), *i.e.* where excise goods are moved under a duty suspension arrangement from a tax warehouse to another tax warehouse, to a registered consignee or to a diplomatic or consular consignee

---

115 All the data elements, as well as the data groups and data subgroups to which they belong, shall be identified by means of the numbers and letters in column A and column B of Table 1 of Annex I to the ECMS Regulation.

116 All the data elements, as well as the data groups and data subgroups to which they belong, shall be identified by means of the numbers and letters in column A and column B of Table 3 or, as the case may be, Table 5 of Annex I to the ECMS Regulation.

or an international organisation (referred to in Article 11(1), see section 3.2.2.3), where the goods are dispatched from another Member State or where excise goods are moved from the place of importation to any of the destinations referred to directly above where the goods are dispatched by a registered consignor, or, where applicable, where the goods are dispatched to a place of direct delivery situated on the territory the Member State of destination, where that place has been designated by the authorised warehousekeeper in the Member State of destination or by the registered consignee, the report of receipt provided for in Article 24(1), see section 3.3.2.8, cannot be submitted at the end of a movement of excise goods within the deadline provided for in that Article, *i.e.* no later than five working days after the end of the movement, either because EMCS is unavailable in the Member State of destination or because, in the situation where EMCS is unavailable in the Member State of dispatch, referred to in Article 26(1), the procedures referred to in Article 26(2) have not yet been carried out, *i.e.* submission of e-document when the availability of EMCS is restored, the consignee must submit to the competent authorities of the Member State of destination, except in duly justified cases, a paper document containing the same data as the report of receipt and stating that the movement has ended.

Except where the report of receipt provided for in Article 24(1), see section 3.3.2.8, can be submitted promptly by the consignee via EMCS, or in duly justified cases, the competent authorities of the Member State of destination must send a copy of the fallback document mentioned above to the competent authorities of the Member State of dispatch, which must forward it to the consignor or keep it available for him.

As soon as availability of EMCS is restored in the Member State of destination or the procedures referred to in Article 26(2) have been carried out, a draft e-AD is submitted, the consignee shall submit a report of receipt, in accordance with Article 24(1). Article 24(3) and (4) apply mutatis mutandis, *i.e.* the competent authorities of the Member State of destination must carry out an electronic verification of the data in the report of receipt and the competent authorities of the Member State of dispatch must forward the report of receipt to the consignor.

According to Article 27(2) of the Recast General Arrangements Directive, when, in the case excise goods are moved under a duty suspension arrangement to a place where the excise goods leave the territory of the Union (referred to in Article 16(1)(a)(iii) or (v)), the report of export provided for in Article 25(1), see section 3.3.2.8 cannot be completed at the end of a movement of excise goods either because EMCS is unavailable in the Member State of export or because, in the situation referred to in Article 26(1), where EMCS is unavailable in the Member State of dispatch, the procedures referred to in Article 26(2) have not yet been carried out, *i.e.* submission of e-document when the availability of EMCS is restored, the competent authorities of the Member State of export must send to the competent authorities of the Member State of dispatch a paper document containing the same data as the report of export and certifying that the movement has ended, except where the report of export provided for in Article 25(1) can be completed promptly via EMCS, or in duly justified cases.

The competent authorities of the Member State of dispatch shall forward a copy of the paper document referred to in the first subparagraph to the consignor or keep it available for him.

As soon as availability of EMCS is restored in the Member State of export or the procedures referred to in Article 26(2) have been carried out, the competent authorities of the Member State of export must send a report of export in accordance with Article 25(1), see section 3.3.2.8. Article 25(3) must apply *mutatis mutandis, i.e.* the competent authorities of the Member State of export must carry out an electronic verification of the data and the competent authorities of the Member State of dispatch must forward the report of export to the consignor.

Article 8(3) of the ECMS Regulation provides that the paper documents referred to in Article 27(1) and (2) of the General Arrangements Directive must carry the title "*Fallback Report of Receipt/Report of Export for movements of excise goods under suspension of excise duty*". The data required must be displayed in the form of data elements, expressed in the same manner as in the report of receipt or the report of export, as the case may be.[117]

3.3.2.19 *Alternative proofs of receipt and evidence of exit*

According to Article 28(2) of the Recast General Arrangements Directive alternative proof od the end of a movement of excise goods may be provided in absence of a report of receipt or a report of export for reasons other than those mentioned in Article 27. In the cases referred to in Article 16(1)(a)(i), (ii) and (iv), Article 16(1)(b) and Article 16(4), alternative proof of the end of the movement may be provided by means of an endorsement by the competent authorities of the Member State of destination, based on appropriate evidence, that the excise goods have reached their destination. A fallback document as referred to in Article 26(1)(a) shall constitute appropriate evidence.

In cases referred to in Article 16(1)(a)(iii) or (v), in order to determine whether the excise goods in the circumstances set out in paragraph 2 have been taken out of the territory of the Union, the competent authorities of the Member State of dispatch shall accept an endorsement by the competent authorities of the Member State in which the customs office of exit is located, certifying that the excise goods have left the territory of the Union, or certifying that the excise goods have been placed under the external transit procedure in accordance with point (a)(v) of Article 16(1) as appropriate evidence that the goods have been taken out of the territory of the Union. Furthermore, the competent authorities of the Member State of dispatch may take into account any combination of the following pieces of evidence:

- A delivery note;
- A document signed or authenticated by the economic operator who has taken the excise goods out of the customs territory of the Union certifying the exit of the goods;

117 All the data elements, as well as the data groups and data subgroups to which they belong, shall be identified by means of the numbers and letters in column A and column B of Table 6 of Annex I to the ECMS Regulation.

- A document in which the customs authority of a Member State or a third country certify the delivery in accordance with the rules and procedures applicable to that certification in that State or country;
- Records of goods supplied to ships, aircraft or offshore installations kept by economic operators;
- Other evidence acceptable to the authorities of the Member State of dispatch.

Where appropriate evidence has been accepted by the competent authorities of the Member State of dispatch, it shall end the movement in the computerized system.

3.4 Mineral Oils

3.4.1 The Original Rules with Regard to Mineral Oils

On 27 October 2003, the Council adopted Directive 2003/96/EC on taxation of energy products and electricity, which restructures the Community frame work for the taxation of energy products and electricity.[118] The Directive repealed Directives 92/81/EEC and 92/82/EEC and replaced the excise on mineral oils by taxation on energy products and electricity. In this section we briefly deal with the original rules with regard to mineral oils.

The Directive on the harmonization of the structures of excise duties on mineral oils (Directive 92/81/EEC) provided for a common definition of (thirty types of) mineral oil referring to the codes of the Combined Nomenclature. For those mineral oils for which no level of duty was specified in Directive 92/82/EEC (see below), the structure Directive stipulated that mineral oil would be subject to excise duty if intended for the use, offered for sale or used as heating fuel or motor fuel. Also, any product not listed as a "mineral oil" must be taxed at the rate for the equivalent mineral oil when offered for sale or used as motor fuel or for heating purposes.[119] However, solid hydrocarbons or natural gas intended for automotive or heating purposes were not taxed with excise duties, but could be subjected to another tax on products as permitted by the horizontal Directive (see section 3.2.1 above). Under the title "Establishment of the excise duty" the mineral oil Directive provided that mineral oils were subject to a specific duty calculated per 1000 litres of product at a temperature of 15 degrees C; heavy fuels are calculated per 1000 kg.

118 Directive 2003/96/EC of 27 October 2003, O.J. 2003, L 283, p. 51.

119 Under German law no use as heating fuel was assumed when the flame comes into direct contact with the substance to be treated, worked or destroyed, for example singeing off textile fibres, flame cultivation, use of oxy-hydrogen torches, heating metals to make them workable, warming roofing felt to make it easier to handle, etc. The ECJ found that the objective of the excise duty on mineral oils as a tax on consumption militates in favour of interpreting the expression 'used as heating fuel' in the first sentence of Article 2(2) of Directive 92/81 as relating to all cases where mineral oils are burnt and the thermal energy thus produced is used for heating, whatever the ultimate purpose of that heating may be, including that of transformation or destruction of the substance absorbing the thermal energy during a chemical or industrial process. In all those cases, the mineral oils are used up and must therefore be subject to the excise duty. Case C-240/01 (*Commission* v. *Germany*), [2004] ECR I-4733.

In addition to the chargeable event, as defined in the horizontal Directive, the structure Directive on mineral oils provided that excise duty becomes due when (certain) products are used for purposes such as heating oil or motor fuel which products are made subject to excise duty.[120] Furthermore, Member States could provide that excise duty comes due when the conditions for exempt use or use at a reduced rate are no longer fulfilled. With regard to these exemptions or reduced rates, which Member States under certain circumstances are obliged or permitted to apply, the Directive provided for a list of activities, including mineral oils supplied for use as fuel for the purpose of air navigation other than private pleasure flying or for the purposes of navigation within Community waters[121] (including fishing), other than in private pleasure craft[122] (Member States must) mineral oils used for the process of producing electricity (Member States may),[123] etc.[124] The Council acting

120 The consumption of mineral oils within the curtilage of an establishment producing mineral oils is not considered a chargeable event.

121 In Case C-391/05 (*Jan De Nul*), [2007] ECR I-1793, the ECJ held that the term 'Community waters' within the meaning of the first subparagraph of Article 8(1)(c) of Directive 92/81 relates to all waters which can be used by all sea-going vessels, including those which have the greatest capacity, capable of travelling maritime waterways for commercial purposes. As to the question whether or not certain operations performed by a hopper dredger may be regarded as coming within the scope of the term 'navigation' the ECJ held that manoeuvres carried out by a hopper dredger during its operations of pumping and discharge of materials, *i.e.* journeys inherent in the carrying out of dredging activities, come within the scope of the term 'navigation' as used in the first subparagraph of Article 8(1)(c) of Directive 92/81.

122 See Case C-389/02 (*Deutsche See-Bestattungs-Genossenschaft*) on the question whether burials on the high seas are trips for pleasure purposes, [2004] ECR I-3537.

123 Member States may reduce the rate of excise duty on mineral oils used for certain purposes, or exempt them from such duty, but must apply a fiscal marker to mineral oils which are so treated. The Netherlands has chosen to reduce the rate of duty on mineral oil used, and hence marks mineral oil for a particular purpose, while Germany has not so opted and prohibits such use of marked mineral oil. In Case C- 292/02 (*Meiland Azewijn*), [2004] ECR I-7905, the ECJ held that Article 8a(1) of Directive 92/81 is to be interpreted as prohibiting Member States from subjecting to excise duty mineral oil, whether marked or unmarked, contained in the standard tank of a commercial motor vehicle, such as agricultural machinery, and used as fuel not only to move the vehicle but also in order to utilize it for other purposes such as agricultural work, when that mineral oil has been lawfully released for consumption in another Member State.

124 Case C-437/01 (*Commission v. Italy*), [2003] ECR I-9861, is similar to Case C- 346/97 (*Braathens*) dealt with in section 3.2.1.1 above. Italian law provided that lubricating oils were subject to a tax on consumption when they were intended for use, offered for sale or used for purposes other than as heating fuel or motor fuel. However under Article 8(1)(a) and Article 2(2) of Directive 92/81, in conjunction with Article 2 of Directive 92/82, lubricating oils may be subject to excise duty only if intended for use, offered for sale or used as motor fuel or heating fuel. In other cases they must be exempt from the harmonised excise duty. The ECJ has already held that to allow the Member States to levy another indirect tax on products which must be exempt from harmonised excise duty under Article 8(1)(b) of Directive 92/ 81 would render that provision entirely ineffective (see *Braathens*, paragraph 24). According to the ECJ the same reasoning may be applied to the exemption laid down in Article 8(1)(a) of Directive 92/81. See also Joined Cases C-145/06 and C-146/06 (*Fendt Italiana Srl*), [2007] ECR I-5869, in which the ECJ concluded that, although mineral oils used other than as motor fuel or heating fuel fell within the scope of Directive 92/81 – since, as the Court held in paragraphs 30 and 33 of *Commission v. Italy*, it was compulsory for those products to be exempt from the harmonised excise duty – it was the intention of the Community legislature, on the occasion of the adoption of Directive 2003/96, to change that arrangement by excluding such products from the scope of that directive. Therefore, since 1 January 2004 – the date from which Directive 92/81 has been repealed, in accordance with Article 30 of Directive 2003/96 – Member States have been able to tax energy products, such as lubricating oils, used other than as motor fuels or as heating fuels.

unanimously on a proposal from the Commission could authorize any Member State to introduce further exemptions or reductions. Based on this provision all Member States were granted the right to continue to apply reductions and/or exemptions.

It was and still is deemed not to be practicable or desirable for the Community as a whole to introduce taxation of aircraft fuel targeting exclusively intra-Community flights operated by Community air carriers at the present time, see the communication on air craft fuel.[125] See also the *Deutsche Bahn* case[126] in which the CFI (now referred to as the General Court) found that the principle of equal treatment has not been infringed, because the situation of air transport undertakings is clearly different from that of rail transport undertakings. As regards their operational characteristics, their costs structure and the regulations to which they are subject, air and rail transport services are very different and are not comparable for the purpose of the principle of equal treatment. The CFI added to this that in any event, it finds that the difference in treatment is objectively justified, having regard to the wide discretion of the Council as regards the objective justification of any differentiating treatment.[127] In the light of the international practice of exempting aviation fuel from excise duties, which is enshrined in the Chicago Convention and in international agreements concluded between States, competition between Community air transport operators and operators in non-member countries would be distorted if the Community legislature unilaterally imposed excise duties on that fuel. Consequently, the exemption provided for by Article 8(1)(b) of the Directive was objectively justified.

3.4.2 *The Rates on Mineral Oils*

Directive 92/82/EEC provided for the approximation of excise duty rates on mineral oils. In contrast to the system as envisaged by the Commission with regard to the approximation of excise duties, the Directive did not[128] provide for a final rate which gradually must be reached by all Member States. The Directive merely prescribed minimum rates which are only applicable to seven of the thirteen types of mineral oil mentioned in the structures Directive.

The most important minimum rates were:

- EUR 337 on leaded petrol;
- EUR 287 on unleaded petrol;
- EUR 245 on gas oil;
- EUR 18 on heating gas oil;
- EUR 13 on heavy gas oil;[129]
- EUR 100 on liquid petroleum gas and on methane.

125 COM(2000) 110.
126 Case T-351/02 (*Deutsche Bahn AG*), [2006] ECR II-1047.
127 Referring to Case T-267/94 (*Oleifici Italiani*), [1997] ECR II-1239, paragraph 47.
128 Directives 92/79/EEC (re cigarettes), 92/80/EEC (re manufactured tobacco) and 92/84/EEC (re alcohol), discussed in the sections below, also did not provide for a final rate.
129 See also Case C-185/00 (*Commission v. Finland*), [2003] ECR I-14189, in which the ECJ held that by maintaining in force the laws and regulations on the use of gas oil as a fuel, as they are applied in practice, the Republic of Finland has failed to fulfil its obligations under Article 8(2) and (3) of Council Directive 92/81 and Article 5(1) of Directive 92/82.

Based on a report of the Commission, the Council was instructed to examine the minimum rates of duty every two years, beginning 31 December 1994 taking into account "the proper functioning of the internal market, the real value of the rates of duty and the wider objectives of the Treaty".

At its meeting in April 2003, the Ecofin Council reached political agreement on the text of a Directive on taxation of energy products and electricity. The Directive repealed Directives 92/81/EEC and 92/82/EEC and replaced the excise on mineral oils by taxation on energy products and electricity. For this taxation there is no longer a separate structure and rates directive. See further section 3.8 below.

3.5 Alcohol and Alcoholic Beverages

It seems to be self-evident that a modern excise on alcohol and alcoholic products be based on the pure alcohol content of a product. History and tradition, however, have made it virtually impossible to come to such a straight-forward approach. The structure Directive on alcohol and alcoholic beverages (Directive 92/83/EEC) is built on the historic distinctions made between beer, wine, fermented beverages other than wine and beer, intermediate products and (ethyl) alcohol. The structure and rates Directives on alcohol and alcoholic beverages are discussed below, based on this distinction. (The exemptions and the requirements with regard to production in a tax warehouse are not discussed here.) See also the Report from the Commission to the Council, the European Parliament and the European Economic and Social Committee (EESC) on the rates of excise duty applied on alcohol and alcoholic beverages (presented pursuant to Article 8 of Council Directive 92/84/EEC on the approximation of excise duty on alcohol and alcoholic beverages).[130] The Report concluded, among other things, that in order to maintain the real value of the minimum excise duty rates, Member States could consider a re-valorisation and so avoid them becoming meaningless over time. In the discussions that followed, the Council, on 12 April 2005, called on the Commission to come forward with a proposal to adjust the minimum rates in order to avoid a fall in their real value and to provide transitional periods for those Member States who may have difficulties in increasing their rates.

In 2006, the European Commission adopted a proposal to increase the minimum rates of excise duty on alcohol and alcoholic beverages agreed in 1992, from 1 January 2008.[131] Considering the need to avoid the EU system of minimum rates becoming meaningless and in line with the request of the Finance Ministers of the Member States to come forward with this proposal, the Commission proposed to increase the minimum rates taking into account the inflation since 1992 and, therefore, restore their real value. The majority of Member States were unaffected by this proposal as their national rates already exceeded the proposed new minimum rates. However, for those Member States that would have difficulty increasing their national rates immediately, transition periods, up to 2010, were proposed. Although the inflation rate from 1993 to 2005 was 31%, the economic and social impact of the proposal could be considered as minimal. For example, for beer, the biggest

130 COM(2004) 223 final.
131 COM(2006) 486.

required increase in national excise duty would be of the order of EUR 0.01 (one eurocent) on half a litre of beer, at the latest by 1 January 2010.

More specifically, for those Member States that were required to increase their national rates by more than 10% but less than 20%, a transitional period to 1 January 2009 was proposed; for those Member States that were required to increase their national rates by more than 20%, a transitional period to 1 January 2010 was proposed.

In its opinion of May 2007, the EESC considered that the proposal should be redrawn. The EESC considered that, among other things, minimum rates should be introduced.

The European Parliament also found that the Commission's proposal could only be endorsed after a number of amendments. According to the EP, it is commonly said that the last 15 years have not achieved convergence of excise duty rates as reflected in consumer prices. The reason behind this fact is not the revalorisation of minimum rates but the very high and even mounting level of tax in different Member States. In order to achieve the goal of converging tax rates and the accompanying relatively moderate distortion in the internal market, a general agreement is necessary to request the heavily taxing Member States to bring down their excise duty rates. GDP per capita varies greatly in the EU. As a result, minimum levels of excise duties have a different impact on different Member States and impose a much higher burden on consumers in countries like Bulgaria and Romania. Increased informal economic activities are the logical consequence. Due to this, the EP proposed certain transitional rules which allow these Member States to increase their rates.

Directive 92/83/EEC was amended by Directive 2020/1151/EU,[132] which will be applicable as of 1 January 2022. Where applicable, this new Directive will be discussed below.

3.5.1 Beer

The object of taxation, according to the structure Directive, is beer covered by CN code 2203 or a mixture of beer with non-alcoholic drinks falling within CN code 2206, both with an alcohol strength above 0.5% vol. The duty is established based on the hectolitre/degrees Plato or hectolitre/degrees of actual alcoholic strength by volume. The rates Directive 92/84/EEC fixes the minimum rate at EUR 0.748 per hectolitre/degree Plato or EUR 1.87 per hectolitre/degree alcohol of finished product.[133]

As of 1 January 2022, all the ingredients of the beer, including those added after the completion of fermentation, shall be taken into account for the purposes of measuring the degree Plato. Member States that, on 29 July 2020, do not take ingredients of the beer

132 Council Directive (EU) 2020/1151 of 29 July 2020 amending Directive 92/83/ EEC on the harmonization of the structures of excise duties on alcohol and alcoholic beverages, O.J. 2020, L256, p. 1.

133 As per the excise duty rate overview published by the European Commission, to be consulted via: https://ec.europa.eu/taxation_customs/sites/taxation/files/ resources/documents/taxation/excise_duties/alcoholic_beverages/rates/excise_duties-part_i_alcohol_en.pdf, only Romania applied (July 2020) a rate below the minimum rate (i.e., 0.743 EUR per hectolitre/degree Plato). This may be caused by a currency conversion difference.

that have been added after fermentation into account for the purposes of measuring the degree Plato, may continue to do so until 31 December 2030.

The structure Directive allows Member States to apply reduced rates of duty, not to be set more than 50% below the standard national rate, in accordance with the annual production of the breweries concerned. The reduction may only be applied to an undertaking, or cooperating breweries, producing less than 200,000 hl of beer per year.[134] In addition, Portugal has a special derogation for beer produced on Madeira.[135]

3.5.2 Wine

The object of taxation, according to the structure Directive, is wine. The Directive distinguishes between "still wine" and "sparkling wine". Still wine[136] has an alcoholic strength between 1.2% vol. and 15% vol. and between 15% vol. and 18% vol. In both cases, the alcohol must be entirely of fermented origin. This distinction is made, so it seems, to allow Member States to continue to apply a higher duty on wine that has a strength of between 15 and 18% vol., although the main rule of the Directive is that still wine should be taxed at a single rate of excise duty. Sparkling wine has an alcoholic strength of between 1.2% and 15% vol. and is mainly distinguished by the use of "mushroom stoppers". The definition of sparkling wine will be changed as of 1 January 2022 to also cover CN codes 2204 21 06, 2204 21 07, 2204 21 08 and 2204 21 09, in addition to the existing definition including CN codes 2204 10, 2204 21 10, 2204 29 10 and 2205. This change relates to a change in CN codes, that now separately distinguish wines with a protected designation of origin, wine with a protected geographical indication and other varietal wines.

The excise duty must be fixed by reference to the number of hectolitres of finished products, in principle the same duty must be applied to all still wines and all sparkling wines, although the Directive permits that the duty on still wines and sparkling wines is not the same.

The rates Directive (Directive 92/84/EEC) offers a surprise, notwithstanding the detailed distinctions mentioned above, it sets the minimum excise duty at zero Euro. An exemption for production by a private individual for consumption by its producer, members of the family or guests may be granted, provided that no sales are involved. The application of reduced rates to apply to independent small wine producers, similar to the existing conditions as for the production of beer, see section 3.5.1 above, will be introduced as of 1 January 2022.

The distinction between alcohol drinks under the EU excise system has been and is an issue for various producers and has played a role in several cases before the ECJ. For example the ECJ decided that indirect fiscal protection under Article 110 TFEU is not permitted and that commonly consumed wines, which in general are cheap wines, have enough characteristics in common with beer to constitute an alternative choice and may therefore be regarded as being in competition with beer for the purpose of the second paragraph of Article 110

134 See Case C-83/08 (*Glückauf Brauerei GmbH*), [2009] ECR I-2857.
135 See Council Decision of 16 November 2020, O.J. 2020, L402, p. 1.
136 Falling within CN Codes 2204 and 2205 with the exception of sparkling wines.

TFEU (indirect protection, see Case C-365/85 (*Commission v. Belgium*)[137]). In other words, on imported wine no higher levy may be imposed than on domestically produced beer, see further below.

Does this mean that Directives 92/83 and 92/84 violate Article 90, since the rate of duty is different? This was suggested by Socridis (an importer of alcoholic beverages into France) arguing that the difference in taxation required and motivated by the directives manifestly exceed the objective differences between beer and wine.[138] The ECJ observed:

> 19. Next, the Court has consistently held that directives do not infringe the Treaty if they leave the Member States a sufficiently wide margin of appreciation to enable them to transpose them into national law in a manner consistent with the requirements of the Treaty (see to that effect Case 5/88 *Wachauf v. Bundesamt fur Ernhrung und Forstwirtschaft*, paragraph 22).
> 20. It is common ground that Directives 92/83 and 92/84 merely require Member States to apply a minimum excise duty on beer. Consequently, the Member States retain a sufficiently wide margin of discretion to ensure that the relationship of the taxes on wine and beer excludes any protection for domestic production within the meaning of Article 95 of the Treaty.
> 21. The plea that Directives 92/83 and 92/84 are invalid because they are incompatible with the second paragraph of Article 95 of the Treaty must therefore be rejected.

Case C-167/05 (*Commission v. Sweden*)[139] deals with differentiated taxation of beer and wine. Alcoholic beverages are sold to the individual consumer in Sweden via a State-owned retail trade monopoly, Systembolaget AB. Strong beer, in other words beer containing more than 3.5% alcohol by volume, and wines are sold through Systembolaget AB. Lighter wines in the middle price range are regarded as being interchangeable with strong beer.

Beer is subject to an alcohol tax which is on average and as a percentage is significantly lower than the equivalent tax on wine. No ground has been put forward which justifies that difference in that selective purchase tax. The difference in the tax affects the price of the respective products. The difference in price is increased by the application of VAT at the rate of 25% to the products.

The effect of the tax on the price of the respective products is likely to distort competition between goods and the internal selective purchase taxes are such as to strengthen domestic patterns of consumption, reduce potential consumption of wine and thus they are likely to afford indirect protection to beer to the detriment of wine.

An action against Sweden was brought before the ECJ on 14 April 2005 by the Commission claiming that the Court should declare that, by applying internal taxes by which beer mainly produced in Sweden is protected indirectly against wine mainly imported from other Member States, the Kingdom of Sweden failed to fulfil its obligations under the second paragraph of Article 90 EC (now Article 110 TFEU). According to the ECJ, the comparison of the relationship between the selling prices of a litre of strong beer and a litre of wine in competition with strong beer makes it clear that the difference in price between those two products is virtually the same before taxation as after taxation. In those circumstances

137 Case C-365/85 (*Commission v. Belgium*), [1987] ECR 3299.
138 Case C-166/98 (*Socridis*), [1999] ECR I-3791.
139 Case C-167/05 (*Commission v. Sweden*), [2008] ECR I-2127.

the Court pointed out that the difference in selling price found in the present case is nevertheless such that the difference in the tax treatment of those two products is not liable to influence consumer behaviour in the sector concerned.

The *Gourmet Classic* case is a reference for a preliminary ruling was made in the context of an appeal brought by the Skatteverket (Swedish tax administration) before the Regeringsrätten (Supreme Administrative Court), seeking confirmation of a preliminary opinion of the Skatterättsnämnden (Swedish Board for Advances Tax Rulings) concerning the taxation of alcohol contained in cooking wine.[140] In support of its application, Gourmet contended that cooking wine falls within the exemption provided for in Article 27(1)(f) of Directive 92/83.

The ECJ observed that although cooking wine is, as such, an edible preparation falling within chapter 21 of the Combined Nomenclature, the fact remains that that edible preparation contains ethyl alcohol falling within headings 2207 and 2208 of that nomenclature. Thus, if the ethyl alcohol contained in cooking wine has an alcoholic strength exceeding 1.2 % volume, that alcohol falls within the scope of the first indent of Article 20 of Directive 92/83. The fact that cooking wine is, as such, regarded as an edible preparation does not affect that assessment. Article 20 of Directive 92/83 applies even when the products covered by that provision form part of a product which falls within another chapter of the Combined Nomenclature. Consequently, the alcohol contained in cooking wine, if it has an alcoholic strength exceeding 1.2% by volume, constitutes ethyl alcohol within the meaning of the first indent of Article 20 of Directive 92/83, which is, without prejudice to the exemption provided for in Article 27(1)(f) of that Directive, subject to the harmonised excise duty.[141]

3.5.3 *Fermented Beverages other than Wine and Beer*

The structure Directive makes a distinction between "other still fermented beverages" and "other sparkling fermented beverages" referring to the relevant CN codes[142] and actual alcohol strengths, the details of which are not discussed here. Some of these products, however, may be treated as intermediate products (see section 3.5.4 below). The provisions on the establishment of the duty of these fermented beverages other than wine and beer are identical to those on wine. The structure Directive provides that for the application of the horizontal Directive and the Directive on rates (Directive 92/84/EEC) references to wine are deemed to apply to the products referred to above, thus, the minimum excise duty of zero Euro is also applicable to fermented beverages other than wine and beer.

The application of reduced rates to apply to independent small producers of fermented beverages, similar to the existing conditions as for the production of beer, see section 3.5.1 above, will be introduced as of 1 January 2022.

140 Case C-458/06 (*Gourmet Classic*), [2008] ECR I-4207.
141 See also Case C-163/09 (*Repertoire Culinaire*), [2010] ECR I-0000.
142 These will be updated as of 1 January 2022 to reflect the same changes as discussed in section 3.5.2.

3.5.4 *Intermediate Products*

Intermediate products are defined on a residual basis, *i.e.* falling within CN codes 2204, 2205 and 2206 and of an actual alcoholic strength between 1.2% and 22% vol., but not covered by the definition of beer, wine or other fermented beverages or treated as intermediate products since Member States may treat certain "other still fermented beverages" as intermediate products. The duty on intermediate products is also based on the number of hectolitres of finished products. The Directive on rates (Directive 92/84/EEC) fixes the minimum rate at EUR 45 Member States may apply a single reduced rate to intermediate products with a strength not exceeding 15% vol. under certain conditions.

The application of reduced rates to apply to independent small producers of intermediate products, similar to the existing conditions as for the production of beer, see section 3.5.1 above, will be introduced as of 1 January 2022.

3.5.5 *Ethyl Alcohol*

Ethyl alcohol covers all products of CN codes 2204, 2205 and 2206 (see the products mentioned in section 3.5.4 directly above) exceeding an alcohol strength of 22% vol., products exceeding 1.2% vol. falling within CN codes 2207 and 2208[143] and potable spirits containing products, whether in solution or not. The excise duty is fixed per hectolitre pure alcohol at 20 degrees C. As in the case with small breweries (see section 3.5.1 above), reduced rates (with a maximum of 50% below the national standard rate) may be applied to alcohol produced by small distilleries, producing less than 10 hectolitres of pure alcohol per year. Based on Article 33 of Directive 92/83, reduced rates may also be applied on certain products not exceeding 10% alcohol vol., on French rum and Greek aniseed flavoured spirit drinks. With regard to the duty, Directive 92/84/EEC did not succeed in imposing the envisaged EUR 1,000 rate per hectolitre of pure alcohol. The minimum rate is EUR 550. Member States applying a rate above EUR 550, but below EUR 1,000 may not lower this rate and Member States applying a rate above EUR 1,000 may not lower the rate below EUR 1,000. This "quasi stand-still" clause[144] indicates that the Commission still aims at eventually achieving a single rate of EUR 1,000.

According to the Directive on the harmonization of excise duties on alcohol and alcoholic beverages, for certain types of product, including ouzo, reduced rates of excise duty may be applied.

In Case C-475/01 (*Commission v. Greece*)[145] in fixing a lower rate of excise duty for ouzo, Greece relied on Article 23(2) of Directive 92/83 and complied with the terms of that provision. The Commission's action, seeking directly to challenge the rate of excise duty that Greece was authorized to apply to ouzo on that basis, indirectly but necessarily amounted to a challenge to the lawfulness of that provision. The ECJ pointed out that measures of the Community

143 Even when they form part of a product mentioned in other chapters of the CN Code.
144 See E. Stubbe, 'Die harmonisierung der besonderen Verbrauchssteueren in der Europäischen Gemeinschaft', *ZfZV* 1993, p. 204.
145 Case C-475/01 (*Commission v. Greece*), [2004] ECR I-8923.

institutions are presumed to be lawful and produce legal effects until such time as they are withdrawn, annulled (in an action for annulment) or declared invalid (following a reference for a preliminary ruling or a plea of illegality). Only measures tainted by a very serious irregularity, which cannot be tolerated by the Community legal order, must be regarded as legally non-existent. However, neither Directive 92/83 as a whole nor Article 23(2) of that directive can be regarded as a non-existent measure. Also, that directive has not been withdrawn by the Council and Article 23(2) has not been annulled or declared invalid by the Court. In those circumstances Article 23(2) of Directive 92/83 produces legal effects which are presumed to be lawful. Since Greece has merely maintained in force national legislation adopted pursuant to Article 23(2) of Directive 92/83 and which complies with that provision it has not failed to fulfil its obligations under Community law. The ECJ therefore found that the Commission's action was unfounded and must be dismissed.

In the *UAB Profisa* case,[146] the ECJ ruled that Article 27(1)(f) of Directive 92/ 83/ EEC should be understood as imposing an obligation on Member States to exempt from harmonised excise duty ethyl alcohol imported into the customs territory of the European Union and contained in chocolate products intended for direct use, where the alcohol content does not exceed 8.5 litres for every 100 kilograms of the chocolate products.

The Finnish Tampere District Court asked for a preliminary ruling on the interpretation of the Sixth VAT Directive, the horizontal Excise Directive, Directive 98/83/EEC on the structures of excises on alcohol and alcoholic beverages and the Community Customs Code.[147] Salumets and accomplices were caught smuggling about 100,000 litres of ethyl alcohol from Estonia into Finland. Part of the alcohol was bottled; the rest was kept in containers in a former stable under unhygienic conditions. They were ordered to pay approximately FIM 38 million. On appeal the Finnish Court was uncertain whether ethyl alcohol (as such not intended for human consumption and the importation is subject to a system of authorizations) ought not to be treated in the same way as the unlawful supply of narcotic drugs and the importation of counterfeit currency. Obviously, Salumets c.s. supported this view!

The ECJ held that, in contrast to narcotic drugs, ethyl alcohol can be lawfully marketed and introduced into economic channels. The circumstances in which the goods were imported in the present case cannot alter that assessment. An intrinsically lawful product such as ethyl alcohol may not be equalled with a narcotic drug for reasons connected with its origin, quality or purity.

3.6 Tobacco

On 21 June 2011, the Council adopted Directive 2011/64/EU on the structure and rates of excise duty applied to manufactured tobacco.

146 Case C-63/06 (*UAB Profisa*), [2007] ECR I-3239.
147 Case C-455/98 (*Salumets*), [2000] ECR I-4993. See also Case C-434/04 (*Jan- Erik Anders Ahokainen, Mati Leppik*), [2006] ECR I-9197.

Directives 92/79/EEC, 92/80/EEC and 95/59/EEC are codified by assembling them in a single act.[148]

Directive 2011/64/EU lays down general principles for the harmonisation of the structure and rates of the excise duty to which the Member States subject manufactured tobacco (Article 1).

3.6.1 Definitions

According to Article 2 of Directive 2011/64/EU *manufactured tobacco* means:
(a) cigarettes;
(b) cigars and cigarillos;
(c) smoking tobacco:
 (i) fine-cut tobacco for the rolling of cigarettes;
 (ii) other smoking tobacco.

Products consisting in whole or in part of substances other than tobacco but otherwise conforming to the criteria set out in Article 3 for cigarettes or Article 5(1) for smoking tobacco are to be treated as cigarettes and smoking tobacco. (Products containing no tobacco and used exclusively for medical purposes shall not be treated as manufactured tobacco.)

According to Article 3, for the purposes of Directive 2011/64/EU *cigarettes* means:
(a) rolls of tobacco capable of being smoked as they are and which are not cigars or cigarillos;
(b) rolls of tobacco which, by simple non-industrial handling, are inserted into cigarette-paper tubes;
(c) rolls of tobacco which, by simple non-industrial handling, are wrapped in cigarette paper.

A roll of tobacco must, for excise duty purposes, be considered as two cigarettes where, excluding filter or mouthpiece, it is longer than 8 cm but not longer than 11 cm, as three cigarettes where, excluding filter or mouthpiece, it is longer than 11 cm but not longer than 14 cm, and so on.

Article 4 provides that for the purposes of Directive 2011/64/EU the following are deemed to be *cigars or cigarillos* if they can be and, given their properties and normal consumer expectations, are exclusively intended to be smoked as they are:
(a) rolls of tobacco with an outer wrapper of natural tobacco;
(b) rolls of tobacco with a threshed blend filler and with an outer wrapper of the normal colour of a cigar, of reconstituted tobacco, covering the product in full, including, where appropriate, the filter but not, in the case of tipped cigars, the tip, where the unit weight, not including filter or mouthpiece, is not less than 2,3 g and not more than 10 g, and the circumference over at least one third of the length is not less than 34 mm.

148 The case-law relating to the replaced directives is not discussed here.

Products which consist in part of substances other than tobacco but otherwise fulfil these criteria must be treated as cigars and cigarillos.

Article 5 provides that for the purposes of this Directive *smoking tobacco* means:

(a) tobacco which has been cut or otherwise split, twisted or pressed into blocks and is capable of being smoked without further industrial processing;

(b) tobacco refuse put up for retail sale which does not fall under the definition of cigarettes in Article 3 and the definition of cigars and cigarillos in Article 4(1) and which can be smoked. For the purpose of this Article, tobacco refuse shall be deemed to be remnants of tobacco leaves and by-products obtained from tobacco processing or the manufacture of tobacco products.

Smoking tobacco in which more than 25% by weight of the tobacco parts have a cut width of less than 1,5 millimetre is deemed to be fine-cut tobacco for the rolling of cigarettes.

Member States may also deem smoking tobacco in which more than 25% by weight of the tobacco parts have a cut width of 1,5 millimetre or more and which was sold or intended to be sold for the rolling of cigarettes to be fine-cut tobacco for the rolling of cigarettes (Art. 5).

According to Article 6, a natural or legal person established in the Union who converts tobacco into manufactured products prepared for retail sale is deemed to be a manufacturer.

3.6.2 *Provisions Applicable to Cigarettes*

Article 7 provides that cigarettes manufactured in the Union and those imported from third countries are subject to an ad valorem excise duty calculated on the maximum retail selling price, including customs duties, and also to a specific excise duty calculated per unit of the product.

Member States may exclude customs duties from the basis for calculating the ad valorem excise duty on cigarettes.

The rate of the ad valorem excise duty and the amount of the specific excise duty must be the same for all cigarettes.

At the final stage of harmonisation of structures, the same ratio will be established for cigarettes in all Member States between the specific excise duty and the sum of the ad valorem excise duty and the turnover tax, in such a way that the range of retail selling prices reflects fairly the difference in the manufacturers' delivery prices.

Where necessary, the excise duty on cigarettes may include a minimum tax component, provided that the mixed structure of taxation and the band of the specific component of the excise duty as laid down in Article 8 is strictly respected.

Article 8 prescribes that the percentage of the specific component of excise duty in the amount of the total tax burden on cigarettes shall be established by reference to the weighted average retail selling price.

The weighted average retail selling price is to be calculated by reference to the total value of all cigarettes released for consumption, based on the retail selling price including all taxes, divided by the total quantity of cigarettes released for consumption. It must be determined by 1 March at the latest of each year on the basis of data relating to all such releases for consumption made in the preceding calendar year.

From 1 January 2014, the specific component of the excise duty on cigarettes may not be less than 7,5% and shall not be more than 76,5% of the amount of the total tax burden resulting from the aggregation of the following:
(a) specific excise duty;
(b) the ad valorem excise duty and the VAT levied on the weighted average retail selling price.

By way of derogation from the above, where a change in the weighted average retail selling price of cigarettes occurs in a Member State, thereby bringing the specific component of the excise duty, expressed as a percentage of the total tax burden, below the percentage of 5% or 7,5%, whichever is applicable, or above the percentage of 76,5% of the total tax burden, the Member State concerned may refrain from adjusting the amount of the specific excise duty until 1 January of the second year following that in which the change occurs.

Subject to provisos regarding the specific component mentioned above, Member States may levy a minimum excise duty on cigarettes.

Article 9 stipulates that Member States must apply to cigarettes minimum consumption taxes which comprise:
(a) a specific excise duty per unit of the product;
(b) an ad valorem excise duty calculated on the basis of the maximum retail selling price;
(c) a VAT proportional to the retail selling price.

Based on Article 10 the overall excise duty (specific duty and ad valorem duty excluding VAT) on cigarettes must represent at least 57% of the weighted average retail selling price of cigarettes released for consumption. That excise duty may not be less than EUR 64 per 1000 cigarettes irrespective of the weighted average retail selling price.

However, Member States which levy an excise duty of at least EUR 101 per 1000 cigarettes on the basis of the weighted average retail selling price need not to comply with the 57% requirement set out in the first subparagraph.

From 1 January 2014, the overall excise duty on cigarettes must represent at least 60% of the weighted average retail selling price of cigarettes released for consumption. That excise duty may not be less than EUR 90 per 1000 cigarettes irrespective of the weighted average retail selling price.

However, Member States which levy an excise duty of at least EUR 115 per 1000 cigarettes on the basis of the weighted average retail selling price need not to comply with the 60% requirement set out in the first subparagraph.

Bulgaria, Estonia, Greece, Latvia, Lithuania, Hungary, Poland and Romania are allowed a transitional period until 31 December 2017 in order to reach the requirements laid down in the first and second subparagraphs. These Member States must gradually increase excise duties in order to reach the normal requirements.

According to Article 11 where a change in the weighted average retail selling price of cigarettes occurs in a Member State, thereby bringing the overall excise duty below the levels specified in Article 10, the Member State concerned may refrain from adjusting that duty until 1 January of the second year following that in which the change occurs.

Where a Member State increases the rate of VAT on cigarettes, it may reduce the overall excise duty up to an amount which, expressed as a percentage of the weighted average retail selling price, is equal to the increase in the rate of VAT, also expressed as a percentage of the weighted average retail selling price, even if such an adjustment has the effect of reducing the overall excise duty to below the levels, expressed as a percentage of the weighted average retail selling price, laid down in Article 10.

However, the Member State must raise that duty again so as to reach at least those levels by 1 January of the second year after that in which the reduction took place.

Article 12 provides for derogations for Portugal and France. Portugal may apply a reduced rate of up to 50% less than that laid down in Article 10 to cigarettes consumed in the most remote regions of the Azores and Madeira, made by small- scale manufacturers each of whose annual production does not exceed 500 tonnes. By way of derogation from Article 10, France may continue to apply for the period from 1 January 2010 to 31 December 2015 a reduced rate of excise duty to cigarettes released for consumption in the departments of Corsica up to an annual quota of 1200 tonnes. The reduced rate must be:
(a) until 31 December 2012, at least 44% of the price for cigarettes in the price category most in demand in those departments;
(b) from 1 January 2013, at least 50% of the weighted average retail selling price of cigarettes released for consumption; the excise duty shall not be less than EUR 88 per 1000 cigarettes irrespective of the weighted average retail selling price;
(c) from 1 January 2015, at least 57% of the weighted average retail selling price of cigarettes released for consumption; the excise duty shall not be less than EUR 90 per 1000 cigarettes irrespective of the weighted average retail selling price.

3.6.3 *Provisions Applicable to Manufactured Tobacco other than Cigarettes*

Article 13 stipulates that the following groups of manufactured tobacco produced in the Union and imported from third countries are subject, in each Member State, to a minimum excise duty as laid down in Article 14:
(a) cigars and cigarillos;

(b) fine-cut tobacco intended for the rolling of cigarettes;
(c) other smoking tobaccos.

Article 14 prescribes Member States to apply an excise duty which may be:
(a) either an ad valorem duty calculated on the basis of the maximum retail selling price of each product, freely determined by manufacturers established in the Union and by importers from third countries in accordance with Article 15; or
(b) a specific duty expressed as an amount per kilogram, or in the case of cigars and cigarillos, alternatively for a given number of items; or
(c) a mixture of both, combining an ad valorem element and a specific element.

In cases where excise duty is either ad valorem or mixed, Member States may establish a minimum amount of excise duty.

The overall excise duty (specific duty and/or ad valorem duty excluding VAT), expressed as a percentage, as an amount per kilogram or for a given number of items, must be at least equivalent to the rates or minimum amounts laid down for:
(a) cigars or cigarillos: 5% of the retail selling price inclusive of all taxes or EUR 12 per 1000 items or per kilogram;
(b) fine-cut smoking tobacco intended for the rolling of cigarettes: 40% of the weighted average retail selling price of fine-cut smoking tobacco intended for the rolling of cigarettes released for consumption, or EUR 40 per kilogram;
(c) other smoking tobaccos: 20% of the retail selling price inclusive of all taxes, or EUR 22 per kilogram.

From 1 January 2020, the overall excise duty on fine-cut smoking tobacco intended for the rolling of cigarettes must represent at least 50% of the weighted average retail selling price of fine-cut smoking tobacco intended for the rolling of cigarettes released for consumption, or at least EUR 60 per kilogram.

The weighted average retail selling price must be calculated by reference to the total value of fine-cut smoking tobacco intended for the rolling of cigarettes released for consumption, based on retail selling price including all taxes, divided by the total quantity of fine-cut smoking tobacco intended for the rolling of cigarettes released for consumption. It must be determined by 1 March at the latest of each year on the basis of data relating to all such releases for consumption made in the preceding calendar year.

The rates or amounts referred to above are to be effective for all products belonging to the group of manufactured tobaccos concerned, without distinction within each group as to quality, presentation, origin of the products, the materials used, the characteristics of the firms involved or any other criterion.

By way of derogation from the above, France may continue to apply, for the period from 1 January 2010 to 31 December 2015, a reduced rate of excise duty to manufactured tobacco other than cigarettes released for consumption in the departments of Corsica. The reduced rate shall be:

(a) for cigars and cigarillos: at least 10% of the retail selling price, inclusive of all taxes;
(b) for fine-cut smoking tobacco intended for the rolling of cigarettes:
   (i) until 31 December 2012, at least 27% of the retail selling price, inclusive of all taxes;
   (ii) from 1 January 2013, at least 30% of the retail selling price, inclusive of all taxes;
   (iii) from 1 January 2015, at least 35% of the retail selling price, inclusive of all taxes;
(c) for other smoking tobacco: at least 22% of the retail selling price, inclusive of all taxes.

3.6.4 *Determination of the Maximum Retail Selling Price of Manufactured Tobacco, Collection of Excise Duty, Exemptions and Refunds*

Article 15 provides that manufacturers or, where appropriate, their representatives or authorised agents in the Union, and importers of tobacco from third countries are free to determine the maximum retail selling price for each of their products for each Member State for which the products in question are to be released for consumption.

The first subparagraph may not, however, hinder implementation of national systems of legislation regarding the control of price levels or the observance of imposed prices, provided that they are compatible with Union legislation.

In order to facilitate the levying of the excise duty, Member States may, for each group of manufactured tobacco, fix a scale of retail selling prices on condition that each scale has sufficient scope and variety to correspond in fact with the variety of products originating in the Union.

Each scale must be valid for all the products belonging to the group of manufactured tobacco which it concerns, without distinction on the basis of quality, presentation, the origin of the products or of the materials used, the characteristics of the undertakings or of any other criterion.

According to Article 16, at the final stage of harmonisation of the excise duty, at the latest the rules for collecting the excise duty will be harmonised. During the preceding stage, the excise duty must, in principle, be collected by means of tax stamps. If they collect the excise duty by means of tax stamps, Member States are obliged to make these stamps available to manufacturers and dealers in other Member States. If they collect the excise duty by other means, Member States must ensure that no obstacle, either administrative or technical, affects trade between Member States on that account.

Importers and Union manufacturers of manufactured tobacco are subject to the system set out above as regards the detailed rules for levying and paying the excise duty.

Article 17 provides that the following may be exempt from excise duty or excise duty already paid on them may be refunded:
(a) denatured manufactured tobacco used for industrial or horticultural purposes;
(b) manufactured tobacco which is destroyed under administrative supervision;
(c) manufactured tobacco which is solely intended for scientific tests and for tests connected with product quality;
(d) manufactured tobacco which is reworked by the producer.

Member States must determine the conditions and formalities to which the above-mentioned exemptions or refunds are subject.

3.6.5 *Final Provisions*

Article 18 prescribes that the Commission must publish once a year the value of the euro in national currencies to be applied to the amounts of the overall excise duty.

The exchange rates to be applied are those obtained on the first working day of October and published in the Official Journal of the European Union and apply from 1 January of the following calendar year.

Member States may maintain the amounts of the excise duties in force at the time of the annual adjustment if the conversion of the amounts of the excise duties expressed in euro would result in an increase of less than 5% or less than EUR 5, whichever is the lower amount, in the excise duty expressed in national currency.

Article 19 prescribes the Commission to submit every four years to the Council a report and, where appropriate, a proposal concerning the rates and the structure of excise duty laid down in this Directive.

The report by the Commission must take into account the proper functioning of the internal market, the real value of the rates of excise duty and the wider objectives of the Treaty.

The report will be based in particular on the information provided by the Member States.

The Commission must, in accordance with the Committee procedure referred to in Article 43 of Council Directive 2008/118/EC, determine a list of statistical data needed for the report, excluding data relating to individual natural persons or legal entities. Apart from data readily available to Member States, the list may only contain data the collection and assembly of which does not involve a disproportionate administrative burden on the part of the Member States.

The Commission may not publish or otherwise divulge data where it would lead to the disclosure of a commercial, industrial or professional secret.

Article 20 instructs the Member States to communicate to the Commission the text of the main provisions of national law which they adopt in the field covered by this Directive.

Directives 92/79/EEC, 92/80/EEC and 95/59/EC, as amended are repealed. Directive 2011/64/EU entered into force on 1 January 2011.

3.7 Environmental Taxation

3.7.1 *Introduction: VAT adjustments to reach environmental objectives*

Article 191 TFEU in combination with Article 192 TFEU (both part of the Title on Environment; introduced by the Single European Act in 1986, and amended by the Treaty on European Union) provide that Community environmental policy shall be aimed at rectifying environmental damage, *inter alia*, the "polluter pays" principle, and that the Council shall take action by unanimous acts. These provisions may become the basis for EU driven environmental taxes ("green" taxes). As early as 2 June 1992, the Commission submitted a proposal to the Council for a Directive requiring Member States to introduce an energy tax, *i.e.* a tax on the emission of carbon dioxide (CO2) and on the (other) use of energy.[149] That proposal was based on both Article 93 and Article 175 EC (now Articles 113 and 192 TFEU). The Commission introduced a revised proposal[150] on 12 March 1997, but no (unanimous) agreement was reached, mainly due to opposition by Spain, which made the harmonization of energy taxation dependent on the liberalization of the energy market. In the meantime, many Member States introduced an energy tax unilaterally.

In its communication on the tax policy in the European Union[151] of May 2001, the Commission mentions the following with regard to energy and environmental taxation:

> Generally, taxation has proved to be an efficient economic instrument for tackling environmental problems. It is a crucial instrument in meeting the commitments of the Kyoto Protocol and has the potential for providing an effective stimulus for policies to dissociate energy use from economic growth, to improve energy consumption patterns and to develop renewable energy sources, like biofuels, as pointed out in the Green Paper on the security of energy supply in Europe.[152] Currently, the taxation of energy builds on three pillars: (i) excise duties, (ii) VAT and (iii) specific levies. Whereas excise duties on mineral oils and VAT constitute Community systems of taxation, no EU-wide framework is applicable to energy products other than mineral oils.
>
> As regards mineral oil products, since 1992 a unanimously agreed Community system provides for a minimum excise rate for each product according to its use (propellant, industrial and commercial uses, heating purposes). Today, however, excise duties are often levied at rates that are significantly higher than the minimum rates, which have not been updated since 1992. Effective excise rates thus differ substantially between Member States. Zero taxation is compulsory for some activities (international air traffic) and national derogations can also be granted for specific policy reasons in favour of, for instance, environmentally-friendly products or economic sectors (agriculture, public transport, road haulage). In many cases, the above-mentioned derogations are granted in order to maintain the competitiveness of local companies when higher energy/environmental taxation schemes are implemented. Moreover the multiplication of national taxes that differ in their scope, methods of calculation, rates, etc. jeopardises the unity of the Internal Market and might negatively affect the functioning of the liberalised gas and electricity markets.
>
> The current mechanisms at both national and Community level thus lead to possible distortions in the consumer choices between energy sources or products and in the conditions of competition. A Community framework for facilitating the approximation of the taxation schemes of Member States would offer the most efficient remedy to these difficulties.

149 O.J. 1992, C 196.
150 COM(1997) 30 final.
151 COM(2001) 260 final.
152 COM(2000) 769.

> Against this background in 1997 the Commission proposed a Council Directive for restructuring the Community Framework for the taxation of Energy Products,[153] with a view to extending the scope of the Directives on mineral oils to a number of other energy sources, e. g. coal, electricity and natural gas, and to increasing the Community minimum excise duties on energy products. In aiming at the gradual introduction of the "polluter pays" principle, this proposal would make it possible to both restructure national tax systems, achieve certain policy objectives in the field of employment, environment, transport and energy, and improve the functioning of the Internal Market. One key element of the proposal is the recommendation that Member States, when implementing the Directive, should avoid any increase in their overall tax burden. Macroeconomic research suggests that a structured reform, involving the introduction of "green taxes" and reducing the tax burden on labour can, under certain circumstances, lead to a double dividend, conferring benefits on both employment and the environment. After a four-year stalemate in the Council, it is essential that progress is now made on the above-mentioned proposal, even if unanimity cannot be obtained. The weaknesses of the current situation have once again been exposed by the range of different measures adopted by Member States, in particular in the road haulage sector, in response to the increased oil prices in 2000. It demonstrates once again that a common framework for the taxation of energy products should be established, not only on the structure of such taxes but also in relation to tax rates. This will prevent distortions in the Internal Market, ensure that prices of energy products reflect their external environmental costs and assist the Community to meet its international environmental commitments.
>
> The shift towards environmental taxes has clearly been a very slow one. A common framework including differentiated rates according to environmental objectives could be very useful. The aforementioned Commission Communication on an EU Strategy for Sustainable Development calls on the Energy Products Directive to be adopted by 2002. An agreed Community framework for energy taxation could help to pave the way for more ambitious environmental targets for energy taxation within two years of the adoption of the Directive, aiming at the full internalisation of external costs.

To a large extent environmental taxation has been focused on VAT rate differentiation.

In 2003, the Commission presented a proposal concerning the review of reduced VAT rates resulting in Council Directive 2006/18/EC of 14 February 2006. The Directive included a request to the Commission to present to the European Parliament and to the Council, by the end of June 2007, an overall assessment report on the impact of reduced rates. (See also Article 101 of the Recast VAT Directive.) This would cover locally-supplied services, including restaurant services, notably in terms of job creation, economic growth and the proper functioning of the internal market, and would be based on a study carried out by an independent economic think-tank.

The Study of Copenhagen Economics

The study contract was awarded to Copenhagen Economics. The study mainly examined the impact of reduced VAT rates and of derogations, not only for locally supplied services, but also more globally. The effects on income distribution, the informal economy and on compliance costs for businesses were also taken into consideration.

On 5 July 2007, the Commission presented its communication[154] to the Council and the European Parliament "on VAT rates other than standard VAT rates".

153 COM(1997) 30.

154 COM(2007) 380 final.

This Communication presents the main conclusions of the above study, provides material for discussion and explores ways forward in the field of reduced VAT rates.

The following points highlight the key results of the study, in particular from the point of view of potential policy implications.

The study stresses that a single VAT rate is by far the best policy choice *from a purely economic point of view*. A move towards more uniform rates has thus considerable advantages. First, a less complicated rate structure would generate substantial savings in compliance costs for business and tax administrations. Second, it could reduce distortions in the functioning of the internal market. Third, it is likely to slightly improve "consumer welfare" compared with the current situation.

However, there may be specific benefits from operating a reduced VAT in carefully targeted sectors. Lower VAT rates can increase overall productivity and thus GDP, as well as tax revenue, in a Member State if they can induce consumers to spend less time on do-it-yourself (DIY) activities and more time on their ordinary job. This behaviour would result in a shift of activities from DIY to the formal economy. *Locally supplied services (and restaurants)* are industries where households have considerable scope for carrying out DIY and therefore the area where such a shift could thus take place. The argument for a reduced rate on locally supplied services is significantly stronger in Member States with higher marginal income taxes and higher VAT-rates and for some sub-sectors within locally supplied services with limited need for formal training and specialised machinery. The same productivity argument holds, albeit to a lesser degree, if lower VAT rates can induce consumers to spend less money on the "*underground*" *economy*. Finally, it appears that different VAT rates applied to locally supplied services are of *no concern for the functioning of the internal market*. Services provided by *restaurants and hotels* are in-between, because they are mainly directed at domestic consumption, but may also affect distribution of tourism between Member States and may have a non- negligible impact in border regions. Lower VAT rates targeting sectors using many low skilled workers, such as locally supplied services, financed for example by higher VAT rates elsewhere can create *permanent* employment gains, but the overall gains are likely to be minor. The net gains stem from the fact that demand for low skilled workers is likely to be boosted and that low skilled workers face more difficulties in obtaining a job than higher skilled workers, as a result of labour market rigidities. However, the gains are minor because the targeted sectors account only for a small proportion of the overall employment in low skilled sectors. So the increase in low skilled employment in these relatively small industries is nearly entirely offset by decreases in other industries hit by the higher VAT rate.

Besides the above-mentioned efficiency arguments in favour of reduced rates, generally the argument of improving equity is advanced. In this respect, the study finds that for the improvement of income distribution in a Member State, reduced VAT rates are effective only when the share of consumption expenditure of goods/ services subject to a reduced rate (out of the total consumption expenditure) differs sufficiently between low and high-income groups and is stable over time. These differences are the largest for *food*. However, in this respect there are relatively large differences between countries. Reduced rates are less potent in countries which already have high income equality. Moreover, in certain cases, policy goals may conflict internally (for example if the objective of a reduced rate is to promote the purchase of certain goods, it is possible that high-income groups benefit more from the reduced rate, which conflicts with the income equality goal).

The study also makes a strong case that reduced VAT rates create significant compliance costs for business and tax authorities, partly at least because of the interpretations which have to be made in respect of borderline cases which are often costly and resource intensive.

Other alternative policy tools, such as direct subsidies for particular activities, in the main achieve the same goals as reduced VAT rates with fewer costs. These subsidy schemes may be better targeted, better designed to avoid negative spill over effects at the EU level and, generally speaking, may be more transparent. They may also incur fewer compliance costs and budgetary losses. However, compared to reduced VAT rates, direct subsidies might appear less secure as a permanent solution for the businesses concerned.

The study recommends that Member States carefully examine all the options available when they want to promote the consumption of specific goods or services: often other tools than reduced VAT rates are more efficient and less costly for the State budget, and this should be taken into account in the decision-making-process.

Reduced VAT for Environmentally Friendly Products

On 19 December 2008, a report again by Copenhagen Economics entitled "Reduced VAT for Environmentally Friendly Products" was published. This report focuses on the role that differentiated VAT rates can play relative to two central policy objectives that have gained significantly in importance in the most recent years. The first policy objective is about reducing emissions of greenhouse gases (GHG) while at the same time reaching goals of energy security within the EU; both of which requires reductions in energy consumption. Should this policy objective be encouraged by way of reduced VAT rates on energy efficient consumer goods? For instance, Member States could encourage consumers to buy a freezer with low electricity consumption relative to other more electricity consuming freezers through a lower purchase price due to a lower VAT rate.

The second policy objective is about distributional concerns and the competitiveness of fragile industries. Rising global energy prices may adversely impact low income families and energy intensive industries as both spend a relatively large share of their budget on fuels and heating. Should this policy objective be encouraged by way of reduced VAT rates on energy consumption? For instance, Member States could shield low income families from the effect of higher energy prices by way of reduced VAT rates on the consumption of heating as it is in fact common in many EU countries.

The main conclusion is that, generally, it is believed that the best approach to reducing GHG emissions is to tax at root.

The report provides three main conclusions on the effectiveness and efficiency of using reduced VAT rates to encourage consumers to save energy.

- First, it is not clear if energy savings will unambiguously follow from such purchase rewards.
- Second, a lower VAT rate is a crude subsidy and may also lead to compliance problems in the real world.
- Third, reduced VAT rates on energy consumption lead to transfers to oil producing countries.

A 2013 study[155] on the economic effects of the VAT rates structure by the Institute for Advanced Studies (IAS) and the CPB Netherlands Bureau for Economic Policy Analysis, adds the following observations:

- Because VAT is calculated as a fraction of the product price, the use of reduced VAT rates provides a larger subsidy to more expensive products than to cheaper ones. Provided that 'green' energy, *i.e.*, energy produced by way of *e.g.*, solar panels and wind or water farms, is more expensive, applying a VAT reduced rate on green energy may make consumers shift more easily from conventionally produced energy to green energy, but it is not likely to necessarily also affect (reduce) their energy consumption behaviour.
- Reduced VAT rates on *e.g.*, energy products can only incentivise consumers, not businesses, because VAT paid on immediate inputs can be deducted by most businesses. Furthermore, this 'VAT as a subsidy' measure cannot be specifically targeted at a certain group of consumers. For example, if over-consumption of conventional energy products in specific areas or by specific households is seen as a problem, a VAT subsidy on green energy will also be enjoyed by those who already mind their energy consumption and those who already switched to green energy products.
- Lastly, and perhaps the most interesting one, applying a reduced VAT rate on the one hand on (part of) product groups which consumption is trying to be reduced or changed through EU policy on the other hand, raises a potential conflict. Both effects may be nullified if the use of (certain) energy products is subsidized by a reduced VAT rate on the one hand, but taxed with an excise tax on the other.

Costs and Benefits Associated with the Use of Tax Incentives

Furthermore, a study was published on the costs and benefits associated with the use of tax incentives to promote the manufacturing of more and better energy- efficient appliances and equipment and the consumer purchasing these products.

The study deals with the fiscal instruments that could potentially be used to promote energy efficiency in the EU. It focuses on direct fiscal incentives (subsidies, tax credits to consumers, tax credits to manufacturers) and compares their costs and benefits with those of conventional tax instruments (energy taxation) and a regulatory measure. The costs and benefits are assessed for four different appliances selected for their high energy saving potential: refrigerators, washing machines, boilers and compact fluorescent lamps (CFLi). In each case the assessment is carried out for two different EU Member States in

155 TAXUD/2012/DE/323.

order to capture the impact of different using patterns, price levels and market penetration of products. The countries included in the analysis are France, Denmark, Italy and Poland.

For each of the eight cases (four products, two Member States) to be assessed two policy options are formed. It is assumed in all cases that the polices are applied on top of the baseline, which implies a 12% energy price increase due to the Emissions Trading Scheme or tax policy.

Policy option 1: A subsidy or tax credit is accorded to those who purchase/ produce a product belonging to the highest energy-efficiency category. In two cases the policy in question is a direct subsidy (refrigerators, CFLi); in one case a tax credit for consumers (boilers) and in one case a tax credit to the manufacturer (washing machines).

Policy option 2: An energy tax leading to the additional increase of electricity/ gas prices by 10% is introduced (refrigerators, boilers, CFLi). In the case of washing machines this policy is replaced by a regulatory measure consisting of removing from the market Band C-class appliances.

In addition to the cost-benefit analysis the study provides information on the following topics:
- The market situation with respect to different energy-efficiency categories of the four appliances in question in Western and Eastern Europe.
- The overview of the current use of subsidies and tax incentives for energy efficiency purposes in the EU and US.
- The review of economic literature concerning the impacts of subsidies and tax incentives used for energy efficient purposes.

The main results of the cost benefit analysis are as follows:
- Energy taxation appears as the most cost-effective policy to promote energy efficiency in the EU. In all the six cases the benefits (the monetary value of CO2 reduction) exceed the costs (welfare and administrative costs) entailed by the policy.
- Subsidies and tax credits have, however, a considerable potential of generating energy savings. In some cases energy savings induced by subsidy schemes (direct subsidies or tax credits) exceed those generated by energy tax increases manifold (refrigerators in France and Denmark, CFLi in Poland). The subsidy schemes tend to have, however, higher welfare costs than the increases of energy taxation, which makes their benefit-cost balance in some cases negative (refrigerators in France).
- The comparison of different incentive instruments reveals that direct subsidies and tax credits to consumers are much more cost effective than tax credits to manufacturers. In the latter case the welfare costs/ton of CO2 (EUR 650 in Italy and EUR 234 in Poland) exceed by far all the reasonable estimates of the CO2 externality, and hence such policies would cost much more to the society than the benefits they could generate.
- The regulatory measure (removing class B or lower form the market) also turns out to have a relatively low capacity to generate energy savings compared with other policy options and therefore a fairly negative benefit-cost balance.

3.7.2 Car Registration and Circulation Tax

Car registration and circulation taxes are increasingly meant to take into consideration the impact on the environment. Currently, there is no (full) harmonization of car registration and circulation taxation at EU level. Guidance on this type of taxation must come, to a large extent, from case law of the ECJ. Some cases are discussed below.

3.7.2.1 Attempts to harmonise passenger car taxation at EU level

Based on Commission Communication of 14 December 2012,[156] we understand that car taxation forms an important revenue source for Member States and the design of national tax regimes is therefore of specific interest for national authorities, as well as for car producers and users. Perhaps that is the reason that only one of three proposals put forward by the Commission has resulted in the adoption of Directive 83/182/EEC.[157] The other proposals, of 1998[158] and 2005[159] have not received unanimous support, as required, of the Member States.

Directive 83/182/EEC is limited in scope and merely requires Member States to exempt from turnover tax, excise duty, other consumption tax and the (car) taxes listed in the Annex to the Directive, temporary imports from other Member States of motor-driven road vehicles, caravans, pleasure boats, private aircraft, bicycles, tricycles and – because it was 1983 when this Directive was adopted – saddle-horses. Private individuals are allowed to use these vehicles in a Member State other than their Member State of residence for not more than six months in any 12 months, without having to pay taxes in the Member State of import/usage. On this basis, the Directive contributes, albeit limitedly, to the prevention of double taxation and potential tax discrimination of cars transported by private individuals from one Member State to another.

The 2005 Proposal for a Council Directive on passenger car related taxes was based on three main pillars:

- The (gradual) abolition of all car registration taxes in all EU Member States, provided that these form an obstacle to the freedom of movement of cars in the EU and negatively affect the competitiveness of the European car industry;
- The establishment of a car registration tax (and annual circulation tax) refund system, applied to passenger cars registered in one Member State and subse quently exported or permanently transferred to another Member State, in order to prevent double taxation;
- The restructuring (on EU level) the tax base for the car registration tax and annual circulation tax to be totally or partially CO2-based, in order to further influence consumer's behaviour towards more environmentally friendly passenger car (usage).

---

156 COM(2012) 756 final.

157 Council Directive 83/182/EEC on tax exemptions within the Community for certain means of transport temporarily imported into one Member State from another, O.J. 1983, L105, p. 59).

158 COM(1998) 30 final.

159 COM(2005) 261 final.

Following unsuccessful negotiations between the Member States, the 2005 Proposal was eventually withdrawn by the Commission in 2015 and no new proposal was submitted to date.

3.7.2.2 *The 2012 Commission Communication*

Despite failed attempts to harmonise car taxation at EU level, in its 2012 Communication, the Commission, as referred to above, the Commission does clarify the EU rules that Member States must respect and makes recommendations to avoid double taxation.

First, the Commission addresses eight cross-border scenarios that cause problems relating to passenger car taxation, being:
- A private individual moves his car as part of the transfer of his normal residence.[160]
- A private individual moves his car permanently to his second residence in another Member state.
- A private individual, living in one Member State, uses a company car registered by his employer in another Member State.
- A private individual, living in one Member State, uses a leased car registered by a lease company in another Member State.
- A private individual, living in one Member State, uses his car frequently to visit his partner or family in another Member State.
- A private individual is going to temporarily study or is temporarily seconded for work to another Member State and brings their car for use in the Member State of study/work.
- A car rental company has registered a car fleet in one Member State and would enter into one-way rental contracts to another Member State, or move part of the fleet to better manage seasonal peak demand.
- A private individual or car dealer of a Member State that levies a registration tax sells a car to a private individual or company established in another Member State where it will have to be re-registered.

With some of these examples being addressed by the ECJ, the Commission still identified the following problems and included corresponding policy options and best practices for each.

Double Taxation
Citizens may be faced with double taxation when moving a car permanently to another Member State or when primarily using it in a country different from the country where the car has initially been registered. Although the EU rules prevent double taxation in some specific situations the problem of double taxation may still arise in many other situations. This problem is predominantly expected in the field of car registration tax and to a lesser extent in the field of circulation taxes. The latter are charged annually and typically refunded (pro rata) in case of deregistration.

160 Council Directive 2009/55/EC of 25 May 2009 on tax exemptions applicable to the permanent introduction from a Member State of the personal property of individuals (O.J. 2009, L145, p. 36) does not apply to vehicle registration taxes.

So as to avoid double taxation or 'over-taxation' in case an EU citizen permanently moves a car to another Member State (cases 1, 2 and 8 above), there exist in principle three policy options:

- The Member State of destination totally exempts the 'imported' car from registration taxes;
- The Member State of departure refunds the part of the registration tax already paid still incorporated in the value of the car (the residual tax);
- The Member State of destination reduces the domestic tax due by the tax already paid in the Member State of departure (imputation system), on top of the depreciation to be applied when taxing used instead of new cars.

The best regime for citizens would be a depreciation-based refund system applied by the Member State of departure combined with an exemption from registration tax in the Member State of destination. In this situation, the ultimate tax burden in the first Member State would always be proportional to the period of use of the car in that Member State (meaning no over-taxation would occur) and no tax burden would occur in the second Member State. The second-best regime would be a combination of refund and imputation schemes. This regime is less beneficial for the citizens as they would not or not fully benefit from such imputation in case they moved to a Member State not charging or charging a lower registration tax.

Lack of clear information

Citizens often complain not only about double taxation but also about the complexity of foreign tax rules and the difficulties in obtaining information on those rules and procedures. These difficulties are partly due to language barriers.

It is the responsibility of the Member States to provide detailed information to citizens and businesses on their application of national taxes and on how they have implemented the principles developed by the Court. It should be available in at least the language(s) of the Member State and the key issues (e.g. in the form of 'Frequently Asked Questions') also in the languages of the citizens that mostly move to this Member State, and in English for all others. The information should be easily accessible on the Internet, adequate and up-to-date and should contain a contact point for more information.

Rules in case of temporary or occasional use

The proper application of Directive 83/182/EEC on the tax treatment in case of temporary or occasional use of a car in a Member State other than the one of registration has been the subject of numerous Court decisions and infringement procedures. Other situations in which the Court has been called upon to decide concern cross-border leasing, company cars used by an employee or an administrator living in another Member State and cars borrowed by a resident of a Member State other than the one of registration. By now, the case law of the Court has crystallised important principles that have clarified the taxing power of Member States, while protecting the rights of EU citizens. It seems, however, to be a challenge for some Member States to bring national legislation and practices in line with these developments. The Commission is continuously engaged in monitoring the compliance of Member States' legislation with the case law of the Court in this field.

It may be a challenge for Member States to bring their car tax legislation in line with the principles laid down in the jurisprudence of the Court. Moreover, discussions with Member States in a technical Working Group could be useful to identify best practices for certain situations.

Already now, some Member States allow that vehicles registered in another Member State are for a relatively short period (maximum two weeks, a month) primarily used by their own citizens without the obligation to pay registration and circulation tax provided certain conditions like an administrative notification are fulfilled. But even this looks quite rigid at times of increasing international mobility and differentiating mobility patterns. Member States should consider allowing a certain period of use of vehicles registered in another Member State by a citizen without the obligation to pay registration tax, provided certain conditions set to avoid evasion or abuse are fulfilled.

Cross-border car rental

Car-rental companies rent out motor vehicles for a relatively short period of time. Car-rental fleets are usually very new, as vehicles remain in the fleet for about 6-9 months and are subsequently bought back by manufacturers. The EU passenger car fleet for short-term rental is estimated at 1.4 million vehicles. A car rental company providing services across the border may face two challenges, i) repatriation in case of one-way rental and ii) coping with seasonal peak demand. Both challenges implicitly restrict the freedom to provide services across borders, increase costs for rental companies and for their customers, or limit the latter's choice of services as such cross-border services may not even be provided at all.

Some Member States have already taken measures to overcome these problems. For example, some Member States allow that vehicles registered in another Member State which arrived in their country as a result of a hire contract, are hired for a certain period to a resident without the obligation to pay registration and circulation tax if certain conditions are fulfilled. This makes it easier to supply one-way rentals although the conditions vary considerably.

Member States applying more flexible arrangements in these two situations can do this on the basis of Article 9(1) of Directive 83/182/EEC. So far, there is no evidence that this flexibility has caused problems. Hence, the Commission suggests that the other Member States introduce similar arrangements, subject to the conditions set by them with a view to avoid any possible evasion or abuse. This would allow car rental firms to optimise the use of their fleets and to reduce costs and, hence, prices for final customers.

Tax-induced market fragmentation

Most Member States levying registration or circulation taxes based on the technical specifications of a car do so by differentiating according to technical performance (e.g. engine size or power) or the amount of CO2 emissions. Often, the thresholds have been set according to national market characteristics or national policy ambitions valid at the time of their introduction, and also having net revenue implications of successive reforms in mind. Car manufacturers have – wherever economically meaningful – adjusted their supply to these design features of car taxes, notably by supplying cars to their main markets that remain just below certain thresholds, such as providing cars with engine sizes of 1599 cm‡ or 1999 cm‡. However, these thresholds differ from country to country. This absence of harmonisation, thus, triggers a 'technical' fragmentation of the Single Market, having a negative impact both on the competitiveness of the industry and the effectiveness of incentive schemes. The cost of cars is also raised as a result. This is because a fragmented system induces car manufacturers to waste resources on fine-tuning cars to different thresholds, and reduces the cost- effectiveness of European climate policy.

Although the 2005 Proposal has not received unanimous support of Member States, it should be recognized that a lot of Member States have since introduced environmental elements in their registration taxes and/or circulation taxes. However, even if Member States apply the same environmental elements, they often use different thresholds resulting in (sometimes huge) differences in the tax levied. Differentiations within car taxation should not be based on technology-specific criteria, such as engine size or engine power, but rely on objective, commonly available and policy-relevant performance data, such as CO2 emissions. Moreover, the thresholds should be regularly updated to keep pressure to buy a clean and efficient vehicle. From this perspective it is suggested that Member States examine in a Working Group how the criteria they use as a basis for calculating registration and circulation taxes can be better coordinated, so that the technical fragmentation of the EU car market is reduced, economies of scale are exploited, and environmental goals are reached in a cost-effective manner.

3.7.2.3 *ECJ decisions on car registration tax matters*

The following cases as decided upon by the ECJ provide additional guidance towards the application of car registration tax, and its impact on EU principles, in the EU. This list is not exhaustive.

In *Commission v. Denmark*[161] Denmark applied a car registration tax of (up to) 180% of the value of the (new) car. At the time, Denmark did not have any domestic production of cars or other products liable to compete with the subjects of car taxation. The ECJ did not find this rate an infringement of EU law, *i.e.*, Member States are allowed to impose car tax rates at any level they seem fit – even if such registration tax exceeds 100% of the value of the car. The tax on imported *used* motor vehicles, however, was based on an estimated value of these cars, that was generally higher than the real value of the imported cars. To the extent that the tax was levied from imported used cars, the ECJ did find the tax an infringement of Article 95 of the EEC Treaty (now: Article 110 TFEU).

In *Cura Anlagen*[162] a lease company entered into a leasing contract with Cura Anlagen for 36 months, concerning a German-registered passenger vehicle. Cura Anlagen was to primarily use the car in Austria, but it would remain registered in name of the lease company and retain its German registration plates. Upon arrival in Austria, Cura Anlagen was unable to use the car, as Austria prohibits driving a vehicle with foreign plates in Austria for more

161 Case C-47/88, [1990] ECLI:EU:C:1990:449.
162 Case C-451/99, ECLI:EU:C:2002:195.

than three days. The ECJ ruled that while Austria was allowed to impose an obligation to register a vehicle to be actually used on its road network, it could not demand for the car to be registered in name of the lessee or an Austrian resident lease company and the fuel consumption tax due must be aligned with the principle of proportionality, and thus reflect, in this case, the duration of the leasing contract.

In *Marie Lindfors*,[163] Ms Lindfors had bought a car in Germany that she had brought into use in the Netherlands, after which she permanently moved to Finland. Ms Lindfors objected against the payment of car tax, arguing it was a consumption tax prohibited under Article 1(1) of Directive 83/183/EEC. The ECJ ruled that, based on the characteristics of the car tax, the chargeable event is the use of a vehicle on Finnish territory, rather than the importation of a vehicle into Finland. Such tax falls outside the scope of Article 1(1) and is therefore permitted. The ECJ however refers it to the national court to decide whether the tax would be allowed in light of Article 18 EC (now: Article 28 TFEU), *i.e.*, the free movement of goods within the territory of the Union.

In joined cases *van Putten c.s.*[164] Mrs van Putten, Mr Mook and Mrs Frank, all Dutch residents, were, during regular checks by the Dutch Tax Authorities, found to using (loaned) cars registered in other Member States on the road network in the Netherlands, without having paid vehicle tax in the Netherlands. All were re- assessed with an amount of vehicle tax without the length of the use of those vehicles having been taken into account. The ECJ first establishes that cross-border rented cars, including those lend free of charge, fall under the freedom of capital movement within the meaning of Article 56 EC (now: Article 63 TFEU). Secondly, loaned vehicles that were registered in the Netherlands would not be subject to the tax, making cross-border movement of capital less attractive and thus, restricting the free movement of capital. The ECJ finally ruled that the vehicle tax may only be levied in the Netherlands in case it takes into account the principle of proportionality, which means it does not allow for the full amount of tax to be due in case the cars are not to be essentially or permanently used in the Netherlands.

In *Vasile Budioan*,[165] Mr Budioan purchased a second-hand motor vehicle that was manufactured and initially registered in Germany. In order to register the vehicle in Romania, environmental stamp duty was due. The ECJ did not find this duty discriminating towards foreign vehicles, but did constitute a breach of Article 110 TFEU in case the tax burden did not take into account any residual tax, included in the value of a second-hand vehicle, that was previously paid and not repaid.

3.7.3 Plastic Tax

Following the (financial) impact of the COVID-19 pandemic, the European Commission presented at the end of May 2020 a financial recovery package under the name Recovery effort under Next Generation (NGEU). These efforts have ultimately led to Council Decision (EU, Euratom) 2020/2053 of 14 December 2020 on the system of own resources of the

163 Case C-365/02, ECLI:EU:C:2004:449.
164 C-578/10, C-579/10 and C-580/10, ECLI:EU:C:2012:246.
165 Case C-586/14, ECLI:EU:C:2016:421.

European Union and repealing Decision 2014/335/EU, Euratom.[166] Based on point 6 of the preamble, to better align the Union's financing instruments with its policy priorities and to better reflect the role of the general budget of the Union in the functioning of the Single Market, the system of own resources is to be reformed and new own resources are to be introduced. Up to that point, traditional own resources comprised of (customs) duty and other duty and levies on the trade with third countries (less 25% collection costs), and a portion of the annual VAT collected, maximized at a fixed percentage of the gross national income of Member States.

Decision 2020/2053 adds to the own resources of the Union a call rate of EUR 0,80 per kilogram to the weight of plastic packaging waste generated in each Member State that is not recycled. According to Article 2(2) of the Directive, the weight of plastic packaging waste that is not recycled shall be calculated as the difference between the weight of the plastic packaging waste generated in a Member State in a given year and the weight of the plastic packaging waste recycled in that year. The contributions will be calculated based on Eurostat data, which typically runs approximately 2,5 years behind. It was therefore agreed that the calculations will be based on forecasts, a method that also applies to other sources of revenue to the EU budget. Once final data becomes available, the contributions are updated accordingly.

It should be highlighted that the addition of a plastic waste related contribution to the own resources of the Union does not give rise to an obligation for Member States to impose a plastic tax on non-recycled waste to be paid by citizens or businesses. While it is expected that Member States are encouraged to reduce packaging waste and stimulate a circular economy, they are free to define the most suitable policies in order to achieve so. Member States are therefore allowed to finance this contribution to the own resources out of their general State budget, which most Member States have announced to do. So far only Italy[167] and Spain have announced plans to introduce a plastic packaging tax in order to finance the contribution to own resources.

3.8 The 2003 Directive on Energy Taxation

At its meeting in April 2003 the Ecofin finally reached political agreement on the text of a Directive on taxation of energy products and electricity, referred to in the communication quoted in the section above. The resulting Directive 2003/96/EC repeals Directives 92/81/EEC and 92/82/EEC, discussed in section 3.4 above, and replaces the excise on mineral oils by taxation on energy products and electricity. For this taxation there is no longer a separate structure and rates directive.

The Directive distinguishes between:

I. The scope (see section 3.8.1);
II. Levels of taxation (see section 3.8.2);
III. Exemptions, reductions and tax refunds (see section 3.8.3);

166 O.J. 2020, L424, p. 1.
167 Dossier 2020 Italian Budget Law, Profili finanziari, A.C. 2305, p. 437.

IV. Holding and movement of products (see section 3.8.4);
V. Chargeable event and chargeability (see section 3.8.5); and
VI. Final provisions (see section 3.8.6).

The minimum levels of taxation as referred to under II are set out in Annex I to the Directive, while the reduced rates and exemptions which Member States may continue to apply are set out in Annex 2.

3.8.1 *The Scope*

Article 1 of Directive 2003/96/EC prescribes that Member States must impose taxation on energy products and electricity in accordance with the Directive.

The products covered are specified in Article 2 with reference to the following CN codes:[168]

(a) products falling within CN codes 1507 to 1518, (*i.e.* various vegetable oils) if these are intended for use as heating fuel or motor fuel;
(b) products falling within CN codes 2701, 2702 and 2704 to 2715 (*i.e.* various mineral fuels, mineral oils and products of their distillation; bituminous substances and mineral waxes);
(c) products falling within CN codes 2901 and 2902 (*i.e.* various hydro-carbons);
(d) products falling within CN code 2905 11 00 (*i.e.* methanol), which are not of synthetic origin, if these are intended for use as heating fuel or motor fuel;
(e) products falling within CN code 3403 (*i.e.* various lubricating preparations);
(f) products falling within CN code 3811 (*i.e.* certain anti-knock preparations);
(g) products falling within CN code 3817 (*i.e.* mixed alkylbenzenes);
(h) products falling within CN code 3824 99 86 (*i.e.*, mixtures consisting mainly of dimethyl methylphosphonate, oxirane and diphosphorus pentaoxide), 3824 99 92 (excluding anti-rust preparations containing amines as active constituents and inorganic composite solvents and thinners for varnishes and similar products), 3824 99 93, 3824 99 96 (*i.e.*, not elsewhere defined chemical products and preparations, excluding anti-rust preparations containing amines as active constituents and inorganic composite solvents and thinners for varnishes and similar products), 3826 00 10 (*i.e.*, fatty-acid mono-alkyl esters; FAMAE) and 3826 00 90 (*i.e.*, other biodiesel en mixtures thereof), if these are intended for use as heating fuel or motor fuel.

The Directive also applies to electricity falling within CN code 2716.[169]

Not for all products mentioned above are minimal levels of taxation specified in Annex I, but when these energy products are intended for use, offered for sale or used as motor fuel

168 A decision to update the codes of the combined nomenclature for the products referred to in the Directive must be taken once every year in accordance with the procedure laid down in Article 27, by the Excise Committee procedure. The decision must not result in any changes in the minimum tax rates applied in the Directive or to the addition or removal of any energy products and electricity.

169 According to the preamble: "As a party to the United Nations Framework Convention on Climate Change, the European Union has ratified the Kyoto Protocol. The taxation of energy products and, where appropriate, electricity is one of the instruments available for achieving the Kyoto objectives".

or heating fuel they must be taxed according to use, at the rate for the equivalent heating fuel or motor fuel. In addition to the taxable products listed above, any product intended for use, offered for sale or used as motor fuel, or as an additive or extender in motor fuels, must be taxed at the rate for the equivalent motor fuel. Also any other hydrocarbon, except for peat, intended for use, offered for sale or used for heating purposes must be taxed at the rate for the equivalent energy product.

Outside the scope of the Directive fall:
(a) output taxation of heat;[170]
(b) products falling within the CN-codes 4401 and 4402, *i.e.* fuel wood and wood charcoal;
(c) energy products used for purposes other than as motor fuels or as heating fuels;
(d) dual use of energy products (an energy product has a dual use when it is used both for heating fuel and for purposes other than as motor fuel and heating fuel. The use of energy products for chemical reduction and in electrolytic and metallurgical processes shall be regarded as dual use);
(e) electricity used principally for the purposes of chemical reduction and in electrolytic and metallurgical processes;
(f) electricity, when it accounts for more than 50% of the cost of a product (cost of a product is defined as the addition of total purchases of goods and services plus personnel costs plus the consumption of fixed capital, at the level of the business, as defined in Article 11 – this cost is calculated per unit on average; the cost of electricity is defined as the actual purchase value of electricity or the cost of production of electricity if it is generated in the business);
(g) mineralogical processes (mineralogical processes means the processes classified in the NACE nomenclature under code DI 26 "manufacture of other non- metallic mineral products" in Council Regulation (EEC) No. 3037/90).[171]

However, the provisions regarding holding and movement of products (see section 3.8.4 below) apply to the energy products, mentioned under (c) to (g).

The title Scope ended with a rather cryptic provision (Art. 3) on "links with Directive 92/12/EC" providing that references in Directive 92/12/EEC to "mineral oils" and "excise duty" (in so far as it applies to mineral oils) must be interpreted as covering all energy products, electricity and national indirect taxes referred to respectively in Articles 2 and 4(2) of the Directive on energy taxation. We understand this provision to mean the following. References to mineral oils in the horizontal Directive cover all energy products, thus, the references in Article 9 of the horizontal Directive (on atypical transportation), Article 15a (on keeping a register), Article 21 (on tax marking in Ireland) and Article 30 (on mutual assistance) were extended from the mineral oils as mentioned in Directive 92/81 to include all energy products and (where appropriate) electricity. Above all the extended definition

170 According to the preamble: "As heat is only subject to very limited intra- community trade, output taxation of heat should remain outside the scope of this Community framework."

171 Now Regulation (EC) No. 1893/2006 of the European Parliament and of the Council of 20 December 2006 establishing the statistical classification of economic activities NACE Revision 2 and amending Council Regulation (EEC) No. 3037/90 as well as certain EC Regulations on specific statistical domains. O.J. 2006, L 393, p. 1.

moves energy products, in so far as they were not covered by the definition of mineral oils, from the ambit of Article 3(3) of the horizontal Directive (Member States shall retain the right to introduce or maintain taxes which are levied on products other than those listed in paragraph 1 provided, however, that those taxes do not give rise to border-crossing formalities in trade between Member States). In the Recast General Arrangements Directive there is only one reference to "mineral oils", in Article 32(4). Provided that this Article refers to excise duty to become due on the acquisition of mineral oils released for consumption in another Member State if these products are transported using atypical modes of transport by or on behalf of a private individual, Article 3 of the Directive on Energy Taxation has become practically obsolete.

Article 4(2) of the Directive on Energy Taxation provides that for the purpose of the Directive on energy products "level of taxation" means the total charge levied in respect of all indirect taxes (except VAT) calculated directly or indirectly on the quantity of energy products and electricity at the time of release for consumption. According to Article 3, references to "excise duties" in the horizontal Directive must be interpreted as covering all these indirect taxes.[172]

3.8.2 *Levels of Taxation*

According to the preamble to the Directive on Energy Taxation, the proper functioning of the internal market and the achievement of the objectives of other Community policies require minimum levels of taxation to be laid down at Community level for most energy products, including electricity, natural gas and coal. Appreciable differences in the national levels of energy taxation applied by Member States could prove detrimental to the proper functioning of the internal market, and the establishment of appropriate Community minimum levels may enable existing differences in the national levels of taxation to be reduced.

Article 4(1) of the Directive prescribes that the levels of taxation which Member States must apply to the energy products and electricity described in section 3.8.1 above may not be less

172 Case C-517/07 (*Afton Chemical Limited*), [2008] ECR I-10427, deals with the question whether Articles 2(3) and 8(1) of Directive 92/81 and Article 2(3) and (4) of Directive 2003/96 are to be interpreted as meaning that fuel additives which are 'mineral oils' within the meaning of Article 2(1) of Directive 92/81 or 'energy products' within the meaning of Article 2(1) of Directive 2003/96, but which are not intended for use, offered for sale or used as motor fuel, must be made subject to the taxation regime imposed by those Directives. According to the ECJ it follows from the wording of the first sentence of the first subparagraph of Article 2(3) of Directive 92/ 81 and the second subparagraph of Article 2(3) of Directive 2003/96 and from the general scheme and purpose of those two directives that those provisions are intended to cover any product used as an additive, whether or not it is a 'mineral oil' or 'energy product' within the meaning of those directives. That conclusion cannot be undetermined by the provisions of Article 8(1)(a) of Directive 92/81 or Article 2(4)(b) of Directive 2003/96, according to which mineral oils and energy products, used for purposes other than as motor fuels or heating fuels, must, respectively, be exempt from the harmonised excise duty or excluded from the scope of Directive 2003/96. Indeed, to apply those provisions to fuel additives, such as those at issue, which are subject to an express requirement for taxation under the first sentence of the first subparagraph of Article 2(3) of Directive 92/81 and the second subparagraph of Article 2(3) of Directive 2003/96 would deprive those provisions of any useful effect.

than the in the Directive prescribed minimum levels.[173] "Level of taxation" means the total charge levied in respect of all indirect taxes (except VAT) calculated directly or indirectly on the quantity of energy products and electricity at the time of release for consumption.[174] The minimum levels of taxation are set for the period starting 1 January 2004 and for the period starting 1 January 2010. Based on the second paragraph of Article 7(1), the Council should have unanimously decided on the minimum levels to apply from 1 January 2013 onwards ultimately on 1 January 2012 – which it never did. At the time of writing, therefore, the minimum levels that were set for the period starting 1 January 2010, still apply.

Before prescribing the minimum levels for motor fuels, heating fuels and electricity, the Directive stipulates that differentiated rates of taxation may be applied by Member States, provided that they respect the minimum levels of taxation set out in the Directive and that they are compatible with Community law, in the following cases:
- when the differentiated rates are directly linked to product quality;
- when the differentiated rates depend on quantitative consumption levels for electricity and energy products used for heating purposes;
- for the following uses: local public passenger transport (including taxis), waste collection, armed forces and public administration, disabled people, ambulances;
- between business and non-business use for energy products referred to in Article 9 and 10, *i.e.* heating fuels and electricity (see section 3.8.2.2 and section 3.8.2.3 below).

3.8.2.1 Motor Fuels

According to Article 7(1) as from 1 January 2010, the minimum levels of taxation applicable to motor fuels must be fixed as set in Annex 1.A.

Leaded petrol[1] (in euro per 1,000 l)	421
Unleaded petrol[2] (in euro per 1,000 l)	359
Gas oil[3] (in euro per 1,000 l)	330
Kerosene[4] (in euro per 1,000 l)	330
LPG[5] (in euro per 1,000 kg)	125
Natural gas[6] (in euro per gigajoule)	2,6

1 CN codes 2710 12 31, 2710 12 51 and 2710 12 59.
2 CN codes 2710 12 31, 2710 12 41, 2710 12 45 and 2710 12 49.
3 CN codes 2710 19 43 to 2710 19 48 and 2710 20 11 to 2710 20 19.
4 CN codes 2710 19 21 and 2710 19 25.
5 CN codes 2711 12 11 to 2711 19 00.
6 CN codes 2711 11 00 and 2711 21 00.

Member States may differentiate between commercial and non-commercial use of gas oil used as propellant, provided that the new Community minimum levels are observed

173 For a waiver of the minimum levels see sections 3.8.3.1 and 3.8.3.2.
174 According to the preamble: "Member States wish to introduce or retain different types of taxation on energy products and electricity. To that end, Member States should be permitted to comply with the Community minimum taxation levels by taking into account the total charge levied in respect of all indirect taxes, which they have chosen to apply (excluding VAT)".

and the rate for commercial gas oil used as propellant does not fall below the national level of taxation in force on 1 January 2003, notwithstanding any derogations for the use laid in the Directive.[175]

Commercial gas oil used as propellant means gas oil used as propellant for the following commercial purposes:

(a) the carriage of goods for hire or reward, or on own account, by motor vehicles or articulated vehicle combinations intended exclusively for the carriage of goods by road and with a maximum permissible gross laden weight of not less than 7.5 tonnes;

(b) the carriage of passengers, whether by regular or occasional service, by a motor vehicle of category M2 or category M3, as defined in Directive 70/156/EEC, including taxis.[176]

Notwithstanding this provision the minimum levels of taxation applicable to products used as motor fuel for specific purposes must, according to Article 8, be fixed as set in Annex 1.B:

Gas oil (in euro per 1,000 l)	21
Kerosene (in euro per 1,000 l)	21
LPG (in euro per 1,000 kg)	41
Natural gas (in euro per gigajoule)	0,3

The specific industrial and commercial purposes are:

(a) for agricultural, horticultural or piscicultural works, and in forestry;

(b) for stationary motors;[177]

(c) in respect of plant and machinery used in construction, civil engineering and public works;[178]

(d) for vehicles intended for use off the public roadway or which have not been granted authorization for use mainly on the public highway.

3.8.2.2 *Heating Fuels*

According to Article 9, as from 1 January 2004, the minimum levels of taxation applicable to heating fuels must be fixed as set in Annex 1.C (business use and non- business use):

175 Member States which introduce a system of road user charges for motor vehicles or articulated vehicle combinations intended exclusively for the carriage of goods by road may apply a reduced rate on gas oil used by such vehicles, that goes below the national level of taxation in force on 1 January 2003, as long as the overall tax burden remains broadly equivalent, provided that the Community minimum levels are observed and that the national level of taxation in force on 1 January 2003 for gas oil used as propellant is at least twice as high as the minimum level of taxation applicable on 1 January 2004.

176 This Directive describes category M as follows. Category M: Motor vehicles having at least four wheels, or having three wheels when the maximum weight exceeds 1 metric ton, and used for the carriage of passengers.
- Category M2: Vehicles used for the carriage of passengers, comprising more than eight seats in addition to the driver's seat, and having a maximum weight not exceeding 5 metric tons.
- Category M3: Vehicles used for the carriage of passengers, comprising more than eight seats in addition to the driver's seat, and having a maximum weight exceeding 5 metric tons.

177 With regard to specific reductions for business use, see Article 17 in section 3.8.3.

178 Idem.

Gas oil (in euro per 1,000 l)	21	21
Heavy fuel oil[1] (in euro per 1,000 kg)	15	15
Kerosene (in euro per 1,000 l)	0	0
LPG (in euro per 1,000 kg)	0	0
Natural gas (in euro per gigajoule)	0,15	0,3
Coal and coke[2] (in euro per gigajoule)	0,15	0,3

1 CN codes 2710 19 62 to 2710 19 68 and 2710 20 31 to 2710 20 39.
2 CN codes 2701, 2702 and 2704.

Member States, which on 1 January 2003 are authorized to apply a monitoring charge for heating gas oil, may continue to apply a reduced rate of euro 10 per 1000 litres for that product. This authorization will be repealed on 1 January 2007 if the Council, acting unanimously on the basis of a Commission report and a proposal, so decides, having noted that the level of the reduced rate is too low to avoid problems of trade distortion between the Member States.

Business use is defined in Article 11. It refers to the use by a business entity,[179] which independently carries out, in any place, the supply of goods and services, whatever the purpose or results of such economic activities. The economic activities comprise all activities of producers, traders and persons supplying services including mining and agricultural activities and activities of the professions.

States, regional and local government authorities and other bodies governed by public law may not be considered as a business in respect of the activities or transactions in which they engage as public authorities. However, when they engage in such activities or transactions, they must be considered as a business in respect of these activities or transactions where treatment as non-business would lead to significant distortions of competition.

Where mixed use takes place, taxation must apply in proportion to each type of use, although where either the business or non-business use is insignificant, it may be treated as nil.
Member States may limit the scope of the reduced level of taxation for business use.

3.8.2.3 *Electricity*

According to Article 10, as from 1 January 2004, the minimum levels of taxation[180] applicable to electricity must be fixed as set in Annex 1.C (business use and non-business use):

179 A business entity cannot be considered as smaller than a part of a company or a legal body that from an organizational point of view constitutes an independent business, that is to say an entity capable of functioning by its own means.

180 With regard to the exemption of energy products and electricity used to produce electricity Member States may, for reasons of environmental policy, subject these products to taxation without having to respect the minimum levels of taxation laid down in this Directive. In such case, the taxation of these products may not be taken into account for the purpose of satisfying the minimum level of taxation on electricity laid down in Article 10. (See Article 14(1)(a).)

Electricity[1] (in euro per MWh)	0,5	1,0

1 CN code 2716.

With regard to the definition of business use, see section 3.8.2.2 above. It should be noted that electricity used principally for the purposes of chemical reduction and in electrolytic and metallurgical processes and electricity, when it accounts for more than 50% of the cost of a product fall outside the scope of the Directive. (Cost of a product is defined as the addition of total purchases of goods and services plus personnel costs plus the consumption of fixed capital, at the level of the business, as defined in Article 11, see section 3.8.2.2. This cost is calculated per unit on average. The cost of electricity is defined as the actual purchase value of electricity or the cost of production of electricity if it is generated in the business.)

According to Article 10(2), above the minimum levels of taxation referred to above, Member States will have the option of determining the applicable tax base provided that they respect Directive 92/12/EEC on the general arrangements for products subject to excise duty and on the holding, movement and monitoring of such products (now the Recast General Arrangements Directive 2020/262/EU). See also the consideration in the preamble: "Member States wish to introduce or retain different types of taxation on energy products and electricity. To that end, Member States should be permitted to comply with the Community minimum taxation levels by taking into account the total charge levied in respect of all indirect taxes, which they have chosen to apply (excluding VAT)".

3.8.3 *Exemptions, Reductions and Tax Refunds*

According to Article 6 Member States are free to give effect to the exemptions or reductions in the level of taxation in the Directive either:
(a) directly;
(b) by means of a differentiated rate; or
(c) by refunding all or part of the amount of taxation.[181]

The title exemptions and tax refunds makes a distinction between compulsory and facultative exemptions.

3.8.3.1 *Compulsory Exemptions and Tax Refunds*

According to Article 14, Member States must exempt:

181 According to Article 21(4), Member States may provide that taxation on energy products shall become due when it is established that a final use condition laid down in national rules for the purpose of a reduced level of taxation or exemption is not or is no longer fulfilled.

(a) energy products and electricity used to produce electricity[182] and electricity to maintain the ability to produce electricity;[183]
(b) energy products supplied for use as fuel for the purpose of air navigation other than private pleasure-flying;
(c) energy products supplied for use as fuel for the purposes of navigation within Community waters (including fishing), other than private pleasure craft.

With regard to the exemption of energy products and electricity used to produce electricity Member States may, for reasons of environmental policy, subject these products to taxation without having to respect the minimum levels of taxation laid down in this Directive. In such case, the taxation of these products may not be taken into account for the purpose of satisfying the minimum level of taxation on electricity laid down in Article 10.

With regard to the exemption[184] of energy products supplied for use as fuels for the purpose of air navigation other than private pleasure-flying[185] and the exemption of energy products supplied for use as fuel for the purposes of navigation within Community waters (including fishing), other than private pleasure craft,[186] Member States may limit the scope of the exemptions to international and intra- Community transport. In addition, where a Member State has entered into a bilateral agreement with another Member State, it may also waive the exemptions. In such cases, Member States may apply a level of taxation below the minimum level set out in the Directive.

182 Article 14(1) gives the responsibility to the Member States for laying down the conditions for the exemption, to ensure correct and straightforward application and to prevent any evasion, avoidance or abuse. It follows from the Case C-355/14 (*Polihim-SS*), [2016] ECLI:EU:C:2016:403 however, that when exercising the power to lay down these conditions, the Member States must comply with the general principles of law, including the principle of proportionality. In the *Polihim-SS* case, heavy fuel oils were sold by Polihim to Petros Oyl OOD and subsequently by Petros Oyl OOD to TETS Bobov dol EAD. The goods were delivered directly from Polihim to TETS Bobov and used by the latter to generate electricity. The exemption applied by Polihim was challenged by the Bulgarian customs authorities on the basis that Petros Oyl did not have the status of end-user exempt from excise duty. The ECJ ruled that denying the exemption on such basis goes beyond what is necessary to ensure the correct and straightforward application of those exemptions and to prevent any evasion, avoidance or abuse.

183 According to Article 21, an entity producing electricity for its own use is regarded as a distributor. Notwithstanding Article 14(1)(a), Member States may exempt such small producers of electricity provided that they tax the energy products used for the production of that electricity.

184 Member States may limit the scope of this exemption to supplies of jet fuel (CN code 2710 19 21).

185 For the purposes of this Directive 'private pleasure-flying' means the use of an aircraft by its owner or the natural or legal person who enjoys its use either through hire or through any other means, for other than commercial purposes and in particular other than for the carriage of passengers or goods or for the supply of services for consideration or for the purposes of public authorities.

186 For the purposes of this Directive 'private pleasure craft' means any craft used by its owner or the natural or legal person who enjoys its use either through hire or through any other means, for other than commercial purposes and in particular other than for the carriage of passengers or goods or for the supply of services for consideration or for the purposes of public authorities.

3.8.3.2 Facultative Exemptions and Reductions

Article 14 of the Directive provides for facultative exemptions or reductions. Member States may apply total or partial exemptions or reductions in the level of taxation to:[187]

(a) taxable products used under fiscal control in the field of pilot projects for the technological development of more environmentally-friendly products or in relation to fuels from renewable resources;

(b) electricity:
- of solar, wind, wave, tidal or geothermal origin;
- of hydraulic origin produced in hydroelectric installations;
- generated from biomass or from products produced from biomass;
- generated from methane emitted by abandoned coalmines;
- generated from fuel cells;[188]

(c) energy products and electricity used for combined heat and power generation;

(d) electricity produced from combined heat and power generation, provided that that the combined generators are environmentally friendly. Member States may apply national definitions of "environmentally friendly" (or high efficiency) cogeneration production until the Council on the basis of a report and a proposal from the Commission unanimously adopt a common definition;

(e) energy products and electricity used for the carriage of goods and passengers by rail, tram and trolley;

(f) energy products supplied for use as fuel for navigation on inland waterways (including fishing) other than in private pleasure craft and electricity produced on board a craft;

(g) natural gas in Member States in which the share of natural gas in final energy was less than 15% in year 2000. The total or partial exemptions or reductions may apply for a maximum period of ten years after the entry into force of the present directive or until the national share of natural gas in final energy reaches 25%, whichever is the soonest. However, as soon as the national share of natural gas in final energy reaches 20%, the Member States concerned must apply a strictly positive level of taxation, which must increase on a yearly basis in order to reach at least the minimum rate at the end of the period referred to above;

(h) electricity, natural gas, coal and solid fuels used by households and by organizations recognized as charitable by the Member State concerned In the case of such charitable organizations, Member States may confine the exemption or reduction to use for the purpose of non-business activities. Where mixed use takes place, taxation shall apply in proportion to each type of use. If a use is insignificant, it may be treated as nil;

187 In Case C-226/07 (*Flughafen Köln/Bonn GmbH*), [2008] ECR I-5999, the ECJ held that the unconditional nature of an obligation to grant an exemption cannot be affected at all by the degree of latitude afforded to Member States by introductory wording such as that contained in Article 14(1) of Directive 2003/96, according to which exemptions are granted by those States 'under conditions which they shall lay down for the purpose of ensuring the correct and straightforward application of such exemptions and of preventing any evasion, avoidance or abuse'. A Member State may not rely, as against a taxpayer who is able to show that his tax position actually falls within one of the categories of exemption laid down in a directive, on its failure to adopt the very provisions which are intended to facilitate the application of that exemption.

188 Member States may also refund to the producer some or all of the amount of tax paid by the consumer on electricity produced from these products.

(i) natural gas and LPG used as propellants;
(j) motor fuels used in the field of the manufacture, development, testing and maintenance of aircraft and ships;
(k) motor fuels used for dredging operations in navigable waterways and in ports;
(l) products falling within CN code 2705 (*i.e.* coal gas, water gas, producer gas and similar gases, other than petroleum gases and other gaseous hydrocarbons) used for heating purposes.

Member States may apply a level of taxation down to zero to energy products and electricity used for agricultural, horticultural or piscicultural works, and in forestry.[189]

Article 16 of the Directive on Energy Taxation allows Member States to apply an exemption or a reduced rate on biofuels and other products produced from biomass,[190] provided such products are made up or contain certain specified products. This exemption or a reduced rate may be applied to all energy products as defined in Article 2 where such products contain water.

The exemption or reduction in excise duty resulting from the application of the reduced rate may not be greater than the amount of excise duty payable on the volume of the specified products present in the products eligible for the reduction. The levels of taxation applied by Member States on the products made up of or containing the specified products may be lower than the minimum as specified in Article 4.

Article 17 of the Directive on Energy Taxation provides for specific reductions for business use. Provided the minimum levels of taxation prescribed in the Directive are respected in average for each business, Member States may apply tax reductions on consumption of electricity and energy products used for heating purposes or for specific industrial and commercial purposes for stationary motors and in respect of plant and machinery used in construction, civil engineering and public works (see section 3.8.2.1 above) in the following cases:
(a) in favour of energy-intensive business;
(b) where agreements are concluded with undertakings or associations of undertakings, or equivalent arrangements, as far as they lead to the achievement of environmental protection objectives or to improvements in energy efficiency.

An energy-intensive business is defined as a business entity where either the purchases of energy products and electricity amounts to at least 3.0% of the production value or the national energy tax payable amounts to at least 0.5% of the added value. Within this definition, Member States may apply more restrictive concepts, including sales value, process and sector definitions.

189 On the basis of a proposal from the Commission, the Council shall before 1 January 2008 examine if the possibility of applying a level of taxation down to zero shall be repealed.
190 'Biomass' means the biodegradable fraction of products, waste and residues from agriculture (including vegetal and animal substances), forestry and related industries, as well as the biodegradable fraction of industrial and municipal waste.

Purchases of energy products are defined as the actual cost of energy purchased or generated within the business. Only electricity, heat and energy products that are used for heating purposes or for the purposes of Article 8(2)(b) and (c) (*i.e.* specific industrial and commercial purposes for stationary motors and in respect of plant and machinery used in construction, civil engineering and public works) are included. All taxes are included, except deductible VAT.

Production value is defined as turnover, including subsidies directly linked to the price of the product, plus or minus the changes in stocks of finished products, work in progress and goods and services purchased for resale, minus the purchases of goods and services for resale.

Value added is defined as the total turnover liable to VAT included export sales minus the total purchase liable to VAT included imports.

Member States may apply a level of taxation down to zero to energy products and electricity, when used by energy-intensive businesses as defined above.

Member States may apply a level of taxation down to 50% of the minimum levels in this Directive to energy products and electricity, when used by businesses entities, which are not energy-intensive as defined above.

Businesses that benefit from those possibilities must enter into the agreements, tradable permit schemes or equivalent arrangements as referred to under (b). The agreements, tradable permit schemes or equivalent arrangements must lead to the achievement of environmental objectives or increased energy efficiency, broadly equivalent to what would have been achieved if the standard Community minimum rates had been observed.

Under the title "Transitional Periods and Arrangements", Article 18 of the Directive on Energy Taxation authorizes Member States to continue to apply the reductions in levels of taxation or exemptions set out in Annex II to the Directive. Subject to a prior review by the Council, on the basis of a proposal from the Commission this authorization will expire on 31 December 2006 or on the date specified in Annex II. Article 18 also allows lower levels of taxation on specific products during transitional periods to Spain, Austria, Belgium, Luxembourg, Portugal, Greece, Ireland, France, Italy, Germany and the Netherlands. Within the transitional periods established, Member States must progressively reduce their gap with respect to the new minimum levels of taxation.

In addition to the differentiations allowed in Article 5, to the facultative exemptions or reductions permitted in Article 15 and to the specific reductions for business use allowed under Article 17, the Council may, according to Article 19, authorize any Member State to introduce further exemptions or reductions for specific policy considerations.[191]

3.8.4 Holding and Movement of Products

Article 20 of the Directive on Energy Taxation lists the energy products[192] which fall under the provisions on holding and movement of products in now the Recast General Arrangements Directive 2020/262/EU.[193] If a Member State finds that energy products other than those listed including electricity are intended for use, offered for sale or used as heating fuel or motor fuel or are otherwise giving rise to evasion, avoidance or abuse, it must advise the Commission forthwith. The Commission will transmit the communication to the other Member States within one month of receipt. A decision as to whether the products in question should be made subject to the control and movement provisions will then be taken in accordance with the Committee procedure laid down in Article 27 of the Directive on Energy Taxation.

3.8.5 Chargeable Event and Chargeability

The Recast General Arrangements Directive 2020/262/EU provides that excise products are subject to excise duty at the time of their production within, or importation into the territory of the Community. According to Article 21 of the Directive on Energy Taxation, in addition to the general provisions defining the chargeable event and the provisions for payment set out in the Recast General Arrangements Directive 2020/262/EU, the amount of taxation on energy products also becomes due on the occurrence of one of the chargeable events mentioned in Article 2(3) of the Directive on Energy Taxation, *i.e.* products for which no minimal levels of taxation are specified in Annex 1, but when these energy products are intended for use, offered for sale or used as motor fuel or heating fuel they must be

191 On 5 October 2006, the ECJ gave its judgment in Case C-368/04 (*Transalpine Ölleitung in Österreich a.o.*), [2006] ECR I-9957, dealing with state aid and partial rebate on energy taxes, failure to give notice of the aid and the powers of national courts and tribunals. The ECJ ruled that the last sentence of Article 88(3) EC (now Article 108 TFEU) must be interpreted as meaning that it is for the national courts to safeguard the rights of individuals against possible disregard, by the national authorities, of the prohibition on putting aid into effect before the Commission of the EC has adopted a decision authorising that aid. In doing so, the national court must take the Community interest fully into consideration and must not adopt a measure which would have the sole effect of extending the circle of recipients of the aid. Since a decision of the Commission declaring aid that has not been notified compatible with the common market does not have the effect of regularising *ex post facto* implementing measures which, at the time of their adoption, were invalid because they had been taken in disregard of the prohibition referred to in the last sentence of Article 88(3) EC, it is of little consequence whether an application is made before or after adoption of the decision declaring the aid compatible with the common market, since that application relates to the unlawful situation resulting from the lack of notification.

192 Article 20 also applies to the energy products which fall otherwise outside the scope of the directive, see section 3.8.1 above.

193 Member States may, pursuant to bilateral arrangements, dispense with some or all of the control measures set out in Title II and III of (now) the Recast General Arrangements Directive 2020/262/EU in respect of some or all of the listed products, in so far as they are not motor fuels covered by Article 7 of the Directive. Such arrangements will not affect Member States who are not party to them. All such bilateral arrangements must be notified to the Commission, which informs the other Member States.

taxed according to use, at the rate for the equivalent heating fuel or motor fuel. In addition, any product intended for use, offered for sale or used as motor fuel, or as an additive or extender in motor fuels, must be taxed at the rate for the equivalent motor fuel. Also any other hydrocarbon, except for peat, intended for use, offered for sale or used for heating purposes shall be taxed at the rate for the equivalent energy product.

According to Article 21 of the Directive on Energy Taxation, the word "production" in now Articles 3(6) and 6(1)(a) Recast General Arrangements Directive 2020/262/EU shall be deemed to include "extraction", when appropriate. Member States need not treat as "production of energy products":

(a) operations during which small quantities of energy products are obtained incidentally;
(b) operations by which the user of an energy product makes its re-use possible in his own undertaking provided that the excise duty already paid on such product is not less than the excise duty which would be due if the re-used energy product were again to be liable to excise duty;
(c) the operation consisting of mixing, outside a production establishment or a bonded warehouse, energy products with other energy products or other materials, provided:
  (i) that excise duty on the components has been paid previously (this condition does not apply where the mixture is exempt for a specific use); and
  (ii) that the amount paid is not less than the amount of the excise duty which would be chargeable on the mixture.

The consumption of energy products within the curtilage of an establishment producing energy products may not be considered as a chargeable event giving rise to taxation if the consumption consists of energy products produced within the curtilage of the establishment. Member States may also consider the consumption of electricity and other energy products not produced within the curtilage of such an establishment and the consumption of energy products and electricity within the curtilage of an establishment producing fuels to be used for generation of electricity as not giving rise to a chargeable event. Where the consumption is for purposes not related to the production of energy products and in particular for the propulsion of vehicles, this must be considered a chargeable event, giving rise to taxation.

According to Article 6(1) of the Recast General Arrangements Directive 2020/262/ EU, excise products are subject to excise duty at the time of their production within the territory of the Community or of their importation into that territory. According to Article 6(2), excise duty shall become chargeable at the time of release for consumption or when shortages are recorded which must be subject to excise duty.

According to Article 21(5) of the Directive on Energy Taxation, for the purpose of applying now Article 6 of the Recast General Arrangements Directive 2020/262/ EU, electricity, and natural gas, are subject to excise duty and becomes chargeable at the time of supply by the distributor[194] or redistributor. Where the delivery to consumption takes place in a Member State where the distributor or redistributor is not established, the tax of the

194 An entity producing electricity for its own use is regarded as a distributor. Notwithstanding Article 14(1)(a), Member States may exempt such small producers of electricity provided that they tax the energy products used for the production of that electricity. See section 3.3.1 above.

Member States of delivery will be chargeable to a company that has to be registered in the Member State of delivery. Tax is in all cases levied and collected according to procedures laid down by each Member State. However, Member States have the right to determine the chargeable event, in the case where there are no connections between their gas pipe lines and those of other Member States.

For the purpose of applying (now) Article 6 of the Recast General Arrangements Directive 2020/262/EU, coal, coke and lignite must be subject to taxation and become chargeable at the time of delivery by companies, which have to be registered for that purpose by the relevant authorities. Those authorities may allow the producer, trader, importer or fiscal representative to substitute the registered company for the fiscal obligations imposed upon it. Tax is levied and collected according to procedures laid down by each Member State.

According to Article 22 of the Directive on Energy Taxation, when taxation rates are changed, stocks of energy products already released for consumption may be subject to an increase in or a reduction of the taxation.

Article 23 of the Directive on Energy Taxation provides that Member States may refund the amounts of taxation already paid on contaminated or accidentally mixed energy products sent back to a tax warehouse for recycling.

Finally, Article 24 of the Directive on Energy Taxation provides that energy products released for consumption in a Member State, contained in the standard tanks[195] of commercial motor vehicles and intended to be used as fuel by those same vehicles as well as in special containers[196] and intended to be used for the operation, during the course of transport, of the systems equipping those same containers are not subject to taxation in any other Member State.

3.8.6 *Final Provisions*

Under the title 'Final Provisions' the Directive on Energy Taxation prescribes that Member States must inform the Commission of the levels of taxation which they apply and on the of measures taken with regard to differentiated rates, limitations of the exemption on energy products for air navigation and navigation within Community waters, facultative exemptions or reductions and specific reductions for business purposes. Such measures

195 'Standard tanks' means:

- the tanks permanently fixed by the manufacturer to all motor vehicles of the same type as the vehicle in question and whose permanent fitting enables fuel to be used directly, both the purpose of propulsion and, where appropriate, for the operation, during transport, of refrigeration systems and other systems. Gas tanks fitted to motor vehicles designed for the direct use of gas as a fuel and tanks fitted to the other systems with which the vehicle may be equipped shall also be considered to be standard tanks;
- tanks permanently fixed by the manufacturer to all containers of the same type as the container in question and whose permanent fitting enables fuel to be used directly for the operation, during transport, of the refrigeration systems and other systems with which special containers are equipped.

196 'Special container' means any container fitted with specially designed apparatus for refrigeration systems, oxygenation systems, thermal insulation systems or other systems.

might constitute State aid and in those cases have to be notified to the Commission pursuant to Article 108 TFEU. Information provided to the Commission on the basis of the Directive on Energy Taxation does not free Member States from the notification obligation pursuant to Art.108 TFEU.

The obligation to inform the Commission does not free Member States from any notification obligations arising pursuant to the provisions of Directive 83/189/EEC laying down a procedure for the provision of information in the field of technical standards and regulations.[197]

Member States had to bring into force the laws, regulations and administrative provisions necessary to comply with the Directive not later than 31 December 2003.[198] The provisions with regard to biofuels and other products produced from biomass and the transitional arrangements (see section 3.8.3.2) could be applied by the Member States from 1 January 2003.

197 O.J. 1983, L 109, p. 8.

198 On 5 October 2006, the ECJ handed down its decision in Case C-360/05 (*Commission v. Italy*), [2006] ECR I-104*, dealing with the fact that Italy has failed to implement Directive 2003/96/EC. The ECJ declared that by failing to adopt, within the prescribed time limit, the laws, regulations and administrative provisions necessary to comply with Council Directive 2003/96/EC of 27 October 2003 restructuring the Community framework for the taxation of energy products and electricity, the Italian State has failed to fulfil its obligations under that directive.

CHAPTER 4

Administrative Cooperation in the field of indirect taxes

Update by Marie Lamensch and Madeleine Merkx

4.1 Legal Basis: 'Internal Market' or 'Fiscal' provisions?

The adoption of harmonized legislation concerning administrative cooperation in indirect tax matters is subject to the unanimity rule in accordance with Article 113 TFEU. The question had been raised whether qualified majority voting should not apply instead of the unanimity requirement for tax measures, as the purpose of administrative cooperation 'is confined to building bridges between tax administrations.'

In the *Gibraltar* case,[1] the ECJ considered

> '44 provisions which merely require cooperation between the Member States, leaving each of them to use their own methods of enquiry and communication of information, cannot be regarded as "acts on the harmonisation of legislation of Member States concerning turnover taxes" within the meaning of Article 28 of the Act of Accession.'

However, in *Commission v. Council*,[2] the ECJ decided that:

> '63 With regard to the interpretation of the words "fiscal provisions", there is nothing in the Treaty to indicate how that concept should be construed. It is, however, necessary to point out that, by reason of their general character, those words cover not only all areas of taxation, without drawing any distinction between the types of duties or taxes concerned, but also all aspects of taxation, whether material rules or procedural rules.
>
> 64 This is also corroborated by the fact that in certain Member States the provisions governing the arrangements for payment and collection of direct and indirect taxes are treated as being "fiscal provisions".
>
> 65 It should further be added that, in accordance with the Court's case-law on Article 90 EC [now 110 TFEU; *authors*], it is necessary, for the purposes of assessing whether or not a system of taxation is discriminatory, to take into consideration not only the rate of tax but also the basis of assessment and the detailed rules for levying the various duties. The decisive criterion for purposes of comparison with a view to the application of Article 90 EC is the actual effect of each tax on domestic production, on the one hand, and on imported products, on the other. Even where the rate is the same, the effect of the tax may vary according to the detailed rules for the assessment and collection thereof applied to domestic

1 Case C-349/03 (*Commission v. UK* (Gibraltar)), [2005] ECR I-7321.
2 Case C-338/01 (*Commission v. Council*), [2004] ECR I-4829.

production and imported products (*Commission v. Ireland*, paragraph 8, and *Grundig Italiana*, paragraph 13, cited above).

66 It follows that the detailed arrangements for the collection of taxes of whatever kind cannot be disassociated from the system of taxation or imposition of which they form part.

67 In the light of those considerations, the words "fiscal provisions" contained in Article 95(2) EC [now 114(2) TFEU; *authors*] must be interpreted as covering not only the provisions determining taxable persons, taxable transactions, the basis of imposition, and rates of and exemptions from direct and indirect taxes, but also those relating to arrangements for the collection of such taxes.'

Accordingly, not only provisions on recovery assistance, but also the rules on assessment assistance are 'fiscal provisions' in the meaning of Article 114(2) TFEU, implying that all EU legislation affecting them must be adopted unanimously.

In 2019 the Commission suggested in a Communication to the European Parliament, the European Council and the Council,[3] to move to qualified majority in certain tax matters, including – and as one of the priorities – for what concerns administrative cooperation,[4] by using either Article 116 TFEU or Article 325 of the TFEU or the Passerelle clauses (Articles 48(7) and 192(2) TFEU). Unsurprisingly the Member States are extremely reluctant to such a move, and no agreement has yet been reached (no formal Proposal by the Commission has actually been submitted).

4.2 The Recovery Assistance Directive (applicable for direct and indirect taxes)

4.2.1 *History, Main Features, Scope*

With growing mobility and European economic integration, Member States recognized that it was increasingly likely that their (tax) debtors, or the recoverable assets of these debtors, were not within their own jurisdiction, but within the jurisdiction of another Member State. Recovery assistance thus became politically feasible.[5] The 1977 Assistance Directive (initially) only provided for the assistance for the assessment of taxes, not for their recovery.[6] For the latter purpose, an existing directive on the recovery of the traditional own resources of the Union was made suitable. The scope of that Directive, on mutual

3 https://ec.europa.eu/taxation_customs/sites/taxation/files/15_01_2019_communication_towards_a_more_efficient_democratic_decision_making_eu_tax_policy_en.pdf.

4 And eventually on more substantive issues such as the VAT definitive system (see Section XX).

5 See, a.o., Marius Vascega and Servaas van Thiel, 'Council Adopts New Directive on Mutual Assistance in Recovery of Tax and Similar Claims,' *European Taxation*, June 2010, p. 231-237. For a discussion of the reasons for the new Directive, see Ilse De Troyer, 'A European Perspective on Tax Recovery in Cross-Border Situations', *EC Tax Review* 2009/5, p. 211-220.

6 COUNCIL DIRECTIVE of 19 December 1977 concerning mutual assistance by the competent authorities of the Member States in the fields of direct taxation and value added tax (77/799/EEC), OJ L 336, 27.12.1977, p. 15.

assistance in the recovery of agricultural subsidies, agricultural levies, and customs duties,[7] was extended first, in 1979, to cover VAT and excises,[8] and later, in 2001, to also cover direct taxes.[9] In 2008, this Directive and its amendments were codified to make it more accessible.[10] Detailed implementation rules were laid down at first in a Commission Directive of 9 December 2002,[11] and later, after the 2008 recasting of the Recovery Directive, in a Commission Regulation.[12] The detailed implementation arrangements concern, *inter alia*, the electronic communication system, deadlines for responses, administrative procedures, and reimbursement arrangements for costs connected to the recovery of debts.

Still, the Directive proved to be insufficient to meet the needs caused by greater taxpayer and capital mobility. Only 5% of the requests for recovery actually lead to recovery. Fraud and budgetary losses were soaring. Important adaptations were needed, both extending the scope of the directive and making recovery assistance more practicable, effective and efficient. This called for a new directive rather than for (again) amending the existing one.

On 16 March 2010, the Council agreed on such a new directive,[13] to be implemented before 1 January 2012 (hereafter the Recovery Assistance Directive or RAD).

The Recovery Assistance Directive covers claims relating to:
(i) *all* taxes and duties of any kind levied by Member States and their territorial or administrative subdivisions, or levied on behalf of the EU,
(ii) EU agricultural refunds, interventions, and the like, and
(iii) levies and duties emanating from the common sugar market organisation (Art. 2(1) RAD), as well as
(iv) connected administrative penalties, fines, fees and surcharges,
(v) fees for connected certificates or documents, and

7 Council Directive 76/308/EEC of 15 March 1976 on mutual assistance for the recovery of claims resulting from operations forming part of the system of financing the European Agricultural Guidance and Guarantee Fund, and of agricultural levies and customs duties, O.J. No. L 73 of 19 March 1976, p. 18.

8 Council Directive 79/1071/EEC of 6 December 1979 amending Directive 76/ 308/EEC on mutual assistance for the recovery of [etc.], O.J. No. L 331 of 27 December 1979, p. 10.

9 Council Directive 2001/44/EC of 15 June 2001 amending Directive 76/308/EEC on mutual assistance for the recovery of claims resulting from operations forming part of the system of financing the European Agricultural Guidance and Guarantee Fund, and of agricultural levies and customs duties and in respect of value added tax and certain excise duties, O.J. No. L 175 of 28 June 2001, p. 17-20.

10 Council Directive 2008/55/EC of 26 May 2008 on mutual assistance for the recovery of claims relating to certain levies, duties, taxes and other measures (Codified version), O.J. No. L 150, of 10 June 2008, p. 28.

11 Commission Directive 2002/94/EC of 9 December 2002 laying down detailed rules for implementing certain provision of Council Directive 76/308/EEC on mutual assistance for the recovery of claims relating to certain levies, duties, taxes and other measures, O.J. No. L 337, p. 41-45.

12 Commission Regulation (EC) No 1179/2008 of 28 November 2008 laying down detailed rules for implementing certain provisions of Council Directive 2008/55/EC on mutual assistance for the recovery of claims relating to certain levies, duties, taxes and other measures, O.J. No. L 319, of 29 November 2008, p. 21.

13 Council Directive 2010/24/EU of 16 March 2010 concerning mutual assistance for the recovery of claims relating to taxes, duties and other measures, O.J. No. L 84, of 31 March 2010, p. 1.

(vi) related interest and costs (Art. 2(2) RAD).

The Recovery Assistance Directive does therefore apply to both direct and indirect taxes but does not apply to compulsory social security contributions, other fees than referred to in paragraph 2, and contractual dues and criminal penalties (Art. 2(3) RAD). A very wide definition of 'person' is laid down, including trusts, foundations, investment funds, contractual partnerships and other 'legal arrangements' owning or managing assets, which, including the income therefrom, are subject to any of the taxes covered.

To improve effectiveness and efficiency, the new directive creates a single European enforcement instrument, which is available in all official languages of the Union and is the sole legal basis for enforcement, thus obviating both cumbersome title recognition or replacement procedures and time-consuming translation (Art. 12 RAD). The new directive also reinforces the possibility to take (early) precautionary measures in another member State, a.o. by similarly omitting procedures for recognition, replacement, or supplementing of the document permitting enforcement in the applying State (Arts 16 and 17 RAD). It further facilitates recovery in practice by introducing spontaneous exchange of information (Art. 6 RAD), relaxing language requirements, especially as regards documents to be notified (Art. 22(2) RAD), introducing the possibility of foreign officials being present during enquiries and proceedings in the requested State (Art. 7 RAD), and introducing a *de minimis* rule (Art. 18(3) RAD): the requested State may decline if the amount of the claim requested for is below € 1500). It further provides a legal basis for direct notification, by registered mail or electronically, of documents to persons in other Member States (Art. 9(2) RAD), also to prevent Member States from using each other disproportionately often as postman.

The RAD provides rules for effective organization, facilitating direct contact between competent officials of different Member States (designation of competent authorities, central liaison offices, liaison departments and liaison officers; Art. 4 RAD), and creating electronic standard forms (Art. 21 RAD). And like that other new Directive, it considerably widens the permissible use of the information obtained under the directive, *e.g.* also for the assessment or enforcement of compulsory social security contributions, for any other use which would be legal in the requested State, as evidence in proceedings, and for forwarding to a third Member state (Art. 23 RAD).

No secrecy for tax defaulters and fraudsters: the RAD prohibits banking secrecy to be used as grounds for refusal to assist.

To be noted that the definitions, limitations on the obligation to assist, admission of foreign officials, organization of the exchange of information, service of documents, standard forms and means of communication, confidentiality and the use permissible of the information obtained, and the comitology procedure of the Recovery Assistance Directive are" aligned to those of the Administrative Cooperation Directive 2011/16/EU (DAC, applicable in the field of direct taxes, see Vol. 1, Chapter 13).

On 18 November 2011, the Commission adopted a new implementing Regulation[14] for the application of the new Recovery Directive, providing, inter alia, detailed rules for various assistance requests, and containing two annexes: a uniform enforcement instrument form and a uniform notification form.

4.2.2 *Types of Recovery Assistance*

The RAD provides for four main types of mutual assistance for the recovery of (tax) claims:

- Exchange of Information:
  (i) mandatory exchange *upon request* of information foreseeably relevant in recovery of a claim covered (if necessary, the requested State must conduct administrative enquiries to obtain the information requested) (Art. 5 RAD);
  (ii) *spontaneous* exchange of information on (upcoming) refunds of tax other than VAT (Art. 6 RAD); and
  (iii) *presence of officials* of the applying Member State in the requested Member State during administrative enquiries and during court proceedings in the latter State (Art. 7 RAD);
- *Notification of Documents*: notification upon request, to the addressee, of documents issued by the applicant Member State and relating to the tax claim or its recovery, such as (additional) assessments, distress warrants, judgments, court orders, writs of attachment, etc. (Art. 8 RAD), in accordance with the national notification rules in force in the requested State (Art. 9 RAD); the request must be accompanied by a standard form (Art. 8);
- *Recovery upon Request, i.e.* collection and enforcement by the requested State (Arts. 10-15 RAD), as if it were collecting its own similar claims (Art. 13(1) RAD; and
- *Precautionary Measures* where the claim or the enforcement instrument is contested by the debtor in the applying State, or where there is no enforcement instrument yet (Art. 16 and 17 RAD).

Every request for recovery assistance must be accompanied by the EU uniform instrument permitting enforcement in the requested State, which reflects the content of the original domestic enforcement instrument. That uniform instrument is the sole basis for recovery and precautionary measures in the requested State (Art. 12(1) RAD), and its validity shall not, therefore, be dependent on any recognition, supplementing or replacement by judicial or other authorities of the requested State. It must be recognized immediately and of itself. As it is also available in all official languages, it may be enforced without delay.

We observe that according to the wording of Article 16 RAD, precautionary measures seem to be limited to only two situations: (i) litigation against the (domestic) recovery title, or (ii) absence as yet of a domestic recovery title. Vascega and Van Thiel[15] wonder whether

14 Commission Implementing Regulation (EU) No 1189/2011 of 18 November 2011 laying down detailed rules in relation to certain provisions of Council Directive 2010/24/EU concerning mutual assistance for the recovery of claims relating to taxes, duties and other measures, O.J. L 302, 19 November 2011, p. 16–27.

15 Marius Vascega and Servaas van Thiel, 'Council Adopts New Directive on Mutual Assistance in Recovery of Tax and Similar Claims,' *European Taxation*, June 2010, p. 231-237, at 237.

that is a mistake or at least a lack of clarity, as it would be desirable that the requested State is able to 'freeze' assets also in many other, 'more normal situations'. They offer that the wording of Article 13(1) RAD ('powers and procedures of the requested Member State') may allow for such freezing in other cases than referred to in Article 16. We believe the requested State's competence to take conservatory measures may be construed more simple. If a writ of execution *is* available (and is not being contested), then the requested State is authorized to attach the debtor's assets. If it has the competence to seize and sell, then it seems reasonable to presume it may also take less radical measures, such as precautionary measures. The power to seize and sell includes the power to take measures of conservation, as an enforceable attachment includes a precautionary attachment: indeed, execution of an enforceable attachment may simply be extended (we do not expect the debtor to object to such extension of enforcement instead of sale of his assets). We find support for this approach in the language of Article 12(1) RAD, stating that the EU uniform enforcement instrument is the basis for 'recovery and precautionary measures' in the requested State.

4.2.3 Limitations on the Obligations to Assist; National Treatment; (No) Preference

The requested State is not obliged to provide *information* requested for, nor to admit foreign officials to that end if:
- it would not be able to obtain the information for its own recovery purposes (Art. 5(2)(a) RAD, but it cannot rely on banking secrecy (Art. 5(3) RAD);
- that would disclose a commercial, industrial of professional secret (Art. 5(2)(b) RAD), but banking secrets are no such secrets (Art. 5(3) RAD);
- disclosure would jeopardize security or public policy (Art. 5(2)(c) RAD);
- the claim is more than five years old (Art. 18(2) RAD);
- the amount for which assistance is requested, is below € 1500 (Art. 18(3) RAD).

The requested State is not obliged to *notify documents* of the requesting State if:
- the requesting State has not used its own notification possibilities (e.g. electronic notification or via registered mail; see Art. 9(2) RAD) or if that would be disproportionately difficult (Art. 8(2) RAD);
- the claim is more than five years old (Art. 18(2) RAD);
- the amount for which notification is requested, is below € 1500 (Art. 18(3) RAD).

The requested State is not obliged to grant a request for *recovery* or to take *precautionary measures* if:
- recovery would, because of the situation of the debtor, create serious economic or social difficulties in the requested State (*e.g.* a bankruptcy and massive lay-offs), provided national law also allows for such exceptions as regards own claims (Art. 18(1) RAD);
- the claim is more than five years old (Art. 8(2) RAD);
- the amount for which assistance is requested, is below € 1500 (Art. 18(3) RAD).

In addition, the Member State considering a request for recovery assistance, may not even *make* such request (and consequently, the requested State is not obliged to oblige) if:
- the claim or the instrument permitting its enforcement is still contested in its jurisdiction by the debtor (Art. 11(1)), unless the laws of both States nevertheless allow

enforcement, and the requesting State pays all damages and refunds if the debtor later wins the contestation (Art. 14(4)(3rd subpara.));
- it has not first exhausted its own recovery possibilities within its own jurisdiction, except where it is obvious that no recoverable assets are there and it has specific information indicating recoverable assets in the requested State, or where using its own remedies would be disproportionately difficult (Art. 11(2)).

Although the foreign claim must be treated by the requested State as if it were a domestic claim ('national treatment') and must be enforced at least according to the domestic rules for personal income tax claims (see Art. 13(1) RAD, the foreign claim does not enjoy the same legal preferences as similar domestic claims (Art. 13(1)(3rd subpara.) RAD), except where so agreed or unilaterally provided. *If* a Member State grants legal preferences to a claim of one particular other Member State, it is required to accord the same preferences to similar claims from other Member States (mostpreferenced-nation clause: Art. 13(1)(3rd subpara.) RAD).

It should be noted that the ECJ's *Pusa* judgment[16] seems to imply that a Member State taking into account domestic tax liabilities in calculating the attachment-free amount of income of a defaulting loan debtor, must take equal account, with equal privileges, of foreign (EU) tax on that income under Article 21 TFEU (freedom to reside).

4.2.4 Miscellaneous

We will not discuss all aspects of the RAD, but to conclude highlight some remaining aspects:

(i) Costs of Recovery
The requested State shall seek to recover from the debtor and retain for itself the costs it incurred in the recovery of the tax, according to its national rules applicable to similar domestic claims (Art. 20(1) RAD). The Member States renounce all claims on each other for reimbursement of costs incurred in complying with each other's requests (Art. 20(2)). They may, however, agree on reimbursement in special cases involving extraordinary difficulties, very high costs or organized crime (Art. 20(2) RAD). If, in retrospect, the tax claim or the enforcement instrument proves to be legally defective, the applying State is liable for costs and losses resulting from actions thus held to be unfounded (Art. 20(3) RAD).

(ii) Legislation Governing Execution, Interest, Payment in installments and Currency
In principle, the execution of the request, the charging of interest, and the granting of payment in installments takes place according to the legislation of the requested State, and in its currency (Art. 13(1), (3) and (4) RAD).

(iii) Litigation; the Competent Forum
In general, disputes regarding the validity of the (tax) claim, of the initial enforcement instrument, of the uniform EU enforcement instrument and of a notification made by the requesting authority itself, must be brought before the courts of the requesting State (Art. 14(1) RAD). This implies that the requested authority may not question the validity

16 Case 224/02 (*Heikki Antero Pusa*), [2004] ECR I-5763.

or enforceability of the measure or the decision of which notification is sought and that in principle, the courts of the requested State have no jurisdiction to hear disputes on the validity of the claim or the instrument permitting enforcement, but the Court of Justice does not exclude that, exceptionally, the courts of the requested State must be considered competent to review whether the enforcement of the instrument is liable, in particular, to be contrary to the public policy of that State and, where appropriate, to refuse to grant assistance in whole or in part or to make it subject to fulfilling certain conditions.[17]

Disputes on the enforcement measures taken by the requested State and on the validity of notifications made by the requesting State, must in principle be brought before the courts of the latter (Art. 14(2) RAD).

If a claim or enforcement instrument is being contested in the requesting State after the requested State has already initiated recovery measures, the former must inform the latter, and the latter must suspend recovery, unless the former is pressing forward and is prepared to carry the risk of having to pay refunds and damages if it loses the litigation (Art. 13(3) and (4)(1st subpara.) RAD).

(iv) Statute of Limitation

The period of limitation of a claim is solely governed by the law of the requesting Member State (Art. 19(1) RAD), but suspension, interruption or prolongation of that period is in principle determined by the law of the requested State, unless that law does not provide for suspension, interruption or prolongation, in which case the steps taken in the requested State are deemed to have been taken in the requesting State in so far as they would produce suspension, interruption or prolongation under the law of the requesting State (Art. 19(2) RAD). This rule serves to avoid that no request is made for fear of losing suspension, interruption or prolongation possibilities.

(v) Delimitation Clause

Like the Administrative Cooperation Directive, the Recovery Assistance Directive explicitly states that its tenor is not to limit in any way the possibilities for mutual assistance under other legal instruments, existing or future (Art. 24(1) RAD).

4.2.5 Evaluation of the RAD

In 2017, the European Commission issued an evaluation report on the RAD.[18]

The main conclusions of the Commission are as follows:

a) The EU legislation and framework for tax recovery assistance has facilitated tax recovery assistance between the EU Member States.
b) In order to guarantee the efficiency and effectiveness of mutual recovery assistance, Member States should strengthen their internal tax recovery systems and deploy

17 Case C-233/08 (*Milan Kyrian v Celní úrad Tábor*), [2010] ECR I-177.

18 Report from the Commission to the European Parliament and the Council on the operation of the arrangements established by Council Directive 2010/24/EU of 16 March 2010 concerning mutual assistance for the recovery of claims relating to taxes, duties and other measures{COM(2017) 778 final}

sufficient resources to deal with recovery assistance requests. In this regard, it should be examined if and how detailed and precise quantitative information can be collected about the administrative burden and costs, and about the correspondence between the workload of incoming requests for assistance and the administrative resources deployed in the requested State.

c) Improving different (legal and technical) aspects of the functioning of the system may still be considered with the Member States and other stakeholders, including taxpayers.
d) More communication to explain and promote this legislation would contribute to increase tax compliance and respect of taxpayers' rights.
e) Recovery of taxes is and remains difficult in case of organised tax fraud by natural or legal persons: natural persons committing fraud or setting up fraudulent tax structures go missing and dislocate their assets; legal persons organise their insolvency and also move their assets. As a consequence of the international development of exchange of information, recovery assistance between the EU and third countries will become a more prominent issue.

4.3 Trade Monitoring Provisions

On 7 November 1991 the Council of the European Communities adopted Regulation (EEC) No. 3330/91 on the statistics relating to the trading of goods between Member States.[19] The introduction of the European single market, on 1 January 1993, allowed for goods freely to circulate among the EU Member States, without border control nor customs formalities. Therefore, since 1993 a clear distinction had to be made in the statistical observation methods and collecting systems between the intra- and extra-Union trade, giving existence to two observation methods: the Intrastat system (direct observation) and the Extrastat system (indirect observation).

Companies trading with countries outside the Union (the Extrastat trade) are declaring (as before 1993) only to the customs authorities and a copy of the customs documents is processed by the statistical authorities. Companies that (also) trade within the Union with other Member States (the Intrastat trade) have seen substantial changes; detected by means of the VAT information, they must declare directly to the statistical authorities.

The Intrastat system is based on the concept of movement of goods between Member States. Accordingly it is applied to the goods which move from one Member State to another. As such intra-EU trade statistics record the arrival and dispatch of movable property recorded by each Member State. 'Arrivals' are analogous to imports; 'dispatches' are analogous to exports. Statistics do not cover goods in transit, that is goods that are merely passing across a Member State, by any means of transport, but are not stored there for any but transport reasons.

Intrastat can be characterized by three main aspects:

(1) The introduction of *the threshold system*. This allowed to exempt 2/3 or more of the enterprises that were trading in the single market. Intrastat had to be conceived as

19 O.J. 1991, L 316, p. 1.

a simplification, and entailed in this way a substantial reduction of the statistical response burden on the SMEs. Since 1993 in several Member States the threshold has been gradually raised reducing the number of declaring enterprises to about 20%–30% of the total number of enterprises trading in the single market.

(2) The *link to the VAT system.* This allowed an easy and continuous identification of the trading enterprises. The link is crucial to maintain the register of the relevant trading enterprises in Intrastat.

(3) The provision of *an electronic reporting tool*, the IDEP/CN-8 software package. This software package was made available free of charge to the reporting enterprises.[20]

On 20 June 2003 the Commission presented a proposal to replace the regulations in force on the trading of goods between Member States as from 2005 in order to improve and adapt the statistical system and address both users' needs and the burden on information providers.[21] This proposal was adopted on 31 March 2004 as Regulation (EC) No. 638/2004 of the European Parliament and of the Council on Community statistics relating to the trading of goods between Member States and repealing Council Regulation (EEC) No. 3330/91.[22]

4.4 Administrative Cooperation and Combating Fraud in the Field of VAT

4.4.1 *Within the EU*

Legal basis

On 7 October 2010, the Council of the European Union adopted Council Regulation (EU) No. 904/2010 on administrative cooperation and combating fraud in the field of value added tax (recast).[23] This recast Regulation supplements Regulation (EC) No. 1798/2003[24] dealing with administrative cooperation on VAT issues by adding provisions for more effective measures against cross-border fraud and better collection of VAT in cases where the place of taxation is different from the place of establishment of the supplier.

The most important changes are the following:

- Member States' responsibility in the field of administrative cooperation is extended to protect the VAT revenue of all Member States.
- The information that Member States must collect and make available to other Member States through an electronic database system is precisely defined. The Regulation also defines access rights to this information in terms of persons and situations.
- A permanent framework is established to guarantee the quality of the information in the databases by laying down common rules on the information to be collected and the checks to be carried out when a VAT identification number is registered in the database. The Regulation specifies the cases in which certain information must be deleted from the databases. It also includes provisions under which Member States

20 See also Paragraph 36 in Case C-114/96 (*René Kieffer and Romain Thill*), [1997] ECR I-3629.
21 COM(2003) 364 final.
22 O.J. 2004, L 102, p. 1.
23 O.J. 2010, L 268, p. 1. Compared to Regulation (EC) No. 1798/2003 'and combating fraud' is added to the Title.
24 O.J. 2003, L 264, p. 1.

are mutually responsible for any erroneous information in their databases or failures to update such information in good time.

- Member States are required to confirm by electronic means the name and address associated with a VAT number. Users are also given guarantees concerning the reliability and use of such information.
- A legal basis is created for establishing a structure for targeted cooperation to combat fraud. This structure makes multilateral, swift and targeted exchange of information possible so that Member States can respond adequately and in a coordinated fashion to combat any new kinds of fraud that emerge. It will be able to draw on jointly organised risk analysis.

In general terms, the Regulation is intended to improve the exchange of information between Member States by defining the cases in which they may not refuse to reply to a request for information or for an administrative enquiry and specifying the cases in which Member States must exchange certain information spontaneously, as well as those in which feedback must be supplied, and laying down the procedures for such feedback. The Regulation also aims to specify the cases in which Member States may and must conduct multilateral controls. Lastly, it provides for the setting of precise objectives for the availability and operating procedures of the database system for the exchange of information.

The following aspects of Council Regulation (EC) No. 1798/2003 remain unchanged:

- the organisation of the departments responsible for administrative cooperation in the Member States;
- the mechanism for requesting information and specific enquiries;
- the request for administrative notification;
- the principle of officials being present in the administrative departments of another Member State and at simultaneous controls;
- the provisions on services supplied by electronic means and telecommunications and radio broadcasting services;
- the provisions on the refund of VAT to taxable persons established in another Member State;
- the principle of the provisions on relations with third countries;
- the limitations on some of the rights and obligations provided for in Directive 95/46/EC of the European Parliament and of the Council of 24 October 1995 on the protection of individuals with regard to the processing of personal data and on the free movement of such data; these limitations are necessary and proportionate in view of the potential loss of revenue for Member States and the crucial importance of the information to effectively combating fraud.

Regulation 904/2010 has been amended in 2013,[25] in 2017[26] and twice in 2018.[27]

---

25 Council Regulation 517/2013 of 13 May 2013, O.J. 10.06.2013, L 158.

26 Council Regulation (EU) 2017/2454 of 5 December 2017 amending Regulation (EU) No 904/2010 on administrative cooperation and combating fraud in the field of value added tax, OJ L 348, 29.12.2017.

27 Council Regulation 2018/1541 of 2 October 2018, O.J. 16.10.2018, L 259 and Council Regulation 2018/1909 of 4 December 2018, O.J. 7.12.2018, L 311.

Analysis per Chapter or per Article

Chapter I establishes the scope of the Regulation, provides definitions and contains provisions on the organisation of the competent authorities under the Regulation.

Article 1: Objectives

This Article reflects the fact that the Regulation covers much more than monitoring the correct application of VAT, particularly on intra-Community transactions, but also combatting VAT fraud and that it lays down rules enabling the competent authorities of the Member States to exchange information with the Commission (para 1).

Member States are expected to assist in the protection of VAT revenue in all the Member States (para 2).

Article 1 also emphasises the fact that the Regulation does not affect the application in the Member States of the rules on mutual assistance in criminal matters (para 3).

Finally, it is clarified that the Regulation also lays down rules and procedures for the exchange by electronic means of VAT information on goods and services supplied in accordance with the special schemes provided for in Chapter 6 of Title XII of the RVD (see Chapter 2.14.6) and also for any subsequent exchange of information. In addition, as far as goods and services covered by the special schemes are concerned, the Regulation also govern the transfer of money between Member States' competent authorities (para 4).[28]

Article 2: Definitions

Article 2 gives definitions of the following concepts used in the Regulation: 'central liaison', 'liaison department', 'competent official', 'requesting authority', 'requested authority', 'intra-Community transactions', 'intra-Community supply of goods', 'intra-Community supply of services', 'intra-Community acquisition of goods', 'VAT identification number', 'administrative enquiry', 'person', 'by electronic means', 'CCN/CSI network', and three new definitions: 'spontaneous exchange', 'automated access', and 'simultaneous control'.

The definitions contained in Articles 358, 358a and 369a RVD (i.e. 'telecommunications services', 'broadcasting services', 'electronic services' and 'electronically supplied services', 'Member State of consumption', 'VAT return', 'Taxable person not established within the Community', 'Member State of identification', 'taxable person not established in the Member State of consumption', 'Member State of identification') also apply for the purposes of the Regulation. Likewise, the definitions contained in Articles 358, 358a, 369a and 369l of the RVD for the purposes of each special scheme also apply.

Articles 3 to 6: Decentralisation of Administrative Cooperation

Article 3 designates as the competent authorities the authorities in whose name the Regulation is to be applied, whether directly or by delegation.

28 These changes were introduced by Council Regulation (EU) 2017/2454.

The Commission must make available to the Member States a list of all competent authorities and publish this information in the Official Journal of the European Union.

The structure of Article 4 is as follows:

- Each authority must designate one central liaison office to be responsible for cooperation. That central liaison office will be responsible for cooperation on request by default (where the requesting authority does not know which local office to contact or where a request is made to a local office which is not competent to deal with it) and will have a central role to play in communicating certain information automatically and spontaneously.
- Each authority will also appoint at least one official per territorial service who will be responsible for information exchange. The concept of territorial service will be applicable by the Member States on a case by case basis, as the situation differs according to the size of the Member State. National control services, where they exist, should also have one official responsible for information exchange.
- Provision is also made for direct contacts between other officials, on condition that the information simultaneously goes through the competent authorities (*i.e.* by delegation via the central liaison offices or the competent officials).

Articles 5 and 6 provide that here a liaison department or a competent official sends or receives a request or a reply to a request for assistance or a request for assistance requiring action outside its territorial or operational area, it must inform the central liaison office of its Member State under the conditions laid down by the latter.

Chapter II concerns exchanges of information on request, and the main change is the limitation of cases in which a Member State may refuse to provide information or carry out an enquiry.

Articles 7 to 9: Request for Information and for Administrative Inquiries

At the request of the requesting authority, the requested authority must communicate the information that may help the correct assessment of VAT, including any information relating to a specific case or cases (Article 7(1)). The requested authority shall arrange for the conduct of any administrative enquiries necessary to obtain such information (Article 7(2)). Article 7(4) provides that a request for information may contain a reasoned request for a (specific) administrative enquiry. If the requested authority takes the view that the administrative enquiry is not necessary, it must immediately inform the requesting authority of the reasons thereof. An enquiry may be refused only on specific grounds, as provided under Article 54 of the Regulation (and sometimes even when an enquiry is refused the Member State has to provide information regarding dates and values of transactions made by a taxable person in the previous 2 years, see Article 7(4) *in fine).*

Article 7(4a) provides that in cases where at least two Member States consider that an administrative enquiry is needed and produce a reasoned request containing indications or evidence of risks of VAT evasion or fraud, the requested Member State may not refuse to undertake the enquiry, again in the specific cases specifically foreseen under Article 54.

Article 7(4a) also provides for the possibility for the requesting Member State to take part in the investigation, which should take place in accordance with the legislation applicable there. This for example means that the authorities of the requiring Member State may be given access to the same premises and documents as the officials of the requested Member State and should be allowed to interview the taxable persons in accordance with the same rules. It is also clarified that the authorities of the requiring Member State may only exercise their inspection powers for the sole purpose of the administrative enquiries for which they have been authorized to intervene. The simple presence of the authorities of the requesting State during the enquiry (still under the conditions laid down under the national law of the requested State), and again only for the purpose of the administrative enquiry itself. See also Articles 28 below on joint audits.

Article 7(5) clarifies that in order to obtain the information sought or to conduct the enquiry requested, the requested authority should act as though acting on in its own account or at the request of another authority of its own Member State.

Article 8 prescribes a standard form for requests for information and administrative inquiries.

Article 9 specifies that information may be requested in the form of reports, certificates and any other such documents or certified true copies or extracts thereof. Original documents will be provided only where this is not contrary to the legislation in force in the requested Member State.

Articles 10 to 12: Time Limits for Providing Information
The three-month deadline set by Article 8 of Regulation (EC) No. 1798/2003 for providing information remains unchanged. Where the requested authority is already in possession of that information, the time-limit is reduced to one month. For certain special cases, in particular involving carousel fraud or complex controls, a different deadline may be agreed upon.

Where the requested authority is unable to respond to the request by the deadline, it must inform the requesting authority forthwith of the reasons for its failure to do so and state when it will be able to respond.

Chapter III concerns exchanges of information without prior request. This chapter has been amended to specify that such exchanges must in any case take place where certain criteria are met. Practical arrangements are established for the exchange of some specific information that meets these criteria.

Articles 13 to 15: Automatic and Spontaneous Exchanges of Information
According to Article 13, in order to increase the possibilities of detecting and preventing fraud in intra-Community trade, Member States must at least exchange information automatically in the following situations:

(a) cases where taxation is deemed to take place in the Member State of destination and the efficiency of the control system necessarily depends on the information provided by the Member State of origin. Examples are intra-Community supplies of new vehicles (land vehicles, vessels and aircraft) or distance sales not taxed in the state of origin;

(b) cases where there is a suspicion of fraud in the other Member State. Examples are intra-Community services of a character deemed irregular (for example, because they are not invoiced to their actual recipients) or discrepancies between intra- Community supplies and acquisitions (cases where the information communicated departs significantly from the declared value of intra-Community acquisitions);

(c) where there is a risk of tax loss in the other Member State, *i.e.* cases which generally represent a higher risk for tax fraud or avoidance in the other Member State. Examples are potential phoenix companies (such as companies which, in their initial years of trading, supply a large number of intra- Community goods and services to customers in another State); VAT refunds to taxable persons not established in the territory of the country (Council Directive 2008/9/EC) or the allocation of VAT identification numbers to operators based in the other Member State; shadow companies which have carried out intra-Community transactions or taxable persons convicted for VAT fraud in intra-Community trade.

The Regulation provides for two types of spontaneous exchange: automatic or spontaneous.

The exact categories of information subject to automatic exchange, the frequency of the automatic exchange for each category of information and the practical arrangements for the automatic exchange of information will be decided based on the committee procedure referred to in Article 58(2).

A Member State may abstain from taking part in the automatic exchange of information with respect to one or more categories where the collection of information for such exchange would require the imposition of new obligations on persons liable for VAT or would impose a disproportionate administrative burden on the Member State.

As from 1 January 2015, the competent authority of each Member State must, in particular, exchange information automatically in order to enable Member States of consumption to ascertain whether taxable persons not established in their territory declare and correctly pay the VAT due with regard to telecommunication services, broadcasting services and electronically supplied services, regardless of whether those taxable persons make use of the special scheme.

Article 15 instructs the competent authorities of the Member States to forward, by spontaneous exchange, to the competent authorities of the other Member States any information which has not been forwarded under the automatic exchange of which they are aware and which they consider may be useful to those competent authorities.

Article 16: Feedback

Chapter IV introduces in Article 16 a feedback requirement, the rules and procedures for which are to be established by the committee procedure. Member States had identified the lack of feedback as a weakness in their information exchanges.

Articles 17 to 24: Keeping Information Up to Date, Complete and Accurate
Chapter V deals with the storage and exchange of information on taxable persons and transactions. It is amended to increase the amount and quality of information exchanged. In particular, it provides that the competent authorities are to be given access to certain information held by the Member States. The Regulation also provides for the establishment of common procedures regarding the information to be collected when a taxable person is registered in the database and the updating of the database system.

Chapter VI concerns requests for administrative notification and has not been amended.

Articles 25 to 27: Requests for Administrative Notification
Articles 25 to 27 provide for notification to the addressee of all instruments and decisions, including those of a judicial nature, relating to a claim or to its recovery, which emanate from the Member State in which the requesting authority is situated. Where no claim has yet arisen, Article 25 provides a clear legal base to provide for notification of the instruments or decisions emanating from the tax authorities of other Member States.

Chapter VII deals with presence in administrative offices and participation in administrative enquires. Some clarifications have been introduced concerning the non exhaustive nature of its provisions.

Article 25: Presence in Administrative Offices and Participation in Administrative Enquiries
Article 25 permits the presence of officials of the tax authorities of one Member State on the territory of another Member State if both the States concerned consider it desirable. At the same time, Article 25 creates a legal structure specifying the rights and obligations of all the parties and the procedures to be followed by the national officials who conduct investigations in another Member State. Article 25(1) provides for the presence of officials of the tax authorities of one Member State in the administrative offices of another Member State. Article 25(2) defines a legal structure governing the presence of the officials appointed by the requesting authority to undertake the administrative enquiries of taxable persons. These Articles constitute a legal base making the tax administration no longer dependent on the consent of the taxable person. As under Article 7 (administrative enquiry and participation thereto), access to premises and documents, etc. should follow the rules of the requested Member State and any inspection powers shall be for the sole purpose of carrying out the administrative enquiry. Article 28(3) also provides that the officials of the requesting authority must at all times be able to produce written authority stating their identity and their official capacity.

Chapter VIII concerns multilateral controls. It has been amended to specify the cases in which Member States must conduct this kind of control.

Articles 29 to 30: Simultaneous Controls
The Regulation provides for an obligation of principle for the Member States to use simultaneous controls wherever these seem more effective than national controls. Member States may agree to conduct simultaneous controls whenever they consider such controls to be more effective than controls carried out by only one Member State.

A Member State must identify independently the taxable persons which it intends to propose for a simultaneous control. The competent authority of that Member State must notify the competent authority of the other Member States concerned of the cases proposed for a simultaneous control. It must give reasons for its choice, as far as possible, by providing the information which led to its decision. It shall specify the period of time during which such controls should be conducted.

The competent authority of the Member State that receives the proposal for a simultaneous control must confirm its agreement or communicate its reasoned refusal to its counterpart authority, in principle within two weeks of receipt of the proposal, but within a month at the latest.

Articles 31 to 32: Validity of Requested VAT Identification Numbers
Chapter IX concerns the information available to taxable persons, and in particular the possibility of obtaining confirmation of the validity of a specific person's identification number, together with the associated name and address. It also provides that the invoicing provisions in force in the Member States that are applicable to taxable persons not established on their territory will be placed on the Commission's website.

Articles 33 to 37: Eurofisc
Chapter X concerns the establishment of a common structure (EUROFISC) which will provide a faster cooperation mechanism for dealing with very large-scale or new fraud patterns. In a nutshell, EUROFIC is a network set up for the swift exchange of targeted information between Member States. Within the framework of EUROFISC Member States commit to:
(a) establish a multilateral early warning mechanism for combating VAT fraud;
(b) coordinate the swift multilateral exchange of targeted information in the subject areas in which Eurofisc will operate (hereinafter 'Eurofisc working fields');
(c) coordinate the work of the Eurofisc liaison officials of the participating Member States in acting on warnings received.

Member States have some flexibility in this framework. They may indeed participate in the Eurofisc working fields of their choice and may also decide to terminate their participation. However, if they participate, they commit to actively participate in the multilateral exchange of targeted information between all participating Member States.

Information exchanged shall be confidential, as provided for in Article 55.

Technical and logistical support should be provided by the Commission, but the latter may not have access to the information which may be exchanged over Eurofisc (Article 35).

In practice each Member State designates at least one Eurofisc liaison official, who remain answerable only to their national administrations (Article 36(1)). Liaison officials should then designate a coordinator for each particular Eurofisc working field (Article 36(2)).

Eurofisc working field coordinators shall:
(a) collate the information received from the participating Eurofisc liaison officials and make all information available to the other participating Eurofisc liaison officials. The information shall be exchanged by electronic means;

(b) ensure that the information received from the participating Eurofisc liaison officials is processed, as agreed by the participants in the working field, and make the result available to the participating Eurofisc liaison officials;
(c) provide feedback to the participating Eurofisc liaison officials.

Eurofisc working field coordinators may request relevant information from the European Union Agency for Law Enforcement Cooperation ('Europol') and the European Anti-Fraud Office ('OLAF') and should make the information received from Europol and OLAF available to the other participating Eurofisc liaison officials; this information shall be exchanged by electronic means (Article 36(4) and (5)).

Eurofisc working field coordinators must submit an annual report (Article 37).

Chapters XI and XII deal with the special one stop-shop scheme and the related issue of refunds. Articles 38 to 42 lays down provisions that were applicable until 31 December 2014. Articles 43 to 47 lay down the provisions applicable since 1 January 2015 (the difference is the broadening of the system to taxable persons established in another Member State) and Articles 47a to 47g lay down the provisions applicable since 1 July 2021.

Articles 47a to 47g: exchange of information, control and enquiries when the special schemes are used

The information provided by the taxable person using one of the special schemes when his activities commence must be submitted by electronic means. The Member State of identification must transmit this information by electronic means to the competent authorities of the other Member States within 10 days from the end of the month during which the information was received from the non-established taxable person (or its intermediary). In the same manner the competent authorities of the other Member States must be informed of the allocated identification number. The Member State of identification must without delay inform by electronic means the competent authorities of the other Members States if a non-established taxable person is excluded from the identification register.

The return with the required details is also to be submitted by electronic means. The Member State of identification must transmit this information by electronic means to the competent authority of the Member State concerned at the latest 20 days after the end of the month during which the return was received (new Article 47d with a prolonged period for submitting declarations).[29]

Member States which have required the tax return to be made in a national currency other than euro, must convert the amounts into euro using the exchange rate valid for the last date of the reporting period. The exchange must be done following the exchange rates published by the European Central Bank for that day, or, if there is no publication on that day, on the next day of publication. The Member State of identification must transmit by electronic means to the Member State of consumption the information needed to link each payment with a relevant quarterly tax return.

29 Council Regulation 2017/2454.

The Member State of identification must ensure that the amount the non- established taxable person has paid is transferred to the bank account denominated in euro which has been designated by the Member State of consumption to which the payment is due, within 20 days after the end of the month during which the payment was received. Member States which required the payments in a national currency other than euro must convert the amounts into euro using the exchange rate valid for the last date of the reporting period. If the non-established taxable person does not pay the total tax due, the Member State of identification is to ensure that the payment is transferred to the Member States of consumption in proportion to the tax due in each Member State. The Member State of identification must inform by electronic means the competent authorities of the Member States of consumption thereof.

Member States must notify by electronic means the competent authorities of the other Member States of the relevant bank account numbers for receiving payments. Member States must without delay notify by electronic means the competent authorities of the other Member States and the Commission of changes in the standard tax rate.

Since 1 January 2019, the Member States are no longer allowed to retain a collection fee.

Articles 47h to 47j lays down provisions relating to the control of the transactions carried out by the taxable persons.

In accordance with Article 47h, Member States are required to carry out an electronic verification of the validity of the I-OSS number when the number is used in the import declaration to obtain an exemption (see Article 143ca RVD).

Article 47i provides that if a Member State of consumption is willing to obtain the records held by a taxable person, it must first make a request to the Member State of identification (by electronic means) and that the request will be transmitted by the Member State of identification to the taxable person (or its intermediary) without delay. The records should in principle be submitted electronically to the Member State of identification and then forwarded to the Member State of consumption (without delay). If the Member States of consumption does not receive the records within 30 days of the initial request, it may take any action in accordance with its national legislation to obtain such records.

Article 47j provides that if a Member State of identification decides to carry out in its territory an administrative enquiry on a taxable person who makes use of one of the special schemes (or an intermediary) it shall inform in advance of the enquiry the competent authorities of all the other Member States. It also provides that if the Member State of consumption decides that an administrative enquiry is required, it should first consult with the Member State of identification on the need for such an enquiry. In cases where the need for an administrative enquiry is agreed, the Member State of identification shall inform the other Member States. Finally, it is clarified that these rules do not preclude Member States to take any action in accordance with their national legislation. However, each Member State should communicate to the other Member States and the Commission the details of the competent authority responsible for coordination of administrative enquiries within that Member State.

Article 47k provides that the Commission will be allowed to extract information directly from messages generated by the computerised system used for the exchange (as organized under Article 53) for aggregated statistical and diagnostic purposes but that this information may not contain data concerning individual taxable persons.

Article 47l provides that the Commission will be allowed to adopt technical implementing measures for the purpose of the uniform application of the Regulation.

Article 48: Exchange and Conservation of Information relating to the Refund of VAT
Article 48 provides that where the competent authority of the Member State of establishment receives an application for refund of VAT pursuant to Article 5 of Directive 2008/9/EC, and Article 18 of that Directive is not applicable, it must, within 15 calendar days of its receipt and by electronic means, forward the application to the competent authorities of each Member State of refund concerned with confirmation that the applicant as defined in Article 2(5) of Directive 2008/9/EC is a taxable person for the purposes of VAT and that the identification or registration number given by this person is valid for the refund period. The taxable person may agree to a compensation in case of liabilities in the Member State of establishment (if the liabilities are dispute, the Member State of establishment may use the funds as a retention measure with the consent of the taxable person, in so far as effective judicial review is ensured).

The competent authorities of each Member State of refund must notify by electronic means the competent authorities of the other Member States of any information required by them pursuant to Article 9(2) of Directive 2008/9/EC. The competent authorities of each Member State of refund must notify by electronic means the competent authorities of the other Member States if they want to make use of the option to require the applicant to provide the description of business activity by harmonised codes as referred to in Article 11 of Directive 2008/9/EC.

Chapter XIII covers relations with the Commission.

Article 49: Relations with the Commission
Article 49 provides for joint evaluation of the functioning of the Regulation by the Member States and the Commission. Member States must provide all the statistical data required for such an evaluation and that the exact detail of the data to be sent is to be decided by the committee procedure. The Member States must also provide any information on methods or practices used or suspected of having been used to circumvent VAT legislation which has helped to reveal shortcomings or lacunae in the arrangements for administrative cooperation provided for in this Regulation. Such information is an indication of how effective the system of administrative cooperation is in combating tax evasion. For the same reason, it might be useful for the Member States to forward to the Commission any other information, including information on specific cases, purely on a voluntary basis.

The Commission must communicate this information to the competent authorities of the other Member States concerned to whom the information has not yet been transmitted.

In accordance with Article 49(2a), the Member States may communicate relevant information to OLAF.

Chapter XIV covers relations with third countries.

Article 50: Relations with Third Countries
Article 50(1) provides a legal base for communicating to Member States information emanating from a non-EU country by virtue of a bilateral agreement (see below the agreement signed on the basis of this provision).

Under Article 50(2), information obtained under the present Regulation may be communicated to a non-EU country with the consent of the competent authorities that supplied it and the third country concerned has given an undertaking to provide the cooperation required to gather evidence of the irregular nature of transactions which appear to contravene VAT legislation.

Chapter XV, which lays down the conditions governing the exchange of information, has been amended to set precise objectives for the level of service of electronic information exchanges.

Articles 51 to 57: Conditions Governing the Exchange of Information
According to Article 51, all information is to be provided, as far as possible, by electronic means under arrangements to be adopted by committee procedure.

Article 52 provides that requests for assistance and attached documents will be accompanied by a translation into the official language or one of the official languages of the requested authority under arrangements to be adopted by the committee procedure.

Article 53 stipulates that the Commission and the Member States must ensure that such existing or new communication and information exchange systems which are necessary to provide for the exchanges of information described in the Regulation are operational and prescribes a service level agreement to be decided in accordance with the Committee procedure.

Article 54 dictates that the requested authority in one Member State shall provide a requesting authority in another Member State with the information referred to in Article 1 provided that:

(a) the number and the nature of the requests for information made by the requesting authority within a specific period do not impose a disproportionate administrative burden on that requested authority;

(b) that requesting authority has exhausted the usual sources of information which it could have used in the circumstances to obtain the information requested, without running the risk of jeopardising the achievement of the desired end.

The Regulation imposes no obligation to have enquiries carried out or to provide information on a particular case if the laws or administrative practices of the Member State which would have to supply the information do not authorise the Member State to carry out those enquiries or collect or use that information for that Member State's own purposes. The competent authority of a requested Member State may refuse to provide information where the requesting Member State is unable, for legal reasons, to provide similar information. Furthermore the provision of information may be refused where it would lead to the disclosure of a commercial, industrial or professional secret or of a commercial process, or of information whose disclosure would be contrary to public policy.

The above provisions should on no account be interpreted as authorising the requested authority of a Member State to refuse to supply information on a taxable person identified for VAT purposes in the Member State of the requesting authority on the sole grounds that this information is held by a bank, other financial institution, nominee or person acting in an agency or fiduciary capacity or because it relates to ownership interests in a legal person.

Article 55 deals with secrecy and the extent in which the information may be used. It prescribes that information communicated or collected in any form pursuant to the Regulation, be covered by the obligation of official secrecy and enjoy the protection extended to similar information under both the national law of the Member State which received it and the corresponding provisions applicable to Union authorities. Such information may be used only in the circumstances provided for in the Regulation. Such information may be used for the purpose of establishing the assessment base or the collection or administrative control of tax for the purpose of establishing the assessment base. The information may also be used for the assessment of other levies, duties, and taxes covered by Article 2 of Council Directive 2008/55/EC of 26 May 2008 on mutual assistance for the recovery of claims relating to certain levies, duties, taxes and other measures. In addition, it may be used in connection with judicial proceedings that may involve penalties, initiated as a result of infringements of tax law without prejudice to the general rules and legal provisions governing the rights of defendants and witnesses in such proceedings.

By way of derogation from the above, the competent authority of the Member State providing the information must permit its use for other purposes in the Member State of the requesting authority, if, under the legislation of the Member State of the requested authority, the information can be used for similar purposes.

Article 56 clarifies the fact that findings, statements, information, documents, certified true copies and any intelligence obtained by the officials of the requested authority and transmitted to the requesting authority may be used as evidence by the competent bodies of the requesting authority on the same basis as equivalent national documents.

Article 57 prescribes Member States shall to take all necessary measures to ensure effective internal coordination between the competent authorities, to establish direct cooperation between the authorities authorised for the purposes of such coordination and to ensure the smooth operation of the information exchange arrangements

Chapter XVI sets out the general and final provisions.

4.4.2 With third countries

Norway

In 2018, the EU and Norway and signed an agreement[30] to establish a framework for administrative cooperation with a view to enable the authorities responsible for the application of VAT legislation to assist each other in ensuring compliance with that legislation and in protecting VAT revenue.[31] Norway is the first country with which the EU has a VAT cooperation agreement.

The agreement lays down rules and procedures for cooperation, including exchange of information and recovery (article 2 of the Agreement). The territorial scope of the Agreement includes Norway and the EU VAT territory (see Chapter 2, section 2.4).

The Agreement follows the same structure as Regulation 904/10 and the Recovery Directive.

In the same way as between the Member States under Regulation 904/2010, exchange of information will, depending on the situation, have to be made on request (Article 7), spontaneously (Article 10) or automatically (Article 11). The conditions governing and surrounding the exchange of information are laid down in Articles 17 to 21 of the Agreement. Other forms of cooperation are foreseen, including presence in administrative offices and participation in administrative enquiries (Article 13), simultaneous controls (Article 14). Norway also participates to the EUROFISC network (see Article 15 and 16).

Rules governing assistance in recovery are laid down in Title II of the Agreement (as mentioned already they are similar to the provisions of the RAD).

Article 41 of the Agreement provides for the setting up of a Joint Committee to ensure the proper functioning and implementation of the Agreement and Article 42 provides that any dispute between the Parties relating to the interpretation or application of the Agreement should be resolved through consultations within the Joint Committee.

The United Kingdom

Under Article 120 of the EU-UK Trade Agreement signed on 30 December 2020, the Parties have committed to:

> "cooperate with each other to ensure compliance with VAT legislation and in recovering claims relating to taxes and duties in accordance with the Protocol on administrative cooperation and combating fraud in the field of value added tax and on mutual assistance for the recovery of claims relating to taxes and duties".

---

30 Agreement between the European Union and the Kingdom of Norway on administrative cooperation, combating fraud and recovery of claims in the field of value added taks *OJ L 195, 1.8.2018, p. 3–22.*

31 Article 1 of the Agreement.

They have signed a specific Protocol,[32] which foresees the exchange (via the EU's common communications network / common systems interface (CCN/CSI -CCN2)) of information for tax assessments purposes and with a view to combat VAT fraud (to be noted that data supplied may be passed onto further states under the agreement without further consent), and the possibility to ask requested states to use their debt recovery processes to be used to collect outstanding taxes and penalties, subject to a request threshold. There is also possible a limit on the frequency of requests, and the possibility to check that the requesting authority has exhausted other sources. Finally, cooperation may be refused when the request would give rise to disproportionate difficulties for the requested state.

In practice, liaison offices should be created and a Specialised Committee (The Trade Specialised Committee on Administrative Cooperation in VAT and Recovery of Taxes and Duties) will be established to meet at least twice a year to review the arrangements. Moreover, a service level agreement will be established between the UK and EU27 to govern the quality and quantity of services.

4.5 Administrative Cooperation in the Field of Excise Duties

On 16 November 2004, the Council adopted Regulation (EC) No. 2073/2004 on administrative cooperation in the field of excise duties[33] in order to simplify, decentralise and reinforce the mechanisms of administrative cooperation contained in Directive 77/ 799/ EEC (eventually replaced by the RAD) and the horizontal excise Directive 92/12/ EEC, later replaced by the General Arrangements Directive 2008/118/EC (see Chapter 3). On the same day, the Council adopted Directive 2004/106/EC modifying Directives 77/799/EEC and Directive 92/12/EEC in order to remove from both of them any reference to assessment assistance on excise duties.

The Regulation had three main objectives:

- To lay down clearer and more binding rules governing the exchange of information;
- To provide for more direct contacts between national anti-fraud agencies;
- To facilitate more extensive exchange of information.

In particular, the Regulation:

- ensured more direct contacts between local offices in Member States, while giving central liaison offices a role in overseeing this decentralised co-operation;
- established a 3 month time limit within which Member States will have to respond to information requests from each other;
- formalised the procedures for officials from one Member State to carry out investigations in another;
- established procedures for simultaneous audits by officials from two or more Member States;
- introduced an obligation for automatic information exchange, without prior request, in cases where there is a risk of serious fraud in a Member State;

32 Protocol on administrative cooperation and combating fraud in the field of value added tax and on mutual assistance for the recovery of claims relating to taxes and duties.

33 O.J. 2004, L 359, p. 1.

- laid down rules concerning time limits for storage and concerning how information held should be exchanged (see also the excise duty computerised monitoring system (ECMS) in Chapter 3);
- provided for transmission of statistical information to the Commission so as to allow the Commission to play a coordinating and facilitating role; and
- provided for information exchange with non-EU countries.

Regulation 389/2012 eventually repealed Regulation 2073/2004. Regulation 389/ 2012 better reflects the introduction of the EMCS in April 2010. Under the regime of Regulation (EC) No. 2073/2004, part of the information exchange between Member States on the movement of excise products (alcohol, tobacco and energy products) was still done manually. Computerising this exchange was meant to make it easier and faster to collect the excise duties that are due.

Regulation 389/2012 also updates the rules on administrative cooperation in order to reap the full benefit of the Excise Movement and Control System. In particular, Regulation 389/2012 replaces manual procedures with automated procedures wherever this information is electronically available within the EMCS. This includes, for example, information on road controls or interruptions in the movement of goods. Regulation 389/2012 also clarifies the rights and obligations of Member States in terms of requests they can submit to each other, information they must provide, deadlines to answer requests, and use of standardised forms for these exchanges. The ultimate objective is to ensure that the process for Member States to collect and retrieve excise duties is as smooth and efficient as possible.

4.6 Administrative Cooperation in the Field of Customs Duties

With regard to administrative cooperation in the field of customs, a distinction can be made between cooperation between customs authorities in the EU, and between customs authorities in the EU and third countries.

Administrative Cooperation in the Field of Customs within the EU
Regulation (EC) No. 515/9718[34] lays down the ways in which the administrative authorities responsible for implementation of the legislation on agricultural and customs matters in the Member States shall cooperate with each other and the Commission in order to ensure compliance with that legislation.[35] It is considered the main legal tool to combat customs fraud through cooperation and the exchange of information between the customs authorities of the Member States.

The first provisions of Regulation (EC) No. 515/9718 set out the purpose of the regulation, the definitions used in the regulation and which data elements the competent authorities

34 Council Regulation (EC) No. 515/97 of 13 March 1997 on mutual assistance between the administrative authorities of the Member States and cooperation between the latter and the Commission to ensure the correct application of the law on customs and agricultural matters (O.J. L 082 22.3.1997, p. 1).

35 The legislation referred to entails both agricultural and customs legislation. For the definition of customs legislation, Regulation (EC) No. 515/97 refers to Article 5 (2) UCC, see also section 1.3.1.1.

may exchange with other competent authorities and the Commission. Data may be shared in particular where no customs declaration or simplified declaration is presented or where it is incomplete or where there is a reason to believe that the data contained therein are false. For those instance, the data that may be shared is listed in Article 2a and concerns the following data:

- business name;
- trading name;
- address of the business;
- VAT identification number of the business;
- excise duties identification number;
- information as to whether the VAT identification number and/or the excise duties identification number is in use;
- names of the managers, directors and, if available, principal shareholders of the business;
- number and date of issue of the invoice; and
- amount invoiced.

The above listed data should relate to goods traded between Member States and third countries and goods traded between Member States in case they have the non- Union status or the goods at stake are subject to additional controls or investigations for the purposes of establishing their Union status.

After the introductory provisions, Regulation (EC) No. 515/9718 provides for more detailed provisions with regard to assistance on request (Title I), spontaneous assistance (Title II), relations with the Commission (Title III), and relations with third countries (Title IV).[36] The data that may be exchanged on request or in case of spontaneous assistance is far more comprehensive than the data elements listed in Article 2a, and concerns basically any information which may enable a competent authority to ensure compliance with the provisions of customs or agricultural legislation.

According to Article 6(1) UCC all exchanges of information between customs authorities should in principle be made using electronic data-processing techniques. Regulation (EC) No. 515/9718 in that respect already provided for an automatic system with the establishment of the Customs Information System (CIS). The CIS was introduced for the purpose of assisting in "[...] *preventing, investigating and prosecuting operations which are in breach of customs or agricultural legislation by making information available more rapidly and thereby increasing the effectiveness of the cooperation and control procedures of the competent authorities referred to in this Regulation.*"[37]

36 The provisions with regard to the relations with third parties mainly deal with how the information can be shared by third countries with the competent authorities of the Member States or the Commission, but does not impose an obligation on the competent authorities or the Commission to share information with third countries.

37 Article 23(2) Regulation (EC) No. 515/97.

Administrative Cooperation in the Field of Customs between the EU and third countries
The WCO and WTO support customs authorities to exchange information.[38] The EU entered into several agreements that facilitate the exchange of information with third countries. It is part of the EU's strategy to seek for customs cooperation with third parties, and the agreements present an important tool for providing a balance between the necessary trade liberalisation and the increasing international trade with the world's large trading partners.

The EU has concluded in that regard several agreements on customs cooperation and mutual assistance implementation with countries like Korea, Canada, Hong Kong, US, India, China and Japan. The obligation to exchange information can also arise from the Partnership and Cooperation Agreements the EU has with a couple of countries like Russia and Ukraine, which also cover customs cooperation and include a protocol on mutual administrative assistance.

38 See Article 12 of the WTO Agreement on Trade Facilitation, the Revised Kyoto Convention (in particular Standard 6.7) and the WCO SAFE Framework of Standards.

ANNEX I - CUSTOMS, VAT AND EXCISE LEGISLATION: TERRITORIAL APPLICATION

EU rules regulating customs, VAT and excise in principle apply on the territory of all the EU Member States. The table below clarifies the status of specific territories related to EU Member States, or with whom a specific link is established for the purpose of the application of the aforementioned legislation.

Territories	*Part of the customs territory*	*Part of the VAT territory*	*Part of the excise territory*
Denmark: Faroe Islands (not on the EU territory)	No	No	No
Denmark: Greenland (not on the EU territory)	No	No	No
Finland; Åland islands (EU territory)	Yes	No	No
France: overseas territories (not on the EU territory)	No	No	No
France: Guadeloupe, French Guiana, Martinique, Réunion, Mayotte, Saint Martin (EU territory)	Yes	No	No
Germany: Island of Heligoland (EU territory)	No	No	No
Germany: Territory of Büsingen (EU territory)	No	No	No
Greece: Mount Athos (EU territory)	Yes	No	Yes
Italy: Campione d'Italia (EU territory)	Yes	No	Yes

Territories	*Part of the customs territory*	*Part of the VAT territory*	*Part of the excise territory*
Italy: the Italian waters of Lake Lugano (EU territory)	Yes	No	Yes
Italy: Livignio (EU territory)	No	No	No
Netherlands: Netherlands Antilles (Not on the EU territory)	No	No	No
Portugal: Azores (EU territory)	Yes	Yes	Yes
Portugal: Madeira (EU territory)	Yes	Yes	Yes
Spain: Ceuta (EU territory)	No	No	No
Spain: Melilla (EU territory)	No	No	No
Spain: the Canary islands (EU territory)	Yes	No	No
Jungholz and Mittelberg (part of Austria)	Yes	Yes (special reduced rate applies)	Yes (but treated as Germany for transactions to and from)
Monaco (EU Treaties do not apply)	Yes (treated as France)	Yes (treated as France, only for transactions to and from)	Yes (treated as France, only for transactions to and from)
San Marino (EU Treaties do not apply)	Yes (treated as Italy)	No	Yes (treated as Italy, only for transactions to and from)
United Kingdom Sovereign Base Areas of Akrotiri and Dhekelia (EU Treaties apply to a limited extent, see Article 355 TFEU)	Yes (treated as Cyprus)	Yes (treated as Cyprus)	Yes (treated as Cyprus)

Territories	*Part of the customs territory*	*Part of the VAT territory*	*Part of the excise territory*
Northern Ireland (No longer an EU Member State)	No (but aligned to a limited set of rules related to the EU's Single Market in order to avoid a hard border – temporary measure based on the Protocol on Ireland/ Northern Ireland)	No (except for goods supplied to and from, temporary measure based on the Protocol on Ireland/Northern Ireland)	Yes (but temporary measure based on the Protocol on Ireland/ Northern Ireland)

INDEX

A
ABC contracts (or chain transactions) 2.7.1, 2.7.2
ad valorem duty 1.4.2.3, 3.6.2
administrative reference code (ARC) 3.2.4.2, 3.3.2.3, 3.3.1, 3.3.2.7
alcohol 3.5, 3.5.2, 3.5.5
application of goods 2.6.1
apportionment method 2.12.1
authorised warehousekeeper 3.2.3, 3.2.4
authorized economic operator 1.3.1.5

B
beer 3.5, 3.5.1, 3.5.2, 3.5.3
binding tariff information 1.3.1.4
border-crossing formalities 3.2.1.1
branch 2.5.5
business asset 2.6.1

C
cancellation message 3.3.2.4
cancellation, refusal or total or partial non-payment 2.9
car registration 3.7.2
car tax 3.7.2.3
car-rental 3.7.2.2
centralised clearance 1.5.2.2
certified consignor 3.2.5.2
classification rules 1.4.2.1
combined nomenclature 1.4.2.1
combinova 1.4.1.3
commercial purposes 3.2.5.2
commission (fee) 2.6.1
commissionaire 2.6.1
commissions and brokerage fees 1.4.2.3
Common Customs Tariff 1.4.1.1, 1.4.2.1
Community Customs Code 1.2.2
compendium of Customs Valuation Texts 1.4.2.3

cost of containers 1.4.2.3
cumulative cascade systems 2.2
customs debt 1.4.1, 1.4.1.1
customs procedure 1.5.2.2
customs status of goods 1.5.2.1
customs territory 1.3.1.1
customs union 1.1, 1.2.2
Customs Valuation Agreement 1.4.2.3
customs value 1.4.2.3
- assists 1.4.2.3
- BMW 1.4.2.3
- buying commissions 1.4.2.3
- charges for construction etc. 1.4.2.3
- charges for the rights to reproduce 1.4.2.3
- Compaq Computer International Corporation 1.4.2.3
- cost of transport and insurance 1.4.2.3
- defected goods 1.4.2.3
- Dollond & Aitchison Ltd 1.4.2.3
- Hamamatsu 1.4.2.3
- import duties or other charges 1.4.2.3
- interest 1.4.2.3
- Mitsui & Co 1.4.2.3
- Overland Footwear 1.4.2.3
- price paid or payable 1.4.2.3
- proceeds 1.4.2.3
- related party transactions 1.4.2.3
- royalties and licence fees 1.4.2.3
- sale for export 1.4.2.3
- software 1.4.2.3
- transaction value method 1.4.2.3
- Unifert 1.4.2.3
customs warehouse 2.11.8

D
debtors 1.4.1.1
destruction or loss 3.2.5.5
diplomatic 3.2.2.4
direct costs 2.12.2
direct delivery 3.2.4.1
discrimination 3.1
disposal of goods 1.5.2.4
distance selling 3.2.5.3
double taxation 3.2.2.2, 3.7.2.2

E

e-commerce VAT package	2.1, 2.6.1
economic activity	2.5.3
electricity	3.8.1, 3.8.2, 3.8.2.3, 3.8.3.2
electronic administrative document (e-AD)	3.2.4.2, 3.3.1, 3.3.2.3, 3.3.2.5, 3.3.2.6, 3.3.2.7, 3.3.2.9
electronic interface	2.6.1
EMCS	3.1, 3.2.4.2, 3.2.5.2, 3.3, 3.3.2.1, 3.3.2.2, 3.3.2.6, 3.3.2.8, 3.3.2.9
energy	3.8.1, 3.8.2, 3.8.3.2
entry in the declarants records	1.5.2.2
entry into free circulation	2.6.4
entry of Goods	1.5.1
entry Summary Declaration	1.5.1.1
environmentally friendly	3.7.1
European Commission's explanatory notes	2.7.1
excise duty	2.9, 3.1
excise goods	3.2.1.1
excise territory	3.2.1.3
exempt	3.2.6.2
exemption	3.2.2.4, 3.8.3, 3.8.3.2
Explanatory notes on VAT e-commerce rules	2.6.1
export	
- exporter	1.5.5
- re-export	1.5.5
extinguishment of a customs debt	1.4.1.3

F

fallback Accompanying Document	3.3.2.9
fallback document	3.2.5.2
fallback procedures	3.3.2.9
fixed establishment	2.5.5, 2.7.3
force majeure	3.2.2.2
free circulation	2.7.4
free trade agreements	1.4.2.2
free zone	1.5.4.3, 2.11.8

G

gas and electricity	2.5.7
general Arrangements Directive	3.1
generalised Scheme of Preferences (GSP)	1.4.2.1, 1.4.2.2
guarantees	1.4.1

H
harmonized System 1.4.2.1
held for commercial purposes 3.2.2.2
holding 3.2.3
holding company 2.5.6, 2.12.1
horizontal Directive 3.1

I
illegal transactions 2.5.3
immovable property 2.11.1
Implementing Regulation 2454/93 (CCIP) 1.2.2
Implementing Regulation 282/2011 2.1
importation of excise goods 3.2.2.1
intermediate products 3.5, 3.5.4
internal supply of services 2.6.3
irregularity 3.2.2.2, 3.2.5.5

J
jointly and severally liable 3.2.2.2

M
market value 2.9
mineral oils 3.4
minimum excise duty 3.6.3
minimum levels of taxation 3.8.3.1
minimum rates 3.4.2, 3.5
modernised Customs Code 1.2.2
motor fuels 3.8.2.1
movement of excise goods 3.2.2.2, 3.2.4.2, 3.2.5.2
movement of excise goods under suspension of duty 3.2.2.2, 3.2.4, 3.2.4.3

N
neutrality 2.2
new means of transport 2.6.6
non-discrimination 3.1
non-taxable legal persons 2.6.2
non-Union goods 1.3.1.1

O
occasional transactions 2.5.4
open market value 2.9
option for taxation 2.11.1
option to tax 2.11.1

origin 1.4.2.2
- non-preferential origin 1.4.2.2
- preferential origin 1.4.2.2
override rules 2.7.3
own resources 3.7.3

P

passenger 3.2.2.4
passenger car related taxes 3.7.2.1
passenger car taxation 3.7.2.2
person liable to pay 3.2.2.2
place of establishment 2.7.3
plastic packaging 3.7.3
plastic tax 3.7.3
plastic waste 3.7.3
platform 2.8.1
Plato 3.5.1
private use 2.6.1
processing 1.5.4.5, 3.2.3
- inward processing 1.5.4.5
- outward Processing 1.5.4.5
production 3.2.3
pro-rata calculation 2.12.1
public bodies 2.5.7

R

recast General Arrangements Directive 3.1
reductions 3.8.3.2
registered consignee 3.2.2.1, 3.2.4.1
registered consignor 3.2.2.1, 3.2.4, 3.2.4.1
registered Exporter system 1.4.2.2
registration tax 3.7.2.2, 3.7.2.3
reimbursement 3.2.2.3
release for consumption 3.2.2.1, 3.2.2.2, 3.2.2.3, 3.2.5, 3.2.5.5
release for free circulation 1.5.3
remission see Repayment of a customs debt
repayment of a customs debt
- defective goods or goods not complying with the terms of the contract 1.4.1.2
- error by the competent authorities 1.4.1.2
- equity 1.4.1.2
- invalidation of the customs declaration 1.4.1.2
- overcharged amount of import or export duty 1.4.1.2

representation 1.3.1.3
representative
- direct customs representative 1.3.1.3
- indirect customs representative 1.3.1.3
retention of goods 2.6.1
reverse charge 2.1, 2.2
right to appeal 1.3.1.6

S
self-constructed goods 2.6.1
self-enforcing effect 2.2
self-supply 2.6.1
simplified administrative document 3.2.5.2, 3.2.5.5
single administrative document 1.5.2.2
single Authorisation for Simplified Procedures 1.5.2.2
single or multiple supplies 2.7.3
special procedures 1.5
special territories 3.2.1.3
specific duty 1.4.2.3, 3.6.2
specific purpose 3.2.1.1
specific use
- end-use 1.5.4.4
- temporary admission 1.5.4.4
storage 1.5.4.3, 3.2.3
- customs warehousing 1.5.4.3
subsidies 3.7.1
supply of fuel 2.6.1
suspensions 1.4.2.1

T
tariff 1.4.2.1
tariff quota 1.4.2.1
tax credits 3.7.1
tax incentives 3.7.1
tax refunds 3.8.3
tax warehouse 3.2.2.1, 3.2.4.1
tax-free sales to travellers 3.2.2.4
tax-free shop 3.2.2.4
telecommunication services 2.5.7
temporary importation arrangements 2.7.4
temporary storage 1.5.1.4, 2.11.8
tobacco 3.6, 3.6.1, 3.6.3, 3.6.4
total destruction or irretrievable loss of excise goods 3.2.2.2

transfer of a going concern 2.6.1, 2.12.8
transfer of stocks 2.6.2
transit 1.5.4.2
- ATA carnet procedure 1.5.4.2
- common transit procedure 1.5.4.2
- external transit 1.5.4.2
- internal transit 1.5.4.2
- new Computerised Transit System 1.5.4.2
- Rhine manifest procedure 1.5.4.2
- TIR Carnets 1.5.4.2
- TIR procedure 1.5.4.2
transitional measures 3.2.8

U
UCC Delegated Act 1.1
UCC Implementing Act 1.1
UCC legal package 1.1, 1.2.2
UCC Transitional Delegated Act 1.1
UCC Work Programme 1.1
UK withdrawal 2.1, 2.4, 2.11.2
undisclosed agent 2.6.1
Union Customs Code 1.1
Union goods 1.3.1.1
unlawful transactions 3.2.1.2

V
VAT Committee 2.11.8
VAT group 2.5.5
vouchers 2.1, 2.6.5, 2.8.1, 2.9

W
warehouse (tax-) 3.3.2.8
warehouses other than customs warehouses 2.11.8
weighted average retail selling price 3.6.2
wine 3.5, 3.5.2
World Customs Organization 1.2.1
World Trade Organization 1.2.1

www.ingramcontent.com/pod-product-compliance
Ingram Content Group UK Ltd.
Pitfield, Milton Keynes, MK11 3LW, UK
UKHW020133290926
15471UKWH00003B/461